ECOLOGY

on the

GROUND

and in

THE CLOUDS

SUNY series in Environmental Philosophy and Ethics

J. Baird Callicott and John van Buren, editors

ECOLOGY
on the
GROUND
and in
THE CLOUDS

Aimé Bonpland and Alexander von Humboldt

ANDREA NYE

Cover, Alexander von Humboldt (1769–1859) and Aimé Bonpland (1773–1858) shown in a romanticised view of their exploration of the Amazon rainforest in 1800, surrounded with various items of scientific equipment. Oil painting by Eduard Ender (1822–1883) painted in 1856. Along with a portion of a plate from Humboldt and Bonpland's *Essay on the Geography of Plants*.

Published by State University of New York Press, Albany

For information, contact State University of New York Press, Albany, NY
www.sunypress.edu

Library of Congress Cataloging-in-Publication Data

Name: Nye, Andrea, 1939– author.
Title: Ecology on the ground and in the clouds : Aimé Bonpland and
    Alexander von Humboldt / Andrea Nye.
Description: Albany : State University of New York Press, [2022] | Series:
    SUNY series in environmental philosophy and ethics | Includes
    bibliographical references and index.
Identifiers: LCCN 2021040873 (print) | LCCN 2021040874 (ebook) | ISBN
    9781438487014 (hardcover : alk. paper) | ISBN 9781438487007 (pbk. : alk.
    paper) | ISBN 9781438487021 (ebook)
Subjects: LCSH: Human ecology—Philosophy. | Human beings—Effect of
    environment on.
Classification: LCC GF21 .N94 2022 (print) | LCC GF21 (ebook) | DDC
    304.2—dc23/eng/20211006
LC record available at https://lccn.loc.gov/2021040873
LC ebook record available at https://lccn.loc.gov/2021040874

10 9 8 7 6 5 4 3 2 1

"The secret of the human condition is that there is no equilibrium between human beings and the surrounding forces of nature, which infinitely exceed them in inaction: there is only equilibrium in action by which human beings recreate their own lives through work."

—Simone Weil, *Gravity and Grace*

Contents

Introduction   1

Part I. Setting Out

1   Close Encounter at a Paris Boarding House   9

2   A Walk across Spain and a Climb Up a Volcano   25

Part II. The Voyage

3   Aerial Views, Nocturnal Birds, and Wild Indians   43

4   The Eel Ponds of the Llanos   61

5   Riverworlds   75

6   The Mountain   95

7   The Changing of the Gods   115

Part III. The Return

8   Coming Home   131

9   Tales of Three Cities   147

10   Botany on Demand   175

11   Taking Leave   195

Part IV. Worlds Apart

12   A Lost Friend   215

13   Warlords and Kings   233

14   Cosmos and Microcosm   261

15   A Last Exchange of Gifts   287

16   Scattered Remains   311

Afterthoughts: A Bonplandian Ethos   325

Notes   333

Primary Sources   349

Bibliography   351

Index   359

Introduction

On August 1, 1804, the frigate *La Favorite* anchored at the Garrone River near Bordeaux, carrying two men who had just completed a four-year exploration of South America. They mapped a reputed link between the tributaries of the Orinoco and Amazon river systems. They climbed the high Andes and crossed the burning desert of the llanos. They brought back 40 crates of animals and plants never before seen in Europe, as well as thousands of pages of notes, drawings, and measurements. Immediately on entering the harbor, Alexander von Humboldt, who had financed the expedition, took charge of what he assumed would be their shared future. In a matter of weeks he selected items from their collections for an exhibit at the Muséum national d'histoire naturelle (National Museum of Natural History) in Paris, impressed the Institut de France with a dramatic talk on the capture of electric eels, lobbied government officials, and began the process of lining up publishers for a long list of volumes that would rival the results of Napoleon's conquest of Egypt. Out and about in fashionable Parisian salons and drawing rooms, he fascinated guests with stories of adventures with wild Indians and on simmering volcanoes.

If Alexander Humboldt stepped eagerly onto the stage of European intellectual history, Aimé Bonpland, the French botanist who had been at his side for five years collecting and describing plants and animals, retreated. When he left Paris with Humboldt in 1798, France was a fledgling republic. Now under the rule of Napoleon Bonaparte, it was an imperial power. Treasure from foreign conquests paraded through the streets. Monumental building projects were under way. No, he would not join Humboldt at Napoleon's coronation as emperor in the Cathedral of Notre Dame, which anyone with any sense would realize was a ridiculous show. Yes, he understood that it was important to profit from a moment of return from exotic locations to attract an audience for one's writings. But botanical work takes time. Each plant has to be carefully cataloged and its classification confirmed. And yes, he would give a paper at

1

the Institut, but its subject would not be howling monkeys or electric eels, but the complex chemistry of a palm high up in the Andes, which produces a vegetal wax that native people use to make candles.

For five years the two had rarely been out of each other's sight. For five years they had worked amicably and productively together. Humboldt recorded temperatures, altitudes, lengths, and pressures with his expensive array of scientific instruments; Bonpland, the botanist, had his eyes on the ground, looking for interesting and useful plants. If Humboldt hoped for something more intimate than friendship with the young Frenchman, he quickly learned to be content with Bonpland's affectionate, energetic, and observant presence. There were no embarrassing passionate misunderstandings, only the pleasure and intimacy of productive life together, the two of them alone, except for guides and porters, negotiating tropical rivers, climbing the Andes, settling down for long periods of time in rented houses. If it was Humboldt's inheritance that had financed the expedition, never did he fail to acknowledge that its success was as much due to Bonpland's energy and competence. Never did he fail to praise Bonpland as a scientific collaborator or hesitate to give him credit for the work of finding, preserving, describing, and identifying plants and animals which provided an important part of the scientific basis for their joint publications. As Humboldt put it in his *Personal Narrative* of the voyage, "I was supported by a brave and learned friend whose keenness and equanimity never let me down despite the exhaustion and dangers we faced" (PN, 5). Unlike the urbane Humboldt in his top hat and frock coat, in forests and on rivers Bonpland was in his element, collecting new and useful plants, talking to locals, rescuing Humboldt from drowning, collecting live animals as pets, disappearing on excursions with local guides.

Back in Paris things changed. Humboldt began his climb to the pinnacle of fame in Europe. Bonpland contemplated crowded, seething, militant Paris with increasing skepticism. He consulted with friends and colleagues at the Muséum national d'histoire naturelle and the Jardin des plantes. He rented an apartment in a quiet neighborhood. He went to work on the thousands of plant specimens in his crates and the hundreds of pages of descriptions and notes in his journals. By December he had arranged and classified a herbarium of 6,200 plants for Humboldt to present to the Muséum. By the next spring he had ready a first installment of plates and descriptions for a two-volume illustrated *Plantes équinoxiales* to appear at the same time as Humboldt's *Essay on the Geography of Plants*. When Humboldt traveled to Italy to see his brother, and then on to Berlin to renew his allegiance to the Prussian King, Bonpland stayed in Paris, taking care of publishing business, negotiating with printers and engravers, editing Humboldt's manuscripts, and correcting Humboldt's French.

Trapped in Berlin during the French occupation, Humboldt continued to turn out copy. He consoled fellow Prussians with romantic descriptions of tropical landscapes in his popular *Aspects of Nature*. He recruited a young astronomer to edit and correlate his astronomical observations for a *Recueil d'observations astronomiques*. Finally permitted to return to Paris, he completed his *Geography of Plants* and published a much augmented version of the *Political Essay* he prepared for the Spanish Viceroy of New Spain. But botanical copy from his coauthor Bonpland was slow to appear. Humboldt was impatient. Where was the second volume of *Plantes équinoxiales*? More important, where were descriptions in Latin of the thousands of new species of plants that would be the basis for Humboldt's theories of nature? Yes, Bonpland was naturalizing many of those plants as director of estates and gardens at Empress Josephine Bonaparte's estate at Malmaison, but was there any reason why an administrative post should interfere with publishing? Finally, with Humboldt hiring other botanists to describe and classify plants that Bonpland collected, Bonpland, having proven himself incompetent, retreated to the wild riverlands of Argentina and Humboldt went on to become one of the heroes of European civilization. As one of Humboldt's admirers cleverly put it: Homer, Hesiod, Humboldt; Aristotle, Aquinas, Alexander.

So the story goes as it is told in recent books celebrating Humboldt as an environmental hero. Aaron Sachs in *The Humboldt Current* compared Humboldt's influence to a mighty river, an intellectual torrent that sweeping through the Western world, flowing into the settlement of North American, the exploration of remote parts of the globe and on into the nature writing of John Muir. According to Gerard Helferich, Humboldt "changed the way we see the world." In a best-selling biography, Andrea Wulf named Humboldt the "Inventor of Nature." Laura Walls heard in Humboldt's prose Nature's very voice: "For the Humboldtian scientist the doing of science combined rigorous and exacting labor with the joy of poetic revelation and an almost spiritual sense of revelation, as if nature borrowed the mind and the hand of the scientist to describe its own most beautiful laws and structures" (Walls, 8). As one reviewer put it, "rediscovering Humboldt is by this point a subgenre unto itself."[1] Bonpland was all but forgotten, mentioned briefly, "gone native" somewhere in South America.

So the story goes, but in the course of doing some research in the history of botany, I began to question it. Nor, I soon found out, was I alone. In the early years of the twentieth century Ernest-Theodore Hamy, editor of Humboldt's *Lettres américaines* and one of the founders of the science of ethnography in France, came to a similar conclusion. As Hamy put it in a preface to his 1906 biography of Bonpland and collection of Bonpland's letters,

I came to know Bonpland through Humboldt. It was gathering materials for my edition of the *American Letters* of the celebrated Prussian savant that I first came across biographical details that made me love his travel companion almost as much as Humboldt himself. The more I went on in my study of Humboldt's *Voyage aux régions équinoxiales du nouveau continent*, the better I came to understand the importance of the role played by our compatriot. . . . In the end I came to have a high idea of services rendered to science and humanity in the midst of many troubles that made me decide to devote to the long and active career of this explorer and naturalist the detailed monograph he merits. (AB, vi–vii)

For me, reading Bonpland's letters, it was his voice, so different from Humboldt's often stilted, formal, flowery French, certainly different from Humboldt's flights of romantic passion, and refreshingly free from the sting of bitter sarcasm found in so many of Humboldt's later letters. Bonpland's prose flowed, easy, expressive, energized by intimate working engagement with the natural world. After decades of separation and deep disagreement as to the aim of botanical science, his letters from South America to Humboldt in Berlin were written with a rush of sympathy for a friend and comrade, who could never be forgotten no matter how far their lives and ideas had diverged. If only Humboldt could be with him in his orange groves at São Borja for the annual making of orange flower water. If only Humboldt could travel up the Paraná River and discover with him plants like the astonishing maize of the water.

It was not long before I was searching in rare book rooms for copies of Bonpland's botanical publications, going from descriptions of plant parts to his commentaries on the origins, local uses, conservation, and beauty of plants. I traveled to Argentina to see some of the sites he explored, spent a month in Paris leafing through his handwritten field journals at the Muséum national d'histoire naturelle. I read his manuscripts on the preservation of wild groves of forest yerba, the companion planting of orchards, the organization of a model farm. All the time I was coming to like Bonpland, not just as much as I liked Humboldt, but more than Humboldt, who in person and in print could be as pompous and irritating as at other times he was endearing and inspiring.

But as time went on, what interested me more than the men themselves was the contrast between two very different approaches to the natural world. In his last, most famous work, *Cosmos*, Humboldt paid tribute to an ecological science focused on universal patterns and correlations. His subject, he said, was not orchards, farms, or forests, but "Nature" as it was viewed and appreciated by "sensitive" and "civilized" European men able to rise above crass utilitarian concerns. As the first volumes of *Cosmos* came off the presses in Berlin and Paris, Bonpland in the river provinces of Argentina was leaving another legacy, not in print but on the ground—a legacy of sustainable agriculture, partnerships between European scientists and native people, development of local products, and community environmental planning. If Humboldt contemplated Nature from the lofty pinnacle of German idealism and European civilization, Bonpland's lost work, *Nomenclature de Bonpland*, walked the rich earth of Argentina, Paraguay, and Brazil with descriptions of five thousand tropical plants, their Latin, French, Spanish, and Guarani names, and new and surprising facts concerning native medicines and indigenous products. As Bonpland's friend and biographer, Adolphe Brunel, put it:

> Humboldt lived, shone, and died in the midst of the salons of the highest. He sought the most refined of the pleasures of civilization. He was the intimate friend of kings who succeeded to the throne of Prussia and had the favor of Emperor Nicolas of Russia. More than once he was proud to be associated with and serve on their diplomatic missions. Bonpland only passed through the honors and pleasures of the "great world" and the political world. Then he returned with delight to plunge back into the heart of untamed nature. (Brunel, 34)

I wondered. Was it Bonpland who was past his time, mired down in the "first half of the nineteenth century" as a last European visitor to Bonpland's property at Santa Ana wrote back to Humboldt in Berlin? Was Bonpland lazy, just not up to the challenge of botanical work as is claimed by many of Humboldt's current admirers? Was Bonpland wrong to put his hopes for the future in the new world of the Americas, rather than in the old world of European "civilization"? Wrong to have seen the key to that future not with the princes of industry or romantic nature lovers, but in restorative, creative, community work on the ground? Or was it Humboldt, champion of trade and development, so certain of the superiority of European civilization, who might need to be left behind if we are to come to terms with our current environmental crisis? History can grow stale, ossify, the same tale told over and over, cited and recited from reputable sources, repackaged to reinforce a message we think we understand. In this twenty-first human century, with the window rapidly closing on the possibility of preventing catastrophic climate change, with forests burning, and industrial farming methods seemingly fixed in place, new inspiration is desperately needed, narratives that might give substance to an environmental message addressed not to a nature-loving elite, but to working women and men struggling to make a living on compromised ground.

PART I

SETTING OUT

1

Close Encounter at a Paris Boarding House

It was the summer of 1798 and things were looking up in Paris. Napoleon Bonaparte's victories in Italy brought a flowering of confidence along with a sweeping vision of European sister republics, all allied with and subservient to France. After a decade of violent revolution, a Directory was in charge of the government. The streets were under control; arrests and beheadings were less frequent. Royalist uprisings of the summer before had been suppressed. Newspapers with monarchist sympathies were closed down, and arrest warrants were out for any aristocrat hoping to return and reclaim a former estate. It seemed the days of revolutionary terror were over. Bastille Day celebrations that summer were particularly splendid. Forty-five wagons draped with giant tricolor flags and filled with looted treasure paraded through the streets. Bands played. Choruses sang. The sad old lion from the zoo of the Muséum national d'histoire naturelle was carted out in a cage, followed by four camels dressed in magnificent harnesses, and then four bronze horses stolen from St. Mark's Basilica in Venice glowing and shimmering in the noonday sun. For Aimé Bonpland, forced to march along as associate of the Muséum, a bright spot in a long weary day were some carts added on at the last moment carrying living trees, tall palms and banana trees, brought back from the West Indies by a renegade ship captain, Nicolas Baudin.

With the exception of a one-year tour of duty as medical officer in the Navy, Bonpland had been in Paris for eight long years. In August he would be twenty-five. With a medical degree in hand he was now expected to return home to provincial La Rochelle and begin a medical practice. It was a prospect that had little appeal. Always he would be a physician, prescribing remedies and tending to the sick, but Bonpland's thoughts were now on lands far beyond the confines of his pharmacist uncles' physic garden and his grandfather's vineyard. In glass houses at the Jardin des plantes and in the herbaria of the Muséum national d'histoire naturelle he discovered plants and animals never dreamed of in La Rochelle. Garden beds, nursery pots, and museum storage shelves swelled with roots, seeds, dried specimens, fossils, insects in jars stuffed birds, and living plants brought back by French travelers abroad. Plants, new in shape and form as well as in behavior and properties, were dried and taped to tissue-thin pages in natural history cabinets, sketched in stacks of travel journals, painted by talented artists. Mystery seeds rested in jars and sealed envelopes brought back by colonial officials, gentlemen travelers, missionaries, sea captains, sailors, and official correspondents of the museum. Botany for Bonpland would never be the same, never again the old categories inherited from Aristotle, Theophrastus, and now Linnaeus. A botanist could no longer merely count stamens or any other dried plant part glued to the pages of a herbarium. He would have to understand the lives of plants, do work in the field, lay out a day's collections, make preliminary identifications, put one plant next to another, note differences, remember terrain, soil, wind patterns, the depth of marshy hollows, the shallows of sandbanks, flooded plains where roots reached down deep for footing. This Bonpland learned not in the medical clinics but with Antoine de Jussieu, Jean-Baptiste Lamarck, and René Desfontaines at the Muséum national d'histoire naturelle, and with André Thouin, master gardener and guardian of the old King's Garden, now a national Jardin des plantes.

The winter before, an invitation to serve as naturalist on a new French "tour de monde" led by the famous Louis Antoine de Bougainville offered Bonpland a reprieve from family obligations that was quickly withdrawn. Notices went out. The Directory was sorry. Bougainville's list of scientists was commandeered for a more important mission. Where? Officially no one would say, but with the French fleet gathering at Toulon, it was not much of a secret. Giving up an invasion of Britain across the channel as impractical, the conqueror of Italy, General Napoleon, was planning to attack British imperial possessions in the east by way of Egypt. Bonpland was approached. Would he join a scientific expedition to Egypt instead? Convinced, as were others at the Jardin and the Muséum, that science was merely added on to give credence to what was in fact a military conquest, Bonpland refused. No, he replied, he was conscious of the great honor, but he would wait for the scientific voyage that was postponed but not canceled. But now with Napoleon floundering in Egypt, new uprisings in Italy, and the Directory short of funds, it seemed that the scientific voyage would never get under way. He would have to give up any hope of travel, return to La Rochelle and life as a provincial physician. With that unhappy prospect in mind, at first he had paid little attention to the stocky, fashionably dressed young man he often passed by in the boarding house where they both had rooms.

Alexander von Humboldt had been in Paris for only a few months, and already he was impatient. He was out of dreary backward Berlin and free from family obligations due to the death of his mother the year before. With money from his inheritance in hand, and no parent to tell him what to do, he had resigned his post as a Prussian inspector of mines and was ready to accomplish something great in science. For once he was in the right place for it, as he put it ecstatically in a letter to his mentor in Geneva, Marc-Auguste Pictet: "Here I live in the midst of science." And what a science it was: d'Alembert plotting the moon's orbit, Clairaut working out the procession of the equinoxes, Lavoisier and Fourcroy in chemistry, Lagrange in mathematics, botanists Jussieu and Desfontaines at the Muséum national d'histoire naturelle, to say nothing of a stunning array of astronomic and geographic measuring devices never heard of in Berlin. He had been out to the Jardin des plantes. He introduced himself to scientists at the Paris Observatory. He gave two talks at the Institut de France, one on nitrous gases and another on a technique he devised for measuring oxygen in the air in mines. He traveled down to Melun to observe a French survey team at work measuring a quadrant of the earth's surface, and got some help using his new sextant. While there he made the acquaintance of the famous Bougainville, who recommended that he join a new French circumnavigation of the earth. But now he too was informed that Bougainville's expedition was postponed. Worse, when it did get under way the leader was no longer to be Bougainville but some Captain Baudin just back from the West Indies, as far as he could see a man of no distinction.

More than anything Humboldt was lonely. His brother Wilhelm and Wilhelm's popular wife, Caroline, were in residence in Paris. He saw them regularly. Every night he was invited out to parties and soirées. But he had no close intimate friend, no one to fill the emptiness around his heart left by the young infantry officer he was sure would be the "love of his life," Reinhard von Haeften, lost to marriage the year before. Standing at the desk of the Hotel Boston chatting with the concierge, it is not surprising that he would notice the young Frenchman hurrying by with a worn botanist's satchel. The healthy exuberance of Bonpland's step, a slight provincial roughness in his diction, his strong build, curly dark hair, and quiet intelligent manner had to be attractive after afternoons and evenings spent socializing with countesses, diplomats, politicians, and portrait artists in sister-in-law Caroline's drawing room. Never did Humboldt have trouble making friends. His bubbling warmth, his often dizzying changes of subject, his tendency to dominate a conversation, all could be off-putting, but he had an ability to charm, especially attractive young men with an interest in science. Nor was he slow to answer when the young Frenchman stopped, politely returned his greeting, and inquired what Humboldt himself was doing in Paris.[1]

What indeed? Humboldt was beginning to wonder. War in Europe had interrupted so many of his plans. His first idea had been to travel to Italy with his brother and his brother's family and study volcanoes. Then he planned to come to Paris, buy the latest in scientific instruments, and look for a ship heading for the West Indies. But everything had fallen through. With Napoleon's troops marching back and forth across Italy, travel was impossible. He spent the winter in the mountains measuring latitudes and practicing with his new sextant and barometer, but it was hardly the grand expedition he dreamed of. And now, just when he had been invited to join a new French scientific expedition, it was postponed, and Bougainville was not to lead it but rather some Captain Baudin of dubious family and unsavory reputation.

At some point, Bonpland would have gotten a word in. He too had been scheduled to sail with Bougainville. He too was waiting for the postponed voyage under the substitute leader Baudin. He too was impatient to be on his way.

For Humboldt it was a delightful surprise. To think that the two of them were signed on to the same voyage and might be shipmates. He had been invited by Lord Bristol—did Bonpland know the eccentric Lord Bristol—invited to go on an expedition down the Nile. Maybe it would have been more a pleasure cruise with ladies on board and a staff of servants, but interesting nonetheless. So he had agreed and came to Paris to buy instruments and say goodbye to his brother, only to find that he had missed an even greater opportunity with General Bonaparte, who had left for Egypt only days before his arrival. And to top it off, now the Nile trip was off. He had put himself on the list for the expedition to be led by Bougainville, but he was not at all sure about going anywhere with Baudin, who, he was told, had already lost a number of ships.[2]

On the subject of Baudin, Bonpland would have been able to offer some reassurance. Baudin might have a dubious past, but he brought back a stunning collection of trees and plants from the West Indies, the flowers and leaves of so many of which were now pressed and dried in the Muséum's herbarium. Had Humboldt not seen the live trees carried on carts through the streets at the Bastille Day celebration and the many others growing in the Muséum's glasshouses—a twenty-foot tree fern, a banana tree, a coconut palm, a pawpaw? All had been allowed to grow freely out of the hatch of the ship, just as Thouin at the Jardin described in his memoranda on collecting plants abroad.[3] And the gardeners signed on for the Baudin expedition were personally chosen and instructed by Thouin himself.

Humboldt could not help but be charmed. Here was a well-connected young scientist who shared his enthusiasm. What could go wrong with such a shipmate? Would Bonpland like to come upstairs and take look at the instruments he purchased for use on his travels? He had even been able to get one of Lenoir's new repeating circles and had to rent an additional room just to accommodate all of his instruments. Still he did not think much of Baudin, who refused to promise him an extra cabin on the ship for his equipment. He, for one, made it clear. If at any time he wanted to leave the expedition he would do so. But now, meeting Bonpland, who trained with Jussieu and Desfontaines at the Jardin and Muséum, and who had such a pleasant and informed manner, he was sure no such escape would be necessary.

Many found Humboldt difficult, especially before fame had given him a degree of confidence and calm. He talked too much; he gave the appearance of always trying to impress. He knew something about everything, but little in depth. He had a nervous intensity not conducive to two-way conversation. That Bonpland and he became friends and comrades, that they would spend the next five years virtually never out of each other's sight, says something about Bonpland's insight into character. Spending time comfortably with Humboldt required weathering onslaughts of talk at the same time as responding to a mute appeal for understanding and acceptance never far from the surface. It meant appreciating the sudden welling up of passion in Humboldt for a friend, an idea, a scenic vista. It meant admiring and drawing on Humboldt's ever-expanding encyclopedic stock of scientific facts and theories. To the end of his life, after years of dispute and separation, Humboldt would pay tribute to the qualities that made Bonpland the ideal friend, companion, and scientific collaborator. Active, observant, independent, and steady of purpose, Bonpland was resourceful, observant, a quiet intelligent listener, brave and resolute in a crisis, and, most important, tireless in the pursuit, discovery, and preservation of rare, useful, and beautiful plants.

The two men's early years could not have been spent more differently. In provincial La Rochelle, Bonpland worked in family vineyards, went to school, wandered hills and limestone cliffs along the western coast of the Bay of Biscay with his older brother, Michel, looking for fossils and watching ships sail in and out of the harbor. His little sister, Olive, adored him. His mother doted on him. The future was laid out for him. He would join his brother in Paris, earn a medical degree, and return home. At first it seemed that the revolution might interrupt those plans. Just as he was about to leave for Paris at the age of seventeen, angry mobs stormed the arsenal at the Bastille, hacked its governor to pieces, and paraded severed heads through the streets. The king wavered in support for a newly elected National Assembly, and thousands of protesters marched to Versailles and escorted the king and his Austrian wife back to Paris. Another father might have had second thoughts about sending a boy to a city seemingly on the brink of violent revolt, but Jacques Goujaud was ambitious for his sons.[4] In the great teaching hospitals of Paris, surgeons were scientists, members of the Royal Academy, researchers developing new therapies and diagnoses. They did not dry homegrown herbs for distillations and tinctures, or bleed and purge their patients as in the past. They diagnosed pathogens and infections. They operated on diseased organs with intimate knowledge of human anatomy. In the future even provincial physicians would need some knowledge of anatomy, organic chemistry, and pathology. And that summer it might have seemed that the troubles in Paris were over. The king was in the Tuileries, willing—or so he said—to accept limits on his royal power. In La Rochelle and other provincial towns festivals of unity were celebrated. Bands played. Citizens raised right hands in allegiance to a new liberal consensus. Letters home from Bonpland's brother, Michel, in Paris were reassuring. The streets were quiet. A National Guard led by General Lafayette was on patrol. An elected assembly was busy drafting legislation. Aimé should come, said Michel, begin his education.

Fresh from a sheltered boyhood in western hills, Bonpland could hardly have imagined what he was about to experience in a city about to explode. Squalor and stench, dead and dying bodies, mobs whipped to frenzy by inflammatory speakers, threats of searches and seizures, strange pointed hats worn by Lafayette's guard. A few months after his arrival, most of Paris's institutions of learning shut down. The Faculty of Medicine at the University of Paris stopped functioning. The old College of Surgery, where barber surgeons were apprentice-trained, closed. The Collège Royal, renamed the Collège de France, held classes but with an outdated curriculum based for the most part on ancient authorities. At meetings of the Royal Society of Medicine, experiments in medical pharmacology and organic chemistry continued to be debated, but established scientists and physicians were invited, not students from the provinces. It would be years before Bonpland would be able to attend a proper medical school with entrance exams and national standards. Stipends from home were worth less and less. Inflation was rampant. Long lines formed at the bakers. Children begged in the streets. Piles of rat-infested garbage accumulated in city squares. There were mass arrests and executions. What instruction there was came in the clinics of charity hospitals like Hôtel-Dieu and Charité, where the internist Corvisart and the master surgeon Desault demonstrated methods and techniques.

In Hôtel-Dieu's long surgery ward, waiting for the surgery to begin, students held handkerchiefs over their mouths and noses against the rank stench of rotting flesh and urine. Poor nutrition and unheated rooms made even small wounds turn gangrenous, and more and more there were wounds. Perhaps it was a leg, crushed by the wheels of a speeding carriage and untreated, so that the wound festered. If the leg did not come off the man would die of blood poisoning. As was his habit, Desault appeared suddenly out of a side door, the circle of students parting respectfully to let him through. He pulled back the stained sheet. An assistant forced a draft of laudanum down the mouth of the patient already half unconscious with pain and shock. From beds lined up along the walls came low moans of anticipation. The next day or the day after it might be one of them on the table. There, working with his friend Xavier Bichat, Bonpland learned the rudiments of dissection, classification of body parts, and repair of damaged limbs. But more and more, when sessions in the clinics were over, he was out at the Jardin des plantes, where he was beginning to fall in love with plants.

Even in the prerevolutionary days of the old King's Garden there was a progressive spirit at the Jardin, a sense that the role of natural history was not discovering new plants and animals for aristocratic curiosity cabinets, but curing human ills. Already in the mid-eighteenth century, directives had gone out to try to preserve the forests of France. Antoine Jussieu was developing his family's new natural system of plant identification. André Thouin gave classes on rural agriculture. Desfontaines classified plants he collected in North Africa to identify trees and shrubs that could be naturalized in French parks. This was natural science as Bonpland was taught it: part wonder at the beauty, complexity, and amazing variety of living beings, part practical knowledge that sustains and conserves those living beings. For Thouin and others at the Museum it was this and not conquest that was the aim of revolution.

Few such progressive ideas reached Humboldt growing up among privileged classes outside of Berlin. There the cry of revolution was barely audible as Frederick the Great's modest program of rational reform withered away under the weak and befuddled Frederick William II. A few liberals might applaud from a safe distance "blows for freedom" struck in France, but no one could think the contagion of violent rebellion would reach as far as the German states. At Schloss Tegel, the Humboldt estate outside of Berlin, young Alexander grew up with everything money and position could buy except affection. His father died when he was nine, leaving him with a cold and demanding mother. Educated by a succession of tutors, sickly as a child, always in the shadow of his older brother Wilhelm, Alexander was the "bad boy," the problem learner who couldn't settle down to concentrate on a subject long enough to master it. By his own admission, he had no interest in science or any other serious subject before the age of sixteen. He dreamed of being a soldier. He liked to draw, a pursuit that, as far as his mother was concerned, was no more than a way to avoid serious study.

There was little enough in the way of intellectual interest. At the time, Berlin was not much more than a country town with unpaved streets and poor drains. A succession of tutors introduced Alexander and his brother Wilhelm to what there was of mental stimulation. At reading clubs and occasional science evenings new ideas from France and England were discussed. On one occasion a demonstration of Benjamin Franklin's lightning rod sparked in Humboldt a lifelong fascination with electricity. Half a year at the nearby University of Frankfurt-on-Oder introduced him to beer-making and a first flush of erotic attraction to a young theology student. But Frankfurt-on-Oder, a popular place of maturing for young aristocrats headed for the state civil service, was hardly what one would call a university. Little science was taught there. None of the professors made significant contributions in their fields. There was a very small library, and in the town only one poorly stocked bookstore. Humboldt's chosen field of study was finance, considered a suitable subject for young men without ambition, and he, like other students, seldom bothered to attend lectures. After six months of study, Humboldt's sober older brother Wilhelm saw little progress in Alexander's intellectual maturity: "His chief failing is vanity, and a love of approbation, the cause of which lies in the fact that his nature has never been stirred by any deep or overwhelming interest" (CB I, 47). But the superficiality of college life and disappointment in love gave Humboldt new resolve. From now on, he swore, he would put "the temptations of life" aside for higher aims.

Sent home to mature for a year while his brother went on to the University of Göttingen, Humboldt met a turning point in the person of Carl Willdenow, a few years older and author of a botanical survey, *Flora of Berlin*. Inspired by Willdenow, Humboldt discovered nature. Exploring the family estate examining mosses, lichens, and fungi, he experienced, as he put it to a friend from Frankfurt, the "complete enjoyment of the purest and most innocent pleasure." Even more exhilarating were times when he and Willdenow would "wander together, hand in hand, through the vast temple of nature." He was, he told his friend, "collecting materials for a work on the various properties of plants, medicinal properties excepted; it is a work requiring such great research, and such a profound knowledge of botany, as to be far beyond my unassisted powers" (CB I, 55–57).

It would not be easy. In Germany science remained closely tied to the needs of a feudal order. Workers had to be fed, so there was concern for agricultural yields. Geology was important because state-owned mines were a major source of income supporting the army and the state bureaucracy. Prussia had no colonies, few explorers, and almost none of the merchants and entrepreneurs so important in the development of science in England. Peasants worked on feudal estates. The landed aristocracy served in the army and civil service. For these pursuits a year at the University of Göttingen was considered sufficient. Once there, Humboldt found more to stimulate his newly active mind: comparative racial anatomy with Johann Friedrich Blumenbach, history of ancient Greece with Gottlob Heyne, and some basic knowledge in chemistry and physics from Karl Kastner and Georg Lichtenberg.[5] Even more inspiring was an escorted tour to England the next summer with Georg Forster, a veteran of Cook's second voyage to the Pacific, as guide and mentor. Listening to Forster reflect on South Sea islanders, visiting Joseph Banks's herbarium, viewing William Hodges's paintings of scenes along the Ganges, Humboldt was inspired with a new ambition. He, too, would become an explorer and a scientist. He would prove his friend Willdenow's mountain-top theory of the creation of regional species. He would collect skulls to send back to Göttingen for Blumenbach's studies of racial anatomy. He would discover strange new plants like a dragon tree he once saw in a Berlin botanical garden.

Returning to Berlin after the trip to London with Forster was a letdown. Humboldt complained in his journal, "The companionship I enjoyed on this journey, the kind interest shown me by Sir Joseph Banks, and the sudden passion which seized me for everything connected with the sea, and for visiting tropical lands, all exerted a most powerful influence in the formation of my projects, which, however, could not be carried out during the lifetime of my mother" (CB I, 92). He was required, said his mother, to have a profession. Dutifully he enrolled in the School of Mining at Freiburg, vowing to pursue science on the side. A monograph in Latin, *Florae Fribergensis*, on fungi, mosses, and lichens found underground in the mines of Freiburg, appeared in print with an attached note on Blumenbach's theory of vital energy. Even more ambitious was a long series of experiments in electrical shock that he hoped would resolve ongoing disputes about galvanism, "lay the foundations of a new way of healing," and make him "the originator of a new science, that of vital energy." Shocking animals, plants, and himself repeatedly, at one point he blistered his back so badly that a doctor had to be called in for consultation. Humboldt published a memoir on his findings—"Experiments on the excited muscle and nerve fiber with conjectures on the chemical process of life in the animal and vegetable world."[6] Fourcroy, professor of chemistry at the Muséum in Paris, criticized his method as unsystematic and faulted him for failing to repeat his experiments. Worse, his thesis turned out to be wrong, and recognition for solving some of the mystery of electricity went instead to Alessandro Volta.

New inspiration came at Jena, when Humboldt was introduced to the circle that gathered around Goethe and Schiller by his brother Wilhelm. Here science was taking another course in response to the philosopher Kant's devastating critique of metaphysics and insistence that empirical science could not reach beyond observed phenomena. The year Alexander arrived, Goethe was attempting to prove Kant wrong with a work in botany. Inspired by plants he saw in an Italian garden, Goethe set out to master Linnaeus's complex system of classifying plants by species and genus. Finding it impossibly tedious and detailed, he changed course. Now in a work he titled *The Metamorphosis of Plants* Goethe hoped to reveal something infinitely greater than any mere catalog of species and genera: an inner essence, a basic plant-form that remained the same even as it varied in different species and environments. And he planned to go on to other areas of science, to the essence of light and color, and of bones in a study that he called "osteology." There was instant rapport, with Goethe impressed by Humboldt's range of knowledge, and Humboldt by the grandeur of Goethe's proposals.

From Friedrich Schiller came other insights. Here the answer to Kant was aesthetics, access to a truth beyond physical phenomena by way of art and poetry. Invited by Schiller to contribute an essay for the first issue of a new literary and philosophical journal, *Die Horen*, Humboldt accepted with enthusiasm:

> Never has my vanity, and that of a noble kind, been so highly flattered as by your invitation to assist you in the dissemination of philosophical ideas . . . Never have my expectations been raised by any literary undertaking as they are by yours, in which from the intellectual powers employed, great results may be anticipated. . . . So long as the present method of studying botany and natural history continues to be followed, in which attention is

directed only to varieties of form, the physiognomy of plants and animals, whereby the study of characteristic distinctions and the law of classification is confounded with the true object of science, so long must botany, for example, fail to furnish a worthy subject of speculation to thoughtful men. . . . But you feel with me that there is something higher yet to be attained, that there is something even to be regained; for Aristotle and Pliny, whose descriptions were addressed to the aesthetic feelings and were aimed at the cultivation of a love of art, undoubtedly possessed a wider range of view than the modern naturalist who contents himself with the mere register of nature. (CB I, 179–180)

Humboldt was encouraged. He too would be no mere "registrar of nature." He too would provide a "wider range of vision." A "bit of rubbish," Schiller commented on Humboldt's essay, "The Rhodian Genius," in which Humboldt depicted vital energy as a dancing spirit redirecting young people's vision up and away from sensual desire. Much as the image may have spoken to Humboldt's ongoing struggle with passionate attraction to young men, for Schiller the essay had an air of artifice. For all his romantic evocations, Humboldt, Schiller suspected, was at heart an empiricist, always wanting to map and measure when nature had to be seen and felt.

In truth, Humboldt was in no way ready to give up the measuring of quantities he was learning at the School of Mines. Always for him, there would be special pleasure in the taking of a reading, the marking down of a figure. The immediate purpose of measuring at the School of Mines might be utilitarian, but why could that probing beneath the surface of the earth not also serve the "higher purposes" conceived by Goethe and Schiller? Might it be possible to map invisible forces and currents not evident to the senses and find the key to Nature's innermost secrets? Humboldt loved his instruments. He loved the feel of them. He loved writing down lists of measurements. Each instrument was kept in its own protective case: thermometers for measuring the temperature of air and water, barometers for determining altitude, devices for fixing geographical location, including a pocket sextant, microscopes, telescopes for looking at stars, scales, compasses, chronometers, a rain gauge, surveyors' instruments, a eudiometer for measuring the amount of oxygen in the air, instruments that could measure not just the surface of the earth, but its atmosphere and waters, its position in the solar system, its distance from the sun. If Lenoir's repeating circle allowed French voyagers to correct maps and check locations, for Humboldt its value went far beyond utilitarian aims.

With it and other instruments he might map the cosmos and reveal the inner heart of nature.

❦

In Paris, the days of August passed by. Humboldt was more and more impatient. In mid-September he would turn twenty-nine. In another year he would be thirty. Why was he in Paris? To make small talk at parties, give yet another talk at the Institut de France, wait for a voyage that might never get under way given the shambles the Directors were making of administration? He had half a mind, he told Bonpland, to go off on his own. They could go together. He had money enough for both of them, and the Muséum would sponsor them in name if not with funding. They could get to Egypt, join up with Napoleon, travel on with him to India, or better still split off and go to China or Tibet. If the Baudin expedition ever did leave port, they could join it en route. And Baudin might never leave at all. The Directorate was out of money. French forces were under attack again in Italy. All available ships were needed to supply the army.

Prospects did not look good for two young men eager to explore the world. News arrived. The French fleet had been destroyed in Aboukir Bay. Official bulletins of victories in Egypt were discounted given rumors of disease among French troops and the mass execution of thousands of Muslim prisoners. Islam had declared war on Europe. Pirates roamed the Mediterranean. In Europe a new coalition was forming against France. If war came, Humboldt, as an enemy alien, would have to leave France. Bonpland would be drafted into the navy. It was not clear how they were to get anywhere with Europe on the brink of war, British warships cruising the seas looking for French ships, passes needed to cross all national and princely borders. And to make it worse, Bonpland was busy with other projects. The day after Humboldt's birthday in September, Bonpland was off with his brother on a ten-day fossil-collecting expedition, and then spent a further week arranging his collections for consultation with Lamarck at the Muséum. Humboldt was left on his own, facing the prospect of spending the winter in Paris with nothing accomplished. If only he had arrived in Paris in time to go with Napoleon. Somehow they had to get to Egypt, and leave before Bonpland was forced to return to La Rochelle.

Suddenly an opportunity presented itself. An acquaintance of an acquaintance, the Swedish consul, was passing through Paris on the way to Marseille, where he was to meet a Swedish ship that would take him to Algiers. Could the ship take two additional passengers? Yes, said the consul, he could probably arrange transport for Humboldt and his friend if they wanted to come with him. And he might also be able to get them permission to visit the Atlas Mountains and then passage from Algiers to Alexandria. But they would have to leave immediately to catch the ship at Marseille. Humboldt went to Bonpland. Pack up, he said. I have money for both of us. I wrote to the Muéeum. Write to Jussieu and ask for a letter of introduction.

To the disbelief and anger of Bonpland's brother, Michel, and to the sorrow of Bonpland's parents and sister in La Rochelle, Bonpland agreed. He wrote to Jussieu, who was away in Lyon:

October 20, 1798.

Citizen:

My immediate departure for a voyage to Africa with M. Humboldt, about which you already know the aim, does not allow me to take directly from your lips and in person the instructions which must serve me as guide in the fine career on which I am about to pursue. I am so bold as to ask you, Citizen, after the friendship which you have never ceased to witness for me in the time I have studied at the Muséum, to include me among your correspondents and give me a letter of introduction to different agents of the Republic that will facilitate my carrying out the task I am undertaking, in relying as much on good will as on my own abilities. (AB, 1–2)

Jussieu's answer was immediate:

Citizen Bonpland:

The professors of the Muséum have been informed of the project that you are undertaking of accompanying M. Humboldt, the celebrated Prussian physicist, to North Africa, and afterward to parts of India, in order to make studies and observations in the fields of natural history and physics. They believe that given your learned studies you will be useful to science and particularly to the Muséum whose collections they wish to augment. . . . We must not then miss the occasion to make new discoveries by maintaining a correspondence with you and inviting you to make known to us any objects which appear to you to be new, as well as any particular facts which may be relevant to the science of the future. Already we have invited M. Humboldt to do the same and we hope he will agree to our request. Having like him a taste for science and a desire to contribute to its progress, you also will serve our cause. We have promised him, in this regard, the assistance of all our French consuls and agents in the diverse locations where he will travel. (AB, 2)

Official sanction for the expedition came quickly from the Directors, happy enough to sponsor a rich Prussian willing to finance an expedition to advance French science. In a rush Humboldt packed up his instruments and hired a coach to carry them and their equipment south. Within the week he and Bonpland were on their way in company with the Swedish consul. Arrived at the port at Marseille, Humboldt sent off a last word to Pictet in Geneva, who had helped with his early attempts at publication. He was about to leave for North Africa. He hoped "tranquility and happiness would reign" in Pictet's country. He hoped Pictet would not forget someone who was "attached to him heart and soul." Furthermore, his chronometer was a marvel, and although the carriage ride was so shockingly bumpy that one of his thermometers had broken, with the chronometer he had already measured the longitude at Marseille to within 8 degrees of error (LA, 7).

But now again came disappointment. They waited. November passed by. No ship arrived. Every day Humboldt and Bonpland climbed the hill of Notre Dame de la Garde to watch for ships entering the harbor. To ease their impatience they took a side trip to Toulon to visit Bougainville's old ship the *Boudeuse* in dry dock. Humboldt was reduced to tears thinking of opportunities missed. Still no packet boat arrived. Then came bad news. The Swedish ship had been damaged in a storm. It would not arrive until spring if it arrived at all. They were left high and dry on the dock with Humboldt's crates of instruments. Would they have to return to Paris? No, said Humboldt, somehow they would find another ship to take them east into the Mediterranean. He booked passage on a small boat headed for Tunis, but again was thwarted when French officials refused to let them leave. Did he not understand? Napoleon was in trouble in Egypt. The British fleet was closing in. The Sultan declared war on France. Pirates roamed the Mediterranean. A Frenchman arriving in Tunis would be immediately thrown into jail. They could go no further.

Humboldt was not one to give up. No boat. No passage with a pilgrim caravan. But nearby Spain was an ally of France. Why not travel overland across Spain with their equipment on pack animals and head for the Spanish coast? From there they could find a ship to take them into the Mediterranean and on to Alexandria and from Alexandria they could get to India or China.

Seven months later, Humboldt described in a letter to Wilhelm not remnants of Napoleon's defeated army, not ancient Egyptian ruins, Hindu temples, or the eastern deserts of China, but the tropical coastline sailed by Columbus three hundred years before.

> What trees! Coconut trees 50–60 feet tall, *Poinciana pulcherrima*
> with bouquets a foot high with flowers of a magnificent deep red;
> bananas and a mass of trees with huge leaves and perfumed flowers
> as large as a hand, totally unknown to us. (LA, 27)

Brilliant white sand beaches lined with palms alternated with green hills giving way to densely forested hills in the distance. Here and there a shrub or small tree made a splash of crimson or orange flowers. Glossy-leaved banana trees, giant feathery date and coconut palms, pomegranates, pawpaws, oranges in flower, all growing freely, not with roots stunted in pots or flowers desiccated and glued to a page, but alive, vigorous, fruitful under a glittering sun.

2

A Walk across Spain and a
Climb Up a Volcano

Setting out on foot from Marseille across the Pyrenees through Catalonia, headed for Madrid and the Spanish coast, Humboldt and Bonpland began a routine they would follow for the next four years. At intervals throughout the day and every evening Humboldt unpacked and set up his equipment. He checked the location of moon, sun, and stars, measured latitudes, noted wind speed and barometric pressure, and recorded rows of figures in his journal. Bonpland looked not up but down, constantly stopping to investigate a new shape of leaf or strange texture of moss. At night he laid out the day's collections on a table or, if no table was available, on a blanket spread out on the ground. He arranged the parts of each new plant on sheets of drying paper, made notes in his journal, tightened his plant presses to preserve what he found during the day. And from the beginning there was much to find. They passed through flowered valleys, plains scattered with cacti and agaves, terraced groves of olives. He sat under glossy-leaved orange trees, breathing in a scent of flowers so much sweeter than the flowers of dwarf trees carted out every summer from the orangerie at the Jardin in Paris. He passed rocky outcroppings covered with roses, stands of palms, watered fields planted in rice, wheat, and cotton. By the time they reached Madrid, Bonpland had a shipment of plant specimens and seeds ready to send back to his brother Michel in La Rochelle along with instructions to forward a selection to Thouin at the Jardin in Paris.

In Madrid, Humboldt presented their credentials to government officials and applied for safe conduct to the coast so they could be on their way to Egypt. Again he had contacts. An old friend of his father, Baron von Forell, was serving as ambassador to Spain from Saxony and immediately took an interest in their plans. Better still, Forell was on good terms with Spain's new secretary of state, Luis de Urquijo, who took even more of an interest. The

25

Spanish empire in the New World was in trouble. Brutal treatment, forced labor, and European diseases were killing off the native workforce. Protest at the immorality of slavery was undermining the morale of colonial officials. Creole leaders quarreled with the Spanish-born administrators sent to guarantee that profits went back to the Spanish crown. To make it worse, the stock of easily extractable precious metals was depleted, mines were not producing, and imported food was becoming more expensive. No foreign scientist had been given free passage in Spanish territories since La Condamine's mission to measure an arc of the meridian in 1735. The coastlines of the empire were closely guarded against intrusion, with ports closed to foreign traders and commercial travelers.

It must have dawned slowly on Humboldt. Here was an unexplored new world. Images of the Nile and Ganges began to fade. Humboldt sent Bonpland to meet Forell at the court at Aranjuez with a letter of commendation, introducing him as "this young man, whose talents, erudition in botany, zoology, and anatomy, and especially his manner have made him dear to me" (LA, 14). He put together a memorandum for Urquijo. Spanish possessions in the New World had never been scientifically surveyed. There was incalculable benefit for colonial powers in such studies. Yes, the French mission under La Condamine had caused only trouble for Spain. But he and his "learnèd secretary," Aimé Bonpland, were different. Their expedition would not be for the glory of France. It would be for science. They would offer their findings to Spain and to the world, geological findings useful in navigation, valuable plants, minerals of potential profit, plants useful for food and fodder, and—most important—better yields from mines.

For Urquijo it was an offer too good to refuse. His position was precarious. He had been secretary of state for only a few months and would be out of office in less than two years. His fervent opposition to the Catholic Church got him enemies. His influence at court was resented by the queen's lover and favorite, Godoy. Here was a well-connected scientist willing to fund an expedition out of his own pocket and pass on to Spain results that might help to increase revenues. The ministers reviewed Humboldt's memorandum. Humboldt waited, hardly daring to think it would be approved. Even before he fully registered the change in their prospects, passports were issued and letters written with the King's royal seal: by *order of his Majesty King Charles IV.* "Never before had such concessions been granted to a traveler, and never had the Spanish government shown such confidence in a foreigner," Humboldt recalled later in his *Personal Narrative* of the voyage (PN, 18). They had been given carte blanche, not only safe conduct, but assistance from civil and military officials in all of Spain's possessions in the Americas. They had permission to make astronomical, physical and natural history observations. They could collect whatever they liked. A world previously closed was opened to them. Almost before they knew it they were on their way to the coast and the port of La Coruña. From there they would sail, not east through the Mediterranean to Asia as planned, but west across the Atlantic to Havana, gateway to the new world of the Americas.

Waiting to embark at La Coruña, Humboldt sent a last letter to his friend from the School of Mining at Freiburg, Carl Freiesleben. Freiesleben had been Humboldt's guide on his first day down into the mines and they became friends immediately. The day after their first meeting they were off together on a week-long trip through the mountains and from then on during Humboldt's time at Freiburg had been inseparable. As Julius Lowenberg, one of Humboldt's biographers, put it, "It was one of Humboldt's characteristics, evinced early in life to select wherever he might be, one particular friend on which to lavish the full force of his affections" (CB I, 109). By now it was clear that, whatever Humboldt might once have hoped, there would be no such intimate friendship with Bonpland. Bonpland is a "good person," wrote Humboldt to Freiesleben, but "he has left me very cold for the past six months, which means I have only a scientific relationship with him" (quoted in Wulf, 95). Perhaps that same disappointment had also prompted a nostalgic letter to Willdenow written back on the trek across Spain:

> Although I have not written a line to you since Marseille, my friend and brother, I have been no less active for you and for your happiness, as you will see from this letter. I am about to close a case for you, containing 400 plants, perhaps a fourth of which have never been described. They come from countries no botanist has ever penetrated before us. When you look over this collection of plants you will persuade yourself of the fact that there did not pass a day when I did not think of you, whether in the forests, on the prairies, or on the shore of the sea. Everywhere I collected for you and only for you, since I do not want to begin my own herbier until I am overseas. (LA, 11–12)

It is hard to know what Bonpland would have made of the letter had he seen it. Whatever it might presage for troubles ahead, it was too late to turn back. The plants he collected on the walk across Spain to be turned over to an unknown botanist friend of Humboldt who had never been out of Europe and seldom

out of Prussia? In the first week or so of their trek, Humboldt had been eager
to do some botanical work of his own, but well before their arrival at Madrid
he was leaving the work of collecting and preserving to Bonpland. His were
higher aims, as Humboldt explained in a letter to the Austrian naturalist and
mineralogist, Karl von Moll, also written just before sailing from La Coruña:

> In a few hours we will be rounding Cape Finistère—I will collect
> plants and fossils. I will make astronomical observations with excel-
> lent instruments. I will analyze the air with the aid of chemistry.
> But all that is not the principle aim of my voyage. I will never
> lose sight of the harmony of concurrent forces, the influence of
> the inanimate universe on the animal and vegetal realm. (LA, 18)

And as he also made clear in a goodbye note to Willdenow:

> I hope we will see each other again, alive and well. All my instru-
> ments are on board. Your memory accompanies me. "Man must
> will the great and the good, the rest is destiny." (LA, 19)

The ship, the *Pizarro*, headed out of the harbor at night. The captain ordered
that no lights be lit on deck to avoid alerting British ships that might be out
patrolling the coastline. Humboldt complained. It made it impossible for him
to set up his instruments and make his observations. Standing with Bonpland
at the rail, staring back as the lights of Europe faded away, he indulged in
melancholy reflection. Did Bonpland feel the weight of the occasion? Did
he sense the great pulse of the universe leading them on into the unknown?
Bonpland nodded amicably. He was watching the faint phosphorescent glow off
the sea rippling in the gentle swell of the waves and thinking about the tiny
creatures that made such displays. Deflated by the meager response, Humboldt
went below to record impressions in his journal:

> The moment of leaving Europe for the first time is impressive.
> We vainly recall the frequency of communications between the
> two worlds; we vainly reflect how, thanks to the improved state of
> navigation, we may now cross the Atlantic, which compared to the
> Pacific is but a shortish arm of the sea; yet what we feel when we
> begin our first long-distance voyage is none the less accompanied

by a deep emotion, unlike any we may have felt in our youth. Separated from the objects of our dearest affections, and entering into a new life, we are forced to fall back on ourselves, and we feel more isolated than we have ever felt before. (PN, 19)[1]

On deck, Bonpland strained ahead to the horizon, thinking of the new land that would be ahead. He watched sea swallows fly and dolphins show their silvery backs in the swell. He admired nighttime meteor showers that increased in intensity as they approached the African coast. But at sea there was little for a botanist to discover. You should write how you feel, record your impressions, Humboldt urged him. You can't rely on memory. But it was impossible to write on deck, and below he found it hard to breathe. Write the facts, said Humboldt, make a story of it. But the bustle of departure and worries about the British—if captured, as a Prussian Humboldt would be set free in some nearby port, Bonpland as a Frenchman and enemy might be locked up or worse—seemed trivial and unworthy of notice in the light of what might be ahead.

One day as Bonpland stood watching, the ship sailed through a colony of jellyfish. It slowed as it passed through shimmering metallic purple, violet, green, yellow, brown billowing filaments coloring the sea in drifting translucent patterns. Bonpland stared down at the blended bodies, at the amorphous mass of organic life, beautiful in its moving parts, and spotted a rare mollusk, *Dagysa notata*. Quickly he called for a line and hauled it on board for Humboldt to draw in his journal, a cluster of small gelatinous bags open at each end, cylindrical and transparent, stacked one on top of another to make a group 6 or 8 inches long. Bonpland filled in the space beside Humboldt's sketch with Latin names and notes, then picked up the gelatinous mass to put it back into the sea. Humboldt stopped his hand and went below to get his Leyden jar. Bonpland shrugged and watched as Humboldt repeatedly shocked the small creature, with little effect beyond a mild phosphorescent glow.[2]

After fifteen days of uneventful transit, they approached the Canary Islands. There the *Pizarro* would catch the currents and trade winds that made for fast passage across the Atlantic. First they were to stop to check for British ships. They anchored offshore, with Bonpland in such a fever of excitement that he climbed up the mast to see better what might be on land. All night he paced the deck in warm tropical air waiting for daylight. Ashy slopes of volcanic mountains rose five or six hundred feet out of a bright metallic silver sea. The sky was streaked with falling stars. Phosphorescence diffused off the water in a soft palpable glow. Then suddenly the sky would change. A strange reddish light came behind the hills in back of masses of black storm clouds. Basalt cliffs cast dark shadows across a sea turned molten copper. Quickly the storm passed with a few spates of rain. Bonpland thought of his sister Olive. He thought of summer nights in La Rochelle and the two of them sitting on the grass watching stars never so bright as they were in this Southern sky. At the first light of dawn, he surveyed the shore with a spyglass but could see no living creature on the volcanic slopes, no plant, no birds even. He had to laugh. So desperate to find his first rare species, climbing masts and staying up all night, and then finding a barren landscape!

The *Pizarro* sailed on cautiously down a narrow channel between the islands with a sailor in the bow plumbing for depth. Bonpland watched as the lead brought up a lobed brown-stemmed creature. Was it an animal or a plant? For a moment he could not tell, so strange was the shape of soft green lobes covered with stiff cream-colored hairs on a brown stem. He and Humboldt pored over it. Most probably a fucus, a seaweed, Bonpland decided. Look, said Humboldt, it comes from the depth of the sea, but the leaves are still green, proof of his thesis in *Florae Fribergensis* that the green of plants comes not only from sunlight. As for Bonpland, he was beginning to experience a strange kind of self-consciousness as if he were looking at himself through the wrong end of a spyglass. Only Olive would understand, and finally he took up paper and pen to begin the letter he promised he would write to the family every week he was gone:

> You can imagine the pleasure one experiences when after 15 days at sea, land is sighted. I climbed up high on the main mast. I looked around with a large spyglass to discover the lay of this land that to me was so new and which would relieve the burning thirst that devoured me to see plants, insects, birds, etc. . . . Unfortunately darkness came and forced me to climb down without having seen anything. All night I walked the deck, I waited for day break with great impatience, looking all the time in my Richard for plants native to the Canaries. Finally came the daylight I so much longed for. We were close to land but still could distinguish nothing but uneven terrain, not very spacious, but elevated and without any greenery, only black shapes on a ground of basaltic rock brought down by volcanic eruptions. (AB, 4)[3]

It was as if he was becoming a different person, the angle from which he saw things curiously altered. After sighting several islands, without being able to find an entrance to Lanzarote harbor, and still without seeing any living being, it came as a relief when the captain put down a boat to send to shore:

> Armed like a "Robinson," I was one of the first to jump into the boat. Soon we were under sail and approaching an opening in the rocks where without doubt we saw a man fishing. Immediately we steered toward him. So concentrated was the man on his task that he did not see us until we were close enough to accost him. Fear that we were English made him try to run away, but we were quicker. We grabbed him immediately and reassured him as best we could.

Desperate for new plants he finds a coast barren of plant life. Excited to set foot on a new continent, the first person he meets is a fisherman speaking Spanish. The irony was not lost on Bonpland. Defoe's cannibals, Cook's South Sea islanders, adventure stories so eagerly consumed by school boys dreaming of travel in foreign lands, all were falling away in the face of this new reality:

> I doubt that the discoveries of Cook in the South Seas could have made as much impression on us as we experienced that day. To have sailed twenty-four hours in sight of land on which there was no living thing, land completely vulcanized, and then approaching this shore to see a single man who fled from our view. All seemed to be the discovery of a land unknown and made even more of an impression given that it was such a short time since we had left civilization and we were not yet accustomed to travel. Having examined this man who dressed just like our country people and spoke very good Spanish, I began to lose the fantasy I had concocted and went out looking for plants. I found only two growing in the sand, for there is virtually no soil in this part of the island. (AB, 4–5)

"Grandiose wild nature," mused Humboldt in his journal as they rounded the tip of Lanzarote, and leaving volcanic slopes behind, approached cultivated fields and what looked like rows of corn: "even the desert is animated when you see some trace of man's work on it." He had to be careful, Humboldt reminded himself, keep to his plan, record on the spot his impressions, but at the same time not neglect to make his scientific measurements. The further they went the more Humboldt had to say and the more Bonpland was silent. That "thirst" for new lands, that eagerness to be the first to go ashore, youthful ambitions nurtured in European hot houses and herbaria, all were coming away like dead skin. Bonpland's letter to Olive ended abruptly. The Captain was keeping his promise to give them time to climb Tenerife's volcano, Pico del Teide, but only for two days. They would have to be quick.

Up they climbed, through orchards where European apples, pears, and peaches mingled with oranges, pomegranates, and date palms, and further to tree-like heaths, lush fern forests, pteris, blechnum, asplenium, and higher yet to stunted wind-twisted juniper and pine. Humboldt measured elevations and mapped zones of vegetation. Bonpland collected plants. Above at twelve thousand feet, mist alternately hid the summit of the volcano and then gave way to reveal the shimmering barren pyramid of the cone surrounded by a severe landscape of pumice and black obsidian punctuated with isolated tufts of gray-brown brome. They camped for the night with the guides, cold, close to freezing, teeth chattering in the shelter of a cave-like hollow in the rock. A cold north wind blew clouds across the moon, ragged shreds wrapped around the cone above them and tore away again so that the shining mass cast a dark triangular shadow over and down on a bank of solid cloud that covered the valley below. Perched on the ledge with smoke from the campfire burning their eyes, hands and feet numb with cold, they experienced the first of many discomforts to come.

The next day on the rim of the crater Humboldt alternated between exact measurement and scenic description. Temperature five degrees. The view "majestic." "The journey to the Tenerife volcano's summit is not solely interesting for the amount of phenomena available for scientific research but far more for the picturesque beauties it offers to those who keenly feel the splendors of nature" (PN, 34). A drawing by Humboldt on the summit, made into a plate for Humboldt's *Views of the Cordilleras*, gives a snapshot of the two of them. Humboldt stands center stage, surrounded by tortured rock furrowed and pushed up into sharpened crags and gazing out into the distance, one hand braced against the ledge that surrounds the crater. Off to one side, Bonpland kneels down on one knee, gesturing to something close to the ground, looking up as if trying to catch Humboldt's attention. In his botanical journal and later in *Plantes équinoxiales*, Bonpland described what he saw there. *Viola cheiranthifolia*, a tiny plant, delicate but still robust enough to survive at an elevation of 3,400 meters, found only there, only on the dry and stony crater of the Tenerife volcano (PE I, 111).

Back down at sea level Humboldt poured out his feelings in a letter to Wilhelm. "What spectacle! What joy! We went into the crater, perhaps further than any other naturalist." He described the sensation of looking down over the edge into the steaming crater with "sulfur vapor burning their clothes" (LA, 21). A similarly triumphant letter went to Baron von Forell in Madrid. He was confident now, he wrote, of important scientific findings. In a letter to Suchfort, rector at Göttingen, he wondered at the magnitude of what he might accomplish. Would he be able to do it? Lay bare the inner secrets of Nature? Could a man do such a thing? Could he come to know the inner heart of something like a volcano?

> Whether it is possible for man to know, with the equality of causation, from where comes the great inequality of actions in nature, I have some doubt. Notably all the ideas that have been expressed on the causes of volcanoes, on the origins of their products, seem to me to be false and unsustainable. And the enigmas we encounter deal not only with the inorganic world, but also to the living world. (LA, 24)

What had become of the native Guanche Indians of Tenerife? Gone, the only proof of their existence mummies buried in caves. How is it possible to understand slavery, understand how civilized nations like Spain and Portugal can treat Negroes like merchandise? Or understand the diseases that kill off whole races of native people? Humboldt finished his letter to the rector with an upbeat account of the climb up the volcano, adding measurements of height and temperature. As for Bonpland's letter to Olive, it was never finished, not even mailed until months later, after their arrival in Cumaná. For the next few years from Humboldt a steady stream of letters would go back to Europe, describing scene after scene, impression after impression, often with pages of measurements of temperature, humidity, elevation, magnetism. From Bonpland would come almost nothing as he absorbed the sights and sounds of a new world.

On they sailed across the Atlantic following the route of Columbus, using the passage sailors called "The Ladies' Route" for its ease of sailing. They passed masses of floating tropical sea-grape, dolphins, sharks, a school of flying fish leaping twelve, fifteen, eighteen feet into the air. At his first sighting of the Southern Cross, Humboldt quoted Dante's pilgrim ascending out of Inferno and approaching Purgatory: "Right-hand I turned, and, setting me to spy that alien pole, beheld four stars, the same the first men saw and since no living eye." He recalled a shipboard scene from Bernardin de Saint-Pierre's romantic travel tale, *Paul et Virginie*, in which the sighting of the Southern Cross is a signal for the heroine to leap into the water to her death rather than return to Europe and a loveless marriage (PN, 43). Did Bonpland repress a smile? Never would he have the heart to tell Humboldt the Muséum's low opinion of Bernadin as a scientist, Humboldt who carried Bernadin's travel romance with him everywhere, reading out passages to Bonpland at odd moments during the day.[4]

Humboldt worked his instruments, recording measurements that he would send back to Europe as soon as they reached port. Days passed. They reached the coast of Brazil and turned north, bound for Havana. The weather was fair. No British ships were sighted. Then came trouble. Just as they were approaching the northern coast of South America, a malignant fever broke out on board ship. The captain is incompetent, fumed Humboldt. He should have fumigated the ship. He should order the ship's doctor to stop treating illness with bleeding and purging. He should carry quinine; certainly every Spanish ship should be provided with Jesuit's bark as a remedy against fever. More of the passengers and some of the crew fell ill. A young man died, only nineteen, sent by his widowed mother to make a fortune in the slave plantations of the Caribbean. Alarmed passengers rebelled, refused to continue on, demanded to be put on shore immediately before reaching Havana. So it was that instead of sailing on to Jamaica, at dawn on the 16th of July, 1799, the *Pizarro* approached the lushly forested coast of Cumaná in Spanish New Grenada, sailed by Columbus so many years before.

As they drew closer to the shore two dugout canoes came out to meet them. In each were eighteen Indians, bare chested, russet skinned, strongly built. A leader stood up, straddling a pile of cedar timbers, tall and regal, sun glinting copper off his torso, holding up a handful of coconuts and a string of brightly colored fishes. Behind him a pile of broad heliconia leaves covered bunches of bananas, the cuirass of an armadillo, and some calabashes used as cups. The captain gestured the man to approach and to come on board. Pleasantries were exchanged. The leader offered his services. If they wished, he said, he would take the ship safely through the entrance to the harbor. He could show them the town, find a house for them to rent, arrange for servants to clean and cook for them. He also could arrange trips into the interior if they so desired. For the next sixteen months, Carlos del Pino would be Humboldt and Bonpland's guide, arranging their living quarters, assembling mule trains and porters to carry Humboldt's instruments, facilitating excursions along the coast and into the interior. Humboldt's comment in his *Personal Narrative*: "It was fortunate that the first Indian we met on arrival was a man whose knowledge was to prove extremely helpful for our journey's objectives" (PN, 48).

As they came near to the harbor entrance, the light began to fade. They would have to wait for daylight to go through the channel, said Carlos. Neither Humboldt nor Bonpland could sleep, but stayed up all night on deck while Carlos entertained them with tales of crocodiles, boas, jaguars, and, of special interest to Humboldt, electric eels. The next morning, safely through the harbor, when they set foot on white sand beach, Humboldt had his thermometer ready to plunge into the sand and record the heat at 37.7° Celsius.

Carlos led the two Europeans and the captain on across the beach and through the Indian settlement along the shore. A woman grinding corn in the shelter of a lean-to porch looked up. A group of wide-eyed children watched as they passed by. With pride Carlos took them through his own garden. "More a copse in the woods than a garden," Humboldt wrote later in his diary. Carlos pointed to the two-foot-wide trunk of a silk wood tree, planted only four years before. "I think the Indian's estimate of the tree's age was somewhat exaggerated," wrote Humboldt. Small plots for vegetables were cleared here and there among the trees. In larger openings maize ripened, ringed with clumps of banana trees. Humboldt hurried on, intent on negotiations ahead. Back in Madrid, Forell had pressed on him the importance of the prompt observance of formalities with local officials. They passed quickly over a bridge across the Manzanares River, then down a stretch of hot and dusty road to the European town. Here damage done by the catastrophic 1797 Riobamba earthquake was still evident. Streets were lined with piles of rubble; hammers and saws sounded as new houses went up over the ruins of the old. For Humboldt it augured well. One of the delights ahead for him in Cumaná would be a feast of seismic phenomena to record and observe: earthquakes, sulfurous gases, meteor showers, and most dramatic of all, the famous "Aguirre's fire," burning spouts that periodically flared up out of the ground, named after the most brutal of the Spanish conquistadors. Arrived at the governor's house, Carlos waited outside while the Europeans went in to present their papers, with Humboldt gratified to find a warm welcome from the governor.

It was not long before the two were in earnest consultation. Did Humboldt think it possible that there was more nitrogen in the air in the tropics than in Spain? Might the rusting of iron be correlated with the high humidity readings shown on a hygrometer? In weeks and months to come, such conversations would be high points of travel for Humboldt. As he put it in his *Personal Narrative*, "The name of his native country pronounced on a distant shore could not please the ears of a traveler more than hearing the words 'nitrogen,' 'oxidation of iron,' 'hygrometer'" (PN, 51). Far from "civilization," to come across a treatise on chemistry or a rudimentary electrical machine, or, here in Cumaná, a provincial governor eager to talk about physics provided for Humboldt a special delight.

True to his promise, Carlos found them a house on the outskirts of town, two stories and a top-floor balcony where Humboldt set up his instruments. On the floor below, Bonpland made a long table with planks so he could lay out his plants. With no glass in the windows and a breeze off the sea, the upper rooms were cool for sleeping and the balcony well situated for Humboldt to view the night sky. Less fortunate turned out to be the view of a plaza below one morning, where Humboldt was shocked to witness a slave auction. "Our house in Cumaná was magnificently placed for observing the sky and meteorological phenomena; on the other hand, during the day, we observed scenes that disgusted us" (PN, 66). A few weeks later as they sailed down the Manzanares River on a moonlit night, the sight of a group of slaves celebrating their day off with music and dancing on the bank provoked melancholy reflection:

> Descending the river we passed the plantations or *charas* where negroes had lit bonfires for their fiestas. A light billowing smoke rose above the palm-tree tops, giving a reddish color to the moon's disk. It was a Sunday night and the slaves danced to the monotonous and noisy music of guitars. A fundamental feature of the black African races is their inexhaustible store of vitality and joy. After working painfully hard all week, they prefer to dance and sing on their fiesta days rather than sleep for a long time. We should be wary of criticizing this mixture of thoughtlessness and frivolity for it sweetens the evils of a life of deprivations and suffering! (PN, 68)

There is an uneasiness in Humboldt's "we." We Europeans might feel repulsion at the "monotonous and noisy" sound of African guitars. "We" might question the "thoughtlessness and frivolity" of dancing all night after a week of hard work. But we must understand the effects of a life full of misery. First intimate glimpses of native Indian life had been equally unsettling, as he related in a letter to Wilhelm:

> Outside of the town live the copper-colored Indians of which the men are almost completely nude. The huts are made of bamboo covered with coco leaves. I went into one of the huts. The mother was sitting with her children, in place of chairs on branches of coral thrown up by the sea. Each of them had before them a coconut

shell in place of a plate out of which they were eating some fish. The plots are completely open, one goes in and out freely; in most of the houses the doors are not closed even at night, so docile is the population. (LA, 26–27)

Still, he wrote Wilhelm, with all the strangeness of it, he and Bonpland were settling down comfortably "with two negresses one of which does the cooking." They planned to stay three months, maybe more, with the governor and other officials pleased to have them as visitors.

The governor was pleased, although when he saw how townspeople rushed to see the new arrivals he had second thoughts. Had the visitors from France brought with them some of the contagion of republicanism? But it was not for politics that locals crowded onto Humboldt's upper veranda. Word spread quickly of his instruments and experiments. Whenever Humboldt set up his apparatus and began his instrument readings there were murmurings. What was this strange man doing peering into the heavens? Was he a necromancer calling forth evil spells? Was this some strange new religion? In Cumaná Humboldt's notoriety became a burden:

> The numerous visitors disturbed us; in order not to disappoint all those who seemed to be so pleased to see the spots of the moon through Dollond's telescope, the absorption of two gases in a eudiometrical tube, or the effects of galvanism on the motions of a frog, we had to answer many obscure questions and repeat the same experiments for hours. (PN, 66)

Most popular was Humboldt's Leyden jar and demonstrations with some dead frogs procured for him by Carlos. See here, the frog is dead, Humboldt would point out to his audience. But look. He administered a shock. The muscles of the dead frog twitched. The audience gasped at the miraculous resuscitation. Local pedants heard about the miracle, came to debate the mysteries of life and death, and went away deflated by a lecture on the principles of physics. Humboldt would try to explain. With modern instruments it is possible to chart accurately the forces of the cosmos. No one can predict events like earthquakes or meteor showers, retorted the locals; it is God's will. In his diary Humboldt vented his irritation with such ignorance, "When we cannot hope to guess the causes of natural phenomena, we ought at least to try to discover their laws and, by comparing numerous facts, distinguish what is permanent and constant from what is variable and accidental" (PN, 59).

Regardless of the distraction of slave auctions, visits from curious locals, electrical demonstrations, and social gatherings with the local Creole aristocracy, Humboldt was filling page after page with measurements of earthquakes, eruptions, pillars of fire, sulfurous gases, inflammable fluids. Soon after their arrival in Cumaná a *Mémoire astronomique* was sent off to Delambre at the Bureau of Longitudes in Paris with instrument readings made on shipboard and at Tenerife. A day later he wrote a long letter to the mineralogist Delamétherie announcing that his instruments had come through the trip undamaged and he was making observations. To the letter were added four pages of observations from Tenerife and Cumaná, and a postscript: "Bonpland, my travel companion, has made a lovely collection of plants."

Every day Bonpland was out exploring the plain around the city. Among patches of foliage he found *Scoparia dulcis*, the sensitive plant with leaves that tremble when touched; lobelias in an endless palette of delicate colors; cassias, many of them unknown; *Brugmansia* with trumpet flowers in yellow, apricot, peach; bromeliads, "heart of flame" with reddish spines and emerging cylindrical flower a foot long in violet and white; "firebrand" heliconia twelve feet high with erect vibrant bracts and blade-like leaves. He traveled the banks of the Manzanares River looking for mimosas, erythrinas, ceibas, explored down to the mouth of a smaller river where mangrove trees waded into the water on long spidery roots. Upriver he found flowering leafy trees, bombax, Brazilwood, tamarind in shaded groves where local dairy farmers kept milk cool in earthenware jugs stored away in reed cages. Entries in his journal those first weeks in Cumaná come one after another as if written by someone too distracted to describe anything in detail, only jotting down notes before moving on to yet another discovery. Soon euphoria gave way to concentration. The entries become longer, with notes added in the margins.

In the arid salty soil of the plain around Cumaná he found more species of cacti than he could count, stately individuals, some of them thirty or forty feet tall with trunks branching like candelabra and habits of flowering utterly different from northern plants. It could be years before a botanist might be able to observe a cactus's flowering parts so as to distinguish one species from another. Twelve years later in the greenhouse at Malmaison, Bonpland would finally be able to coax one of his Cumaná cacti to produce the large red "very beautiful" flowers that allowed him to identify it as a new species:

> *Cactus speciosus* has much analogy in its bearing with *Cactus phyllanthus* and *Cactus alatus*, with which it was at first confused. But it was not until the month of March 1811 when this new candelabra

species gave flowers at Malmaison, that it was possible for me to establish the differences that exist between these three plants. (PR, 9)

Humboldt was happy to leave such botanical detail to Bonpland, as he made clear in a letter to Wilhelm:

> Bonpland assures me that he will lose his mind if the wonders do not cease soon. But what is more beautiful than any particular marvel is the impression produced by the ensemble of this powerful vegetal nature, exuberant and yet so gentle, so easy, so serene. (LA, 27)

For Bonpland, images of home were fading. No reports were going back to his friends and colleagues in Paris, and after the one shipment of plants and seeds sent to Michel from Madrid and the letter from Tenerife finally mailed to Olive, no letters were arriving in La Rochelle. To say what? The weather is rainy. Humboldt employed two servants to take care of us. I am collecting plants. This morning out on the plain I came upon . . . and he would tear up the paper and go out with his plant boxes and his journal. The plants that he was collecting, preserving, and describing would have to speak for him, and he would give them that voice. After the one letter describing his transformation from eager Crusoe to immersion in a new world of experiences, his family would have no word from him for more than a year.

PART II
THE VOYAGE

3

Aerial Views, Nocturnal Birds,
and Wild Indians

In the surrounding mountains there are caves inhabited by thousands of nocturnal birds; and, what struck our imagination more than all the marvels of the physical world, even further up we found a people until recently still nomadic, hardly free from a natural, wild state, but not barbarians, made stupid more from ignorance than from long years of being brutalized. (PN, 77)

So Humboldt described the wonders inland that were talked about in Cumaná. They had rested now for two and a half months with only one short trip up the Manzanares River to the Araya Peninsula, and it was time to begin their travels. A pressing problem was portage. Humboldt's equipment required lines of porters and pack animals, and later, when traveling on rivers, fleets of canoes. He was advised by Carlos. Inland from Cumaná it would not be possible to take so much. The roads were steep and difficult. He could take no more than two or three mules. In his *Personal Narrative* Humboldt described at length the painful decisions he had to make, listing his instruments again by name: sextant, dipping needle, magnetism gauge, thermometers, Saussure's hygrometer to measure humidity. "Choosing the instruments caused us most problems on the short journeys," he wrote (PN, 79).

Whether Bonpland should have been included in Humboldt's "us" is doubtful. Years later in Argentina Bonpland would travel days and weeks on horseback alone or with one assistant, visiting remote patients and collecting plants. Papers for drying and a press with multiple leaves, a box for storage, a journal to write down plant descriptions, weather, locale, growing habits, local knowledge: a botanist needed little else. Humboldt's larger vision, what

43

he now called his "physique générale," required considerably more in the way of baggage: sextant, barometer, and thermometer ready to hand to check the altitude, the air temperature, the oxygen in the air, the temperature of water when they stopped to drink from a spring—cooler than the air temperature—all noted and sent back to Forell in Madrid, von Zach in Germany, Fourcroy at the Muséum, and astronomers at the Observatory in Paris.

Humboldt made his difficult selection and they set off, first along the banks of the Manzanares River, then east up into thick forest, where Humboldt commented on some small cleared *conucos* or agricultural plots:

> We passed some huts inhabited by mestizos. Each hut stands in the center of an enclosure containing banana trees, papaw trees, sugar cane and maize. The small extent of cultivated land might surprise us until we recall that an acre planted with bananas produces nearly twenty times as much food as the same space sown with cereals. (PN, 79)

He noted the isolation of the small compounds with a shiver:

> Without neighbours, virtually cut off from the rest of mankind, each family forms a different tribe. This isolated situation retards the progress of civilization, which advances only as society becomes more populous and its connections more intimate and multiplied. (PN, 80)

Clearing temporary garden plots in fragile tropical forest soils was a practice used for centuries in the Caribbean and northern South America, but on Humboldt's mind was still that sense of tropical vegetation charged with resurgent growth that struck him so forcibly those first days in Cumaná: "Within the Tropics agriculture occupies less land; man has not extended his empire, and he appears not as the absolute maker who alters the soil at his will but as a transient guest who peacefully enjoys the gifts of nature" (PN, 80). He contrasted the monotony of cultivated European fields plowed and planted with grains:

> If in our temperate regions the cultivation of wheat contributes to the spreading of dull monotony over the cleared land, we cannot doubt that, even with an increasing population, the torrid zone will keep its majesty of plant life, those marks of an untamed, virgin nature that make it so attractive and picturesque. (PN, 80)

Might there be method in this kind of planting? Might there be value to life in a native *conuco*, in harmony with nature and at peace with one's surroundings? Might one live in such a place with an independence of spirit not possible among plowed fields? Acknowledging that possibility in his *Personal Narrative*, Humboldt referred that independence of spirit not to indigenous traditions but to Spanish blood—"on the other hand, solitude develops and strengthens liberty and independence; and has fed that pride of character which distinguishes the Castilian race" (PN, 80).

Even more striking, at the top of a sandstone hill, was a first aerial view of tropical rainforest:

> From our feet an immense jungle spread stretched out as far as the ocean. The tree-tops, intertwined with lianas and their long tufts of flowers, formed an enormous green carpet whose dark tint increased the brilliancy of the light. This picture struck us more powerfully as it was the first time we had seen tropical vegetation. (PN, 81)

Higher up the view was even more expansive, and again Humboldt turned to images from European art—"The extraordinary view reminded us of the fantastic landscape that Leonardo da Vinci painted in the background of his famous portrait of Mona Lisa" (PN, 82). Always, after such revelations, the precision of instrument readings was reassuring, the manipulation of each apparatus, the writing down of fixed quantities. Arriving on another high ridge just before sunset, Humboldt hurried to get out his chronometer to calculate the latitude before the light failed.

Coming down from the heights into dense rain forest evoked different emotions. The sky disappeared behind a thick canopy of leaves. In a strange glow of green light, flowering vines twined up gigantic trees with black trunks, lianas, pothos, shining-leaved dracontium, draped in festooned garlands over the narrow footpath to make an archway overhead. They climbed through tangled vegetation, over deep crevices made by rushing streams, tree growing on tree, vine clinging to vines. Here was a nature that no image from European art and literature could contain:

> When a traveler recently arrived from Europe steps into South American jungle for the first time he sees nature in a completely unexpected guise. The objects that surround him only faintly bring to mind those descriptions made by famous writers of the banks of the Mississippi, of Florida and of other temperate regions of the

New World. With each step he feels [he is] . . . in a vast continent
where everything is gigantic; mountains, rivers and the masses of
plants. If he is able to feel the beauty of the landscape, he will
find it hard to analyse his many impressions. He does not know
what shocks him more: whether the calm silence of the solitude,
or the beauty of the diverse, contrasting objects, or that fullness
and freshness of plant life in the Tropics. (PN, 83)

A high canopy closing off the sky, no way to orient or measure longitude, silence
broken only by the constant drip of water, the unnatural thickness of leaves
and stems, the confusing profusion and diversity of species: all were unsettling.

For Bonpland the botanist it was different. Under some large-leafed plants,
he found his first *Melastoma*, known in Europe for its bright purple flowers
but never seen by European botanists in a native habitat. In that first year he
would gather so many and in such variety that back in Paris he would be able
to reclassify and reorder an entire family of plants. In the canopy a hundred
and more feet above, epiphytes and lianas wove together, drawing up moisture
from the dark leaf-littered forest floor. Orchids were everywhere, hundreds of
them, endlessly varied in form and habit, difficult to classify until you had
a great number in hand and could lay them out in order, each with its own
peculiar beauty and unique habit and form: *Epidendrum grandiflorum* with large
beautiful flowers with yellow and purple markings; the strange *Epidendrum
antenniferum*, shaped like an insect, named the mosquito plant by locals, here
described by Bonpland in *Plantes équinoxiales*:

A sham parasite, that takes pleasure in the shade at the bottom of
shrubs and likes to hide its flowers between the branches with a
cluster of six to eight flowers, remarkable for spots of a beautiful
violet color with which it is graced and for two strands in the
form of antennae that give to the flower the appearance of an
insect. (PE, 98)

For Bonpland, plants were neither visual elements in a landscape nor tropical
vegetation, but living things with needs and habits. Vines reached down from high
crevices of branches, laid down buttresses and anchors in thin soil, sheathed the
trunks of host trees with long slanting arms. Creepers pushed networks of white
finger-like roots into bark. Liana ropes reached high into uppermost branches to
support inaccessible aerial gardens where parrots and macaws flitted, and orioles
built their hanging nests. Troops of howler monkeys passed overhead with their

distinctive hooting cries. At intervals Bonpland disappeared into openings in the undergrowth, exasperating Humboldt, who was forced to wait with Indian bearers at the side of the trail or on the bank of an insect-infested stream until his botanist companion staggered back with more plants.

At one point they emerged from forest into open humid countryside and splashed in water up to their ankles through aquatic plants. Bathed in sweat, they walked down an allée of giant tree-like grasses. "It is hard to imagine anything more elegant than this arborescent grass," wrote Humboldt; "the form and disposition of its leaves give it a lightness that contrasts agreeably with its height" (PN, 84). Bonpland's attention was on a new species of bamboo, and in his journal and later in *Plantes équinoxiales* he reflected at length on the endless local uses of *Bambusa guadua*. Fast growing, it made a renewable building material better for building houses than timbers taken from larger forest trees. Easy to cut and transport, it did not have to be split, and did not break or rot. It could be used for doors, tables, and beds as well as to build houses. Larger pieces were used for walls and smaller pieces to support a roof, itself covered with bamboo shoots that made a layered thatch. Protected from the sun by a thick roof, bamboo houses maintained their coolness even in the hottest times of the day. And, Bonpland noted, bamboo provided an added benefit for thirsty travelers: water inside the stalks made a clear and refreshing drink, so intimately was this one plant involved in the lives of a community (PE, 71).[1]

But now, after a long day of walking, they were nearing one of the "marvels" Humboldt had been told about in Cumaná: Cuchivano's Crevice, a deep slit cut into the side of a cliff, approachable only by a deep narrow gulch. From rocks at the end periodically belched out plumes of fire so bright and high they illuminated the surrounding mountains in pyrotechnic shows. Staying with a local farmer who had traveled with them from Cumaná, Humboldt called for an expedition. Impossible, said the farmer, the gulch is impassable; jaguars live there that can tear a horse apart. Humboldt would not be put off. If an excursion could not be gotten up, he would go on his own. He set out for the crevice with the farmer and Bonpland following reluctantly behind. Immediately a thick tangle of vegetation prevented them from reaching even the entrance to the gulch, and they were forced to turn back. Still Humboldt was insistent, and the next day a team of Indians was gotten together to cut a path into the gulch with machetes.

Chopping away at roots and vines, the Indians led the way along a stream that flowed at the bottom of the deeply shaded ravine, murmuring to themselves about the gold that must be in rocks ahead. Why else would a German make such a trip? It would have to be for gold. The lead Indian stopped. A strong smell of cat urine and a fresh carcass of a small animal signaled that jaguars were nearby. They would have to turn back. No said Humboldt, they must go on. A compromise was made. They would wait, send back for dogs. The dogs would go ahead and be attacked first, giving the humans time to escape. After a wait the party was joined by barking dogs, and they continued on. When undergrowth along the stream became impassable, they climbed, clinging to the rocky cliffs on either side of the ravine, contemplating a drop of 200 to 300 feet while teetering along a narrow ledge. The ledge narrowed further and disappeared. They climbed down, forded the stream and scaled the cliff on the other side to find another precarious foothold. Back and forth they went, wet and exhausted with sliding and with climbing, all the time cutting away vines and creepers, holding on to roots of trees that clung to the rocks. Suddenly one of the Indians ahead let out a cry. A vein of something shiny was sighted in the rock. Farm workers scrambled up to chip out bits of sparkling pyrite with Humboldt shaking his head impatiently below, trying to explain that no, this was not gold, but only iron sulfide.

I cannot think it was Bonpland's choice of excursions. There would have been more plants to find in forests and open areas, but he lagged behind with some of the guides, arms full, more than any of them could carry: cannas, a strange violet flowering heliconia, *Brownea racemosa* in brilliant purple, an unknown euphorbia with red sap. Tree ferns, costus ten feet tall, a twenty-foot *Eupatorium laevigatum* grew in pockets of soil in the cliff. Bonpland watched guides find footholds in the rocks and climbed up after them, learning Indian names for some of the plants. Short with muscular legs and broad shoulders, one of guides climbed, braced himself against the rocks, reached up to cut into a tree trunk, bring down a sample so Bonpland could admire the close grain and deep russet color of native wood. Bonpland tried out the name on his tongue, repeating it until he had it to the guides' satisfaction. He watched another take a leaf, crush it between his fingers, lift it to his nose, breath in deeply, take a piece of stem and chew, releasing flavor, spitting out the pulp after a few minutes ready to give a confident identification. Later, even Humboldt was forced to admit that the Indians agreed—"at least among themselves"—on a plant's identification.[2]

But if the expedition up the crevice turned out to be success for the botanist, it was a disappointment for the geologist. The rocks from which the fires erupted remained a mystery. As the party struggled through a last tangle of roots, a perpendicular rock face thousands of feet tall loomed up before them. High up and completely inaccessible were the openings from which the fires came. The party had to make their way back down the ravine with Indian guides carrying Bonpland's baskets of plants, but without the rock samples Humboldt had hoped to collect.

More successful for Humboldt would be caves further up in the highlands near the Capuchin hospice that was their farthest destination. Built against a sheer cliff of white rock, less humid and healthier for convalescence, the hospice served as both a rest home for sick and ailing priests and a training station for new missionaries. There, after a week of hard trekking, the travelers found some welcome amenities. Food grown in the fathers' communal gardens was fresh and varied. A large stand of coffee trees provided stimulating beverages. The Father Superior's library had books, including, to Humboldt's delight, several on electricity and chemistry. Humboldt was allowed to set up his instruments in the open cloister without interference and sit up at night waiting for clouds to clear so he could make his observations. By day he registered impressions in his journal:

> The site has something wild and tranquil, melancholic and attractive about it. In the midst of such powerful nature we felt nothing inside but peace and repose. In the solitude of these mountains I was less struck by the new impressions recorded at each step than by the fact that such diverse climates have so much in common. . . . Despite these exotic sounds, and the strange plant forms and marvels of the New World, everywhere nature allows man to sense a voice speaking to him in familiar terms. The grass carpeting the ground, the old moss and ferns covering tree roots, the torrent that falls over steep calcareous rocks, the harmonious colours reflecting the water, the green and the sky, all evoke familiar sensations in the traveller. (PN, 109)

If for Humboldt everywhere nature was the same grass, moss, water, and calcareous rock, for Bonpland there was always so much that was new. He explored high up the cliff in back of the hospice where trees grew in little pockets of trapped soil, cieba and praga palms watered by the many springs that trickled and flowed down the rock. *Evosmia caripensis* had fruit that when rubbed between the fingers gave off a delicious odor. Red-flowered *Rhexia rotundifolia* grew on the steep slopes of the hills behind the monastery beside a magnolia-like white *Clusia*. More and more he was adding Melastomata-ceae to his growing collection. He climbed high up on the cliff to examine small groves of bananas and papaw, lush clumps of tree ferns, thick swathes of vegetation that followed small water channels that flowed down through crevices of rock. On their return to Cumaná, Humboldt would report to the astronomer von Zach that on the trip inland they had collected 1,600 plants, many of them new.

But foremost on Humboldt's mind at the Capuchin mission was another excursion, this time an attraction that was described to him at length in Cumaná: the Cave of the Guácharos, home to flocks of strange nocturnal fruit- and seed-eating birds. Never leaving the caves by day, on moonlit nights the birds flew out in great dark flocks, hundreds and even thousands of them, feeding on hard nuts and seeds, cracking them open with their strong beaks. The fathers were agreeable. There would be a cost, they said, but yes, an expedi-tion to the caves could be arranged for the visitors. Amazing birds. From the fat pad between the legs a full pint of fat could be rendered from one bird, odorless and tasteless oil that kept fresh for more than a year. They used it at the hospice for all their cooking, and the food never tasted oily or rancid.

A large party was assembled for what would be a day-long expedition. Any missionary able to make the journey joined in, along with Indian super-visors and bearers with pack mules carrying torches to light the inside of the cave, as well as lunch to be laid out at the mouth of the cave. First came several hours of walking through meadow along a wide, swiftly flowing river, then yet another descent down into a deep gorge cut through rock by a flow of rushing water. At first the banks were wide enough for a line of mules and men to pass. Soon fallen boulders and uprooted trees blocked the way and they were forced to walk in the stream, splashing through several feet of water. It grew darker. Rock ledges above cut off all but a sliver of sky. They were in a kind of echo chamber for the gurgling of rushing water choked by debris and fallen rocks. The crevice narrowed. Again they were forced to climb up along a narrow ledge angling higher and higher above the stream. Below, the water foamed and rushed, the current broken by huge boulders. But this time there was no disappointment. As they turned the last corner they saw, not an unscalable cliff face, but a giant vaulted entrance, larger than even Humboldt could have imagined. No cave in Europe could compare, Humboldt would write to Forell back in Madrid. "Nothing is as majestic as the entry to this cave crowned with the most beautiful vegetation" (LA, 67).

The entrance was deeply shaded, surrounded by trees that flourished in mist thrown up by the cascading stream. Large shiny leaves reached against the sky and sheltered a lower canopy of smaller trees. Flowering vines festooned the entrance, framing a dark interior. Crevices in the surrounding rocks held out bouquets of orchids and oxalis; vines dripped blue violet jacaranda with clusters of bell-shaped flowers, solandra with large orange trumpet flowers streaked with black. Heliconia eighteen feet tall, their yellow and tangerine bracts needles of color against the dark foliage of palms and arums. Bonpland looked up at a heliconia, deep blood red with branched bracts, inside the crook of each rod a tender furl of yellow green, and farther up to orchids growing out of reach high in the rocks. Humboldt was busy with his measuring devices, recording the results in his pocket journal: the width of the cave, the width of the underground river that flowed out of the cave, the height of the ceiling.

Inside the entrance, they paused in the sudden hush of the dark interior, listening to the murmur of moisture dripping onto leaves, mist rustling one petal against another, the tap-tap of the Indian guides' sticks against the rocks ahead. Go, go on, the monks urged them, anxious to get on so they could sit down to lunch. The air flowing from the interior of the cave was cool laced with a smell of mud, rotted leaves, and excrement. Light from the entrance shimmered on the creamy crust of giant stalactites that hung down from the ceiling and blocked the banks so that they were forced to wade in the stream. At one point they stopped to look back at the brilliant green of the entrance framed in vines against dark columns of the stalactites.

Little by little the light faded, and in the darkness began to come the calls of the *guácharos*, "ones who cry and lament." The screeching grew louder. High above from crevices in the rock came a wild panicked flapping and beating. Birds began to strike into their faces, brushing their cheeks with their wings. The guides lit flares, pushing them up into the heights of the cave, driving off the birds so the visitors could see the nests built high above in funnel-shaped holes in the rock and the parent birds flying off in panic. The Indians tied copal torches on long poles, reached up high with the light. The parent birds shrieked. In the wavering blood red light of the torches, blind bald heads and oversized beaks appeared over the nests like giant malformed embryos. Trunks of palm trees were placed ready against the walls. Using notches where branches had been cut off for footholds, one of the Indians climbed up. The palm trunk was wet; he slipped back. Indians holding the torches laughed and hit at the birds beating around their heads. The screaming was deafening, echoing and reechoing against the rock walls, loud cries of parents, frantic peeps of chicks. Wings flap and grate, feathers into their mouths, terrified birds tumbling out of the nests and hitting against the walls in panic. Humboldt pulled at Bonpland. Give me the gun. I need a bird down to sketch it. Humboldt shot wildly into the air, unable to aim in the screeching flying confusion of birds. Bonpland took the gun, ordered one of the Indians to hold up the torch, fired and fired again. Two birds fell, and immediately Humboldt was on his knees, examining the carcasses, spreading the legs to see the protuberant fat pouch, pulling open the curved seed-cracking beak. Bruised gray feathers glowed with a rose tint in the torchlight as the eye of the dying bird gyrated and went still.

The dead birds were packed away in a canvas bag, but Humboldt insisted. They had to go further into the cave. He started out with the Indian guides following reluctantly behind. At 472 meters—measured by Humboldt from the entrance with a cord—they came to a fall of water where the floor of the cavern slanted upward. "Angle of 60 degrees," Humboldt wrote in his notebook. The Indians drew in their breaths. They would go no further. Humboldt looked back to the missionaries. One of their bishops had penetrated even further into the cave and still had not come to the end. Make them go on, Humboldt told the fathers. Still the Indians held back. Humboldt gestured impatiently. The missionaries drove the Indians, who reluctantly dragged their feet on to the top of the small waterfall where the cave narrowed. Underfoot was no longer rock but black mud slippery and rank with rotted vegetation. The screaming of the birds echoed in the lowered height of the ceiling. The torches gave off acrid smoke that burnt the eyes so that it was hard to see where to place one's feet.

Now in the murky smoke-filled darkness ahead forms begin to appear, wavering in the draft from the torches, wraithlike figures, two feet tall, ghostly white and sinuous, hovering in the breeze made by the torches. The Indians gasped, eyes wide at the pale, skeletal, plantlike forms, and abruptly turned, disappeared back into the darkness. It was a few minutes before even Humboldt was able to make out what he was seeing, not shades or spirits, but albino plants, sown by seed brought to the chicks by parent birds, similar to underground plants he found down in the mines of Prussia and wrote about in his first youthful publication. Why were the Indians so frightened? he asked the fathers. The missionaries explained. For the Indians the caves beyond the waterfall were sacred ground, a land of the dead, a place of shades and ghosts. Humboldt's comment in his *Personal Narrative*:

> Despite their authority the missionaries could not persuade the Indians to go any further on into the cavern. The lower the vault the more piercing the screaming of the *guácharos* became. Thanks to the cowardice of our guides we had to retreat. (PN, 106)

Back at the mouth of the cave, lunch was laid out on banana leaves. As they sat eating, the fathers described the harvesting of the oil. Once each year, Indians with missionaries supervising came up to the caves in a large party. Indians climbed up the palm trunks with clubs to beat down young birds, preferred for the quality and quantity of their oil. Feathers flew, bits of flesh, the noise of the birds deafening, the smell of flesh, of rot, of terrified birds. The torches cast a strange light on the clubs used to strike down the birds, the bare copper backs of the Indians running with sweat and blood. Hundreds, even thousands of birds fell and were packed into baskets. Out at the mouth of the cave a brushwood fire was lit. Indians cut open the bellies of the birds, took out the fat from between the legs to be melted down in a great kettle and transported back to the mission in clay pots, leaving behind a great pile of discarded flesh and feathers for vultures and jaguars. Along with the fat pouch came another prize: With missionaries supervising, the Indians cut open the gullets of the young birds to extract the undigested seeds later ground up and sold in towns as a medicine for fevers, "semilla del guácharo."[3]

In his *Narrative*, Humboldt meditated on the "primitive superstition" and "cowardice" that had prevented the Indians from going deeper into the cave, comparing it to the enterprising spirit that inspired his own youthful research into underground plants:

> These traces of plant life in the dark struck the Indians, usually so stupid and difficult to impress. They examined the plants in a silence inspired by a place they fear. You could have said these pale, deformed, underground plants seemed like ghosts banished from the earth's surface. For me, however, they recalled one of the happiest days of my youth when during a long stay at the Freiberg mines I began my research into the effects of blanching plants. (PN, 106)

At many points in the several published volumes of *Personal Narrative* taken from his travel journals, Humboldt inserted treatises on particular topics: forty-nine pages on the geography of the Canary Islands, forty-two pages of tables of astronomical and atmospheric observations, long lists of instruments, dissertations on plants that exude milky substances, venomous insects, cultivation of cacao, twenty pages on the source of the River Negro, and twenty-five more on South American river systems, to mention only a few. One of the longer of these mini-dissertations—"Physical Constitution and Customs of the Chaima Indians"—followed his account of his and Bonpland's visit to the oilbird caves.

Describing the Chaima Indians, Humboldt struggled to find the right words. "Savage," "barbarian," "civilized": these were terms currently in use in Europe to describe what were taken as progressive stages in human development. Savage hunter-gathers give way to barbarian tribal chiefs, then comes civilization, which spreads from its Greco-Roman beginnings first to Italy with Dante and Leonardo da Vinci, and then on to Western Europe with Newton, Goethe, German mineralogy, and French chemistry. With the discovery of the Americas, "civilization" was presumably crossing the Atlantic to the eastern coasts of the New World, from which it would slowly move inland. As Humboldt put it,

> As the missionaries struggle to penetrate the jungles and gain the Indian land, so white colonists try, in their turn, to invade missionary land. In this long-drawn-out struggle the secular arm continually tends to take over those Indians tamed by the missions, and missionaries are replaced by priests. Whites, and mestizos, favored by *corregidores*, have established themselves among the Indians. The missions are transformed into Spanish villages and the Indians soon forget even the memory of their own language. So civilization slowly works its way inland from the coast, sometimes hindered by human passions. (PN, 118–119)

There were few "savage" Indians still living near the region inland from Cumaná, reported Humboldt, but he immediately confessed that he used the term "savage" grudgingly. Indians living outside the missions were not exactly what he would call wild, but nor were they what he would call "barbarous" even though they might live in villages under chiefs and practice a form of agriculture. But nor could he say that Indians in the missions were civilized. If "civilization" was spreading inland in the Americas, at the Capuchin mission it did not seem to be taking hold. This Humboldt attributed to something resistant and stubborn in the Indian race. In their two-week stay at the Capuchin hospice while Bonpland searched for plants, Humboldt made it a point to observe the Chaima as they worked in communal gardens and took religious instruction. He had encouraged them to visit him in his quarters and answer his questions, offering them brandy as enticement. But when questioned about their beliefs and customs, the Indians had often refused to answer, or when they did answer, answered with whatever they thought he might want to hear.

They showed little interest in his astronomical instruments and were happier sitting in their rural *conucos* in the rain then they were in his comfortable room drinking brandy. Even more surprising, regardless of the safety and comfort of the mission, they often slipped away into the forest for months on end:

> [The Indian's] thinking has not increased with his contact with whites; he has remained estranged from the objects with which European civilization has enriched the Americas. All his acts seem dictated by the wants of the moment. He is taciturn, without joy, introverted and, on the outside, serious and mysterious. Someone who has been but a short time in a mission could mistake this laziness and passivity for a meditative frame of mind. (PN, 120)

> Though life is less comfortable in the *conuco* they prefer living there as much as possible. I have already alluded to their irresistible drive to flee and return to the jungle. Even young children flee from their parents to spend four or five days in the jungle, feeding off wild fruit, palm hearts and roots. (PN, 123)

As for the Indian "magistrates" or supervisors who organized work crews in the missions, and who carried proudly the cane that symbolized their traditional authority:

> Their pedantic and taciturn seriousness, their cold and mysterious air, and the zeal with which they fulfil their role in the church and communal assemblies make Europeans smile. We were still unaccustomed to these nuances of Indian temperament, found equally on the Orinoco, in Mexico and in Peru, among people totally different from each other in customs and language. (PN, 101)

Nor did religion seem much of a civilizing influence. As far as Humboldt could see, the Indians were impervious to Christian teaching. Christianity was taught in Spanish, a language not their own, but it seemed clear to Humboldt that religious concepts would have made little sense to the Indians in any language:

> The tamed Indian is often as little a Christian as the free Indian is an idolater. Both, caught up in the needs of the moment, betray a marked indifference for religious sentiments, and a secret tendency to worship nature and her powers. (PN, 118)

Even more troubling for Humboldt was that as far as he could see, Indians had little grasp of numbers. When asked to be precise about an amount, they seemed unable to count or do simple addition, a defect which could not come from the poverty of Indian languages, since those languages had names for larger numbers, but rather, he thought, from native resistance to rigorous thought: "we observe in the copper-coloured men a moral inflexibility, a stubbornness concerning habits and customs, which, though modified in each tribe, characterize the whole race from the equator to Hudson's Bay and the Strait of Magellan" (PN, 119).[4]

If Humboldt had little good to say about the Chaima, he was no more impressed by the missionaries who were their teachers. If the Indians were "stupid" and "cowardly," he held the fathers at least partly to blame. As he saw it, the missions might provide a place of safety and shelter for the Indians, but they had done little to improve Indian minds:

> But these institutions, useful at first in preventing the spilling of blood and establishing the basis of society, have become hostile to progress. The effect of their isolation has been such that the Indians have remained in the same state as they were found before their scattered huts were grouped around the missions. Their number has considerably increased but not their mental development. They have progressively lost that vigour of character and natural vivacity which everywhere comes from independence. By subjecting even the slightest domestic actions to invariable rules the Indians have been kept stupid in an effort to make them obedient. (PN, 78)

Some of the low spirits of Indians Humboldt blamed on the rigid routines of mission life: prayers first thing in early morning with sometimes the addition of a catechism lesson in the church, then breakfast and work parties of men and women dispatched to communal fields. Then came lunch for each family in their quarters and rest, after which they were free to go to individual plots allotted to each family. To Humboldt it all seemed impossibly dreary, the same routine day after day, though perhaps unavoidable given what he saw as the low state of development of native peoples.

A supposed trait of the Indian race Humboldt came back to again and again was stupidity. "You would think their mental stupidity greater than that of children when a white asks them questions about objects that have surrounded them since birth" (PN, 123). Also irritating was what he called "a cunning courtesy common to all Indians," which made them give whatever answer was suggested by a questioner (PN, 124). Humboldt remarked on what he saw as a lack of animation and curiosity. The Indians were gloomy, abstracted, unwilling and uninterested in his researches. They had a way of saying "no Father" or "yes Father" to everything he said, which infuriated him. Yes, he admitted, probably they had no Spanish, but why pretend to answer? The urge to disappear back into the jungle was only further proof of native irrationality. Given that away from the missions they were prey to slave traders, given that much of their ancestral lands had been lost to European settlement, would not the intelligent recourse have been to settle down to civilized life in the missions or in Spanish towns?

Informing these observations was the racial template Humboldt learned from a professor at Göttingen whom he would always call his "master," Johann Friedrich Blumenbach. Blumenbach was a monogenist. On his view, human races come from one original white-skinned "Caucasian" stock. But migration and then climate and environment brought about a degeneration from species-type that resulted in different subspecies or races. These Blumenbach divided into five major groups: first the undegenerated Caucasian, and then Mongolian, Ethiopian, American Indian, and Malayan, with groups and subgroups closer or further away from the original Caucasian.[5] Humboldt's descriptions of the physical and mental characteristics of the Chaima echo Blumenbach's descriptions of the distinctive and "less beautiful" physical and mental characteristics of the American Indian race:

> The Chaimas are usually short and thickset, with extremely broad shoulders and flat chests, and their legs are rounded and fleshy. The colour of their skin is the same as that of all American Indians from the cold plateau of Quito to the burning jungles of the Amazon. (PN, 120)

Indian skulls, said Humboldt, showed a mixture of "Mongolian" traits (hair, eyes, cheekbones), but also a remnant of the "Caucasian" (the nose), with teeth "attractive and white" but "not as strong as negro teeth."

Like Blumenbach, much of what he interpreted as Indian torpor Humboldt blamed on climate, on the ease and exuberant growth of the tropics where fruit supposedly falls spontaneously off the trees and seeds sprout as soon as they are sown without the farsighted storing and fertilizing necessary in northern climates:

The Indians of the missions, remote from all civilization, are influenced solely by physical needs, which they satisfy very easily in their favourable climate, and therefore they tend to live dull, monotonous lives, which are reflected in their facial expressions. (PN, 121–122)

Tropical degeneration, as Humboldt saw it, also occurred in people of original Caucasian stock who spent long periods of time in tropical climates. On an excursion from Cumaná to inspect salt works on the Araya peninsula, Humboldt found the manager spending the heat of the day in a hammock and attributed what he saw as laziness to "tropical torpor." Salt deposits that would have made other European countries jealous, he lamented, had not led to the building of a town (PN, 68–69). He also saw tropical "degeneration" in "second-hand" republican ideas discussed among Creoles in Cumaná along with dog-eared copies of Rousseau's *Social Contract* and Locke's *Second Treatise on Government*. Did anyone read these tracts, much less understand them?

"Degeneration" caused by climate could to some degree be reversed. Guaiquerí Indians at the coast like Carlos who lived with and worked for the Spanish, said Humboldt, became more "civilized." They spoke Spanish, professed loyalty to the Spanish king, lived peacefully alongside Europeans, working as guides and servants:

The Guaiquerí belong to a tribe of civilized Indians inhabiting the coast of Margarita and the surroundings of the town of Cumaná. They enjoy several privileges because they remained faithful to the Castilians from earliest times. Also the King names them in some degrees as 'his dear, noble and loyal Guaiquerías.' (PN, 47)

These Guaiquerí are an intelligent and civilized tribe of fishermen, notably different from the wild Guarano from the Orinoco who build their houses up in the mauritia palm trees. (PN, 54)

In contrast, further up coast away from the Spanish towns, Indians retained ways of life that "flatter idleness." Guaiquerí there did not take the trouble to grow vegetables, but sold fish they caught in the town, purchased what they needed in the way of produce, and went back up the coast (PN, 71). On one hot and shadeless trek up the coast, their Indian guide kept wanting to stop and rest, offering an irritated Humboldt further proof of Indian laziness and lack of ambition:

We observed this characteristic trait whenever we travelled with Indians; it has given rise to the most mistaken ideas about the physical
constitutions of different races. The copper-coloured Indian, who is
more used to the burning heat of these regions than a European,
complains more because nothing stimulates his interest. Money is
no bait, and if he is tempted by gain he repents of his decision as
soon as he starts walking. (PN, 73)

Visiting a pottery works where Indian women used centuries-old techniques
rather than new methods, Humboldt made a similar observation: "This reveals
both the infancy of this craft and that immobility of manners so characteristic
of American Indians" (PN, 73).

From the beginning, Bonpland saw native people very differently. Blumenbach's racial theory was not taught at the medical schools in Paris or by
professors at the Muséum national d'histoire naturelle. There, natural history
took a different course. French botanists used Linnaeus's Latin binomial nomenclature for species, but Linnaeus's four varieties of human species were based
on geography and were listed with "African" first, then "European" and on to
"American Indian" and "Asian." Not only did Blumenbach add a fifth racial
variety, the "Malay," to Linnaeus's four, but he rearranged races hierarchically,
with Caucasian as the original human, and the other four varieties listed in
order of degree of "degeneration" from an original type due to emigration and
adaption to environment. Much as Blumenbach, like Humboldt an opponent
of slavery, tried to mitigate the perception of inferiority, racial hierarchy was
embedded in the order of his categories as well as in his description of racial
characteristics, with white-skinned "Caucasian" Europeans the original most
"beautiful creation" compared to less attractive traits in other races.[6]

Botanists at the Muséum in Paris took taxonomy in a very different
direction. Jussieu, like his predecessor Michel Adamson and his Uncle Bernard,
retained the binomial Latin style of naming, but rejected Linnaeus's artificial
counting of sexual parts of plant species, in favor of a "natural" multi-character
system of identification based on close observation. Doing field work with Jussieu and debating with Lamarck the fossil history of shells, Bonpland inherited
no racist template within which to place human kinds. Nor after eight years
in the mean streets and clinics of Paris during the French Revolution was
he under any illusion that Europeans were more beautiful or intelligent than
other peoples. What he learned from Jussieu, Desfontaines, and Lamarck was
careful observation, not only of form, but of intricate and infinitely variable

organic functioning. In this endeavor native people were not his subjects but his allies. Describing plants in *Plantes équinoxiales* he added from his journals the names given plants by local people, valuable information he gathered from them on the extent of the range of a species, its growing habits, and its local uses. He referred to his local informants simply as "inhabitants," those who live in a place and have intimate knowledge of its plants and animals. Never would he be the ethnographer, observing and categorizing exotic races. The Chaima were people with whom he had much in common, people who had information of importance: new medicines, dyes, extracts, valuable plants. Here were the wild delicacies introduced to the fathers by the Chaima, the delicious heart of the pragma palm, wild berries and fruits, sweet varieties of wild bananas grown in some of the remote rural plots. Here might be fruitful partnership, with Europeans providing techniques that could make the work of tropical cultivation easier and bring new imports to be interplanted with traditional native maize and cassava. Here might be furniture made of native woods, fences of bamboo, oranges and lemons cultivated, pigments extracted, medicines researched.

4

The Eel Ponds of the Llanos

Returned to Cumaná after the trip inland, Humboldt declared that another rest period was needed before they continued on. An additional reason for delay was the prospect of a solar eclipse predicted for the end of October, which came and was observed by Humboldt with great interest. Several afternoons later, under dark skies and rumbling thunder, a seismic shock woke Humboldt while he napped in his hammock and almost threw Bonpland to the ground as he stood below at his work table. Such experiences made a great impression on Humboldt. As he explained it, "When shocks from an earthquake are felt, and the earth we think of as so stable shakes on its foundations, one second is long enough to destroy long-held illusions" (PN, 130). In Cumaná there were many such phenomena: red mists, waves of heat, dust in the air, crackling in the sky, brilliant sunsets. Late in the night after the earth trembling had stopped, Bonpland, unable to sleep, walked out on the upper balcony to find the sky full of shooting stars. "From the start of this phenomenon there was not a patch of sky the size of three quarters of the moon that was not packed with fire-balls and shooting stars," he reported to Humboldt, who back in Paris would add to his *Personal Narrative* a lengthy treatise on bolides and shooting stars.

Already in Cumaná Humboldt was thinking of publication. Two packets of astronomical and geodesic measurements made on shipboard and in Cumaná had gone off to the Bureau of Longitudes in Paris before they left on their trip inland to the missions. Now Humboldt wrote to Baron von Zach, director of the observatory at Seeberg. He was keeping an astronomical journal, he said. He hoped that if he died in South America before he returned to publish his results, someone would take his findings, correct them, and publish them in his name. He told Zach,

It requires superhuman patience to make astronomical observations with exactitude and "con amore" in such heat. You see, however, that the crushing heat has in no way inhibited my activity. (LA, 39)

He ended the letter with an apology; he would have been able to do so much better if he had been part of a proper governmental expedition. Writing to Zach again after observing the earthquake, Humboldt expressed new confidence. They carried with them "Berthoud's chronometer and the sextants of Ramsdan and Troughton." He had fixed longitudes and latitudes at fifteen locations and had measured heights with his barometer. He observed a solar eclipse in Cumaná and in the process burned his face and eyes so badly that he had to go to bed and take pain killers. He witnessed an eclipse of a moon of Jupiter, an earthquake, fire balls in the sky, and was passing on a long list of magnetic readings made with his "Borda compasses." Soon they would go down the coast to Caracas, would remain there until January, and from there continue on into the interior to the Apure River, the Río Negro, and the Casiquiare.

There were disappointments. Word arrived that the ship carrying his measurements to the Bureau of Longitudes had been lost in a storm. Immediately Humboldt sat down to make new copies to send by other means. And with one phenomenon he was having no success at all. From the beginning of their stay in Cumaná he had urged Carlos to get him live electric eels, the famous *Gymnotus electricus* that lived in nearby rivers. To his frustration no eels had been forthcoming, perhaps because no one took his request seriously:

I had busied myself daily over many years with the phenomenon of Galvanic electricity and had enthusiastically experimented without knowing what I had discovered; I had built real batteries by placing metal discs on top of each other and alternating them with bits of muscle flesh, or other humid matter, and so was eager, after arriving at Cumaná, to obtain electric eels. We had often been promised them, and had always been deceived. (PN, 169)

Now they could delay no longer; it was time to move on. Money and letters of credit were procured for the trip on the Orinoco; instruments were packed so as to fit into narrow canoes. The plan was to travel by ship to Caracas and wait there until the rains stopped. When dry weather came, they would travel inland through a region of mountains and fertile valleys to arrive at the llanos, a vast empty flatland stretching from the Andes to the Atlantic Ocean, and from the Caracas Mountains to the forests of Guiana. Once across it, they would come to the Apure River. From there they would go up the Apure to the Orinoco, and if all went well, they would find and map a long-rumored link between the Orinoco and the Amazon river systems located somewhere deep in the jungle.

The sea journey to Caracas was rough and stormy. Some of the passengers insisted on disembarking and going by land. Bonpland, tired of the tedium of sea journeys and eager to look for new plants, went with them. Humboldt stayed on board to supervise the unloading of his instruments at the harbor at La Guaira and see them safely on pack mules up over the hills to Caracas. It was a tedious business. In the harbor the sea was choppy, making unloading difficult. Overland transport up to Caracas was slow. The group stopped at an inn to rest the mules, and Humboldt was forced to listen to locals talk on and on about the execution of the leader of a failed republican conspiracy: "The excitement and bitterness of these people, who should have agreed on such questions, surprised me" (PN, 134).[1] All they did was argue, Humboldt recalled in his *Personal Narrative*: argue about the hate mulattos felt for freed blacks, about the wealth of monks, about how hard it was to own slaves. In that mix of racial tensions, with church allied with state and the brutality of slave labor, he could see only confusion and unrealistic ideals. It came as a relief when thick mist down off the mountain drove the disputants into the inn. There, Humboldt reported, an old man "with great equanimity" told the company that it was best not to discuss political matters since there might always be spies. "These words, spoken in the emptiness of the sierra, deeply impressed me; I was to hear them often during our journeys," commented Humboldt (PN, 135). Talk of republican revolution might be bandied around, but as he saw it, there was little chance that South Americans would be able to govern themselves.

In Caracas, away from any talk of revolution, Humboldt was more comfortable. He found the hospitality of the Creole elite delightful. He noted a refreshing egalitarianism among people of white blood:

In the colonies skin colour is the real badge of nobility. In Mexico as well as in Peru, at Caracas as in Cuba, a barefoot man with a white skin is often heard to say: 'Does that rich person think himself whiter than I am?' . . . We do not find among the people of Spanish origin that cold and pretentious air which modern civilization has made more common in Europe than in Spain. Conviviality, candour and great simplicity of manner unite the different classes in the colonies. (PN, 136)[2]

And in Caracas there was "culture": music, literature, lively conversation. As Humboldt put it, "nowhere else in Spanish America does civilization appear so European" (PN, 136). During the day he worked on his correspondence. Copies of the astronomical observations lost at sea were sent off, this time addressed directly to Jerome Lalande, chair of astronomy at the Collège de France—"Allow me to address myself to you, citizen, to inform, you about my work . . ." Again came the apology—"A voyage undertaken by an individual who is not very rich and carried out by two persons, zealous, but very young, could not promise the same results as the voyage of a society of savants of the higher order, sent at the expense of a government." Again came reminders of the ambitious aim of his voyage—"You know that my principle aim is a 'physique du monde,' the composition of the globe, the analysis of the air, the physiology of animals and plants, and finally the general relations that link organized beings to inanimate nature" (LA, 56). He reviewed for Lalande what had already been achieved:

> We have dried more than 1,600 plants and described more than 500, and collected shells and insects. I have made some 50 drawings. I believe that considering the burning heat of this zone, you will think we have done much work in four months of time. Days have been consecrated to physics and natural history, nights to astronomy. I give you this sketch of my activities not to glorify myself by what we have done, but to get your and our friend Delambre's indulgence for what we have not done. (LA, 56)

Once again he named his instruments and described his diligence in making observations.

In the letters Bonpland was mentioned briefly. In his September letter to von Zach: he and his companion Bonpland, "tireless naturalist," were in good health. To Lalande at the Institut went more formal commendation: "Citizen Bonpland, student of the National Museum well versed in botany and comparative anatomy and other branches of natural history, assists me with his talents with indefatigable zeal" (LA, 56). To the chemist Fourcroy at the Muséum in Paris, who knew Bonpland personally, went warmer, if somewhat condescending, praise:

> My travel companion, citizen Bonpland, student at the Jardin des plantes, becomes each day more and more precious to me. He joins very solid knowledge in botany and comparative anatomy with an indefatigable zeal. I hope in him one day to return him to his country a savant worthy of public attention. (LA, 59)

More often Bonpland is the silent other of Humboldt's botanical "we." To Zach: "*We* have dried more than 1600 plants; *we* have described close to 600 for the most part new, and *we* have collected lovely shells and insects. I have made 60 drawings" (LA, 45) To Lalande: "*We* have dried more than 1,600 plants and described more than 500, and collected shells and insects. I have made some fifty drawings" (LA, 56).[3] To Fourcroy: "In the seven months in which *we* have been on this beautiful continent, *we* have dried (with doubles) near to 4,000 plants, written more than 800 descriptions of species new or little known (especially new genera of palms, cryptogams, new melastomes), and also insects and shells" (LA, 60). The "we" in these letters is misleading. Although it is often "we" who collect plants, and "we" who describe them, the great part of the entries in the *Botanical Journals* are in Bonpland's handwriting, with paragraphs added here and there in Humboldt's easily identifiable microscopic script.[4] After a first few weeks of walking across Spain, Humboldt was happy to leave the tedious work of collecting, drying, mounting, and describing plant specimens and botanical journal writing to Bonpland.

Each individual plant specimen, including doubles, had to be mounted and labeled with a number corresponding to the applicable entry in the botanical journals, a preliminary identification, the date, and the location found. Entries in the journals were numbered chronologically starting from plants found at the beginning of their trip through France and Spain and ending with those found at their last stop at Mexico City. Each journal entry included a description of a plant's physiology, habitat, sensory qualities like scent and taste, and the shades of color important for later illustrators. In addition to the standard Linnaean binomials, Bonpland added local names and information gotten from local inhabitants. Unlike the collecting of unusual or pretty plants for the natural history cabinets popular in the eighteenth and nineteenth centuries, Bonpland's journals, along with the collections that went with them, would represent a new standard in botanical record keeping, making possible the systematic scientific study of plants collected. Not only was information on each plant easily retrievable, the collection could be divided, allowing research to go on in different locations and by different researchers without the confusion in naming and identification that made coordinated botanical research so difficult. Given the uncertainty of transport abroad, with many letters and shipments lost and the fragility of dried specimens, it allowed for backup copies of plants. Because all copies were-number keyed to journals that Bonpland kept in his possession, questions about a labeled plant could always be referred back to Bonpland or to the journals wherever they were kept. It was laborious work. Entries in the journal were made in ink and with little crossing out or correction, which meant that each night Bonpland copied from his rough notes in the field. Leaves, bark, flowers were carefully unwrapped from where they were roughly folded in paper during the day and mounted with both sides of leaves visible and all the flowering parts. Thick fruits were sliced through. Careful notes were made at the bottom of each specimen sheet, date and place of collection and number reference to the journal's detailed notes. Duplicates were prepared with copies, each delicate specimen pressed between sheets of porous paper and dried over gentle heat. In Caracas there was more to do. Given the upcoming river voyage, specimens would have to be stored in waterproof packets and wrapped to travel with them. While Humboldt socialized with the local aristocracy, Bonpland concentrated on his plants. When Humboldt announced that they were to climb Mt. Silla, a peak visible from their rented house, it had to come as something of a distraction.

Mountains would always draw Humboldt. Even without the drama of possible volcanic eruption there was the arduous climb, the achievement of height, the moment when the view opened out at the peak. But he had work to do to persuade officials at Caracas to arrange an expedition up Mt. Silla. The trail was rough, he was told, and treacherous with mud. Clouds made visibility uncertain. Once more Humboldt insisted, and a party of "negroes" was gotten together to carry his instruments and some reluctant Indian guides recruited to show the way, giving Humboldt yet another opportunity to comment on racial differences between the "taciturn seriousness" of Indians and the "familiar chatting" of the negroes (PN, 137).

Starting out, they followed a well-worn smugglers' trail, but after only a short way the path narrowed and became rough and slippery. When bearers carrying instruments lagged behind, Humboldt forced them to walk in front of him so he could bar their escape back down. Soon they were walking in a cloud. Thick mist obscured the view below. The peak of the mountain was only intermittently visible in the distance. At times the fog was so thick that Humboldt had to use his compass to avoid the precipice that on one side dropped 6,000 feet to the sea. Arrived at the top, Humboldt made his magnetic and barometric observations. Most painful was the way back down, slipping and sliding, having to take off their shoes to keep their footing, feet torn and bleeding from rocks and sharp grasses. At the bottom Humboldt was cheered by locals, who had watched their progress with binoculars, although they were less happy to hear that by his measurements La Silla was nowhere near as high as mountains in the Pyrenees.

But now the rains were over. The preparations had been made. It was time to move on. With a large party of guides, porters, pack mules, and dogs procured for Humboldt by the governor general of the province, they began their trip south through the mountains and valleys that separate the coast from the arid plains of the llanos. At first it was a comfortable even luxurious journey. On the shores of Lake Valencia, a high inland body of water surrounded by mountains on one side and cultivated land on the other, they enjoyed a pleasant recreational interlude. Paths bordered with *Cestrum*, azedarach, and other perpetually flowering shrubs linked isolated farms. Humboldt and Bonpland bathed together near to shore, momentarily surprised by several giant three- to four-foot lizards. They lazed in hammocks wrapped in towels at a forest spa run by a local healer. Six years later, writing *Aspects of Nature* in occupied Berlin, Humboldt would remember the lake as one of the most pleasing scenes in any part of the globe, with banks "thickly clothed with plantains, mimosas, and triplaris," and "small islands, which, as the loss of water by evaporation exceeds the influx, are increasing in size" (AN, 45).[5] They visited the town of New Valencia and its therapeutic hot spring. They stayed at a sugar plantation owned by a wealthy family. Standing on its veranda Humboldt admired the aesthetic beauty of the cane fields at the same time as he registered again his disapproval of slavery:

> The sugar-cane fields with their tender green leaves seem like a great plain. Everything suggests abundance, although those who work the land have to sacrifice their freedom. (PN, 155)

Finally they were at the edge of the llanos, where the real voyage would begin across an expanse of empty grasslands to the rivers. In the rainy season as much as 80 percent of flat land might be under water; now in the dry season the ground cracked open with drought.

They traveled with a mule train plagued by tricks of light. Phantasmal forms rose out of the mist to hang suspended in air above shimmering glassy surfaces. Without warning a wandering cow would appear out of the heat haze for a moment only to vanish back into the dust-clogged air. A lone leafless palm reared up like the mast of some ghostly ship. The ground—Humboldt ever ready with his instruments—registered 122 degrees. The air at midday—106. Everywhere rippled water-like mirages. Hot wind burned their faces like fire. It is a land, mused Humboldt, "estranged from the destiny of mankind."

Bonpland searched for signs of life: shadows of vampire bats that flew around their heads at night, tracks of leaf-cutting ants, holes of snakes, lizards, small mammals that burrowed into the ground to reach some bit of cooling moisture. The pack mules pawed at the stems of cacti to get at the moisture inside. When it got too hot during the day they walked at night under a sky bright with stars, stopping to sleep as soon as an enormous orange sun doubled by refraction rose above the horizon. From a makeshift lean-to shelter they watched the sun shrink down to a red hot molten ball and then rise to flood the plains with white and blinding light, obliterating form and shape, erasing the line between sky and land. No horizon now, only a pink choking dust haze and occasionally the swirl of a tumbleweed, or the faint swift shadow of a small rainless cloud passing over head. In a small grove of chaparral, on the suggestion of the porters, they stopped to pick leaves and stuff them into their hats to insulate their heads from the burning sun.

Little tufts of grass were crisp, brown, inedible. Stepping on them felt like crunching dry cinders. Dust burned their skin and reddened their eyes. They rode sometimes with no visual mark of progress, only the needle of a compass almost too hot to hold, straining ahead into white haze stretching into the distance, out of which could appear a great shimmering expanse of what looked like a lake. "Could be water," commented one of the porters. "Is water when it rains," commented another. And indeed they could see channels in the dust, slightly darkened remnants of dried up watercourses, sometimes even a muddy stagnant pool left behind as the waters receded.

At a small cattle station, El Cayman, "Alligator Farm," they stopped to rest. The owner was gone, leaving the small ranch house in the care of an elderly Negro servant, who greeted them with amazement. On the plains there were few visitors, certainly not visitors with a train of mules and porters. In rough shacks lived the *llaneros*, bare-chested cowboys, skin burnt livid red by the sun, bowlegged and awkward out of the saddle, subsisting on a diet of dried beef and maté. Water? Could they have a drink? And a place to rest? The servant bought out a cup of muddy water and a piece of linen and showed them how to drink through the cloth to filter out the mud, a process they would repeat in months to come on the Río Negro when there was nothing to drink but river water. Humboldt complained. Had the owner not taken the trouble to dig a well? Water could not be far underground. The drink of warm fetid water was hardly satisfying. They had been on horseback for two days now with their skin blistering and burning with dust. Was there not fresh water somewhere?

Why not use the llanos method of finding water, suggested one of the porters, half serious: don't take water to the mules; let them loose and they will find it for you. Immediately, Humboldt ordered two of the thirsty mules unpacked and let loose. The mules galloped off. The two Europeans followed at a run, watched by incredulous porters. The mules slowed. Their pursuers caught their breaths. The mules raised their muzzles and sniffed the air, looking here and there for signs of vegetation. Bonpland and Humboldt imagined the feel of cool water on their skin, layers of dried sweat and encrusted dust sluicing off. The water hole was not far, or at least in their eagerness it did not seem far, a small fetid pool with a palm tree at one end for shade, the ground around it churned up in mud where animals came to drink. The mules jostled for position at the edge and drank deeply. Humboldt and Bonpland peeled off their clothes, with Bonpland laughing to see the bright red of their hands and neck against the white of belly and buttocks. With sighs of pleasure they slid into the muddy water, felt the coolness on their skin, crouched down in the mud. In a moment Bonpland's head reared up.

"Did you hear it?"

He pushed at Humboldt, always slower, always somewhat distracted. "Out, out." He pulled and pushed Humboldt in the direction of the bank. The mules resting under the tree looked up and shied off, kicking their heels as the two men scrambled out of the water onto the muddy bank. Standing covered with mud, Bonpland pointed out the reason for the alarm: a shadow sliding through the water on the other side of the pool, an alligator.

But now there was another problem. They could not be much more than a mile from the ranch house, but in which direction? The mules were gone, frightened off by their sudden leap out of the pool. In their eagerness for a bath they had failed to keep track of the direction they had come, so Humboldt's compass was no use. They cleaned themselves as best they could, dressed, and set out. After an hour or so of walking, they were hopelessly lost. With the sun setting behind them they sat down in a patch of dry grass alone in the desert. Look, Bonpland pointed. Was that a welcoming fire on the horizon? But it was only a rising star made enormous by vapors from the heated ground. Dead silence. Surely someone must have missed them by now and would come to look for them.

A lone figure emerged slowly in the dim starlight, an Indian on horseback. He looked down at them impassively as they explained their plight in broken Spanish. The Indian sat immobile until they finished, nodded, and started off at a trot. They jumped up, afraid he might disappear as quickly as he had come. Following at a run, they panted to keep up, not sure where, following nonetheless. The Indian took no notice of them, only looked straight ahead, trotting along at his own pace, and once in sight of the ranch house, he disappeared back into the night. Bonpland and Humboldt headed for the smoke of the fires. Guides and porters looked up from a dinner of corn cakes and tales of travelers lost on the plains. "We were worried for you," said one of them with a chuckle. "Who knows what might happen to Europeans out there alone at night." But there was more in the stagnant pools of the llanos than hungry alligators. A little further on at the dusty desert town of Calabozo, Humboldt would finally get his chance to study the *Gymnotus*, the electric eel, the "galvanic tornado."

Calabozo had been the first settlement on the llanos, eleven Spanish families in 1548, far from any other settlement, marooned in a wilderness of burnt grass and blinding sun. So it remained. But here Humboldt found another one of those outposts of European science that so delighted him. A local inhabitant, Carlos del Pozo, had constructed a rudimentary electrical machine using only an outdated *Treatise on Electricity*, some treatises of Benjamin Franklin, a few simple materials, and two metal plates ordered from Philadelphia. In a little shack-like house on the edge of town, an electric generator clinked and sparked away, with its maker surprised and delighted to have an important European visitor. Del Pozo explained. At first he experimented with cylindrical machines made from large glass jars with their necks cut off. But plates ordered from Philadelphia had allowed him to make a proper disc machine. Reverently he picked up and examined one by one Humboldt's stock of European instruments.

Bonpland wandered off. Were there were no gardens, nothing growing in the hard-baked soil? At the ranch where they stayed the food was monotonous, dried beef, beans, roasted cassava. Nothing will grow here, he was told. Even in the rainy season? Yes, even then because of the ants, giant red leaf-cutting ants with enormous heads and sharp jaws. In nests deep in underground gardens they fed the leaves they harvested to their food of choice, beds of fungi kept captive below. Was there no way to be rid of the ants? The monks had a method, said the locals. They dug down into the nests, destroyed the fungus gardens and the ant larvae, sprayed the nests with poison. But the Jesuits were long gone, expelled from South America by the Spanish. The practice had died out. Now it was cattle only. The ants returned, eating every small shoot of green.

Back with Pozo, Humboldt was again sending out orders for frogs. Again locals gathered to watch as Humboldt killed them, cut them up, and made the severed sinews twitch with his Leyden jar. And more important, del Pozo knew about the electric eels, knew they burrowed in great numbers in mud pools like the one where he and Bonpland took their interrupted bath. The creatures had a bank of muscles running down each side of their bodies that released a charge of electricity powerful enough to kill a horse and stun a man unconscious. Send out the word, said Humboldt: any Indian who brings me a live eel will get generous payment. At first there was little result. For the Indians, eels were hated enemies. Eels tormented the pack horses they used to cross streams in the rainy season. Their shocks reverberated through the water and killed fish needed for food. No one took up Humboldt's offer. Again Humboldt railed at native backwardness. Again Indians had proved indifferent to monetary reward. One half-dead eel arrived with no charge left.

If eels would not be brought to him, he would go to them. Where were they to be found, asked Humboldt. There were many, he was told, at a place called Caño de Bera, a stagnant pond not far outside of town surrounded by flowering trees. But how was he to catch them? Perhaps he could use the native *barbaseo*, suggested one of the Indians, a poison made from phyllanthus roots that stunned the eels and made them harmless. No, fumed Humboldt, could they not understand, he wanted the eels alive, as alive as possible, not drugged. Perhaps, said another hesitantly, there might be a way, but it would cost. Go on, Humboldt urged them. The Indian continued: It might be possible to use horses and mules as bait. The injured animals would drain off some of the electric charge, but only enough so the eels could be caught.

Finally, with the outlay of a considerable sum, Humboldt would now have his eels. A few days later, a mixed troop of Indians and Creoles assembled at the edge of a pool of mud-thick foul-smelling water. Standing in the shade of straggling trees, Humboldt watched with excitement as from a distance came the sound of stampeding hoofs. A red-orange whirl appeared on the horizon. Closer and closer, thirty horses and mules were herded toward the pool in a cloud of suffocating dust to arrive in a confusion of rearing and pitching hoofs on the far side of the pool. Shouting, hitting the animals with clubs and whips, the Indians forced the animals into the water. Eyes wild, manes tossing, the horses reared back. More docile, no less frightened, mules dug in their heels. Mud flew, spattering men and horses. Animals slipped and struggled on the wet ground. The Indians beat at their flanks. One by one the horses were driven into the water, churning up the mud with pawing hoofs. Humboldt's description from *Aspects of Nature*:

> The capture of the gymnoti affords a picturesque spectacle. Mules and horses are driven into a marsh which is closely surrounded by Indians, until the unwonted noise and disturbance induce the pugnacious fish to begin an attack. One sees them swimming about like serpents, and trying cunningly to glide under the bodies of the horses. Many of these are stunned by the force of the invisible blows; others, with manes standing on end, foaming and with wild terror sparkling in their eyes, try to fly from the raging tempest. But the Indians, armed with long poles of bamboo, drive them back into the middle of the pool. (AN, 22)

The eels' long yellow-spotted bodies were clearly visible in the muddy water. In swarms they dove under the horses' soft bellies attacking their organs. The animals reared up in agony. Over and over the eels attacked panicked horses, churning the surface of the water into a turmoil of blood-tinged foam and seething bodies. When a horse or mule tried to climb out and up the slippery banks, as soon as it got a foothold the Indians were ready with sticks and clubs to force it back into the water. Several of the horses collapsed in the water. One went under, struggled a few moments, then floated to the surface. On and on went the battle, the crazed eyes of the tortured horses, the slimy streaks of the eels as they attacked, a confusion of limbs, horse manes standing straight up on their backs in terror, teeth and jaws open. Coils of swarming eels surrounded each animal while Humboldt and Bonpland watched from the bank.

Little by little the turmoil died down. The eels had expended some of their charge, said the Indians. They would not regain their strength until they rested. This was the moment when they could be caught. A dead horse floated on the water. Another paralyzed by shock lay half in and out of water on the bank. Two horses that made it out of the water past the Indians lay on the dried grass with only the slight rise and fall of their bellies to indicate that they were alive. The fishing could begin. The Indians used harpoons on long strings to hook and pull the lethargic and exhausted eels near to shore, from where they could be hauled up on pieces of dry wood pulled by heavy string, the ends of which stayed dry so as not to conduct the eel's remaining charge. Soon five eels lay on the bank, with more to follow. An eel close to the water looked like it might escape. In his excitement, Humboldt stepped on it and immediately felt a paralyzing shock in his knees and feet. Never, he reported, had he gotten such a shock from his Leyden jar. "With each stroke," Humboldt reported, "you feel an internal vibration that lasts two or three seconds, followed by a painful numbness" (PN, 171). Stepping back, he poked and prodded the eels with sticks and even with his bare hands. Hold him there, he called to Bonpland. Here, over here. As incredulous Indians looked on, Humboldt put frogs and toads on an eel's back and watched the result as the frogs shot up and fell to the side motionless. After four hours of experiments, he and Bonpland felt a weakness in the muscles, a pain in the joints, and a general malaise that lasted until the following day. Captured eels, half dead after their ordeal, were killed, dissected, drawn, and their innards described. Months later, returned to the coast, Humboldt described his experiments to the Captain General of Caracas and Venezuela:

> In the plains of the Apure, we made some very curious experiments
> on the powers of the gymnoti (*tembladores*), six or seven of which

killed two horses in a few minutes. The results of these experiments were very novel and contrary to what one had thought up to now in Europe, due to the lack of good instruments that were available in the Indies. This fish is not really charged with electricity, but with a galvanic fluid, about which I told you several times and which I described in my work on the nerves and principle of vitality. (LA, 99)

To his more dramatic description of the scene in *Aspects of Nature*, Humboldt added a cosmic gloss.

That which forms the invisible but living weapon of this electric eel;—that which, awakened by the contact of moist dissimilar particles, circulates through all the organs of plants and animals;—that which, flashing from the thunder cloud, illuminates the wide skyey canopy;—that which draws iron to iron and directs the silent recurring march of the guiding needle;—all, like the several hues of the divided ray of light, flow from one source; and all blend again together in one perpetually, every where diffused, force or power. (AN, 23)

Moving on from Calabozo and the adventure with the eels, covering the last stretch of desert, there was one last adventure. They came across a young Indian girl alone in the desert lying almost dead in the sand. Dismounting, getting out their canteens, they revived her and filled her water jar. She worked as a servant in a neighboring hacienda, she told them, had fallen ill and been cast out. She should come with them, they told her. They would get her to the missions on the river Apure and to a place of safety. But once on her feet, over all their objections, she insisted on going on alone, giving Humboldt one more opportunity to comment on characteristics of the Indian race. "Our threats and requests were useless; she was hardened to suffering, like all of her race, and lived in the present without fear of the future" (PN, 172). They could do nothing but continued on a last few miles to the suffocatingly hot border station of San Fernando, where Capuchin monks provided them with chickens, eggs, bananas, cassavas, and fruit, as well as canoes and guides for the trip up the rivers.

5

Riverworlds

Imagine them. The heavy-laden pirogue is rowed by four Indians. A pilot stands straight and vigilant in front on the lookout for floating logs and sandbanks. In the back a low cabin shelter thatched with palm leaves extends several feet beyond the sides of the long narrow canoe; Humboldt and Bonpland lie down and rest there during the heat of the day. Every available corner and surface in the boat is crammed with Humboldt's instruments, Bonpland's papers and presses, crates for specimens, Schreber's *Genera plantarum*—eventually lost overboard in a storm—and Bernadin's *Paul et Virginie*, from which Humboldt reads aloud at moments during the day. Sitting at attention behind the pilot, a large dog accompanies them until one dark night on shore he is carried away by a jaguar. Everywhere, in cages lashed to the shelter's framing, loose on the canoe, huddled among the baggage, are Bonpland's birds and monkeys, to the amusement and sometimes irritation of Humboldt. A beautiful little titi monkey with a childlike face chatters on the roof of the shelter. For a joke they teach him to recognize the pictures of insects in Humboldt's copy of Cuvier's *Tableau élémentaire de l'histoire naturelle des animaux.* Cages for birds hang from the crossbeams, a macavahu monkey with a pale masklike face sits alert in the bow, a purple macaw preens brilliant feathers, and there are seven parrots, two jungle hens, a motmot, two guans, and eight monkeys, some in cages, some loose, and a pair of brilliant jokester toucans with white-bordered backs, lemon-yellow bibs, and blue-shadowed eyes.

For this first part of the trip they would be alone. Only in the rainy season, they were told, was there depth enough for the larger boats that went upriver to the Orinoco to supply remote outposts and bring away jungle products. On the river they entered a dream world, moving up a corridor of brown water between high walls of thick impenetrable vegetation out of which flashed brilliant red bromeliads and pairs of hyacinth macaws. Schools of freshwater dolphins spouted silver in the sun. Giant snakes fourteen or more feet long kept pace treading the surface. Pale ochre sandbanks opened where crocodiles lay half buried in the mud with open jaws in front of a backdrop of mimosas and palms. Suddenly an island shimmered pearly pink with flamingos and pink pelicans. Herons stood in the shallows. Hocco birds strolled the bank with heraldic black feathers and tufted heads. Tapirs and peccaries came down narrow tracks through forests of cedar to drink and stare up at the strange apparition gliding by with its thatched canopy and rowing figures. Across the sky came sudden storms, dark banks of clouds with sunlit edges, a spate of rain on the opposite bank and then a pink-and-purple-tinged torrent and the bottom of the boat awash with water. As suddenly the storm would end. Steam rose off huge glossy leaves and enveloped the canoe in thick mist as cooler air hit warm water.

At times they passed down narrow canals, trees close on either side covered with velvety moss and hung with clusters of white sweet-smelling orchids. Herds of rabbit-like capybaras watched motionless from clearings in the trees. Once a giant jaguar looked up at them from the bank, one paw resting on a freshly killed capybara while not far away a flock of vultures waited for their turn at the kill. Camped out one night on a sandbar, they looked out into darkness to see the eyes of crocodiles glistening in the firelight watching them from the shallows. There was discomfort and sometimes misery. The heat was suffocating. The provisions given them by the fathers were soon depleted. At times all they had to eat was dry unsweetened cocoa powder mixed with river water. They were tormented by insects. Mosquitoes swarmed around their heads. Biting flies attacked any exposed skin. When they camped, six-inch cockroaches invaded their supplies. Sweat poured down their bodies in equatorial heat. Mosquitoes raised painful welts on exposed skin. Small bloodsucking plume flies left rashes of irritated bites; chiggers dug under their toenails and laid eggs. There would be no cooling swims, not with alligators waiting in the shallows and piranhas known to take a chunk of flesh. After days rowing on the Apure they would reach the Orinoco. There they would turn, not east downstream into the trading channel, but northwest up against the current into unexplored territory.

Described by Columbus as one of the four rivers of Paradise that divide and water the world, the Orinoco rises in the Guiana Highlands and swells gently as it flows northeast, periodically expanding into clear lakes and scattering into fingers of black water tributaries. Many of its twisting channels are seasonal, leaving behind stagnant lakes, host to ephemeral species of plants that vanish when the rains come and waters rise. Here was a land of mystery, protected by seemingly impassable rapids, seldom traveled even by native people, attempted only by a few Europeans. From its upper reaches came back tales successively embellished as they were passed down the rivers, through the ports, and across the ocean to Europe. From the brutal Spanish conquistador Acuña in his *New Discovery of the Great River of the Amazons* came stories of giants, dwarfs, and fierce women warriors. From Sir Walter Raleigh: headless men with eyes in their shoulders and mouths in their chest. From Condamine on his way back from measuring the earth in Peru: Amazon warrior women, two-headed men with a third eye on each forehead, and a man-ape who stole and raped women, and always shocking, tales of man-eating cannibals.

On the mile-wide Orinoco the water was rough and broad like a sea, with banks hardly visible on either side. Their boat was tossed on white cap waves whipped up by the mixing of river currents and strong winds. The Indian rowers strained to make headway against the current. Eventually they would reach the Atures and Maypures cataracts, miles of rapids, barrier between explored and unexplored territory, hazardous entry to unmapped canals, rivers, waterways, swamps and marshes that knit together the Orinoco and Amazon waterways. Here was jungle that killed off hordes of gold-hunting conquistadors and confounded attempts of Portuguese on the Amazon and Spanish on the Orinoco to lay claim to defendable boundaries. For Humboldt, finding a passage between the rivers would be a great achievement, facilitating the fixing of a border between Spanish and Portuguese America, facilitating trade and the spread of civilization.

At one point their pilot boasted that he could tack directly upstream. He steered close to the wind. A sudden gust took the sail and tipped the boat over so that one side was submerged, and in an instant the canoe filled with water. Humboldt and the Indians cried out. The boat would sink. They would be lost. The Indians prepared to abandon ship, dive into the water and swim to shore. Humboldt, who couldn't swim, was paralyzed with fear. He would drown if the canoe sank. There was panic, until Bonpland, who had been napping under the thatched shelter, woke up. Humboldt described the incident in his *Personal Narrative*:

> Bonpland was sleeping in the middle of the boat. Woken by the flooding water and the shrieking Indian he immediately took charge of the situation with that coolness he always showed in danger. As one side of the boat rose up out of the water he did not think the boat would sink. He thought that if we had to abandon boat we could swim ashore as there were no crocodiles about. Then the ropes holding the sails broke, and the same gust of wind that

almost sank us now helped us recover. We baled the water out with gourds, mended the sail, and in less than half an hour we were able to continue our journey. (PN, 192)

And described it again with considerably more drama in a letter to Fourcroy at the Muséum in Paris:

Never will I forget [Bonpland's] devoted attachment of which he gave me the greatest of proof in a storm which hit us on April 6, 1800, in the middle of the Orinoco. Our pirogue was already two thirds full of water and the Indians who were near to us were already beginning to throw themselves into the water to swim to the bank in the storm. My generous friend spoke of following their example and carrying me with him to shore. . . . Our situation was truly terrifying. The shore was more than a half-mile from us and a quantity of crocodiles showed themselves half-submerged in the water. Even if we had escaped from the fury of the waves and the voracity of the crocodiles and gotten to solid ground, we would have been prey to hunger or jaguars because the forest is so dense on these banks and interlaced with so many lianas it is impossible to penetrate it. (LA, 88–89)

It was not the only time Bonpland proved his skill and courage in times of danger. Returning from the Rio Negro, they were crossing over some steep rapids at Atures with a loaded canoe when the Indian rowers decided they would have to take the canoes around another way, leaving Humboldt and Bonpland to embark with the heavier cargo and to be picked up on the other side. Humboldt and Bonpland followed a rare and fierce *Pipra rupicola* with a double crest of golden feathers into a hollow behind a fall of water and waited for the canoes to come back. They waited. It began to rain. Night was coming, light fading. The monkeys in their wicker cages chattered in fear, attracting crocodiles. Still the Indians had not returned. Had they been abandoned? Again Bonpland took charge. He would swim to shore, he assured Humboldt, and go for help. Before he could carry out his rescue, the Indian rowers had returned.

At the cataracts at Maypures giant rocks and islands break the course of the Orinoco. In a width of more than 8,000 feet of rocks and foam, sometimes only one channel, twenty feet of rushing roaring water, remains open. Here they would have to leave the large comfortable pirogue behind for smaller slender canoes dug out of tree trunks. They watched with the local missionary as a team of conscripted Indians dragged, rowed, and pulled canoes up the rapids.

The Indians waded out into waist-deep water, swam ahead, with difficulty attached a rope to a rock, hauled the canoe forward through narrow deep channels only a few feet wide, held it off from boulders where it could break into splinters, pulled it inch by inch and mile by mile, dragged it with muscles straining through miles of falling water, up giant chains of black granite outcroppings, up miles of steps and dams that broke and tore apart the river's flow. It was a dangerous business. If the Indians were unlucky the canoe could break up, knock them senseless, pull them under the water. They would have to scramble to get away from the wreck, swim to shore, and then run away from the wrath of the missionary. It was better in earlier times, one of the guides told Bonpland, pointing out to him the tracks of wagon wheels still visible along the shore. The Jesuits, before their expulsion, used oxen to drag canoes up the slope on wheeled supports.

But the Jesuits were long gone, expelled from South America in 1756. Other missionaries were now in charge, and it was no longer easy to keep Indian workers to the task. One night the missionary shackled two Indians he relied on as interpreters to be sure they would be there in the morning. At dawn Humboldt and Bonpland were woken by screams of a another young Indian being brutally whipped. "Not without difficulty did we obtain his pardon," commented Humboldt in his *Personal Narrative*. " 'Without severity,' we were told, 'you would get nothing' " (PN, 198). Humboldt went on to explain what he saw as the missionary's mistake. The father treated the Indian as if he was a "civilized man" who understood that "to enjoy the advantages of a social state he must give up some freedom." Not being civilized, the Indian, "wise in his simplicity, retains the wish to return to the forest that gave him birth." Just as with a child, the proper remedy was not force but rather "moral influence": "Whatever may be the state of weakness or degradation in our species, no faculty is completely annihilated. The human understanding exhibits only different degrees of strength and development," concluded Humboldt.[1]

Meanwhile Bonpland was in a flurry of collecting. In the mist that came off the cataracts, rainbows appeared and disappeared. On rock islands emerging from foam and spray grew flowerbeds of melastomes, ferns, and silver-leaf mimosas. Pools warmed by the sun formed between boulders surrounded by greenery. Wandering in the forest near the Orinoco, he came upon a fifty-foot jacaranda in full flower, its tubular flowers quivering against bright blue sky, a tree which, as he put it in *Plantes équinoxiales*, "pleases the eye":

> From far off, by its foliage and size, one thinks one sees one of
> those sensitive plants (Mimosas) which are the ornament of thick
> tropical forests, but as one approaches double flowers of a beautiful

violet color arranged in panicles put it rather among the *Bignonias*.
The wood of *Jacaranda obtusifolia* is blond, soft, and very flexible.
The Indians who live along the banks of the Orinoco use it to line
their pirogues, and make *canaletes* of it—this is the name they use
for their oars, which are differently formed from ours and which
they use differently. (PE I, 64)

Geoffraya superba was a new species similar to the tamarind. He found it first
near Cumaná, and then came upon it again at the Orinoco cataracts growing
to twenty or thirty feet in height.

> *Geoffraya superba* is a truly magnificent tree for the thickness of
> its trunk, the arrangement of its branches covered with leaves of
> a beautiful green, for the quantity of its flowers with which it is
> almost constantly covered, for its numerous fruits, and finally for
> the shade it offers for travelers in a country as hot as the one in
> which it grows. (PE II, 71)

Its wood is hard, Bonpland went on to note; it takes a nice polish and is used
in construction. The fruit when he tasted it was not very agreeable, but it was
savored by parrots, monkeys, and other small animals that clustered on the
ground beneath its branches.

In the rapids between Atures and Maypure, he found a new genus,
Platycarpum, growing out of pockets of soil in granite rocks that rose up out of
foaming cataracts. Also at the rapids, verrucaria, lichens, along with clumps of
purple-flowered melastomes in island gardens, and rock basins behind curtains
of giant ferns where he and Humboldt bathed in botanical splendor. Debris
caught in basins between the rocks made flowerpots blooming bright with
arums, yellow bannisterias, heliotropes. Out of the swirling mist rising and
falling from the constant spray and wind emerged and disappeared tall tops
of trees, ninety new species of palm alone. Hyacinths, water lilies, moss like
the rootless *Podastemaceae* clinging to bare rocks. Small trees rooted in rotting
tree trunks floated in pools surrounded by ink-black rocks. Inland from the
cataracts, on excursions with Indian guides, Bonpland walked through forests
of myrtles and polyanthus, kapok trees with red pods ripening and bursting
in a silken mist of flying seeds. He added to his growing collection of *Rhexia*,
so many and so charming.

Above the cataracts they took directions at a small mission at San Fernando de Atabapo. Yes, they were told, it was possible to reach the Amazon.

They would have to continue up the Orinoco, then up the Atabapo, the Temi, and the Tuamini. From there, if they had made each right turning, they could take a portage through swampy jungle overland, hauling the canoes, to a narrow stream called the Pimichin, which would take them to the Río Negro, a tributary of the Amazon. Once there they would have to make a circle to avoid passing into hostile Portuguese territory, taking the meandering Casiquiare canal from the Negro back to the Orinoco. The directions might have seemed all but impossible to follow in narrow twisting channels and side channels of dark water, but Humboldt was determined. Once he found the link, a canal might be built at the Pimichin portage. Commerce between Portuguese and Spanish territories would be facilitated, hostile territory opened to trade bringing civilization to the jungle.

As always he was busy with mapping and measuring. He recorded the depth of the river, the width of the flow, the speed of the current. He measured barometric pressure and static electricity. He was now able, he wrote in his *Narrative*, to hold his electrometer up six feet from the ground for 20 minutes at a time to record changes in electric charge. Always in addition to measurements, he was writing down his impressions and sensations:

> I made the effort to note down in writing, every day, whether in the canoe or at night camps, anything that happened which was worthy of note. The heavy rain and incredible amount of mosquitoes crowding the air on the Orinoco and Casiquiare obviously left gaps in my chronicle, but I always wrote it up a few days later. . . . What is noted down while actually viewing the described objects keeps a semblance of truth (dare I say 'individuality'), which gives charm even to insignificant things. (PN, 177–178)

And Bonpland? Perhaps he was too deeply immersed in this new world to worry about capturing the imaginations of future readers? So it would seem from a few snapshots of him provided by Humboldt in his *Personal Narrative*.

Bonpland looking up at gigantic *Ocotea*, laurels, and trees without English or Latin names, trees that support epiphytic orchids and ferns 100 feet up in the forest canopy, so high the Indians refuse to gather samples, and even Bonpland balks at the climb. As usual Humboldt was impatient with the Indians. They cared nothing for flowers; they could see no point in climbing; all they cared about was timber for their boats. But as interesting to Bonpland as orchids were less showy plants growing on the forest floor. Competing for available light and nutriments, in reach of foraging animals, plants in the understory developed toxic defenses, plant phenolics, tannins, alkaloids that were the stock in trade of native healers who used them as analgesics, stimulants, and hallucinogens. Medicines and poisons, teas and tisanes, saps with anti-venom effects, downy excrescences that stanch bleeding, barks that cure fever, curare from the boiled down sap of a bejuco vine: along the Orinoco Bonpland began a lifelong course of research into plant-based medicines.

Bonpland interrogating some Indians. What was the plant source of the brilliant red dye called *chica* so important to the Indians that the mission fathers made it into cakes and sold it back to them at exorbitant prices? Could they show him the plant so he can identify the species? He knows the common and less intense annatto dye that comes from *Bixa orellana*, but he also knows that the chica preferred by the Indians for body paint is from another plant, perhaps one of the *Bignonia* or trumpet vines that he sees growing so rampantly and beautifully in the seasonally moist and dry forests around the rapids. Its vines climb up the tallest forest trees, with double flowers an inch long with unfurling tendrils. He questions the guides, makes notes on native processes of extraction—leaves crushed in water, mixed with oil, and pressed into cakes—already thinking of experiments that could be run in Paris at the Muséum to determine chemical properties (PE I, 109). Might it be used, he mused, not only for skin painting but as a safe dye for fabric and foodstuffs? Clearly it was not toxic to the Indians who covered their bodies with it.

Bonpland botanizing deep in the forest with Indian guides. They warn him to hide behind a tree as a band of grazing wild pigs passes by, an order he obeys immediately and without question. He has learned to trust the Indians, who not only protect him from the razor-sharp teeth of small forest animals, but show him remote groves of trees covered with golden cassia panicles, and *Clusia grandiflora*, the strangler plant, so lovely with white outer petals and a coral heart. They lead him up a small stream off the Río Negro among the fibrous half-submerged stems of small palms to *Galeandra devoniana* with purple perfumed flowers. They take him into tangled vegetation where bands of excited squirrel monkeys whistle through the trees. They show him colonies of birds with hanging nests.

Bonpland working with a native hunter, a "zambo" of mixed African and Indian blood, preparing a special weak preparation of curare, a jungle poison that Bonpland uses to capture small animals alive. He and Humboldt watch as the "amo del curare," the curare master, prepares the stronger lethal hunting poison, watch him grate and crush the sapwood and bark of the *bejuco de mavacure*, boil it down, spread it in trays to evaporate, mix into the thick yellow liquid coagulants from other jungle plants to make it thick enough to adhere to arrows. Bonpland touches a drop of the poison to his tongue. If it tastes bitter it will be too strong. He has the master's assurance: Curare is only dangerous when it enters directly into the bloodstream, a fact of particular interest to Bonpland as a physician. He knows by now that an extract is used medicinally by local healers, and is studying species of bejuco used in different villages and differing methods of preparation. Later in Paraguay and Argentina he will use curare in his medical practice to ease intractable stomach ailments.

At a narrows on the Orinoco in the blistering heat of midday, Bonpland hunts in rocks along the shore for signs of plant life while Humboldt dozes in the shade. Objects only a few feet away undulate in waves of heat and dissolve into red haze. Iguanas, geckos, salamanders lie motionless on the rocks, mouths open breathing in the fiery air. Foraging in the rocks Bonpland finds a new species of *Apocinea* beside some silver-leaved croton bushes. At night, plagued by mosquitoes as he tries to dry and press his plants, he climbs into one of the Indian *hornitos*, low closed structures cleared by smoke to be free of mosquitoes. "Bonpland, with a praiseworthy courage and patience, dried hundreds of plants shut up in these Indian *hornitos*," reported Humboldt (PN, 210). As important and delicate as the collecting of plants is their preservation, a task that in the hot humid air of the jungle required endless care and precaution. At the rapids Bonpland spent a night on a missionary's tree house platform, happy for once to be able to lay out the day's find on a dry surface away from damp ground. Arrived back in Cumaná, Humboldt would announce to Fourcroy, "In the sixteen months we covered the vast territory between the coast, the Orinoco, the Río Negro, and the Amazon, citizen Bonpland has dried, with copies, more than six thousand plants" (LA, 80).

There was a price to pay. At the delta of the rivers Horeda and Paruasi covered with dense vegetation, Bonpland could not resist a botanical excursion. He soaked himself several times in streams and emerged covered with mud. A few days later in Angostura when he set up his worktable to begin the difficult business of putting his specimens in order, he staggered. Gravely ill with fever, he nursed himself through a dangerous month-long illness, extracting medicines from plants he learned about from native guides.

On the Casiquiare canal came a major discovery. Reduced to eating bad cocoa and rice cooked in river water without butter or salt, they passed a canoe of Indians coming from harvest deep in the forest and quickly devoured handfuls of large nourishing nuts given them by the Indians. The nuts were delicious, fresh, with no rancid taste. From then on, Bonpland watched closely along the banks. One of the rowers pointed out a sixty-foot-tall tree. Bonpland questioned him. Was that the normal height of the tree that gave the nuts?

Were there groves nearby? No, he was told. He was lucky to see a tree so near the river. Bonpland listened attentively as his informants speculated on the possible origin of one lone individual close to the river. Unlikely to have been sown by a randomly dropped seed, they said. Experiments in the villages showed that seeds seldom germinate on their own because of the hardness of the shell and the great quantity of oil in the seed, which quickly turns rancid. Instead groves were inland on dryer land where trees grew with trunks one or two meters in diameter and as much as 120 feet tall, towering over other trees. So it was that trekking deep into the forest with the guides, Bonpland was the first European to see and describe the tree that bears Brazil nuts.

Two-foot-long ovate leaves form a dense canopy high overhead. Flowering panicles of large yellow flowers with many stamens produce an ovary that becomes a large brown hard-skinned capsule weighing as much as three kilos. From the ovary comes, not nuts, but large edible seeds. In *Plantes équinoxiales*, Bonpland reviewed the colonial rivalries that kept this valuable tropical tree a mystery for so long. For some time, the seeds, or "nuts" as they were called, had been known in French Guiana, Lisbon, and at the Jardin in Paris, but not the tree that bore them. Marketed in Europe by a Portuguese trader, its location was kept a secret. A French ship captured a British merchantman, and a cargo of the nuts was sold in Rouen. The buyer made oil from the seeds he proclaimed was as good or better than anything available in France. He wrote to Jussieu and Desfontaines at the Muséum. Where was this tree found? What was its name? Even they could not give him an answer. No one had ever seen the tree, they told him. It was somewhere in Brazil, but no one knew where.

It was an important discovery and Humboldt took full advantage of it, naming the new genus *Bertholletia excelsa* in honor of Claude Louis Berthollet, the influential French chemist and founder of the prestigious Arcueil Circle of scientists. For Bonpland, more important than strategic naming was information from native growers about the tree's habits and cultivation. As he put it in *Plantes équinoxiales*, here were nutritious seeds with a mild taste and copious oil that deserved not only to be gathered in the wild, but to be grown with "as much care as almonds or walnuts are in France." The best and only really reliable sources of knowledge of that successful cultivation were the native people, whose relations with the tree were intimate and long-standing. For the harvesting of such a valuable product, men "of good will and intelligence" should be sent into the forest, not random foragers. Those who hoped to naturalize the plant should follow native advice. They should not rely on bringing out seeds, which would not germinate under artificial conditions. They should collect seeds already sprouted. Guided by natives, they should put seedlings into cases filled with some of the same earth in which they started to grow and carefully transport them down the river on trains of rafts in cases covered with palm leaves to protect them from the sun. What was needed, in other words, were qualities in short supply among Europeans on the rivers: the "intelligence" to take advantage of local knowledge, and the "good will" not to endanger a useful and beautiful species for quick profit. There should be no indiscriminate cutting and gathering. Native groves should be left to thrive in forests so that cultivated stock could be replenished when necessary. Above all, specified Bonpland, transport of precious seedlings must be left to native inhabitants who know the river and appreciate the value of tropical products.

> The natives, skillful in navigation on the Orinoco and accustomed to leading these trains, should be the pilots. They are intelligent and one can leave the care to them. They know the extreme utility of this plant because every year they make long trips to get the nuts. Missionaries and the Indians who live along the banks of the Orinoco and neighboring rivers, each receive a quantity of young *Bertholletia* that they without doubt cultivate with as much care as the sugar cane, bananas, pineapples and manioc from which they get their main nourishment. (PE I, 126–127)

With th,eir help, he reported, he himself carried *Bertholletia* striplings down the river from the cataracts to San Tomás de la Nueva Guayana. No damage at all had been done to the young trees, any more than it had to *Coumarouna odorata*, the source for tonka beans that his native aides also transported and transplanted down river with complete success.[2]

If Bonpland was in his element on the river, judging from some of the passages in his *Personal Narrative*, Humboldt often found his surroundings disturbing:

> The uninhabited banks of the Casiquiare, covered in jungle, busied my imagination. In this interior of a new continent you get used to seeing man as not essential to the natural order. The earth is overloaded with vegetation: nothing prevents its development. An immense layer of mould manifests the uninterrupted action of organic forces. Crocodile and boa are the masters of the river; jaguar, peccary, the dante and monkeys cross the jungle without fear

or danger, established there in an ancient heritage. This view of a living nature where man is nothing is both odd and sad. Here, in a fertile land, in an eternal greenness, you search in vain for traces of man; you feel you are carried into a different world from the one you were born into. (PN, 233)

Recalling their Jesuit-trained Indian boatman's reverent chant "Es como en el Paraíso" in *Aspects of Nature*, Humboldt demurred: "The peace of the golden age was, however, far from prevailing among the animals of this American paradise, which carefully watched and avoided each other" (AN, 269).

Equally disturbing to him were human inhabitants who at times posed a challenge to Humboldt's high-minded humanitarianism. Here he watches a gathering of Indians resting from digging turtle eggs on an island in the Orinoco:

> The gathering of Indians at Pararuma again afforded a fascinating chance for civilized men to study the development of our intel-lectual faculties in savages. It is hard to recognize in this infancy of society, in this gathering of dull, silent, impassive Indians, the primitive origins of our species. We do not see here a human nature that is sweet and naïve as described by our poets. We would like to persuade ourselves that these Indians, squatting by the fire, or sitting on huge turtle shells, their bodies covered in mud and grease, fixing their eyes stupidly for hours on the drink they are preparing, belong to a degenerate race rather than being a primitive type of our own species that, having been dispersed for ages in jungles, have fallen back into barbarism. (PN, 194)

Could what Blumenbach called "degeneration" from a common origin in fact be evidence of another species altogether? Given his description, the possibility might have crossed Humboldt's mind and crossed it again when they passed a party of Carib Indians on their way to the same turtle hunt. The canoe appeared out of the mist. The leader, his body painted head to toe in traditional red chica, stood stiffly in the bow. "Smooth, thick hair cut in a fringe like choir boys', eyebrows painted black, and a lively and gloomy stare give these Indians an incredibly hard expression," noted Humboldt. The Carib leader gave the Europeans no greeting, only looked straight ahead. In back of the canoe rode some women: "fat, disgustingly dirty," commented Humboldt (PN, 187).

Spanish incursions left little dignity to the once flourishing Orinoco inhabitants. At San Borja near the confluence with the Apure there were six huts and a few "uncatechized" Indians who lived no differently than "wild" unconverted Indians. The annual egg harvest on the Orinoco's "turtle island," presided over with efficiency by the Jesuits, was now a disorderly affair under Franciscans who had allowed the beach to be dug up so badly that each year there were less and less turtles, explaining perhaps the depression and despair observed by Humboldt. But the decline, as Humboldt saw it, was not due to European diseases, which had decimated Indian populations elsewhere, or to hostile invasion, but rather to the Indians' aversion to mission life—"Jungle Indians have a horror of the life of civilized man and desert when the slightest misfortune befalls them in the mission"—and to the "unpardonable custom that Indian mothers have of using poisonous herbs to avoid pregnancy" (PN, 205). Again he found little to admire in the missionaries either. They exploited the Indians in petty ways. They sold the chica body paint, without which the Indians felt naked, at a large markup. They bought rare animals from the Indians at "disgustingly low prices" and resold them down river. They charged Indians dearly for small items needed for fishing and hunting and used the proceeds for their own comfort and the decoration of their churches. But, as Humboldt saw it, the Indians were no better. They were passive. They went through the motions of Christian worship without attempting to understand. They were unable to answer the simplest questions.

In truth, what was left of indigenous river culture was a sad remnant, the result not of degeneracy or passivity, but of violence, disease, greed, slave raids, and the destruction of traditional ways of life. After the expulsion of the Jesuits many of the missions melted away into the jungle. Others were taken over by orders with little knowledge or interest in native culture. Reminders of the past survived, a heavy silver lamp half buried in sand in a small chapel at Atures, some mango and citrus trees growing wild in a clearing, a ruined blacksmith's workshop at San Fernando de Atabapo. Alien invasion pressed down on a people whose cultural and physical roots had been torn away. A few decades before their visit, noted Humboldt, 600 Indians lived in the Jesuit mission at the Maypures cataract, 300 in the mission at Atures, even more beyond the cataract at San Carlos. Now barely sixty sad-faced Indians remained at Maypures under the fathers of the Observance, and at Atures Indians came to the mission only occasionally, were given a few colored beads, fishhooks, and knives, and retreated back into the jungle. Little was left of what river culture might have been like before Spanish incursions.

At the same time, as even Humboldt noted, these were not the silent defeated Chaima:

> The Guamo tribe refuse to be tamed and become sedentary. Their customs have much in common with the Achagua, Guahibo and Otomac, especially their dirtiness, their love for vengeance and their nomadic life-style. (PN, 182–183)

Caribs were taller than other tribes, "their physiognomy less Mongoloid. Their eyes, blacker than is usual among the Guiana hordes, show intelligence, almost a capacity for thought" (PN, 274). Were the Orinoco Indians guilty of that most savage of practices, cannibalism? In letters back to Europe Humboldt insisted that they were. To Willdenow:

> One sees there nations who cultivate the earth, who are hospitable, who appear gentle and humane, just like the inhabitants of Tahiti, but who are, like them, anthropophages. Everywhere in free South America (I speak of the part south of the cataracts of the Orinoco, where no Christian had set foot before us except five or six Franciscans) we found in huts horrible traces of anthropophagy. (LA, 112)

In his *Narrative* Humboldt repeated tales told them by one "Captain" Javit, an aged Indian who took them on botanizing expeditions on the river Negro: "In his youth he had seen all the Indian tribes of the region eat human flesh," reported Humboldt (PN, 227). Other stories came from a "good missionary" who told them stories of an Indian chief who fattened up his wife and ate her, and of tribes who rounded up families in the jungle out of "perverted greed" taking them back for a midnight feast. Could a race be truly human that treated other humans as prey?

> Civilization has led men to sense the unity of the human race, the bonds that link him to customs and language which he does not know. Wild Indians hate all those who do not belong to their tribe or family. Indians who are at war with a neighbouring tribe hunt them as we would animals in the wood. (PN, 245)

It made for exciting copy, but whether anthropophagy existed in any form at the time of Humboldt and Bonpland's voyage is extremely doubtful. If it ever had existed, it was never the wholesale killing and eating of alien tribes or the harvesting of wives, but rather ritual acts of consuming part of the body of a dead enemy, or in rare cases a dead relative. Years later, in Paris, publishing the second volume of his *Narrative*, Humboldt had revised his story. "Carib," he now informed his readers, was not the name of any Indian tribe, but rather a synonym for "cannibal," a designation that by Spanish decree had been given to certain Indians to sanction the use of corporal punishment and forced enslavement: "All the tribes that Figueroa called Carib were condemned to slavery; they could be sold at will or exterminated" (PN, 277).[3] Even if the Caribs were not cannibals, Humboldt continued to see a need for physical discipline:

> It would be better if the priest did not impose corporal punishment as soon as he left the altar; he should not witness the punishment of men and women in his priestly robes; but his abuse arises from the bizarre principles on which missions are based. The most arbitrary civil powers are tightly linked to the rights exercised by priests; yet, though the Caribs are not cannibals, and you would like them to be treated gently, you do realize that some violence is necessary to maintain order in a new society. (PN, 278)

An occasion for such discipline came at Atures on their way back to the coast from the rivers.

Humboldt and Bonpland climbed up through giant granite boulders and crystals of feldspar to where Humboldt had been told there was an ancient Indian burial cave. At a summit of rock outcropping they paused, looking down on a mist-shrouded riverbed and up to the peaks of mountains beyond on which balanced huge spheres of rock. Below them, deep in a thick expanse of wooded forest, was a cave where the last 600 Atures Indians had been laid to rest. Led by their Indian guides, they passed down a narrow overgrown path and approached a vaulted overhang concealing a hidden entrance. Humboldt went quickly inside while Bonpland held back, botanizing among the *Bignonia* vines, fragrant vanilla, yellow *Banisterias* that festooned the entrance.

Inside the cave the skeletons were lined up in rows, reverently prepared, flesh rotted away, bones cleaned, wrapped, and laid in palm-leaf baskets, or placed in large family urns decorated with carvings of animals, meanders, and labyrinths. The Indian guides stepped back murmuring as Humboldt began to rummage in the baskets, opening palm leaf coverings, pulling out skulls. Some of the skulls, he thought, would make good examples of Blumenbach's "American Indian" racial characteristics; others were more "Caucasian." Ignoring the growing "indignation" of the guides, he made a selection to take away: three skeletons, one of a child and two of adults, and a number of skulls. Carrying out his finds, he ordered them loaded onto one of the mules. In deference to what he called the "superstitious aversion that Indians have about corpses," he laid over them woven mats to obscure the cargo (PN, 264). He recalled the moment in *Aspects of Nature:*

> we turned our steps in a thoughtful and melancholy mood from this burying-place of a race deceased. . . . Thus perish the generations of men! Yet when each blossom of man's intellect withers,—when in the storms of time the memories of his art moulder and decay,—an ever new life springs forth from the bosom of the earth; maternal Nature unfolds unceasingly her germs, her flowers, and her fruits; regardless though man with his passions and his crimes treads under foot her ripening harvest. (AN, 231)

But the subterfuge with the mats was not successful, which Humboldt blamed on the Indians' "acute sense of smell." The porters backed away, refusing to lead the loaded mules. It had not helped to tell them that under the mats were animal bones. What they smelled was not rotted flesh but the sacred resin with which the bones had been prepared. Later, leaving the Carib mission where they stopped to take on provisions for the trip to the coast, again Indian bearers refused to drive mules that carried the bones "of their old relations." This time it was necessary to invoke the "authority" of the missionary to force them to go on. In the end it all was to no avail. Skulls and skeletons, with the exception of a skull Humboldt kept with him in his luggage, were lost in a shipwreck on the way to Europe. One skull only, which Humboldt carried with him, would make it back to Blumenbach in Göttingen to be measured and racially classified.

Back at the coast after their adventures on the rivers, Humboldt was exuberant. The trip had been a marvelous success. He had gone where no European had ever gone before. He located and mapped the canal that links the upper Orinoco to the Río Negro and the Amazon River system, with all that meant for trade on the rivers. He added to his astronomical and geodesic observations and had pages of numbers to send back to Paris. They collected plants, skulls, animals, and rocks. Best of all, after seventy-five days of camping along rivers and a long trek across the eastern llanos he was safe and back in civilization.

In the coastal town of New Barcelona, he and Bonpland spent a recuperative month as guests of a wealthy French merchant, enjoying, as Humboldt put it, "all the comforts of town" before continuing back down the coast to Cumaná. Humboldt's plans were ever more ambitious. From Cumaná they would sail to Havana. From there they would travel up the west coast of North America as far as it was possible to go. They would then head south through Spanish territory to the Ohio and the Mississippi rivers, down to Mexico, and finally across the Pacific to the Philippines, returning to Europe from the East, completing the "tour du monde" promised so long ago in Paris.

But in Cumaná came delays. British warships were barricading the coast. No Spanish ships were leaving port. Fuming, eager to continue, Humboldt occupied his time writing letter after letter, describing miles covered, discoveries made, observations recorded, cases of plants, rocks, dead and live animals, human remains brought back from the rivers, page after page in small closely written handwriting. To Fourcroy at the Muséum in Paris on the scope of his scientific mission:

> To study the formation of the globe and the layers of which it is composed, to analyze the atmosphere, to measure with the most delicate of instruments its elasticity, its temperature, its humidity, its electrical and magnetic charge, to observe the influence of climate on the animal and vegetable economy, to approach "en grand" the chemistry and physiology of organized beings, this is the work I set myself. (LA, 79)

To the physicist Delamétherie: "Although I have had many hardships in the territory I am covering, my existence is nevertheless delicious because everything here is new, grand, and majestic" (LA, 90). To Delambre: "I have slept for the past three months outside in the woods, surrounded by tigers and hideous serpents or on beaches covered with crocodiles. Bananas, rice, and manioc have been our only food, because all provisions rot in this hot and humid country. . . . What a variety of Indian races! All free, governing themselves, and eating each other" (LA, 92). To his brother Wilhelm:

> I cannot tell you how much I am happy in this part of the world. I am so much used to the climate that it seems I have never lived in Europe. There perhaps exists no place in all the universe where one can live more agreeably and in a more tranquil and agreeable fashion than in the Spanish colonies where I have traveled for

fifteen months. . . . Nature is rich, varied, immense, and majestic beyond all expression. (LA, 86–87)

He described all that they endured:

> I have overcome all the difficulties of these painful voyages. For four months we have suffered cruelly from rain, terrible mosquitoes and ants, and especially hunger. We have slept always in forests. Bananas, manioc, and water, and sometimes a bit of rice has been our only nourishment. (LA, 88)

And he had survived, survived better than Bonpland, who had fallen ill from fever at Angostura:

> I cannot describe to you the anxiety I felt during his illness. Never could I have found a friend so faithful, active, and courageous. . . . Never will I forget his devoted attachment of which he gave me the greatest proof in a storm which hit us April 6, 1800, in the middle of the Orinoco. (LA, 88)

He recounted for his brother the almost-capsized pirogue: the "fury of the waves" and the "voraciousness of the crocodiles." But with all the enthusiasm for travel, Humboldt was also thinking about return to Europe and civilization. As he put it to Wilhelm,

> The only thing to regret in this solitude is to remain estranged from the progress of civilization and science in Europe and to be deprived of the advantages that result from the exchange of ideas. Even though this would be a reason not to want to spend the rest of one's life here, one can pass several years here in a very agreeable fashion. The study of diverse human races mixed together, the Indians and especially the savages, would itself provide enough work to occupy an observer. (LA, 87)

The letters were all written. Still no Spanish ships were getting through the British blockade to take them to Havana so they could continue on with Humboldt's ambitious itinerary. Humboldt gave up on finding a Spanish ship and paid for passage on an American ship leaving from New Barcelona with a cargo of salt. Waiting to embark, he wrote a formal report of his discoveries on the rivers to the Governor General of the Province of New Grenada in Caracas:

Permit me to offer to you my respectful homage for the favors you have shown me and for the good reception you were willing to give to me in that capital during the time I stayed there and the protection you deigned to give me in all the provinces under your rule to which I owe in a large part the good results I have achieved. If the travails of a naturalist expose him to many privations and great dangers, such an enterprise offers at the same time ample recompense when those who govern are just appreciators of services and favor those who render them. (LA, 97)

He reviewed their many adventures: the capsized pirogue, the electric eels, Don Carlo's electric machine, astronomical observations, hardships on the river, and promised more discoveries to come. He outlined the great advantages for Spain in the information he was gathering: better mapping of the rivers so useful "in times of war" when ports are blocked by enemies, a clearer and more profitable boundary between Portuguese and Spanish territory, identification of fertile areas inhabited only by Indians which could be developed for agricultural cultivation by Spanish settlers.

6

The Mountain

A few months later in Havana, writing to Willdenow, plants were on Humboldt's mind. If they were going to go on to years more of difficult travel, something would have to be done about the many plants already collected:

> At a moment when the sea festers with pirates, when one little respects passports or neutral ships, nothing preoccupies me more in my voyage around the world as obstinately as saving my manuscripts and herbaria. It is very uncertain, almost inconceivable that both of us, Bonpland and I, will return, safe and sound, from the Philippines and the Cape of Good Hope. Given this state of things, it would be sad to think that the fruits of the labor were lost. (LA, 107–108)

Humboldt reviewed for Willdenow the plans they were making for safekeeping the collections. Copies had been made of Bonpland's botanical journals, two volumes so far, describing 1,400 new and rare species. One would be sent by way of the French vice-consul to Bonpland's brother in La Rochelle for safe keeping. The originals would go with them on their travels. Out of thousands of plant specimens, they were making three separate collections: one to take with them for reference, another—"that of Bonpland with whom I share everything"—that would be sent to La Rochelle, and a third collection that would go to London with the naturalist John Fraser, who would get it to Willdenow in Berlin when it was safe to do so. There was some urgency to such a plan:

> Alas! It is almost in tears that we open our cases of plants. Our herbaria share the unfortunate lot of those of Sparmann, Banks, Swartz, and Jaquin. The immense humidity of the American climate, the exuberance of the vegetation—which makes it so difficult to find

mature and well-developed leaves—has spoiled more than a third
of our collections. Each day we encounter new insects that destroy
both paper and plants. All the devices found in Europe fail here,
such as camphor, turpentine, glue on planks, and the suspension
of cases in air, and we lose patience. (LA, 111)

Still, Humboldt reassured Willdenow, he was intent on keeping the promises
he made to him in his letter from Spain.

I remain true to my word. All the plants collected on the voyage
that are mine are destined for you. I want to keep nothing. As I
reserve for myself the publication of my herbarium after my return,
I ask only that you not mix them with your own collection before
that publication or before my death. (LA, 109)

Of course, he went on, botany was only one part of a long series of publications he was planning to publish on the results of his voyage. There would be
popular narrative travel accounts that would appeal to any "man of culture."
In these he would describe general conditions, the look and character of the
Indians, languages, customs, commerce, the height of mountains, topics to attract
a wide audience. Other volumes would be scientific, validating conclusions
reached in more popular editions, works in geognosy, geography, astronomy,
physics and chemistry, zoology, and botany. Again came a rush of nostalgia
for the days when he brought offerings of mosses and flowers to Willdenow
to identify and name:

I have said . . . that I plan to publish my plants myself after my
return, but meanwhile if, in the two cases Fraser will forward to
you, you find some new species that attract your attention, you
could, you understand, take them, only not many and not all of
them, in order to incorporate them into a new edition of your
species. On the contrary, Bonpland and I would count it an honor
to be cited by you in your work.

And as quickly a note of caution:

I say intentionally "not many and not all" because it is impossible
to describe as exactly from dried specimens as it is from what one

has drawn from nature. Bonpland and I believe that we have made exact identifications but we cannot be sure of the number of new species. (LA, 110)

He reassured Willdenow. He said the same thing to the astronomers to whom he sent his atmospheric observations. Use could be made of his findings but with the understanding that he plans to publish them himself when he returns to Europe. Of course, if he does not return alive, publication can go on with others editing his notes and maps. He named for Willdenow those who might take over his publications in case of his death: in astronomy Delambre, in geognosy von Buch, in zoology Blumenbach, and "for my botanical studies you, or at least so I hope so, in my name, and also in the name of Bonpland."

Matters of publication out of the way, Humboldt gave way to euphoria. So many plants! More than anyone could collect! More than he ever thought could exist!

> What a treasure of marvelous plants are found in the country between the Orinoco and the Amazon! . . . At present I am completely convinced of what I did not want to believe in England and that I doubted even after seeing the herbariums of Ruiz, Pavon, Nées, and Henken. I am, I say, at present convinced that we know only three fifths of the species of plants existing. (LA, 111)

He described dangers he had endured—snakes, tigers, shipwrecks, fevers—and how well he weathered them: "I was born for the tropics, never have I felt so well" (LA, 112). Nor had the voyage been expensive, considering he hired twenty-four Indians on the river, and fourteen mules carried the equipment whenever they traveled overland. And the Spanish had been wonderful to them—"the most aristocratic and vain of men could not have desired more." He had been left free to do whatever he liked—"Never in the memory of man, has a naturalist been able to act with so much freedom." There was one caveat. He has heard that the English are saying he is a Spanish agent:

> If the German newspapers translate an English article—otherwise flattering to me—but saying that I travel by the orders of the Span- ish government and that I am called to occupy a high position on the Council of the Indies, one should laugh at it as I do myself. If ever I return to Europe, other projects will occupy me than a

position on the Council of the Indies. A life begun like mine is
made for action, and if I must succumb, as all those like you dear
to me know, I pursue no common aim. (LA, 113)

In praise for the Spanish, Humboldt was effusive: "Despite the despotism of
church and of state, this nation is advancing in giant steps toward development,
toward a formation of great character. Bonpland and I have all reason to be
extremely content" (LA, 114).

Conflicting currents of emotion—resurgence of his old feelings for
Willdenow, the thrill of danger survived on the rivers, exuberance at the
thought of achieving "no common aim," gratification at the reception he is
receiving from Spanish officials—animate this long letter to the friend who
first introduced him to the joys of nature. Willdenow should count himself
lucky, Humboldt concluded. Never having seen the forests and waters of
the Orinoco, Willdenow can rest happily in his quiet retreat. If he had seen
them, never would he be content with Prussian pine trees. Humboldt ended
on a romantic note:

If I dream sometimes of a happy end to this perilous odyssey, I see
myself in that old room on the corner of Freidrichstrasse, always so
well loved by you. If I picture that situation too vividly, I might
truly be ready to advance the end of this voyage, forgetting that in
great enterprises it is necessary to listen to reason and not to the
heart. An inner voice tells me that we will see each other again.
(LA, 114–115)

"My herbier," "I" collected, botanical work done "with Bonpland," "I share"
with Bonpland, "'not many and not all' because it is impossible to describe
as exactly from dried specimens," "all my plants are yours"—Was Bonpland
aware that Humboldt was claiming credit for a good part of the botanical
work? Was he aware that Humboldt had given Willdenow permission to name
and publish plants Bonpland had collected and described? Certainly Bonpland
approved and perhaps suggested, the making of duplicate collections and sending them to different locations for safe keeping. But to tell someone who had
never seen the plants in question or any tropical plant in its native habitat to
make a final distinction of species: this no botanist trained at the Muséum
and Jardin in Paris could have countenanced. Willdenow's *Flora of Berlin* was
a competent survey of mostly familiar ground. Naming exotic new species

required detailed knowledge of plants and their habitats and comparison with the findings of other botanists, and Willdenow, who had never never been out of Europe and rarely out of Prussia, had none of the resources of the Muséum and the Jardin des plantes.

Perhaps Bonpland was simply working too hard sorting plants and dividing his collections to pay much attention. If they were to go on to North America and cross the Pacific, there was no way he could carry with him the thousands of specimens he had collected. Cases had to be opened, damaged specimens discarded, doubles sorted out, decisions made to insure that as much as was possible of the collection survived. But between the lines of Humboldt's letter, one can hear his cautioning voice. Willdenow can publish plants he finds interesting?—Perhaps, maybe one, or two, but certainly not many. Why? Because, as any botanist trained by Jussieu knew, it is impossible to describe a plant accurately from dry specimens alone. Even field descriptions are provisional and need to be verified. Plants must be compared with similar plants described and named by other botanists; otherwise, confusion results, with plants misidentified and given different names. It might be possible for Humboldt to turn over his lists of atmospheric readings to the astronomers at the Paris observatory to correlate and correct; it was not so easy to do the same with plants. Bonpland wrote on the inside cover of his journal the numbers of all plants sent to Willdenow, just as he had for those he himself sent to Cavanilles in Madrid. He also sat down to write a letter to his brother in La Rochelle announcing the upcoming shipment of plants and journals.

Michel was not the best of choices. The earlier shipment of seeds and plant specimens Bonpland sent to him from Madrid with instructions to forward a selection to Thouin at the Jardin aroused more irritation than interest. Or at least so it would seem from an offhand postscript added at the bottom of a letter from Michel to Thouin about an exchange of plants between a newly founded botanical garden at La Rochelle and the Jardin in Paris:

> My brother still voyages with Humboldt. They are in America. They are now traveling the banks of the Orinoco and will send seeds and plants next March. They will send them first to Saint-Thomas of Porto-Rico or to Saint-Domingue so they arrive more directly in France. I have a numerous collection of dried plants they sent to me from Madrid. There are also some seeds that I have not had time to look at and for which I will send you the catalog should you desire it. (AB, 218)[1]

Only a few phrases from Bonpland's letter to Michel from Havana survive, quoted sardonically in a note sent by Michel to their sister Olive to let her know that their brother was alive:

> Prepare your herbaria, let your museums take in the forms, the development, the attitude of America. . . . The soon arrival of three cases sent from Cumaná, in which you have a share, requires some preparations. . . . etc. (AB, 6–7)

One can only guess what Bonpland went on to convey. "The forms, the development, the attitude of America." "Prepare your herbaria." Prepare for what? For new plants or for something more? New ways of thinking, new possibilities, new forms of life? Whatever Bonpland said in his letter, it made little impression on Michel, still resentful of what he took as desertion on Aimé's part and not at all sympathetic with foreign adventures.

But now in Havana came news that would radically alter Humboldt's plans. Before leaving Madrid, he had written to Wilhelm in Paris asking Wilhelm to let Jussieu at the Muséum know he was leaving for South America and to tell Jussieu that if the Baudin expedition was scheduled to leave in the spring or at any time during the next year he would return immediately to France. Now a notice appeared in one of the French newspapers. Baudin had left France for the Pacific the previous fall with two ships and twenty-four scientists, artists, geologists, botanists and gardeners. The grand expedition Humboldt had hoped to join was under way without him.

It had to have been galling. So often in letters to scientists back in Europe Humboldt apologized. He was not a trained astronomer. His was only a private expedition. So many times he noted how much more he could have accomplished on a government-funded voyage with experts in different fields at his disposal. Immediately he made new plans. They would not go on to North America as planned. Baudin's announced itinerary was to reach the Pacific by going around Cape Horn, and they could intercept his expedition at Valparaiso or at Lima as it made its way up the Peruvian coast. They would take a ship from Havana back to Cartagena on the mainland. They would sail from there to the east coast of Panama and cross the isthmus, an added benefit because he could make measurements for the canal that was so often talked about. From there they would sail down the coast and intercept

Baudin. But time was short. Bonpland would have to hurry with his plants. Again Humboldt fumed at the delay:

> While Bonpland worked day and night dividing our herbal collections, thousands of obstacles prevented our departure from Havana. No ship would take us to Porto Bello or Cartagena. People seemed to enjoy exaggerating the difficulties faced crossing the isthmus and the time it takes to go by ship from Guayaquil to Lima. (PN, 287)

At Cartagena there were more problems. No, Humboldt was told, it was the wrong season to sail south. The currents were adverse. A trip down the Peruvian coast could take as long as three months and he would miss Baudin. Humboldt was not one to be thwarted. If they could not go by sea, they would go overland, up and over the Andes traversing the chain of high cordilleras that extend the length of South America from the Caribbean to Tierra del Fuego. All the better. On the way they could visit Santé Fé de Bogotá, explore the volcano rich region around Quito, perhaps climb Chimborazo, the tallest mountain in South America, if not the world.

It is doubtful Bonpland made any complaint. Higher elevations only meant more new species and genera, many more than he could have found in populated regions of Mexico or the Philippines. Better still, at Santé Fé de Bogotá, he could consult with José Celestino Mutis, the renowned Spanish botanist who founded and led the Spanish Royal Botanical Expedition to New Grenada, and whose collection of South American plants and botanical drawings was famous. Now almost seventy, Mutis had come to Peru as a young man to serve as physician to the viceroy of New Grenada and botanized around Santé Fe. Eventually he convinced the Spanish crown to fund an official scientific expedition now headquartered in Bogotá. Once there, Bonpland could compare his descriptions with those of Spanish botanists. He could begin to determine which of the plants he collected were actually new. Already he had in his collection all of the melastomes listed by Linnaeus and more; only by collaboration with other botanists and access to their collections could he tell which of those he had collected had not been described by others. Nor did he have any objection to six weeks rowing up the River Magdalena against the current, plagued with constant rain and insects—not when he could disappear into openings in the thick vegetation along the banks and look for plants.

It would prove a difficult journey. By now Humboldt had lost much of his enthusiasm for river travel and was irritable with bearers and guides. There were no leisurely readings from *Paul and Virginie*. Some of the Indian rowers dropped out from exhaustion. Others developed painful ulcers from the damp. As always, Bonpland learned what he could from guides. *Matisia*: he would name it after Francisco Matis, one of Mutis's gifted botanical artists; it was a beautiful luxuriant tree with wide leaves and low-hanging globes of fruit found along the banks of the Magdalena. Try it, said one of the guides. He bit into the thick leathery greenish rind; inside, the orange-yellow flesh was sweet and juicy. Did it taste like apricot, or maybe pumpkin, or something else, a new taste, not one he knew? It grew spontaneously in the hot and humid valleys at the fifth latitude, and, Bonpland noted, the inhabitants of Peru and new Grenada cultivated it with care:

> We observed it the first time on the Magdeleine River going from Carthagène-des-Indies to Santa Fé. It was near the end of May, the fruits were already formed. In the course of June we found it at Mariquita in a state of perfect maturity, and it was not until we were in Peru that we had the leisure to examine the flowers in the first days of April. The inhabitants of the Magdeleine call it *chupachupa*, the Peruvians *sapote*. (PE I, 12)

It was a majestic and beautiful tree and with useful fruit. He thought it might well be transplanted to French colonies and other tropical regions.

At Honda they left the river behind and began the climb up a mule trail 9,000 feet to Bogotá. Here came hardship of another kind. Humidity and heat were gone, but the path was rough, at times no more than giant boulders into which were cut some rudimentary steps. Higher and higher they climbed through thick forests of bamboo, walnut, nutmeg, and cinchona, Humboldt dressed as usual in top hat, rumpled striped trousers, and cutaway jacket, barometer in hand, unwilling to entrust it to the luggage on the backs of mules; Bonpland a less distinctive figure in rough trousers and shirt, still carrying the battered leather satchel from his days at the Hotel Boston. Behind them struggled pack animals, pressed on by Indian drivers. Up and then down into moist marshy valleys and a patch of bright yellow flowers rising out of the mud on long thick stems. *Limnocharis*, Bonpland named it: "lover of mud."

As they came near to Bogotá Humboldt sent a messenger ahead to announce their arrival. When they came into the main street, a crowd of dignitaries waited to greet them. Humboldt described the scene in a letter to Wilhelm:

> Our arrival at Santa Fé resembled a triumphal procession. The arch-
> bishop sent his carriage for us, along which came all the dignitaries
> of the town. We were given lunch two miles from the town and we
> proceeded there with a troop of sixty men on horseback. (LA, 126)

Humboldt was pleased. A house outside of town was made ready for them
with all the amenities. Mutis was waiting there to greet them with colonial
officials and lunch. There was an awkward moment when Humboldt stepped
out of the carriage carrying his barometer and immediately began talking to
Mutis about science. Tactfully he was deflected, and conversation was diverted
to general topics so as not to offend dignitaries less interested in rocks or the
heights of mountains.

Once more they settled down with servants to see to their needs. Humboldt was invited to lunch with the Viceroy and passed on to him a map he
made of the Magdalena River. He began a survey of coal deposits, toured a
salt works, gathered rock samples, found some mastodon bones buried out on
the plain. Bonpland, suffering from a recurrence of the fever he contracted on
the Orinoco, rested in Mutis's library, herbarium, and museum, studying the
most extensive collection yet in existence of South American plants: 24,000
plant specimens and as many botanical paintings and drawings done by Mutis's
talented team of thirty artists. When Humboldt announced that they would
stay a while, Bonpland made no complaint. Not only was Mutis's library
and collection there to explore, but there were plants to discover. *Marathrum
foeniculaceum*, a new genus, found high on the dangerous cliffs of Salta de
Tequendama, drawn for him by one of Mutis's artists. A new species, *Loasa
ranunculifolia*, with poisonous spines. *Culcitium canescens*, covered in a white
down, called the bedding plant. *Espeletia grandiflora* with large yellow daisy-like
flowers—it would provide interest in French gardens, he thought. *Mikania*
guaco, its sap with a strong nauseating odor, but useful, he was told, as an
anti-venom, orally and as a poultice.

But the plant of particular interest to Bonpland was *Cinchona*, source
of the famed "Jesuit's bark" sold in Europe as a cure for malaria. On the way
up to Bogotá he and Humboldt explored groves of trees said to be one of
its sources, and Bonpland gathered specimens. Now in Mutis's library he was
able to examine and compare them to a large collection of dried parts and
drawings of different species. Here was a plant of great importance. Long
used by local people against fevers, it had the potential to make the tropics
safe for travelers, but carelessness in naming and identification caused endless

problems. Bark marketed in Europe was from uncertain sources, arriving by ship and labeled by clerks who knew nothing about the trees from which it came. With the resources of Mutis's library and further collecting, Bonpland now hoped to make a start at a more accurate identification of species and products. Labeled samples could be sent back to France, tests run for chemical properties by Fourcroy at the Muséum, different species tested for effectiveness, different ways of gathering bark and preparing extracts compared. Before they left Bogotá Bonpland would have a preliminary collection of specimen species and barks ready to be sent back to the Institut and the Muséum along with a copy of notes on quinquina written by Hippolito Ruiz, one of the botanists associated with Mutis's Botanical Expedition.[2]

Nor was *Cinchona* the only local anti-fever remedy of interest. There was also *Symplocos alstonia*, with bright green leaves out of which was made a bitter infusion that stimulated digestion and promoted sweating. They must take it with them, said Mutis, when they left to travel up to Quito and then down to Lima. Going up across the high Andes and then abruptly down into hot rainy valleys, changes in altitude and frequent soakings could cause fever. Here again the combination of local and European knowledge might result in a valuable medical remedy, but also again, a tangle of nomenclature and description had resulted when European botanists classified plants from dried specimens sent to them by untrained collectors. In the case of *Symplocos*, botanists, many of whom had never seen the living plants, disagreed as to whether there were several genera or one, different flowering habits or the same. Until plants could be reliably identified no tests could be run that were of any use. Using his notes and observations, comparing the species published by other authors, Bonpland went to work to try to clear away some of the confusion surrounding a native American drink with many of the refreshing and restorative properties of tea. As he put it in *Plantes équinoxiales*:

> The plant grows in a cold climate and would do well in that of France. Use of its leaves should attract the attention of doctors and soon enrich medicine with a new remedy that joins to the advantage of being good that of being agreeable to drink. (PE I, 185)

Much as Bonpland might have liked to stay even longer, Humboldt was ready to move on, eager to get to Quito and then down to the Pacific coast in time to meet Baudin.

Traveling out of Santa Fé they walked comfortably in a narrow valley along a winding river and through a grove of palms to the small town of Ibagué. There they gathered provisions and made final preparations for the hard climb up over the Andes. Bonpland watched bearers cut huge leaves of a species of *Heliconia* to carry with them to make shelter for times when it rained. He examined the underside of the leaves, silvery white and covered with a starchy material that came off when he scratched with his thumbnail. He watched guides make large piles of leaves, roll each lot up into a cylinder, and load them onto oxen along with Humboldt's instruments and his plant boxes. After Ibagué would come a long week and a half of hard climbing through deep wet forest, packing along with their equipment provisions for as much as a month in case they were stopped by a blizzard or torrent of water.

At times the path was only a few feet wide at the bottom of a deep slit in the rock open only to a ribbon of sky high above, so that they slipped and slid in semi-darkness on mossy rocks. If they met a train of oxen coming the other way there was nothing to do but to go back and wait for it to pass or to climb up the steep sides to find some sort of foothold and hold on to vines to be out of the way of oxen passing below. Climbing up out of one such ravine onto a dry plateau, Bonpland saw a new species of cocoa, *Theobroma bicolor*. Bitter, he was told by the Indians, but if cultivated and mixed with the more common *Theobroma* it made a good blended chocolate. Bonpland made a note: it could be grown in France's warmer colonies for its foliage, and the quality of beans might be enhanced with careful cultivation. They crossed over into Peru. Near the village of Lucarque he came upon another new genus, a pretty tree, remarkable for its silvery tuft of leaves, its trunk with large spines, and for its hard wood. It was used, he was told, for making furniture and looms for weaving. He would name it *Turpinia*, after the artist who prepared many of the engravings for his botanical publications back in Paris. There was a spectacular *Mutisia grandiflora*, with flowers 16 centimeters long and a brilliant red, and *Erythroxylum coca*. He made a note in his journal: "when chewed lightly aromatic and increases saliva indicating medicinal value" (MNHN, ms 2534, 1767).

It threatened to rain. The bearers unwrapped the cylinders of heliconia leaves. Branches were quickly cut for a frame. Lianas and cords made from agave were strung to make a kind of netting with leaves laid on top, overlapping like roof tiles to make a temporary shelter big enough for six or eight people. On one occasion, he and Humboldt sat in such a structure in torrential rain for several days, preparing and drinking Mutis's tea, writing up their notes. When the rain stopped they continued on up to Quindío Pass with bearers cutting a way through thick stands of bamboo. Sharp rocks on the path cut the leather of their shoes. They tracked through mud, sometimes waist deep in freezing mountain streams. Now certainly Humboldt would want to be carried on the backs of the porters, said the guides. It was expected of European travelers, whose tender feet could not be expected to walk on such terrain. No, said Humboldt, it was degrading to think a man was a beast of burden. The porters grumbled at this white man in his striped trousers who refused to them the trade on which their living depended. More and more Bonpland blended into the background; almosthe could be taken for a guide or porter with his wide straw hat and stooping botanist's gait.

Down from the heights, they headed south along the Cauca Valley to the town of Popayán, where they planned to rest a few weeks and meet Francisco José de Caldas, recommended by Mutis as a local scientist with interests in astronomy and physics. Caldas was away on business, he left word. He would meet them in Quito. But at Popayán there was another mountain for Humboldt to climb, Puracé, nowhere near the height of mountains to come near Quito, but an active volcano emitting puffs of smoke. That accomplished, they started out again up across a high barren frigid desert littered with the bones of dead pack mules. Shivering in constant mist and cold damp, Humboldt strained ahead, waiting for the moment when he would catch glimpses of smoke rising from the peaks ahead. Puracé was no great height, but ahead were mountains much taller, many of them volcanic. It would never leave Humboldt, this fascination with height and trapped simmering volcanic energy deep in the earth. Always he would be drawn wherever there was word of a coming eruption, to wait for that climatic rumble, watch for that rush of steam and fire.

Up on the high plateau Bonpland was marveling at the tallest palm he had ever seen, *Ceroxylon andicola*, the Andean wax palm growing at an altitude it was thought no palm could survive, 180 feet tall, leaves twenty feet long. Bonpland ran his finger along the trunk to find an area between scars left by old leaves covered with a thick waxy veneer. They made candles of the substance, the guides told him, good candles for churches and houses. He scraped off a bit with his knife, rubbed it between his fingers: more brittle than beeswax but of the same consistency. High up, feathery fronds were silhouetted against the sky with bunches of white flowers. He would have to find a way to see the flowers closer, determine if they were female, male, or hermaphrodite, and get Humboldt to make a drawing of them. He took a sample of the wax, wrapped it carefully in a paper to send it back to the museum for analysis. A plant source for wax, a substitute for expensive beeswax, would be of interest in Europe. He picked up one of the fruits fallen on the ground and bit into the sweetish but also bitter flesh. Perhaps useful for food—if not for humans, for animals and birds. Why was such a tree not widely known? A survey of the surrounding area provided an answer. The tree, he was told, grew nowhere else, only on this one high rocky swathe of mountainside—a fact of interest to Humboldt, who contributed a page of observations in Bonpland's botanical journal, noting the area's temperature, elevation, and soil, as well as "the fact curious for the geography of plants" that a plant could grow only in one unique locale (MNHN, ms 2534, 1884).

Higher and higher they climbed. An engraving in Humboldt's *atlas pittoresque* gives us a God's-eye view of them, two tiny figures in a vast landscape, looking up and ahead at a tall peak rising in the far distance. Humboldt's accompanying text:

> One sees Chimborazo appear like a cloud on the horizon,:it detaches itself from the neighboring peaks; it rises above all the chain of the Andes like that majestic dome, the work of the genius of Michelangelo, rises over the ancient monuments that surround the Roman Capital. (VC, plate 16, 288)

Here was a prize as grand as St. Peter's Basilica in Rome, a mountain not known to be volcanic, but the tallest of the peaks ahead, perhaps even the tallest on earth.

Arrived in Quito, Humboldt wrote to Wilhelm expressing satisfaction. Quito was a delight, the sophisticated capital of the province and home to the local aristocracy. Again a house was made ready for them with all the amenities. They were welcomed with parties and receptions. They were invited to stay at the country house of the provincial governor, the Marqués de Selva Alegre. From its veranda Humboldt could look up at the peak of a volcanic mountain, Pichincha. Caldas, the local savant they failed to find in Popayán, was waiting to greet them. Lawyer, businessman, self-taught in many branches of science, he was eager to learn from important European visitors. Mutis had encouraged him, thinking that perhaps Caldas might join Humboldt's party, travel on with him to Lima. Back in Bogotá Mutis was already raising money to pay Caldas's expenses, delighted that one of his local researchers might collaborate with a visiting scientist, bring the knowledge gained back to the province, not carry it off to Europe. There were meetings, some initial discussions, with Caldas dazzled at the breadth of Humboldt's knowledge. But Humboldt's attention was elsewhere, not on an aspiring fellow scientist, but on the marqués's dashing young son, Carlos de Montúfar.

It had been a long time. Any hope Humboldt might have once had for a passionate relations with Bonpland had long since faded away. Caldas's eagerness to learn was briefly flattering, but Caldas was a year older than Humboldt and a solid, serious, married man. He could hardly compete with cultivated, charming, handsome Carlos, who knew nothing about science and who was, as one Paris acquaintance would quip, "very expensive." Study sessions with Caldas were canceled. Caldas wrote to Mutis in Bogotá in alarm. Did Mutis know the reason for Humboldt's sudden lack of interest in him? Had he offended somehow? Had he proven too dull, too plodding in his thinking? Mutis sent a formal letter to Humboldt recommending that Caldas become a member of Humboldt's party and guaranteeing funding. Humboldt put the letter aside. Caldas inquired. Had a letter from Mutis been received? No, Humboldt told Caldas, he had received no such letter. Caldas protested. Humboldt was forced to remember—yes, perhaps he had, but he was not interested at the moment in adding anyone to his party. When Caldas heard that Montúfar was to travel on with Humboldt, he vented his feelings in a letter to Mutis: "The baron enters this Babylon, becomes friends with a few dissolute obscene youths; they drag him to houses where tainted love reigns" (Appel, 30). Writing to Wilhelm about the constant threat of volcanic eruption at Quito, Humboldt gave a similar, if more positively worded, description of the social circle frequented by Montúfar:

> In spite of the horrors and dangers with which nature has surrounded
> them, the inhabitants of Quito are gay, lively, and amiable. Their
> town breathes nothing but voluptuousness, luxury, and nowhere
> perhaps does there reign a taste so determinedly and universally
> bent on self-diversion. (LA, 131).

For five years Montúfar would be Humboldt's companion, accompanying him on the rest of his travels, to Mexico and Philadelphia, and returning with him to Paris. As for Caldas, he was stunned, and resentment at his treatment by Humboldt only slowly dissolved.

To all appearances Caldas was remarkable. With little access to books or journals, resolutely working on his own, he had achieved a high degree of knowledge and expertise in many areas of science. He made and correlated astronomical observations. He knew local plants and could distinguish between them; he observed relations between plants and climate. The difference in temperament between him and Humboldt was stark. As one contemporary observer of the drama put it,

The personalities of Humboldt and Caldas are very different. The former possesses a liveliness that borders on restlessness, loquacious, love of society and amusement. The latter with a background of activity maintains a certain slowness in his operations: taciturn and with a somewhat austere lifestyle and a love of privacy. (quoted in Appel, 30)

Caldas worked alone, slowly and meticulously. Humboldt wrote and moved quickly from subject to subject, relying on second-hand material, never going deeply into any one subject. In the end it was not with Humboldt but with Bonpland that Caldas found common ground.

Understanding Caldas's disappointment, seeing that Caldas was unfamiliar with botanical nomenclature, Bonpland invited him to share his study at the Marquise's house, and for Caldas, Bonpland was the ideal mentor. As Appel recounts, "while Humboldt dealt with a great range of subjects—geology, botany, zoology, astronomy, and so forth—and while the baron displayed an incredible amount of energy in his study of the vast sweep of nature, it was Bonpland who pursued the study of plant life in a meticulous, detailed, and persistent manner" (Appel, 40). Caldas reminisced: "Bonpland, that sage and profound Bonpland, has lent me his books, his immense herbarium, his counsel; allowing me to take a place in his study and copy all I want" (quoted in Appel, 40).

Bonpland set out a course of botanical study, gave Caldas lessons in Greek and Latin, studied with him *Flora Peruana*, a regional study produced by Mutis's Botanical Expedition. Together they collected plants. Caldas would write a description and Bonpland would go over it with him as they looked at the plant together. Little by little Caldas's resentment dissipated. His spirits revived. "I go out with this friendly and sage botanist to collect plants. I am building an excellent herbarium; he puts the names and has given me paper to dry the plants" (quoted in Appel, 41). In the end rejection by Humboldt had its advantages. After the Europeans left, Caldas, with his new proficiency in botany, joined Mutis's Botanical Expedition in Bogotá and earned a generous salary traveling the Andes researching cinchona. Based on his plant studies, his lessons with Bonpland, and his talks with Humboldt, he made maps of the Northern Andes. His essay on the geographical distribution of plants included extensive notes on cinchona. In 1805 he was back in Bogotá directing the expedition's new astronomical observatory.

Meanwhile there was more bad news for Humboldt. Baudin would not be coming up the coast of Peru after all. He had gone the other way around by way of Cape Horn. There was no way they would be able to join the expedition. New plans would have to be made, but for the moment, when Humboldt's mind was not on Carlos, it was on mountains. He had climbed Puracé at Papayán. Next would be Pichincha, the peak visible from the marqués's house.[3] It would never be easy for Humboldt to recruit companions for these excursions. Caldas and Bonpland were busy with their plants. Hard climbs were hardly Carlos's favorite pastime. His first time climbing Pichincha, Humboldt set off alone. Reaching a height midway up to the peak he felt dizzy and nauseous, all but fainted, and barely made it back to town safely. On a second try up Pichincha he took an "Indian guide." Just as they were nearing the summit, the guide sunk down into chest-deep snow. They had wandered onto a precarious ice bridge extending over the cone of the volcano. As Humboldt told it in a letter to Wilhelm, he "rescued" the Indian and found a rocky ledge from which they could look down into the crater: "I do not believe that any image could capture something more sad, more lugubrious, and more frightening than what we saw there" (LA 132). Humboldt crouched down. The ledge trembled with recurrent earth trembles. Sulfurous fumes suffocated him whenever he took a breath; blue flames shot up here and there. With all the shaking it was impossible to take proper readings.[4]

A third climb up Pichincha was more successful. This time both Bonpland and Montúfar were pressed into service along with Humboldt's servant José, who had been seeing to Humboldt's personal needs since his first stay in Cumaná.[5] More instruments were taken, divided between four of them. At the top, Humboldt was able to lie down on the rock ledge and take readings, and compare his ascent favorably to La Condamine's. "Until now no one, that I know of except La Condamine has seen [the summit] and La Condamine himself only arrived there after five or six days of useless searching, and without instruments, and was only able to stay twelve or fifteen minutes because of the excessive cold there" (LA, 131). Even more gratifying was another peak, Antisana, where Humboldt made it to the summit with bleeding lips and eyes, beating La Condamine's previous record of height on the peak of Corazón at 15,793 feet. But the prize was Chimborazo, some distance from Quito, possibly volcanic, taller than any of the others, perhaps taller than any mountain on earth. Here too La Condamine had gone before, but had failed to reach the summit. To reach the peak of Chimborazo would be to go higher than either Saussure or La Condamine, perhaps as high as it was possible for a man to go. A long futile trek was still ahead of them down to the coast and Lima to pick up equipment Humboldt shipped there for the voyage with Baudin, but Humboldt was determined. He would not leave the Andes until he climbed the highest peak.

Humboldt left Quito ready for this final challenge, accompanied by Montúfar and Bonpland, José entrusted with the heavy barometer, and a large company of bearers and mules carrying the rest of the equipment. Caldas sourly noted the date of their departure: "Baron von Humboldt left here on the eighth [June 1802] in the company of Bonpland and of his Adonis who does not interfere with his trip as does Caldas" (quoted in Appel, 30).

❧

Humboldt was by now a celebrity. News spread of their arrival and a reception committee was waiting at the foot of the mountain to cheer him on. The party along with guides and bearers started up the lower slopes with Bonpland taking notes. At 13,000 to 15,000 feet there were a few flowering plants growing on rocks that stuck up among patches of snow. At 15,320 feet even moss had disappeared. At 15,626 feet, they spotted some yellow butterflies flying close to the ground against the snow, at 16,000 feet fly-like dipterans swarming out of reach down a rock face. By 17,300 feet it was hard to see ahead in the mist. Their eyes started to bleed. They suffered from nausea and headache. The mist cleared for a moment, and there was a quick glimpse of what might be the summit. Humboldt was determined to go on. At 17,400 feet came hail and then blinding snow. A last few lichens were sighted on some rocks. The Indian guides would go no further.

In a letter to Wilhelm Humboldt recounted the rest.

We were able to get to just about 1,470 feet short of the summit of the immense colossus of Chimborazo. A string of volcanic rocks, bare of snow helped us make the ascent. We climbed on to a height of 19,381 feet, where we felt ill as we had on the summit of Antisana, a condition that remained with us even two or three days after our return to the plain, a sickness we could only attribute to these high regions which, when analyzed, measured only 20 centimes of oxygen. The Indians that accompanied us had already left us before reaching this height, saying that we were trying to kill them. We rested there alone: Bonpland, Carlos Montúfar, myself, and one of my servants who carried some of my instruments. We would have gone on to the top if a crevasse had not opened too deep to cross and it seemed better for us to go down. So much snow fell on our descent that we could hardly see each other. Little protected us against the piercing cold of these high regions, we suffered horribly, and me in particular because I had the problem of an ulcerated foot from a fall several days before which hurt horribly on a path where each instant you were hitting your foot against a sharp rock, and where you have to calculate each step. (LA, 133–134)

Back down they stumbled in a blinding snow storm, Humboldt limping with pain. Still, he reported to Wilhelm, he had made an important discovery. It seemed from some of the rocks he saw that Chimborazo might indeed be volcanic, and if there was ever an eruption it would be sure to destroy the province. A letter written two months later to Delambre at the Institut de France was somewhat more positive. He had proven that it was possible to withstand a height 3,031 feet higher than La Condamine had been able to go. Unlike La Condamine, he carried instruments and made measurements. He had not made it to the top of Chimborazo, but back down on the plain of Tapia he was able to measure its height more accurately than he could have on the summit, choosing a time when the air was crystal clear and the snowcapped summit a brilliant white against deep blue sky. From below he accurately drew the snow line as well as successive bands of vegetation, ligneous plants, trees, alpines, grasses all clearly marked.

Still, the sense of something less than heroic about it would worry at Humboldt. Later writing a description to accompany an engraving of Chimborazo in *Views of the Cordilleras*, he played down the importance of height:

> These painful excursions, stories of which generally excite such interest in the public, offer only a small number of results useful to the progress of the sciences. The traveler finds himself on ground covered with snow, in air whose chemical mixture is the same as that underground, and in a situation in which delicate experiments cannot be made with the required precision. (VC, 286)

Even later, in response to a report that one of his young protégés, Jean-Baptiste Boussingault, had gone higher than he had on Chimborazo, Humboldt made an attempt to put the record straight in an address to the German Assembly of Naturalists, and in an essay entitled "On Two Attempts to Ascend Chimborazo." "Chimborazo," he complained, "has been the tedious subject of all the questions that were posed to me when I first returned to Europe." Nothing else, not his discovery of "important laws of nature," or his "vivid description of plant zones," or the "effect of climate on agriculture" ever seemed to take the public's attention away from this mountain whose peak he failed to reach.

Once again he told the story of the climb, this time copying directly from his diary all the less-than-heroic details: the ulcerated foot, the stumbling, Bonpland unable to find a way across an ice bridge as Humboldt had been able to do on Antisana, swirling mists, the impossibility of seeing anything at all, no sign of life, nothing but rock and ice, a story more of folly, suffering, and disappointment than heroic achievement.[6] One could climb, it seemed, to the top of the world and find nothing to there to record, or if there was something to see, be too blinded by mist to see it.

Disclaimers had little effect. The heroic image of Chimborazo would return, appear, reappear throughout Humboldt's lifetime and after his death, in writings by him, about him, in portraits made of him. In a fold-out "Tableau physique des Andes et Pays voisins" attached to Humboldt's *Essay on the Geography of Plants*, Chimborazo loomed up, a giant vertical tablet ruled with lines of successive ascent, along with the lesser summits of the peak of Mont Blanc achieved by Saussure, the height reached by Condamine just barely to the snow line, and highest of all, the height reached by Humboldt and his companions on Chimborazo. On one side of the mountain successive zones of vegetation are colored in. On the other side, the slope is written over in tiny script with hundreds of plant names taken from Bonpland's journals. Panels on either side list Humboldt's measurements: elevations, temperatures, barometric pressures, corrected and correlated by scientists at the Paris Observatory.

A much-publicized drawing of Chimborazo by Goethe, to whom Humboldt dedicated his *Geography of Plants*, pictured comparative heights reached by Saussure on the summit of Mont Blanc and Humboldt on the slope of Chimborazo. Jean-Thomas Thibault made a painting, "Chimborazo from the plateau of Tapia," for Humboldt's *atlas pittoresque*, adding grazing llamas and Indians on the plain below (VC, plate 25). An 1810 commemorative painting by the German court artist Friedrich George Weitsch showed Humboldt standing on the plain in front of the massive rise of Chimborazo, passing back his barometer to the servant José. In the bottom corner of Weitsch's painting, in the shade of a blanket rigged up on the branches of a tree, sits Bonpland, journal on his knee, specimen box at his side, quietly recording what he has seen.[7]

7

The Changing of the Gods

As Humboldt began the journey down from Chimborazo and the high plain of Tapia to the coast, he had some reason to be content. He would miss Baudin, but he had found the link between the Orinoco and the Amazon river systems. He had not reached the peak of Chimborazo, but he had gone higher than anyone else. Pages and pages of observations had been sent to the Paris Observatory and the Bureau of Longitudes. As far as he knew, skulls and skeletons from the burial cave of the Atures Indians were on a ship bound for Spain along with Bonpland's plants and animals. Ruiz's notes on cinchona with specimens and barks, a generous gift of botanical illustrations from Mutis, and a case of volcanic rocks had been sent off to the Muséum in Paris. The way down was gradual. There was no more climbing over rough boulder steps or following narrow trails along sheer cliffs. They traveled on stable roadways with no need to worry about shredded shoes or dangerous precipices. The baggage was carried comfortably on twenty mules changed every eight or nine days at convenient way stations. Mountain views, mile-high waterfalls, natural rock bridges over vertiginous drops to torrents below, provided striking subjects for his sketch book. A first stop at Riobamba with Montúfar's brother offered comfortable accommodations, as well as a new discovery.

At Riobama Humboldt was introduced to a local Indian leader, Leandro Zapla, who, as he put it in a letter to Wilhelm, "had for an Indian a singularly cultivated spirit" (LA, 135). Zapla showed him manuscripts written by one of Zapla's ancestors in the sixteenth century in an Indian language, Purugnay, older even than the Incan Quechua, along with a Spanish translation. The manuscripts told an amazing story. Back in the distant pre-Columbian past, a volcanic mountain taller than Chimborazo had collapsed in an eruption so violent that for seven years after there had been perpetual night. Even more surprising, the manuscripts told of priests who predicted and observed the eruption, and who declared it a divine omen, warning the king who ruled at

115

that time, telling him "The face of the universe is changing. Other gods chase ours. Do not resist what fate ordains." Humboldt was surprised and impressed. It seemed that well before the Spanish conquest there had been native historians and astrologists who recorded and predicted natural phenomena.

And there was more. As they continued on up over the Andes it became evident that they were traveling on roads supported by well-laid foundations and paved with large flat stones, roads more advanced in construction than Roman roads still visible in parts of Italy. "We were surprised," wrote Humboldt in *Views of the Cordilleras*, "to find there, at a height that surpassed even the summit of Tenerife, the magnificent remains of a road constructed by the Inca of Peru" (VC I, 290–291). There were remains of structures built of cut stone, guard houses and accommodations for travelers, and on the way from Riobama to Cuenca the ruins of a well-built lodging house and a huge granite rock incised with an image of the sun. At one point they were shown an elaborate park-like enclosure once used for some kind of princely game with balls. In Coxamarca he was introduced to an Inca family who told him of gold relics and palatial edifices buried in the ground under their houses.

Humboldt wrote to Wilhelm about these new discoveries, recalling remnants of ancient Indian culture he saw earlier in his travels: hieroglyphic-like figures carved on rocks high above the Casiquiare, a stone from Bogotá that he thought might be an ancient calendar:

> The manuscript, the traditions I gathered at Parime, and the hiero-glyphics that I saw in the Casiquiare desert where today there exists scarcely any vestige of man, all combined with the ideas of Clavijero on the emigration of Mexicans toward the middle of South America, has given rise in me to ideas on the origin of these people that I propose to develop when I have the leisure. (LA, 135)[1]

In his letter, Humboldt made special mention of language, a subject that was now taking up much of his brother's energies:

> I am also much occupied with the study of American languages and I have seen how much of what La Condamine said of the poverty of these languages is false. The Carib language, for example, is at the same time rich, beautiful, energetic, and polished. It does not really lack expressions for abstract ideas; one can talk in it of pos-terity, eternity, existence, etc., and it has numerical signs sufficient to

indicate all possible combinations of numbers. I am applying myself especially to the Incan language, which is commonly spoken here in society. It is so rich in fine and varied locutions that the young men, when they speak sweet things to women, start to speak Inca when they have exhausted the resources of Castilian. (LA, 135–136)

For Humboldt it caused some puzzlement. Where had these seemingly sophisticated people come from with their expressive language? European theorists like Buffon, who had never been to the New World, claimed confidently that reports of ancient American civilizations from missionaries and conquistadors were no more than travelers' tales, but the ruins he was seeing told another story. Could they be the work of ancient emigrants from China or India who established colonies in South America at some early time?

Meanwhile on Bonpland's mind as they traveled down from Quito was not ancient history but cinchona, the plant with such potentially important medical uses. Here again La Condamine had gone before, giving a first botanical description of the tree that was the source of the anti-fever remedy. His 1738 *Sur l'arbre du quinquina* was based on information gathered by his travel partner Joseph Jussieu and on what La Condamine himself learned during a two-day stop at Loxa, the most important regional source for the "Jesuit bark" marketed in Europe. At Loxa, La Condamine talked to gatherers and traders about uses of the bark and methods of distinguishing and cutting barks. He was told that stocks of the preferred species were becoming depleted and that to keep up with demand from Europe barks with little or no efficacy were being mixed in with superior bark. He was also told that as a result there was worry that Loxa "quinquina" was in danger of being discredited and an important element in the local economy would be lost. La Condamine did drawings of the flowers and the seed of the tree pointed out to him as the source of the bark. He collected and dried specimens of that tree's flowers, seed, and bark. When he returned to Europe, he sent the drawings and his memoir to Linnaeus at Uppsala and to the king of Spain, who funded his explorations. In his memoir, La Condamine called for two initiatives. First, botanists should work to clearly establish genus and species and their characteristics. Second, Spain should find a way to verify the authenticity of shipments of bark arriving from South America. As La Condamine put it diplomatically to the king, "Wise regulations assuring the good faith of this unique commerce so useful to the conservation of the human race, would be an object not unworthy of the consideration of His Catholic Majesty."[2]

Since La Condamine's visit to Loxa the situation had only worsened. Linnaeus christened the genus *Cinchona*, a misspelling of name of the Spanish Countess of Chinchón, who popularized the bark as a cure for fever. Because La Condamine's specimen seemed the only example he named the species *Cinchona officinalis*. But by now it was clear that there were other species with varying properties. For any progress to be made on La Condamine's initiatives, a stop at Loxa was essential. Even Humboldt, who downplayed the "mere registering of nature," made an exception for such an important plant, recording in Bonpland's journal elevations where trees were found, the composition of the soil, the average day and night temperatures. Humboldt also noted evidence of the depletion of mature trees due to cutting, and registered "astonishment" at the lack of output. Only 110 hundredweight of bark was collected annually, none of it in general commerce and all of it going to the Spanish court.

For Bonpland, more important than the quantity and destination of this colonial product was reliable identification of species and understanding of the plant's complex chemistry. A confusion of names, claims, and counter-claims had resulted in indiscriminate and uninformed European trade in the bark of a plant of great potential medical value, long known to and used by native people in remote forests of the Andes. La Condamine titled his memoir "On the Quinquina tree," but it was clear that this common name caused confusion as demand for fever bark grew in Europe and gatherers and traders began to mix in barks from different species, labeling the product indiscriminately "Quinquina de Loxa." Linnaeus's choice of a name for the genus, *Cinchona*, coupled with *officinalis* was of little use once news reached Europe of other species. Confusions and errors multiplied, with different species given the same name, and the same species given different names by different botanists. Linnaeus's *Cinchona officinalis* dropped out of use in favor of a variety of poorly described species, including *Cinchona condaminae* because La Condamine had been the first to give a botanical description.

At Loxa Bonpland was determined to make a beginning addressing La Condamine's neglected initiatives. He gathered specimens of species most used in commerce. He spoke at length to workers who were paid to collect and harvest bark. He gathered specimens of flowers and flower parts to compare to plants sent or brought back to Paris by La Condamine and Joseph Jussieu. In the forests around Cuenca he collected another species he named provisionally *Cinchona ovalifolia*. In addition to detailed botanical descriptions he paid special attention to bark itself, taking samples of both old and new bark, and bark from trunk and branches, noting not only color and texture but smell and taste (astringent and slightly aromatic) when put in the mouth. Further on at Jaen he discovered an additional species, known locally as *Cascarilla bora*, not much used in commerce. Adding to the species he knew from Mutis, and comparisons he would make in Paris, he hoped to both improve the reliability of cinchona as a fever remedy and facilitate sustainable production of an important indigenous product.[3]

Arrived in Lima, they found a small backward town with few amenities. There was little to do but to retrieve the instruments and supplies Humboldt shipped there and wait for transport back up the coast. By now Humboldt had given up any plans he might once have had for further travel. As he put it to Wilhelm,

> I plan to go from here in the month of December to Acapulco and from there to Mexico, in order to get to Havana by the month of May 1803. There, wasting no time, I will embark for Spain. I have abandoned, as you see, the idea of returning by way of the Philippines. I would have had to make an immense sea crossing without seeing anything but Manila and the Cape, and if I wanted to tour the East Indies I would lack the necessary supplies for the trip, which would be impossible to get here. (LA, 137)[4]

Return to Europe and his reception there were now much on Humboldt's mind. To Delambre, secretary of the Institut de France, he wrote expressing relief that just as he was leaving Quito he had finally received word from the Institut:

> How can I tell you, Citizen, the joy with which I read this letter from the Institut with its repeated assurances that you had not forgotten me? How sweet to know that one lives in the memory of those whose work never ceases to advance the progress of the human spirit! In the deserted plains of the Apure, in the dense forests of the Casiquiare and the Orinoco, everywhere your names were present to me, and remembering various stages of my wandering life, I would stop with joy at the thought of that year of 1798 when I lived in the midst of you and Laplace, Fourcroy, Vauquelin . . . (LA, 140)

After continuing on with a long list of the many other Paris scientists he thought about while traveling, Humboldt reviewed shipments sent to the Institut about which he had heard nothing. Three long packets of observations had gone to the Department of Physics and Mathematics, as well as a gift of botanical illustrations from Mutis and a selection of rocks from Quito to the Muséum. Nor had they heard anything about three shipments of seeds sent to the Jardin. Humboldt rehearsed for Delambre their long "painful" journey to try to catch Baudin at the coast. He expressed pride in the way his health stood up through it all in comparison to Bonpland's. "My companion, whose talents, courage, and immense activity have been the most help to me in botanical researches and comparative anatomy, citizen Bonpland, has suffered recurrent fevers for three months" (LA, 142). He told of his research on volcanoes and the climb up Chimborazo, adding pages of readings of elevation and temperature. Foremost on his mind now, he concluded, was return to Paris and publication:

> I am not going to the Philippines. . . . I will be in Mexico in February, in June in Havana, for I think of nothing but of conserving the manuscripts I have in my possessions and publishing. How I long to be in Paris! (LA, 147)

In Mexico City in April after a short stay in Acapulco to measure longitude and latitude, Humboldt was happy to be back in a European-style city:

> The new city, which has nearly one hundred and forty thousand inhabitants, was built by Cortes over the ruins of the old, following the street patterns; but little by little, the canals that crossed the roads have been filled in, and Mexico, singularly embellished bythe Viceroy, Count Revillagigedo, is comparable today to the most handsome cities in Europe. (VC I, 57)

Letters of introduction from Madrid gave him immediate entry to colonial circles. The director at the School of Mines turned out to be an old classmate from the mining school at Freiburg. Immediately on arrival, he was called in to consult at the Academy of the Arts on the casting of a giant equestrian statue of Charles IV, king of Spain. It is a statue with a "great purity of style," wrote Humboldt in commentary accompanying a drawing of the statue included in his *Views of the Cordilleras*. "One does not know which one ought to admire more, the talent of the artist or the courage and perseverance of those who deployed it in a country where all remains to be created and in which it is necessary to surmount so many obstacles" (VC I, 59). He had arrived in Mexico City, he recounted, just in time to assist with the difficult mechanics of mounting the giant statue up on its pedestal in the city square. Looking up at rider and horse against the deep blue sky, he wrote, "produces a very picturesque effect" (VC I, 59–60). When word came of fever at Vera Cruz, the port from which he planned to leave for Havana and the journey back to Europe, Humboldt opted to stay in Mexico City until the danger was over. He was invited to the best houses. He was sought after for advice on improving yields from Mexican mines. He had free access to government records and archives and was compiling a report for the Viceroy on improving profits from colonial holdings. He was given tours of ruins in the surrounding countryside more impressive than even those of the Inca.

In Mexico City he was happy to finally receive a letter from Willdenow. His "joy," he wrote back to Willdenow, was all the greater given since it was the first letter from Willdenow that reached him on his travels, although he was sure that Willdenow must have written to him many others. They sent off ten or twelve large shipments of seed to the Jardin in Paris and to Madrid, he told Willdenow, but Willdenow need not worry; he would receive his share: "I have dried them all with extreme care" (LA, 155).

A report went to Cavanilles, head of the Botanical Garden in Madrid, with Humboldt describing the difficulty of the journey and the extent of their discoveries. They were in good health "in spite of the lack of shelter and the hunger we experienced in the deserts, the change in climate and temperature, and the excessive fatigue of our painful travels":

> Many Europeans have exaggerated the influence of climate on the spirit and have claimed that it is impossible to do intellectual work here, but we must proclaim the contrary; never have we had so much energy as in contemplating the beauties and the magnificence that nature here offers. Its grandeur, its infinite and novel productions electrify us, one might say, filling us with rejoicing and making us invulnerable. It is thus that we work exposed for three hours at a time to the boiling sun of Acapulco and of Guayaquil without experiencing any notable inconvenience. It is thus that we strode through the icy snows of the Andes, that we crossed joyfully deserts, deep woods, shores and quagmires. (LA, 148–149)

Special commendation went to Bonpland, who had met and worked with Cavanilles in Madrid.

You know the ardor and enthusiasm of my friend and companion Bonpland and, knowing that, you can calculate the riches we have gathered traveling countries never visited before by botanists, countries where nature is pleased to spill out her favors, multiplying plants in new vegetal forms and unknown fructifications. The result is that our current collections exceed 4,200 plants. . . . Even though botany is an accessory part of the principle aim, as is comparative anatomy of which we also have many pieces prepared by my companion Bonpland. (LA 149–150)

Once again Humboldt made it clear. The "principle aim" was not plants or animals, but something more universal, maps and profiles keyed to electrometric, eudiometric, hydrometric features that influence "vegetation." "I am now able to indicate," said Humboldt, "the altitude of every tree in the tropics." At the same time, Humboldt added a note of caution: mistakes might have been made. Anyone who wished could read his materials, but there should be no publishing until he returned and his findings were verified.

Attached to Humboldt's letter to Cavanilles was a note from Bonpland, drawing Cavanilles's attention to some particular plants they had collected and acknowledging the honor of having had a plant named after him by Cavanilles: "Coming from Acapulco to this city, I had the pleasure of encountering the plant *Bonplandia* with which you have wanted to perpetuate my name." Among the plants in the cases they were sending to Spain, Bonpland told Cavanilles, were species of that plant and also of *Phlox* and *Hoitzia*, which would help to show more clearly differences between the genera (AB, 7–8). More and more, Bonpland had been impressed by the work of Spanish botanists, and in Mexico City he was given the opportunity to work with another of them, Vicente Cervantes, whose collection of Mexican plants he had seen and admired in Madrid. Cervantes came to Mexico in 1787 on an official botanical expedition led by Martín Sessé charged with making an extensive survey of Mexican plants. Together they founded the Royal Botanical Garden of Mexico City and on the basis of their research published an authoritative *Flora Mexicana*. When Sessé returned to Spain, Cervantes took over as director of the garden, and Bonpland found they had much in common. Trained in pharmacology like Bonpland, Cervantes was interested not only in new species but in plant physiology. Of particular interest was a native tree famous for the strange form of its flowers, much cited by ancient native historians and venerated by local Indians.

Legend made the tree one of a kind, a lone individual growing near the town of Tolca, a tree with long waxy red stamen shaped like the fingers of a spidery hand that never reproduced itself. For years Cervantes had tried to prove the legend wrong, taking cuttings and seeds and planting them out in the Botanical Garden. Finally now he was able to show Bonpland a second individual grown from one of his cuttings and also to pass on news that some of his students found groves of the tree in the province of Guatemala. The failure of the lone individual at Tolca to reproduce with the exception of this one progeny remained a mystery, and Bonpland gathered 100 seeds to take back to Europe so that he too could experiment with propagation. He also suggested a better name: not *Cheiranthodendron*, "flower in the shape of a hand," but the more anatomically correct and pronounceable *Cheirostemon*, "stamen hand" (PE I, 81–83).[5]

More important to Humboldt than unusual trees was adding to the list of new species discovered on their voyage, and here there was some disappointment. Due to the monumental work of collecting and describing already done by Spanish botanists in Mexico, it was not always easy for Bonpland to find new plants. Traveling with Humboldt on visits to mines and monuments, he did his best. There were species he was sure were new, small charming trees like *Dalea mutabilis* with striking blue flowers highlighted with tints of rose and white, and *Dalea bicolor* less showy but with a fragile beauty. *Lobelia fulgens* he found growing up in the high plain of Valladolid with multiple flowers in a shimmering red. Others he would have to be sure had not already been identified by the Spanish botanists.

Returning to Mexico City in June after a survey of Mexican mines, Humboldt was worrying again that Paris had forgotten him. This time he wrote directly to the Institut de France, reiterating that "they had never ceased working for France." Again he listed astronomical data, shipments of plants and cases of rocks, all sent to Paris, but no word ever reached them that anything had arrived. He assured the officers of the Institut; both he and Bonpland were persisting valiantly in their efforts:

> Accustomed to privations and reverses even greater, we continue without any pause in labors we believe to be useful to mankind, and we hasten to profit from the occasion which presents itself at this moment, reiterate to you, citizens, assurances of the devotion for which your goodness always obliges us. (LA, 158)

He explained their delay in returning. Yellow fever broke out in Vera Cruz, where they were to get a ship for Havana. To avoid illness he thought it better to wait out the epidemic in Mexico City. When it passed he would immediately return to Europe. He reviewed again his reasons for not to proceeding on to North America and the Pacific: damaged instruments, difficulty of procuring replacements, the prospect of a long ocean trip with little of interest to science, and "above all rapid progress in the sciences and the necessity of remaining current on new discoveries after four to five years' absence" (LA, 163).

Writing a month later to Delambre, still he had no response: "I do not know what to think; it troubles me all the time" (LA, 164). He works without ceasing. He has determined the longitude at Jaen de Bracamoros, "which Condamine was unable to do." He has corrected the longitude of Mexico City. He is about to leave for the Guanaxato mines, which bring in millions of piasters a year. He is analyzing lake water for carbonate of soda and suphurous hydrogen. He is preparing a profile of the landmass along the coast, studying mineralogy and analyzing the air. He has access to government records and statistics and is preparing a report on the economic, geographic, agricultural resources of New Spain with long sections on mining and profits from mining that he will give to the viceroy before he leaves. He is hard at work compiling information from government records to which he is adding his own observations on mines and geographical measurement. Always, he reiterated, his motives are humanitarian. "Any man must put himself in the position in which he believes himself to be the most useful to his species." But much as the adventurous life suits him, he is ready to change his ways:

> I think that for me, I must perish either on the edge of a crater or drowning in the waves of the ocean; such is my opinion at the moment after five years of fatigue and suffering; but I well believe that advancing in age and enjoying again the charms of European life, I will change my opinion. *Nemo adeo ferus est, ut non mitescere possit.* (LA, 167)

The quote was from Horace's *Epistles*—"No man is so wild he cannot be tamed."[6] Savage though he might consider himself to be, Humboldt was more than ready to return to civilization.

At the beginning of the New Year with the plague now over, they were on their way to Vera Cruz, stopping to see the volcanoes of Iztaccíhuatl and Popocatépetl and the Pyramid of Cholula on the way. By March they were on a ship bound for Havana and an opportunity for one last American adventure. When they arrived in the city, the United States consul, Vincent Gray, introduced himself. He had heard about Humboldt's economic report for the Spanish viceroy, he said. Might Humboldt be willing to make a stop at Washington on his way back to Europe? If so, a meeting with President Jefferson could perhaps be arranged. Given the recent "Louisiana" purchase of a vast stretch of unexplored territory adjacent to Mexico, the president would no doubt be interested in seeing Humboldt's maps and surveys of economic possibilities in Mexico. Immediately Humboldt changed his plans, and along with Bonpland, Montúfar, and the ever-faithful José, he was on his way to Philadelphia.

In Philadelphia, Humboldt wrote to Jefferson with flattering deference:

> Having arrived from Mexico on the happy soil of this republic . . . I have the pleasant duty of paying my respects to you and testifying to the great admiration your writing, actions, and breadth of ideas have inspired in me since childhood. . . . I could not resist the moral interest of seeing the United States and benefiting from the consoling nature of a people who know how to appreciate the precious gift of liberty. I hope I can have the good fortune of paying my respects to you in person. (Philadelphia, May 24, 1804)[7]

Following that introduction came a long account of his travels, his knowledge of the South American Indians, his work on economic resources in Mexico. Perhaps Jefferson had heard of his experiments with galvanism. Might Jefferson be interested in seeing the mammoth tooth he discovered in the Andes?

Jefferson's response was brief and to the point. The United States would be happy to receive information on Mexico if Mr. Humboldt found it convenient to add to his journey and make a trip down to Washington (May 28, 1804). A second note to Humboldt two weeks later made that interest specific, citing boundaries in dispute with Spain in regard to the territory called Texas. An aide passed on to Humboldt specific questions President Jefferson would like answered: "Can the Baron inform me what population may be between those lines, of white, red or black people? and whether any & what mines are within them?" (June 9, 1804) Was the territory in question worth fighting for? Were the Indians living there as menacing as reported? Were there mineral deposits in the region of any importance?

It was not long before Humboldt and his party were on their way to Washington, where Humboldt met several times with Jefferson. He also passed on to him a hastily done French translation of the economic report he prepared for the Viceroy in Mexico, to which had been added material on the uncertain borders of Spanish territory and the geological and agricultural value of regions contiguous with territory now controlled by the United States.[8]

Back in Paris, augmented with additional research in Paris and Berlin, the report prepared for the viceroy and passed on to Jefferson would become one of Humboldt's most successful publications, the *Political Essay on the Kingdom of New Spain*. In a long subtitle Humboldt summarized the benefits scientific travel like his could bring to the New World:

> Researches relative to the Geography of Mexico, the Extent of its Surface and its political Division into Intendancies, the physical Aspect of the Country, the Population, the State of Agriculture and Manufacturing and Commercial Industry, the Canals projected between the South Sea and Atlantic Ocean, the Crown Revenues, the Quantity of the precious Metals which have flowed from Mexico into Europe and Asia, since the Discovery of the New Continent, and the Military Defence of New Spain.

For a frontispiece to the *Geographical and Physical Atlas* that accompanied the *Political Essay* Humboldt commissioned a drawing from his friend the Parisian painter François Gérard: A defeated Aztec warrior half falls, half kneels exhausted on the steps of a ruined pyramid while, standing over and above him, two Greco-Roman gods offer solace and assistance. Athena holds out to him her olive branch of industry and craft. Hermes with winged feet and herald's staff of trade and commerce reaches down to take the warrior's arm as if to help him to his feet. Behind them in the far distance rises the high peak of Chimborazo. In place of a caption suggested by Gérard—"America rescued from ruin by commerce and industry"—Humboldt substituted the more erudite touch of a quote from Pliny, "Humanitas, Literae, Fruges": Humanism, Literature, Crops. He also added a detail that was not in Gerald's original drawing. In the dust at the bottom of the steps of the ruined temple, barely noticeable given the drama being acted out above, lies a broken shattered female idol.

Unmentioned in Humboldt's letters from Mexico City to Willdenow, Delambre, and the Institut de France were discoveries he made there, which were not so easy to categorize. "Surprise" at the pre-Incan manuscripts shown to Humboldt at Riobamba and at the remains of Inca roads in the Andes gave way to consternation with remnants of Aztec art shown to him in Mexico City. Visiting the house of a Spanish army captain he was shown a carved female figure crouched sphinxlike with a solemn and staring visage. Describing it in *Views of the Cordilleras* Humboldt struggled to find the words. The headdress worn by the female figure, he thought, perhaps looked something like the veil on the heads of Egyptian statues of Isis. And the string of pearls on the woman's forehead? Might it be similar to decorations on the robes of Jewish high priests? But the figure was "grotesquely carved" with no hands and only stylized digits that must be toes. Certainly here was the infancy of anything one could call art, but at the same time the carving was done with skill and fine detail (VC, I, 54). Could it be some sort of deity, Humboldt wondered, given the pearls? But no, he decided, "the ornament around the neck and the not prodigious form of the head made it more probably simply the bust of an Aztec woman" (VC I, 55). In his commentary, he used the title given by its owner, "Bust of an Aztec Priestess."

Even more disturbing was a monumental Aztec sculpture considered so dangerous to Catholic eyes that it was buried underground in a special vault closed to all but official visitors. Thirteen years before Humboldt's stay in Mexico city it had been dug up in the course of excavating a drainage line under the central square: a twenty-foot monolith in basaltic porphyry carved with gigantic figures covered with snakes and surrounded by bits and pieces of bodies. It was an image, Humboldt was told, of the barbarous Aztec war god Huitzilopochtli and his wife. Humboldt was shocked. This was hardly the innocent "infancy" of art but rather total "ignorance of the true proportions of the human body" along with "crudeness and incorrectness in design." But again there was also that unexpected expertise in carving. How was he to make sense of it? Worse, what was to be said of such images? The Aztec were a people with institutions and rituals that would have to be called religious, who produced a wealth of artifacts, but artifacts that had little affinity with anything one could call "art," certainly not in the sense of Greek or Roman art he studied at Göttingen, but not like Asian art either. What would you call such carvings? And where would one place a people that produced such objects on the standard European scale of human development from hunter-gatherer savagery, to barbarous theocracy, and on to "civilization." If had been hard to place the Chaima on a scale between savage and barbarous, the Aztec presented even more of a puzzle. There were exceptions. He was shown a relief carving at Oaxaca less "crudely" done and with human figures more realistically executed. Was it European influence, Humboldt wondered, that accounted for this artistic "advance?"

There was much that escaped Humboldt's notice. He tested the water in the lakes around Mexico City for chemicals, but took little interest in remnants of the complex system of canals and lakes that once worked to purify the waters and preserve the ground on which the pre-Columbian Aztec city of Tenochtitlán was built. Nor, on his way out of Mexico City to visit the mines, did he take notice of remains of lowland terraced agriculture adapted to local conditions of seasonal precipitation. Looking across now-deserted fields, Humboldt saw only undeveloped land where he imagined future European settlers and cattle grazing.[9] Nor was the idol discarded in the dust at the feet of the defeated Aztec warrior a priestess. It was the water goddess Chalchiuhtlicue, who presided over the waterworks and waterways of the ancient Aztec city buried under the Spanish Mexico City. She was the spirit behind the canals that had made all parts of the old city accessible both by boat and on foot, and behind the dikes that kept back brackish water from inland lakes and purified the waters surrounding the city. She was the spirit behind the aqueduct that brought fresh water from springs in the mountains, the giant cisterns that stored that water for bathing, the floating gardens covered with mud and planted with vegetables and flowers that came regularly to stock the markets. Nor was the massive basalt monolith dug up from under the central square the war god Huitzilopochtli and his wife Teoyamiqui. It was the powerful earth goddess Coatlicue, source of life as well as of death.[10]

Ironically the quotation "Humanitas, Litteras, Fruges," chosen by Humboldt from Pliny's letters as caption for the frontispiece to his *Atlas* might have carried a meaning other than the one Humboldt intended. Maximus, the recipient of Pliny's letter, had just been named Roman governor of the conquered province of Achaia, including the once-great city-states of Athens, Corinth, and Sparta. The gifts—culture, letters, grain—that Pliny warned his friend to remember were not the gifts brought by victorious Romans. They were gifts that the Greeks had given to humanity in the past, and might continue to give if they were treated by their conquerors with dignity and respect.

PART III

THE RETURN

8

Coming Home

Humboldt and Bonpland returned to a Paris very different from the one they left five years before. A few months after they sailed from Spain, Napoleon limped back from defeat in Egypt and participated in the coup that made him consul and then first consul. A second Italian campaign brought Italy under French control. Austria was defeated. A truce was signed with Britain. The Netherlands were under French control. Government administration was centralized. Banking, taxation, and commerce were reorganized. A law code was written and imposed by military command on conquered territories and puppet states. Just before their ship docked at Bordeaux, Napoleon had the senate and the tribunat proclaim him emperor. France was an imperial power. Storerooms in the Louvre overflowed with captured antiquities from Egypt, paintings taken from Italy and Austria, tapestries from Belgium and Holland. Monumental public works were commissioned and under construction: grand avenues, public buildings, triumphal arches. Once, in a small village on the llanos, Bonpland and Humboldt were shown a magic lantern show of European scenes, one of them the new façade and formal gardens of the Tuileries. In that vast open land it hardly seemed real. Now for Bonpland it was the reverse. Surrounded by imperial grandeur, memories of the ease and freedom of life in the tropics could seem no more than storybook images.

In the harbor off the coast of Bordeaux, waiting out the quarantine, Humboldt went immediately to work, preparing the ground for their arrival. He wrote to his old classmate Freiesleben, now director of silver and copper mines at Eisleben. He was sorry, he said, not to have written all the time he was away. His voyage was wonderful. He was in fabulous health; had met President Jefferson, who received him with great honor; was bringing back many treasures and would take a few years to publish the results of his voyage. "I was sorry to leave that Indian world, so splendid, but the idea of getting together again with you, to embrace you again—to dig up with you the gold of Katzenfels—has for me infinite attraction." As soon as the quarantine was over, he told Freiesleben, he would begin work. There came a shadow of doubt. Had he been away too long? He could not be sure what he would find on shore. Confidence immediately returned: "The idea alone of being saved is consoling" (LA, 169).

Writing to the family retainer and steward of the Humboldt estates, Gottlob Kunth, Humboldt was on surer ground. He had escaped the dangers of travel. In Washington he was treated with "most signaled recognition." He had heard nothing about family affairs and would like an accounting of his revenues (LA, 170). A letter of correction went to a Paris newspaper in response to an article announcing his arrival. No, he did not make it to the peak of Chimborazo, but he carried instruments higher than anyone had before him. And no, he was not in the pay of the Spanish government. The Spanish gave him safe conduct but he paid all the expenses of the voyage himself. It was an accusation he would often have to parry. Had he been financed by the Spanish? Was it to serve Spanish interests that he traveled?

Out of quarantine and arrived in Paris at the beginning of September, he wrote to the king, Frederick William III of Prussia, formally announcing his return and affirming his allegiance to the Prussia throne:

> After an absence of eight years from my country, having escaped dangers that threaten the health of Europeans in the Tropics, I believe that it is my first and my most sacred duty to lay at the feet of Your Majesty my most profound devotion. The generous protection of the sciences, the influence of gentle laws, the free intercourse of society and of justice, have elevated the Prussian monarchy at the beginning of the nineteenth century to a high point of moral well-being and external glory. (LA, 173)

He played down his connection with the French, referring to Bonpland as "a French savant I took along at my expense." If in coming years Humboldt would be suspect in Paris as a Prussian national, in Prussia he would suffer from association with the French. Already Wilhelm, serving as Prussian ambassador to the Vatican in Rome, was sending urgent appeals. Given deteriorating relations between France and Prussia it was imperative that Alexander come back to Berlin and establish himself as a Prussian citizen. It did not look good for him to publish in French and seem to prefer Paris to Berlin. But regardless of official eulogies to Prussian enlightenment, Humboldt was in no way ready to leave Paris. He was sending gifts, he wrote to the king, cases of rocks for the

Museum of Natural History, and also a large block of platinum as a special gift for the king himself. And, yes, he wanted very much to return and live "under the benevolent protection of a wise and paternal government," but given considerations of health he had decided that it was best to spend the winter in Italy.

In Paris Humboldt was an instant celebrity. He was invited everywhere. At soirées he was the center of attraction, entertaining guests with stories of adventures with savage Indians and on the craters of erupting volcanoes. Wilhelm was away serving as Prussian minister in Rome, but Wilhelm's popular wife, Caroline, stayed on in Paris waiting for the birth of a child. She wrote to Wilhelm. Alexander, she said, was not at all aged after six years of travel. "His vivacity in speech and manner is if possible increased" (CB I, 344). Writing again a few days later, she expressed some worry. Was Alexander letting himself be swept off his feet by French charm with newspapers hailing him as the "Second Discoverer of America," a superhero who had climbed higher than anyone dared to go? Indeed Humboldt was in a frenzy of activity. In a matter of weeks he had arranged an exhibition at the Jardin des plantes, including some of his drawings, a collection of rocks, and the surviving skull from the Indian burial cave. He sent observations to the Paris Observatory to be analyzed and correlated. He opened negotiations with publishers. In October he presented a preliminary account of his voyage to the Institut de France. In December he attended Napoleon's coronation as emperor in Notre Dame, dressed in a new frock coat especially embroidered for the occasion. A memoir followed, read at the Institut in January, on a new species of monkey, and then another on the dramatic trapping of electric eels. Berthollet, the chemist in whose honor Humboldt had named Bonpland's Brazil nut tree, declared him to be a "one-man academy."

In one department, Humboldt was having little success. He and Bonpland were welcomed by Josephine Bonaparte at her estate at Malmaison. Bonpland had been invited back to plant out any of his rare plants he might wished to cultivate in her greenhouses. But any approach Humboldt made to Napoleon was rebuffed. At a reception at the Tuileries, Napoleon passed Humboldt and Bonpland with a few curt words—"So you are interested in botany?"—turned his back and walked away, muttering, "So is my wife." As Humboldt described the incident: "The Emperor behaved with icy coldness to Bonpland and seemed full of hatred for myself" (CB I, 344).

In respect to botany, Humboldt gave Bonpland full credit. In a letter to the Muséum accompanying the selected herbarium of South American plants that Bonpland prepared for the Muséum's collections, he acknowledged the debt he owed him:

If my expedition had some success, a very great part of it is due to
M. Bonpland, who was, so to say, educated in your establishment
and walked in the footsteps of his masters. We gathered together
the plants that we brought back. I have drawn a great number, but
it is M. Bonpland who alone described four fifths of them, and it
is he alone who made the herbarium. (LA, 176)

As for Bonpland, two problems were taking most of his attention. First there
was organizing and preserving the plants he had collected; second was finding
a means of support that would allow him to continue his work. A paper read
at the Institut on the wax palm *Ceroxylon* discovered on the Quindio Pass
aroused little interest:

If it is a striking phenomenon to find a palm that grows to such
a height, it is even more striking to see it exude a mélange of wax
and resin. This extremely inflammable substance, which covers all
the plant like a polished veneer, is the product of a vegetal sap
which appears as thin and aqueous as what comes from the wood
of the coconut palm. But this vital action, this game of chemical
affinities of which we see only the effect, gives rise in the same
plant to very different products. (PE I, 6)

Wax? Native peoples? They were hardly as dramatic as Humboldt's stories of
electric eels and amusing monkeys. Was it not surprising, Bonpland continued,
surprising to find wax, always before thought to be an animal product, coming
from a plant in such quantity, a vegetal source of wax, abundant, similar to
beeswax, but easier and cheaper to process? And more than the wonder of
this one palm there was the endless diversity of this vast family of plants so
intimately involved in human life in the tropics:

In some palms, the flowing sap is carried to the flowers, which
give sugars and emulsions similar to almond milk, in others like
the *pirijao* [peach palm] of the Orinoco the fruits are encased in a
farinaceous material, similar to the *Jatropha manihot*, the *Solanum
tuberosum* [potato] and other plants with tuberous roots. Others
still, like the coconut and especially the *Cocos butyracea*, give oil in
abundance and because of that are of interest in commerce. The
Mauritia, on which the Guarani rely in building scaffolding for
communication from summit to summit during the flooding of

the Orinoco, has in its trunk a starch as nourishing as that of the sago palm of Asia and the *Sagus* of the Moluques. A number of other palms give a sap very high in sugar and because of that are well suited to fermentation, but the sugar is only in abundance at the moment when the racemes of flowers form, as if nature uses in the making of flowers and especially of their pollen that very substance which makes the sap so easy to ferment. (PE I, 6)

Not only could a waxy substance be scraped off the wax palm and mixed with suet to make candles to light houses and churches, the wood of the tree was hard enough to be used for canals and aqueducts and, due to the width of its trunk, for building houses. And the tree was beautiful, growing to 160 to 180 feet, the tallest palm seen on all their travels and one of the largest trees ever reported by anyone anywhere. Feathery leaves six to seven meters long. Clusters of flowers at the intersection of its branches. Polygamous, self-fertile, and complete in itself, with feminine, masculine, and hermaphrodite flowers on spreading branches. As the female flowers dropped, the ovary swelled to become a nut with a fleshy covering and a sweet taste relished by birds and squirrels that depended on it for food. Tests should be run, concluded Bonpland, trials to determine the mechanisms that produce this vegetal wax and that might help to identify other plant sources of wax.[1] For him there was marvel to it: "Thus nature produces in a family of plants and in organs, whose structure appears very uniform, mixtures that are very heterogeneous, as if playing at varying the combinations of elements and the mysterious games of their affinities" (PE I, 7).

If Bonpland's presentation to the Institut was a disappointment, so were relations with his brother at La Rochelle. Bonpland wrote, hoping to smooth over their disagreements. In return came back only a few curt words of acknowledgment. Yes, Michel had received Bonpland's shipment of plants and seeds. Yes, he had written a note to Thouin at the Jardin telling him that his brother was on the Orinoco and would be sending on more plants and seeds. Bonpland wrote again. This time there was no response. He and Michel had always been together, collecting plants as boys and taking the same courses in natural history and medicine in Paris. So constantly were they together that professors at the Muséum took to referring to Michel as Goujaud and to Aimé as Bonpland in order to distinguish them. Michel might be forgiven for thinking that theirs was to be a shared life. Bonpland would return to La Rochelle; they would work together as provincial leaders in medicine and natural history. The family heard little from Bonpland in the five years he was gone.

In the summer of 1803 there were reports of Humboldt's, and presumably also Bonpland's, death. In June, just before their return, again rumors circulated that they were dead of fever. If Bonpland imagined a loving and celebratory reunion in La Rochelle, he was disappointed. While he was gone, his mother had died. Had he even gotten the letter? And why had he not written so that they could at least know he was alive?

In the end it was Bonpland's sister, Olive, now married to a respectable magistrate and living with two children on a pleasant estate in the countryside near La Rochelle, who broke the ice. Why hadn't Aimé written to her? She loved him and longed to hear from him and was eager for news of Paris. Relieved to find that he had not been rejected by all of his family, Bonpland answered at once and at length, addressing his letter both to Olive and to her husband, apologizing for his silence:

> My very good friends: I received your letter yesterday morning and if you had seen me, I was full of shame, reproaching myself greatly. I confess my wrongs. It was unpardonable of me not to write to you, and all the more so in that, having had only a tiny bit of a note from La Rochelle since I have been in Paris (even though I wrote at least eight letters), I should have written to you sooner to see if you were also as negligent. Each mail I said to myself: I must write now to the good inhabitants of Chauvins, but then I would put the idea aside, and with each mail I would put it aside to the next. It will be different from now on, not that I want to burden you with my letters, but at least I will write to ask you not to forget me and to give me your news. (AB, 9)

Apologies out of the way, Bonpland went on to do his brotherly best to satisfy Olive's request for news of life in the new imperial Paris. Paris, he said, was much changed: "One has done here and done again just about everything that it is possible to do in the way of embellishment." Galleries at the Louvre, he went on, were full of paintings and antiquities brought back from Napoleon's conquests in Holland and Italy. As for the year's Art Exposition, it was not worth seeing:

> Little that is good, a lot bad, some portraits of actresses, of ministers, and of gatherings of distinguished men, battles of Marengo, Egypt, Arcole, etc., but for all that, one ten-foot painting has everything good in art. It shows a woman (more beautiful than any woman

one knows) leaning against a rock and mixing her tears with the waters of a small rivulet that flows at her feet. She is dressed in a dress of black velvet, her hair is disordered, and she has a portrait of her lover in her hands. (AB, 10)

Poor Olive, longing for a firsthand account of grand entertainments and fetes; mock-serious portraits of grieving maidens would hardly suffice. What about *Les Bardes*, the play that was all the rage in fashionable circles with a libretto written by Napoleon's protégé Jean-Marie Deschamps, secretary to the Empress Josephine, with a plot taken from Napoleon's favorite "Tales of Ossian"?[2] Bonpland answered as best he could:

> As for the theaters, I am out of it; I am very busy and don't go very much. They have had my money only three times. The first day I arrived in Paris our Peruvian companion [Carlos de Montúfar] needed absolutely to see the Comédie Française, and I went there with him. . . . *Les Bardes* has many partisans and the newspapers are paid to say that there is nothing as good. . . . Still here it is necessary to say much that is negative. This is to make oneself interesting since everyone is crying out in opposition. Howl with the wolves, bite with the dogs. This is what is done here all the time and what must be done. There is no middle ground! (AB, 10–11)

So much grandeur and embellishment! Humboldt busy, Montúfar at loose ends and needing to be entertained. Greek statues and old masters in the Louvre, painting after painting depicting military victories, courtesans, bourgeois display. Bonpland, tongue in cheek, answers a sister's questions about his love life. Does he have a sweetheart now that he is back in Paris?

> The impartial interest you take in my situation, in the state of my affairs, etc. gives me pleasure, but the desire you have to see me married, father, and grandfather etc., etc., is too much. Me, without a fortune, to choose a wife in this bosom of corruption!!! If I felt a disposition to marriage, I would go, I swear to you, to the provinces and find a woman in some corner of Saintonge or Poitou. I am not perhaps so far from doing just that, but above all, I know what I owe to my elders, and our brother must give me an example. If he marries I promise to go to his wedding (if he asks me) and then perhaps I will make a firm resolution. (AB, 11)

In short, there was to be no flirtation with society belles in low-cut dresses in fashionable salons. Nor is he willing to "howl with the wolves and bite with the dogs" long enough to endure polite society and make the acquaintance of eligible young ladies. Short of funds, without a source of reliable income, faced with shelves and shelves of unclassified plants, he was hard put to keep his clothes decent enough to appear in the streets. First would come fulfilling his obligations to Humboldt and then, well, one would see. As for the future, he told Olive, nothing was settled. Friends were working on his behalf at the Muséum and with the publicity their voyage was getting in the newspapers, there were possibilities that might insure his independence:

> All the professors at the Muséum are very attached to me and want, as much as anyone could, that the government do something for me. I am only waiting for the arrival of M. Jussieu, who at the moment is in Lyon, to find me some employment that will give me enough to live on and support myself in Paris without any assistance. . . . I have always thought of having a free and independent station in life, and I dream of it that much more seriously today in that I have a certain project in mind which is my secret. I can see you burning with wanting to know, and it seems to me from here that you might suspect me of having some travel plans? (AB, 12)

Kindhearted Olive must have read this last with alarm. Her brother had been back in Europe for only a few months. Could he be thinking of disappearing again? But however much Bonpland might play with the idea of immediate return to the New World it would be difficult to manage. There was talk of a post as traveling botanist supported by the Muséum, which would give him an income and allow him to go where horticultural interests took him. But given the cost of Napoleon's military adventures, the Muséum was short of funds. There was nothing to do but wait and work on his plants.

He was settled in Paris at least for the winter, he told Olive. Humboldt wanted him to join him in Berlin in the spring but he was doing nothing about it. The first installments of a botanical work, *Plantes équinoxiales*, were almost ready for publication. He would continue work in Paris during winter and spring, although draftsmen and engravers were constantly holding him up with their slowness even when he had eleven new plants ready to be engraved. He ended his long letter with a playful invitation and a description of his living quarters:

You talk of coming to Paris, but you don't say when. For sure it won't be this winter, but maybe in the spring, and if the job I get does not oblige me to change lodgings I can offer you a pied-à-terre. My apartment is big enough to hold all of us and with ease. But I warn you that since you are fond of looking at yourself in big mirrors, you must bring your own. (AB, 13)

Bonpland continued with a humorous inventory of his furnishings: marble fireplace, antique bed, pillows with fringes and tassels, all lent to him by a relative in Paris. Most important, he said, was his workspace: a writing table, three big work tables, and a lot of shelves to display "our riches."

At the beginning of January, Bonpland wrote again to Olive in response to a query about the coronation:

We have had, you know as well as me from the papers, much amusement with the coronation. I let it all be told to me, I saw nothing, so I can't tell you anything about it. (AB, 14)

He was working without ceasing, he told her, still without the certainty of any recompense. He met with the minister of state. A post was talked about at 6,000 francs a year. The price was knocked down to 3,000. He joked: Might it go as low as 100 louis? Then perhaps he would be brave enough to refuse. In any case work with the plants was ongoing—"Whatever the compensation, it is work that is agreeable to me, and there will remain for me the joy of having done it." Even with losses from mold and insects, his shelves and cupboards overflowed with barks, bulbs, leaves, flowers, seeds, cross sections of tree bark, all needing to be sorted, listed, classified, described, drawn, duplicates separated: 150 melastomes, 86 magnolia, 52 calceolaria, 58 psychotria, 40 lobelia, 400 grasses, related plants sorted and laid out together so it was possible to look in a glance down a series, note subtle gradations in shape, form, seed and leaf.

At hand were his journals, so essential in bringing back memories of living plants. The *Jussiaea* species he collected in the Orinoco swamps might be used to settle the poorly distinguished species of that genus, especially if the seeds he gave to the Jardin and to Josephine at Malmaison sprouted. Seeing living plants again would allow him to be sure about *Limnocharis emarginata*, found in the Guaduas Valley, its thick stem and leaves rising out of the water supporting yellow flowers. Yes, the plant was known before, but now he could make certain it was a new genus and name it officially, "lover of mud." Jussieu had named another genus *Buguinvillea* from one dry specimen, but in Peru Bonpland saw the small living tree profusely flowering in tender rose and could now determine whether it was a different species of the same genus. Above all there were the melastomes. Here there was much work to do, hundreds—maybe thousands—of examples gathered in the vicinity of Cumaná, on the steaming banks of rivers, up the slopes of the Andes. They would be the basis for a separate *Monographie des melastomacées* because he was now sure that the entire order had been wrongly divided. Rare species identified from a few dry specimens had been misdescribed, small differences between species ignored. Aublet's *Melastoma grandiflora* and *scandens*, for example, he is convinced are *Rhexia*, as are Mutis's *grassa* and *strigosa*. And the Muséum has assured him. He can have all the melastomes in France: Candolle, Desfontaines, Jussieu, Ventenat, Thouin, all have said they would open their collections to him. The beauty of some of the hardy *Rhexia* would grace any garden: small bushy trees with brightly colored frilly flowers and anthers ending in bizarrely and diversely shaped appendices that gave off an enchanting efflorescence.

Meanwhile Humboldt had a new intimate friend, Joseph Louis Gay-Lussac, a young French physicist to whom he was introduced at one of Berthollet's gatherings of scientists at Arcueil. Some of those present might have worried that the meeting would not be so amicable. Not only had Gay-Lussac mercilessly criticized in print Humboldt's lecture on eudiometry back in 1799, he had just topped Humboldt's Chimborazo record for height in a hot air balloon. As always Humboldt was charming, and Gay-Lussac was black-haired, handsome, and a gifted physicist and chemist. It was not long before Montúfar was on his way back to Quito, and José was sent home to Cumaná. Humboldt and Gay-Lussac were constant companions, working together in the laboratory of the École Polytechnique, with Gay-Lussac tutoring Humboldt in the latest oxygen testing techniques.

With festivities surrounding the coronation over, Humboldt's main concern was publication. In January, he wrote to Cotta, a friend of Schiller's and co-founder with Schiller of the journal *Die Horen*, in which Humboldt's youthful "The Rhodian Genius" appeared. He was in need of money, he told Cotta. Not only had the voyage been costly, publishing was proving even more expensive: "Who better to enter into relations with than you, who are friend of my friends? My voyage is dedicated to Schiller" (LA, 177). A dedication to Schiller, he wrote, would put the voyage on the proper footing in Germany, and he was sure a deal could be made with profit for both of them. Yes, he was under some obligation to Schöll in Paris, to whom he had promised his *Geography of Plants* and also his *Observations on Astronomy*, but a multi-volume *Narrative* account of the voyage was still available. Admittedly, he was only on the first volume of a long list of projected publications, but much more was to come, and the botany publications were well in progress. A few weeks later an irritated note went to Willdenow, who wrote with questions about plants in the duplicate collection that had finally reached him in Berlin:

> In spite of the pêle-mêle of my own affairs, I will find the time to
> do your commissions. I will go today myself to Dupetit-Thouat,
> who is a very stiff man. It is a terrible shame that your good genie
> did not bring you this year to Paris rather than sending you to
> Trieste. Here you might have had at your disposal the herbier of
> Bonpland's and mine, and also those of Lamarck and Jussieu. You
> could have chosen yourself anything of use to you. (LA, 180)

Humboldt had too much on his mind to think about plants. Due to all the "running and mixing," he was, however, able to announce to Willdenow with some satisfaction that a little more than six months after his return, installments of a *Tableau physique*, *Observations on Zoology*, and *Observations on Astronomy* were ready to go to the printer along with the first folios of *Plantes équinoxiales*. All his works, he assured Willdenow, would be published in German as well as in French.

Three days later he was back in communication with his old mentor Pictet in Geneva. In 1795 Humboldt had written to Pictet, introducing himself as a young man wanting to be instructed. Soon he was sending Pictet results from his studies of galvanism and electrical shock and Pictet was responding with suggestions and additions. He asked Pictet for advice. If he wrote and sent more results, might it be possible to get a French bookseller to print and sell his writings together as a collection, perhaps calling it "Letters on Physics addressed to M. Pictet?"[3] Now well past such juvenilia, Humboldt hoped to enlist Pictet's help with an unprecedented omnibus publication on the results of his five years of travel, as many as 30 volumes on different subjects and in different formats. The best-selling official *Journal* of the third Cook expedition, prepared and edited by the Admiralty from the journals of various crew members, had been a modest three volumes totaling 1617 pages, illustrated with eighty-seven plates. Cook's personal journal of the voyage and other informal accounts of the voyage written by members of the expedition were single volumes. Humboldt's *Voyage* would include in botany alone two volumes of *Plantes équinoxiales*, a *Monographie des melastomacées*, a *Geography of Plants*, and a multi-volume *New Genera and Species*. There would be works on zoology with Cuvier and other zoologists at the Muséum contributing. There would be astronomical observations with correlations and calculations, observations of magnetism, a geological pasigraphy, a geological atlas, a multi-volume *Personal Narrative* of his travels. It was an immense undertaking, but Humboldt was confident. He would finish it in two or two and a half years.

Again there were moments of doubt. Unprepared for the expense of hiring artists, draftsmen, printers, translators, and engravers, he worried about money. He feared that completing the slate of publications might take longer than he projected. Doubts were transitory. Of course his works would make money, as did Cook's and Forster's, and even moreso due to both the scientific basis of his publications and the cosmic scope of his subject matter. He was sending on, he told Pictet, an expanded version of his political and economic report on Mexico. "I doubt that there is anything more complete on the population, area, finances, and commerce of any country in Europe" (LA, 182). He was about to leave for Rome to be reunited with his brother. Once there he would put together a formal prospectus for an ensemble of works to be published in six languages. Did Pictet think such a menu of works might interest an English publisher? Might it be possible to sign a contract and be paid for each work separately, while promising in time to deliver the entire list? The whole ought to be worth some millions of pounds sterling, and the material was there and ready, but it was important that works appear in order, to begin by interesting "people of taste" not just with facts and figures, but with literary style and descriptions of the look of a country, its ways of life, commerce, intellectual culture, and antiquities, as well as all the "little adventures" had by voyagers.

Humboldt ended an already long letter to Pictet, but, as would so often happen, immediately found he had more to say. Writing in the margins and at the bottom of pages, he added additional queries. What should be the order of publication? As he saw it, two contradictory things had to be taken into consideration. Given that he is being honored with so much attention, he must do nothing to damage his reputation. Atlas, maps, and graphs should not be published before he has his lunar distances verified to be sure that he has not made mistakes. On the other hand, it is important not to make readers wait too long. He needs to publish something now to keep his name in play, to "amuse the public," something "general," which meant either the *Geography of Plants* or a collection of his presentations to the Institut about catching eels or life on the Orinoco. On the whole, perhaps, the *Geography of Plants* with its

Tableau physique of Chimborazo with its lines of vegetation and comparison of heights reached by himself and by other climbers would be best:

> I think it is more philosophical to choose to take Nature as a whole rather than to recount one's own adventures. . . . [The Geography of Plants] indicates what I have done and proves that my researches have embraced the ensemble of phenomena, and especially it speaks to the imagination. Men want to *see* and I give them a macrocosm on one page. I think that in this way literary charlatanry meets up with the utility of the thing. (LA, 183–184)

The dilemma went deeper than any "charlatanry" of marketing strategy. On the one hand there were the endless tables of measurements written off from his many instruments and sent back regularly to the Observatory to be verified and correlated. But these were just numbers. Without any larger aim, without that vision of higher spiritual meaning evoked in "The Rhodian Genius," they had little meaning. On the other hand, without "facts and figures" any higher vision could be dismissed as no more than subjective illusion. The problem was how and in what sequence to splice these two together in mutual support.

In addition there were shoals of controversy to be navigated. Religion was a touchy subject given Prussia's Protestant orthodoxy, and Humboldt had no interest in engaging the issue directly. Much of the ongoing work on the geography and the distribution of plant species had bearing on the controversial question of divine creation. Willdenow had taken safe middle ground, proposing multiple creations on different mountain tops, accommodating distinctive regional flora without calling God into question. In his *Geography of Plants*, Humboldt avoided the issue, opting instead for the mapping of vegetal "physiognomies" suited to particular climatic zones. Another touchy issue was colonialism. Humboldt's Mexican "statistics" emphasized gradual reform rather than revolution. Slavery should be phased out to prevent rebellions such as in Haiti. Emphasis on local agriculture would better support a working populace. The mining of useful metals could supplement gold and silver. As far as revolution against colonial authorities went, there was no suggestion that such a move could be successful.

To Pictet Humboldt gave specific instructions. Pictet's name would add importance to his work. Pictet should actively promote publication in Britain. He should feel free to correct copy and make notes for English translations. Humboldt added a final marketing suggestion. When Pictet writes to publishers in London giving them Humboldt's "restaurant menu" of works, it might be politic to send a goodwill offering, perhaps the gift of a pretty engraving, perhaps his drawing of the "Aztec Priestess" shown to him in Mexico City. At the same time, he cautioned, also send a gift of the same drawing to either Banks or the Antiquarian Society in case someone might try to reproduce the image clandestinely.

Nor was Europe the only market for his works:

> Also you might insinuate that I am planning an edition for North America, where I dare say among the Anti-Federalist Party there reigns a certain enthusiasm for my expedition as the newspapers of that country bear out. The yield in the United States would be very big; one wants subscribers there (a method that otherwise does not appear to me to be the most delicate), Jefferson, Madison, Galatin, Whistler, Barton, etc. will procure a great number of same. (LA, 184)

Bravado, hubris, shrewd marketing strategy; a week later writing to Friedlander some of the excitement had diminished:

> My life here is as laborious as it is sad; since my return to Europe, I have started more things than I am in any state to accomplish. Three of my works are at the printers, naturally in German and French. I say "naturally" for I have learned to my stupefaction that in Germany there is a rumor that I had to have my work translated into German. Such a rumor comes from spite. I think that at the moment it is Spanish that I write most fluently. But I am proud enough of my country to write in German, however badly. (LA, 184–185)

There were times when for Humboldt there was little "joy" in it. He knew what was being said about him in Prussia. He was a number-crunching Francophile, traitor to his German heritage, incapable of writing the language of Goethe and Schiller. Just as he alternated between passionate evocation of the beauties of nature and cold numerical fact, so he was pulled back and forth between Prussia and France, suspect in Paris for being German, suspect in the German states for being French. Added was what was turning out to be the terrific expense of it all. Regardless of the confidence he expressed to Cotta and Pictet, few subscribers would ever sign on for the slate of publications with its expensive atlases and graphs. Only large well-funded libraries, a few crowned heads of state, and wealthy individuals would make such a commitment. There would be sales, but sales of cheaper single-volume abridged editions, printed for a mass market.

At the beginning of March, Humboldt, still in Paris, wrote in a rush to Pictet, who was also in the city. His plans had changed. He was not going to be able to stop in Geneva and settle their business there. Instead he was crossing the Alps with his friend Gay-Lussac and going to Rome to see his brother. Could he come to where Pictet was staying in Paris to settle their affairs? At the bottom of Humboldt's letter preserved in his archives, Pictet made a note of the gist of what was discussed at their meeting. Humboldt wanted him to do translations into English. The manuscript would be sold in London and the proceeds divided between Humboldt, Pictet, and Bonpland. Installments would be sent to Geneva as soon as they were finished, and Pictet would make the sales in London volume by volume, starting with Humboldt's *Geography of Plants* and Bonpland's *Plantes équinoxiales*.

In a rush to get ready to leave for Italy, Humboldt sent a last conciliatory communication to Prussia, addressed to Karsten, Privy Counselor of Mines. All the minerals he had collected were for Karsten and for Prussia, he wrote. He has sent seven cases of them. If it seemed too little, it was important to remember he traveled at his own expense, and he had to carry what he collected over the Andes and give half of everything to Bonpland. They had collected 60,000 plants, 6,300 of them new. Karsten needed to remember how hard it had been to make room for them, how often he had to leave some of the rocks behind, tossed away to lighten the load. Still he was sure Karsten and his colleagues would see the value of what he had to offer to Prussia:

> If this geognostic collection is small in number, I believe it is all the more important for the progress of science. I can give for each exemplar the elevation, the strata, and position. There exists nothing like it in any existing collection from Chimborazo, Cotopaxi, or Pichincha, and many things which might appear to you insignificant at first will gain in importance when you have read my treatise. (LA, 186)

For good measure, he told Karsten, he was sending more gifts, some gold medallions, some old Mexican statues, and a picture made with feathers. Again came the warning: Keep his collections apart. He will want to publish them himself. Again came afterthoughts in the margins: His health is good. He works with more effort than before, but he hopes his work will be more mature. He is preparing for a trip to the far north of Asia, will not be able to go for two or three years. As for the "spiteful rumor" that he has remained in Paris because he is a Francophile: "The emperor has just granted a pension of 3,000 francs to Bonpland; the principle aim of my sojourns here was that of obtaining this pension for him." In other words, if he lingered in Paris it was not out of any love for the French, or admiration for French science, but to help out a needy and bereft assistant. A few days later he was on his way with Gay-Lussac across the Alps measuring the oxygen in the air and leaving Bonpland to see to the day-to-day business of publishing.

9

Tales of Three Cities

In March, just as Humboldt was preparing to leave Paris with Gay-Lussac for reunion with his brother in Rome, a decision was made on recompense to Bonpland for his contributions to science and the Muséum:

> ARTICLE 1 The collection of plants collected by MM. Humboldt and Bonpland in their voyage to equatorial America and offered by them to the Museum of Natural History is accepted by the government.

> ARTICLE 2 In recognition of this gift and conforming to the desire expressed by M. Humboldt, an annual pension of THREE THOUSAND francs is awarded to M. Bonpland, who shared the work of his voyage, to be paid from pension funds. (LA, 233)

Not the post of traveling naturalist as Bonpland had hoped, but a regular source of income in recognition of the first extensive South American herbarium labeled and described, preserved in the Muséum archives as a permanent resource for future botanists: endless species of palms, 150 melastomes, 86 species of *Molina*, 88 of *Eupatorium*, 52 *Calceolaria*, 58 *Psychotria*, 40 lobelia, 40 *renoncules*, 400 *graminées*, 6200 plants in all, three-fourths of them new species or genera.

Bonpland passed on the news to his family with self-deprecating irony:

> Congratulate me. I am sheltered from the cold, the north wind, the rain, etc., in the end for all the little causes which often make a cultivator fear for his harvest. The government has just accepted the offer that we have made—M. Humboldt and I—of our collection of plants and has given me in recompense for this gift, and

for pains I have taken on this long voyage, an annual pension of
3,000 francs. This sum plus money from publications will give me
a small fortune, which perhaps will take away all desire to return
to America. (AB, 15)

The joke was for Olive. She knew her brother well enough not to take him
seriously when he suggested that a steady income might take away all desire
to leave Paris. He now had money enough to support himself frugally, but
knowing him as she did she could not have thought that he had given up
all plans of travel. For Bonpland, more immediate was what he owed to
Humboldt:

I have always spoken of the kindness M. Humboldt shows me,
of his great generosity, of the intimacy in which we lived for six
consecutive years. For almost two years we have been occupied with
publishing and the manner of dividing the work.

Bonpland outlined for his family the generous division of profits promised
him by Humboldt. He was to get half the proceeds from all publications that
came from the voyage whether he contributed to the writing of them or not.
He would do all of the botanical work and get all of the proceeds. He tallied
up the plates and commentaries already paid for and the long delays caused
by the engravers—"It takes, as a result, at least two months to publish an
installment of ten plants, the engraving is so slow." With Humboldt gone the
business of publishing had been left to him, but he acknowledged, he himself
had made the decision to stay behind:

I had for a long time hesitated to accompany him. The trip to
Italy was tempting, but it would be very hard for me not to be
able right away to publish my plants. For this reason I preferred to
wait here a year and then join M. Humboldt if he has not already
come back here.

Yes, he wants very much to see the family and to meet his new nephews and
nieces:

I make great plans to come and see your pretty little family and
bring in the harvest with you, but hardly would I have time to
embrace you. If I followed my own taste, I would have come back

to see you as soon as we returned, but so much advice was given
me that I had to profit from the "moment of enthusiasm," and that
if I wanted to draw any profit from the voyage it would be have
to be in the first days of my arrival etc. etc. (AB, 16)

Again he catches himself. "I have gained, it is true. And I owe all to the activity of my friend and to the perseverance with which he has been soliciting."

Writing again in April he described for Olive new living conditions. With no more need to accompany Montúfar to the theater or appear in public with Humboldt, he was able to move to a less fashionable neighborhood where he could rent a large space cheaply and remain "chez moi" when it pleased him and work required it. He had a maidservant who came in to do housekeeping, brush his clothes, make him meals, and keep him clean. Still, money was tight. The few times he had to revisit "le grand monde," just making a decent appearance cost him small sums that added up at the end of a year. And there was much to do, not only the botanical work, but editing and correcting references to plants in Humboldt's *Geography of Plants*, transcribing Humboldt's difficult handwriting and correcting Humboldt's French, working with engravers for plates in *Plantes équinoxiales*, arranging matters with printers, and writing letters to Humboldt to keep him informed. Olive, he told her, was most fortunate to live far away from high society in a pleasant countryside surrounded by her pretty, charming children:

> What more could you want? To come here to this whirlwind of
> intrigues! On this stage where all is represented without exception,
> where it seems to be a crime to say the truth and where it is always
> necessary to dissimulate and pretend . . . To live near you, to share
> your country life, or to return to see the savages of the Orinoco, of
> the river of the Amazonians, is all that I desire in the world. . . . If
> I complete my projects, I will come. I will come and make the
> harvest with you. I will go out to the vineyards in the morning and
> supervise the harvesters, at midday I will hunt and collect plants,
> at night I will turn the winch, and open the ball with my nieces
> and we will be the zeros of the party or, if you like it better, the
> heroes. (AB, 17–18)

Return to La Rochelle, settle down to life as a country physician, help Michel organize a Botanical Garden of La Rochelle, herbalize and socialize with the local gentry: was it really a possibility?

For the moment publishing took precedence, and Humboldt was turning out copy. His *Essay on the Geography of Plants* with its graphing of isothermal lines on the slopes of Chimborazo would soon be in print. With the help of astronomers at the Observatory and Guy-Lussac, his astronomical and meteorological observations were being tabulated and correlated ready for publication. A first volume of *Observations on Zoology and Anatomy* was in preparation, with specimens prepared by Bonpland and added commentaries by Cuvier and Latreille at the Muséum. When Humboldt arrived in Rome a pile of letters were there waiting for him from Bonpland. "How amiable you are, my good and tender friend," Humboldt wrote back. "How good you are to write to me so often and in a manner so interesting." Regardless of the distance between them, there were still the long years of travel together, the intimate being-as-one that neither had with his own brother. Little jokes and lighthearted banter still went back and forth between two friends with every reason to think they knew each other well.

In his answering letters, Humboldt got down to business. First citations. In the botanical publications Bonpland should cite and praise the Spanish botanists as often as possible; in fact it would be best to make a list of those it was necessary to perpetually praise and praise again: Née, Zea, Mutis, Cavanilles, Pavon, and Ruiz. There was a note of urgency. In the preface Humboldt wrote for Bonpland's first installments of *Plantes équinoxiales,* Humboldt acknowledged the contributions of Spanish botanists, but he also emphasized the limits of their achievements. Joseph Jussieu went to Loxa, but much of his work had been lost. Mutis covered ground but he had never been up the Quindío Pass or into Popayán and de Pasto. Ruiz and Pavan made some discoveries but they had not gone east of the Cordillera or to Jaén de Bracamoros and the Amazon. Cervantes and Sessé made a survey of Mexican plants, but he and Bonpland found plants that "escaped their sagacity" (PE I, iii). Yes, said Humboldt, it was possible that he and Bonpland might list as a new species a plant already known to other botanists, and yes they could not be sure without further research which of their plants was in fact "new." *Plantes équinoxiales* was, after all, a preliminary publication, a compromise between not rushing too fast with the main part of their botanical work and the need to offer something immediately to the public. If they made mistakes they would correct them later.

It was just this sort of confusion that a botanist trained at the Muséum was taught to avoid, and the first installments of *Plantes* had brought complaints about Humboldt's treatment of the Spanish botanists in his preface. Humboldt's answer was diplomacy. The two of them must be in harmony,

Humboldt warned Bonpland; theirs was to be one body of work. "Answer Pavon with much friendship; it would be difficult to have issues with him and Ruiz and we can avoid it." And entertain Née's nephews, take them out for dinner, or "buy them something on my account." "It will give Née pleasure and make us seem to him less aristocratic than Ventenat, whom Née always complains about." The nuisance of botanical courtesy over, Humboldt returned to business. He thanked Bonpland for editing his manuscripts. "This is not agreeable fun work, but you are so good, and no one but you could read so well my scrawl." He made an urgent request:

> You must, you must give me some coleopteran insects. I have a friend, Count Hagen, who would kill for this vermin. He has a very large cabinet, but not a single coleoptera from Peru. See with Pavon if you can't get me some insects from their voyage, seven, eight, twelve, and I will be content. As for the list of who should get complementary copies—Jussieu, Desfontaines, Ventenat, Richard, Zea, Empress Josephine, and your father, also include an advance copy for my brother. And what about your own brother Michel? Is he to share a copy with your father? (LA, 190–194)

That last question might have touched a nerve. A cordial and regular correspondence was now kept up between Bonpland and both his father and sister in La Rochelle, but between the brothers was still icy chill. And Bonpland hardly needed reminders about the contributions of Spanish botanists. He worked with Cavanilles in Madrid, Mutis in Bogotá, and Cervantes in Mexico City. He constantly credited their work in commentaries in *Plantes équinoxiales*. As for Luis Née, his researches were in the Pacific, and taking someone's nephews out to dinner was an irritation, as was also hunting down insects for wealthy patrons. Still, compromises could be made. Other conflicts would prove more difficult to resolve. In answer to Bonpland's query whether Humboldt had kept notes on tropical skin diseases, Humboldt was dismissive. Certainly Bonpland knew as much about the subject as he did, and anyway—"It is not necessary to go so much into descriptive natural history; it is enough to describe the genera, in that there are certainly many very different species that cause the trouble" (LA, 192). For Humboldt, botany was data, names written on the side of Mount Chimborazo on his *Tableau physique*, listed as genera for his *Geography of Plants*, and added to their list of new species. Specific details and local uses of plants were of little importance beside his "general physics" of Nature and the need to complete a slate of publications. In the opening paragraphs of his introduction to the *Geography of Plants*, Humboldt reiterated what he saw as the shortcomings of what he called "descriptive natural history":

> One must see it as indispensable for sciences that deal with the medical properties of plants, their culture, or their application to the arts, but even if it is worthy of occupying a great number of botanists and even if it might be seen from a philosophical point of view, it is no less important to identify the Geography of plants as a science, existing up to now only in name, but which is nevertheless an essential part of general physics. (GP, 13).

As he also made clear in the preface, his "general physics" had more than any mere utilitarian value:

> In Europe a man isolated on an arid coast can enjoy in thought the aspects of faraway regions. If his soul is sensitive to works of art, and if his cultivated spirit is extended enough to rise to the grand conception of a general physics, in the depth of his solitude without leaving his home he can appropriate everything that the intrepid naturalist has discovered in climates and seas, in subterranean caverns, and on icy summits. It is in these things without doubt that the light of civilization influences most our individual happiness. They make us live both in the present and in the past. They surround us with all that nature has produced in indifferent climates, and put us into communication with all the peoples of the earth. Sustained by discoveries already made, we can thrust ourselves into the future and foreseeing the consequences of phenomena, fix forever the laws to which Nature is subjected. It is here in these researches that we prepare for ourselves an intellectual jouissance and a moral liberty that fortifies against the blows of fate and which no external power can threaten. (GP, 34–35)

From such a perspective, Bonpland's worries about mistakes in naming species had to seem hopelessly pedestrian, stripped of glamour, lacking in significance.

Humboldt was even more dismissive of another issue raised by Bonpland in the letters waiting in Rome. Cavanilles, director of the Royal Botanical Garden in Madrid, renowned for his work in taxonomy, died shortly before their return to France. As he said in the note attached to Humboldt's letter to Cavanilles from Mexico City, Bonpland had been very much honored by Cavanilles's naming a genus in his honor, *Bonplandia*. But now in Paris, going through Humboldt's plant references, Bonpland found cited by Humboldt a different *Bonplandia*. Had Humboldt mixed up the names? Could he have forgotten Cavanilles's *Bonplandia*? The reason for the duplication, once Bonpland pieced it together, was even more troubling. At some point in their travels, Humboldt had the idea of himself honoring Bonpland with the naming of a plant. Thinking that they had discovered near Cumaná a new genus in the form of a tree that was the source of a reputed anti-fever remedy, *Cortex angostura*, word went to Willdenow that the supposed new genus might be named *Bonplandia*. Not only had the name *Bonplandia* already been used by Cavanilles, but the tree named by Humboldt was not a new genus but a species of the known genus *Galipea*. Now in Paris, correcting and editing Humboldt's references to plants, Bonpland came across a reference to Willdenow's *Bonplandia*. Surely, he questioned Humboldt, you knew about Cavanilles's *Bonplandia*? Humboldt's response was casual.

> Tsk, it is very bad of you to think for a moment that I knew it. What purpose could such monkey business serve? How could I have known it? . . . In the end, I am *content*. You have the most handsome genus, the most interesting genus, the genus most often cited, that any botanist could have. Your ugly old *Bonplandia* (Cavanilles)? can at present be destroyed. The dead are wrong. And you can publish yourself the *Hoitzia* and this *Bonplandia*. (LA, 193)

Yes, Humboldt went on, he had written to Willdenow from Havana, and sent him some plants, saying that he could name 4 or 5 of them on the condition that he name one of them after Bonpland. The solution was simple. They would simply change the name of Cavanilles's *Bonplandia*. Humboldt ended his letter with a prudent proviso. Just be sure to list it *Bonplandia* (Willdenow) so as to make it clear that no one thinks we named it ourselves. Bonpland included Willdenow's *Bonplandia trifoliata* in the second volume of *Plantes équinoxiales*, but in this case left the commentary to Humboldt:

> We recognized, M, Bonpland and I, that the tree called Cuspare by the locals, formed a new genus and wrote it down as such in our botanical journals. Our respected friend M. Willdenow, to whom I owe my first knowledge of botany and to whom I sent my collection of plants gathered on the river Oronoco, the Rio Negro and the Casiquiare, described the Cuspare in the Memoirs of the

Academy of Berlin and dedicated the new species to my travel companion, M. Bonpland. It is to conserve the name given by this great botanist, that I here list the Cuspare under the name *Bonplandia trifoliata*, changing the ***Bonplandia geminiflora*** of Cavanilles to *Caldasia geminiflora*. (PE II, 61)[1]

In this quarrel of names perhaps it is Willdenow who is most to be pitied. Judging from Humboldt's letters, Willdenow might have been entitled to think that a considerable portion of the botanical work of the voyage was to be turned over to him to arrange and publish in his, Humboldt's, and perhaps also Bonpland's names. From the beginning of his travels, Humboldt seemed to say as much: "Everywhere I have collected for you and only for you" (LA, 112). And in Paris Humboldt had renewed that promise, complaining to Willdenow that Willdenow had not come to Paris to work on the plants: "Here you would have had my herbier and Bonpland's, and those of Jussieu and Lamarck at your disposal; you could yourself choose what is useful." As for Bonpland, what was he now to make of the expectation that he would come to Berlin? Was it to bring his collections and journals and turn them over to Willdenow, like the twenty-year-old Humboldt brought rocks and flowers to a mentor to name? To someone who had never seen a tropical plant? It was not a comfortable situation for either Willdenow or Bonpland.

For a time no letters arrived in Rome from Bonpland in Paris. Writing from Naples at the beginning of August, Humboldt complained,

> You are so cruel to me in not writing, This must not be. I scold you in all its forms. It is necessary that we never be more than fifteen days not writing. I impose that rule on myself in the future and you love me too much to refuse me that consolation Alas! Could you be sick . . . or your father in La Rochelle? I give you the grace of all the excuses, letters lost, gone astray, not knowing if I am still in Italy. But I call to you, write to me, tell me that you have not forgotten me, that your *Plantes équinoxiales* advances. (HCH, 20)

As always came instructions. Correct Latin names, money matters, wording on title pages, and a demand that would now continually be made: send plants to Berlin that are missing from the collection here.

> I flatter myself, dear Bonpland, that you have thought of the little collection of plants, of melastomes, of graminées that I asked to be

sent to me in Berlin by Schöll by October 9 at the latest. As for the designation of all my share of the plants, I give you as term Oct. 1 and I flatter myself that you will make this separation with M. Desfontaines to satisfy your conscience. (HCH, 22)

In his new lodgings, correcting proofs, making out Humboldt's all-but-unreadable handwriting, finishing descriptions and commentaries for *Plantes équinoxiales*, Bonpland tried, not always successfully, to let the matter of the misuse of the name *Bonplandia* pass. Regardless of the importance of Willdenow to Humboldt as the person who introduced him to the joys of nature, Willdenow was a minor figure compared to the legendary Cavanilles. To so causally rename one of Cavanilles's genera, even in honor of the spurned Caldas, hardly made turning over more plants attractive. Having done the botanical work, as Humboldt had himself acknowledged, Bonpland could not but think that the plants collected were, if not his, his as the trained botanist who collected and described them, to put in order and describe. Of course collections and descriptions would be shared with the Jardin and with other botanical establishments. He prepared sets of doubles for Humboldt and for offering to qualified others, and of course he would consult with other botanists, with Jussieu and Desfontaines at the Muséum, Thouin at the Jardin, Candolle at Montpellier. His numbering system and his botanical journals allowed research to continue on different fronts without confusion. But he could hardly have thought that his collection of tropical plants would be turned over to a Prussian botanist who had never been out of Europe, rarely out of Germany, and who had never seen a tropical plant in its own habitat. In his apartment in Paris, with the pages of his botanical journals from the voyage open on his table, files of dried specimens at hand, and memories still fresh in his mind, Bonpland tried to settle back to work, dedicating *Plantes équinoxiales* to Don José Celestino Mutis, who had greeted him so cordially in Bogotá and who had been so generous with gifts of botanical art and plant specimens.

Never again will works like this appear in print: folio volumes, two feet long and fifteen inches wide, in series of installments. Bound into volumes, they were displayed in the houses of wealthy collectors and heads of state, products of a rich confluence of science, art, and skilled engraving. It might be a celebration of one genus or family of plants, as with Bonpland's *Monographie des melastomacées*, or Redouté's *Liliacées*, or a selection of plants of a particular geographical region or climate as in *Plantes équinoxiales*. Original watercolors on vellum, worth a fortune, were painstakingly reproduced in stipple engravings and sometimes recolored by hand. Flowers were depicted life-sized in colored plates, supplemented with intricate line drawings of each plant part—stem, seedpod, fruit, leaf, capsule, nut—art and science collaborating with both beauty and meticulous detail. To turn the pages is to enter a virtual world of plant celebrities, to live among plants as kindred personalities with complex lineages and natures.

Bonpland's "plantes équinoxiales" came from varying habitats, from flat lands and riverbanks near Cumaná on the coast of Venezuela, from hot steaming jungles along the Orinoco, from the vast plains of the llanos and high mountains ranges of the Andes. Many of the genera and species he described were new, and their discovery helped to reorder orders or families, but seldom did newness alone determine his choices. There was beauty—flowers that might be cultivated in European gardens outdoors or under glass: the pure white *Passiflora* found on the slopes of Mount Quindío, a hardy *Desfontainia splendens* with red tubular flowers. He noted decorative uses of tropical foliage. In a greenhouse the gray-white leaves of *Leucophyllum ambiguum* or the whitened leaves of *Rhexia canescens* would be a welcome contrast with the unrelenting green of cool weather plants, as would many of the new Rhexias he collected.

> *Rhexia multiflora* is one of the prettiest species of the genus. It
> would be most desirable if it was brought to Europe to be cultivated
> in our greenhouses. It would be more pleasing to see than any of
> the great trees of hot regions that we try so hard to cultivate and
> which never give flowers or fruit and not even agreeable foliage. It
> is the job of naturalists who travel at the expense of governments
> to make in these far off lands the choice of plants that can offer
> charm and utility or at least one of these advantages. (Bonpland,
> *Monographie des melastomacées* II, 43)

The spectacular and bizarre *Cheirostemon platanoides* with its stamen hands had never been successfully propagated. He planted some of the seed given him by Cervantes at Malmaison and at the Jardin. In twenty-four months none had germinated, but he had hopes that with proper treatment some might sprout and allow propagation so that the plant could be grown in southern gardens.

Bonpland featured plants that could be naturalized outdoors in Europe to provide shade and timber as well as beauty. He collected enough species of *Symplocos* to show that several reputed genera could be gathered into one, facilitating the identification and culture of this useful tree. The hard blond wood of *Symplocos rufescens* would be good for furniture making. *Symplocos coccinea* with its beautiful foliage and flowers would do well in European woodlands. The *Matisia* found on the Magdalena with its sweet apricot-tasting fruit, native to warm humid valleys, would not survive in France, but this "majestic" tree with its useful fruits might be transported to French holdings in North Africa. What was at stake for Bonpland was not consoling rapport between Nature and the souls of "sensitive" men, but the inexhaustible and essential ways in which human well-being is dependent on complexities of plant chemistry.

And then there was *Cinchona*. Working from notes in his journals, using what he learned with Mutis and later in Paris, Bonpland did what he could to further Condamine's initiatives. With his field notes and his researches in Paris, he was able to describe four species of *Cinchona* with various degrees of confidence. First came Linnaeus's original *Cinchona officinalis*, renamed *C. condaminae*. Then *Cinchona ovalifolia*; under its local name *cascarilla* he had been told that it was not much valued by traders around Quito, who preferred the *quina jaune*, or yellow quina, named by Mutis *C. cordifolia*, and he was also told that for the past twenty years much had been cut and sold. He had good samples of both barks and described each in detail as to color, texture, thickness, dry and wet, taste when put on the tongue so that shipments could be better verified. Again came the caveat: plant species cannot be determined by bark alone, nor can the efficacy of the bark be determined by its "physiognomy." Not only might trees with similar bark be different species, but bark from young trees could differ widely in properties from bark of older trees of the same species. What was needed was consultation with local experts, bark gathered from known species and tested scientifically for medicinal properties. It was of little use to know that a particular bark was effective, unless one could determine the species and renew the supply. Of his description of *Cinchona scrobiculata* he was the surest. It was similar to *C. condaminae*, but different in important respects. He found it in the forests around Jaén. He had been able to observe it both in flower and in fruit. Known in the province as *quina fina*, the superior quina, its bark was locally the most valued and the most traded and the most valuable for medical use (PE I, 33, 65, 136).[2]

Meanwhile, back in Rome, Humboldt was becoming more and more impatient. In a letter to John Vaughan in Philadelphia, he apologized for being unable to fulfill his promise to send to the American Philosophical Society copies of any of the many publications he talked about during his visit to Philadelphia in 1804:

> Engraving is so slow that there is still only the first volume of my *Plantes équinoxiales* finished, and it has not yet been sent to me from Paris. I am waiting for it and the last print of my *Tableau physique des régions équatoriales* to send both to you and to your most respected president and to M. Barton. (LA, 188)

He reviewed for Vaughn his immediate plans. By September he would be "at rest" in Berlin—"The King has called me to an Academy that is a dilapidated hospital. Am I not killed with kindness!" His intention, he wrote, was to stay there only long enough to finish his publications, and then be off on a new voyage to Missouri, the Arctic Circle, and Asia. "It is necessary to profit from one's youth," he quipped, "and only in later life die a citizen of Fridonia." "Fridonia": in other words Berlin, land of frost.

Meanwhile in Rome, with the help of Wilhelm, Humboldt was taking back up that troublesome question of Incan engineering and Aztec art. In Wilhelm's drawing room he was introduced to artists who could be hired to turn his sketches of Andean scenes and Aztec monuments into engravings for his *Atlas pittoresque*. And Wilhelm, deep into his research in comparative linguistics, passed on to him material on Indian languages and arranged entry to the Vatican library, whose director once served as head of Jesuit missions in South America. In the library Humboldt was shown Aztec codices depicting histories, mythologies, cosmologies, social customs, complex legal disputes, lunar calendars, games, elaborate rituals of naming and feasting. How to present images like the "Aztec priestess" or the monolith shown him buried in the vault in Mexico City remained a puzzle. Humboldt knew better than to dismiss Spanish and missionary reports of the grandeur of South American institutions and edifices as invented or imagined, as did some European writers. And he knew from Wilhelm to reject the common claim that Indian languages had no words for large numbers and a limited vocabulary. Certainly he knew that Buffon's assertion that America was a young continent recently emerged from the sea and too swampy to support large animals and robust humans was not supported by any evidence. The quandary remained. What was to be made of cultures that could not be called "primitive" or "savage," but at the same time could not be placed on any accepted progression of human development from savage, to barbarian, and then on to "civilization?" If anything, the Americas seemed to reveal the very lack of such a history of "development." As he put it in the preface to his *Personal Narrative* of the voyage,

If America does not occupy an important place in the history of
mankind, and in the revolutions that have shattered the world, it
does offer a wide field for a naturalist. Nowhere does nature so
vividly suggest general ideas on the course of events, and their
mutual interrelationships. (PN, 12)

At the same time there was clearly more to America than "overpowering
vegetation" or "rock formations." He studied a copy of the *Codex Mendoza*,
prepared by Aztec scribes in 1541 for the first Spanish viceroy sent out to try
to institute more humane policies in the Spanish territories. But he could find
little to admire in the elaborate rituals depicted there of Aztec dynasties, industries, domestic life. He singled out the harshness of some of the punishments:
children pricked with a pin, penalty of death by strangulation given a governor
who rebelled against one of the kings. As he saw it, if there was affinity with
"civilization" it would have to be with some ancient Asian civilization. As he
put it in his preface, "One is surprised to find toward the end of the fifteenth
century in a world we call 'new' ancient institutions, religious ideas, forms of
edifices that would seem to go back in Asia to the first dawn of civilization"
(VC I, 8).[3] At the same time, Aztec and Incan art and monuments could not
be simply dismissed as "unworthy of attention."

Since the end of the last century, a happy revolution has come
in in the manner of envisaging the civilization of peoples and the
causes that halt or favor progress. We have come to know nations
of which the customs, institutions, and arts differ almost as much
from those of the Greeks and Romans as the primitive forms of
extinct animals differ from those species which are the object of
descriptive natural history . . . My researches on the native peoples
of America come at era when one does not regard as unworthy of
attention all that departs from that style of which the Greeks have
left us such inimitable models. (VC I, 11–12)

The problem remained. If Greek and Roman models are the basis for "civilization," what is to be said about an ancient American people, whose art and
institutions are completely different in "style" from anything Greek or Roman?
The question was debated with regard to the Egyptian art that Napoleon's
expedition brought back to Europe. Now what were "civilized" Europeans to
make of Incas and Aztecs whose way of life and cultural icons had even less
affinity with Greece and Rome than Egypt's? Where were they to be placed
on the scale of human development from savage hordes, to barbarian tribes, to

classical Greece and Rome, and on to civilized Europe? One thing was clear to Humboldt: If there were native American "civilizations" they were not civilized in the same sense as Europe was civilized.

> In using in the course of these researches the words "monuments of the new world," "progress in the arts of design," "intellectual culture," I do not mean to designate a state of things that indicates what one calls, a bit vaguely, a very advanced civilization. The Mexicans and Peruvians should not be judged after principles taken from the history of peoples that our scholarship recalls to us constantly. They are as far from the Greeks and the Romans as they are closer to the Etruscans and Tibetans. (VC I, 39–40)

Rejecting Buffon and de Pauw's dismissal of American cultures as primitive, Humboldt took a position similar to that of the American historian William Robertson, who in in his influential *History of America* described South American cultures as stalled somewhere between barbarism and civilization, unable to develop further due to a lack of metal and large animals, and to the "infancy" of their civil life. On the one hand, Robertson argued, pre-Columbian South American cultures appear to have had some of the factors associated with "civilization": private property, cities, division of labor, skilled crafts, social classes, taxes, and laws. On the other hand, they had no "fine" arts, they were always waging war, and their agriculture was not "productive" like European agriculture. In the end Humboldt dodged the issue. What was important, he emphasized, was to be clear on his reasons for bringing monuments of the Incas and Aztecs to the attention of the public. It was not that objects of Aztec art should be taken as models of beauty or goodness in the same way a statue of Apollo excites "admiration for the harmony and beauty of its form" and is a work of "artistic genius":

> Such is the privilege of that which has been produced under the sky of Asia Minor and part of southern Europe. On the contrary, the monuments of peoples who have not arrived at such a high degree of intellectual culture, or that—whether from religious or political causes, whether from the nature of their organizations— have appeared less sensitive to the beauty of forms can only be considered as historical monuments. (VC I, 44)[4]

If the art of ancient America was deficient in beauty, even worse, in Humboldt's view, was pre-Columbian American social life and politics:

Enchained by despotism and the barbarism of social institutions, without any liberty in the most trivial actions of domestic life, the entire nation was brought up in the sad uniformity of habitudes and superstitions. The same causes have produced the same effects in ancient Egypt, in India, China, Mexico, and Peru, everywhere men present only a mass animated by the same will, everywhere laws, religion, and usages run contrary to individual perfection and happiness. (VC I, 222–223)

In these "not very advanced" or "semi-civilized" nations, "theocratic" governments favored progress in industry and public works by way of a "civilisation en masse" that "impeded the development of individual faculties." The Incan government, said Humboldt, was like a giant monastic establishment. Each member of the congregation was told what to do for the public good, fostering "general ease but little private happiness." The result was "resignation to the decrees of the sovereign rather than love of country" and "passive obedience rather than courage for daring enterprise." "The spark of human liberty was stifled" (VC I, 41). It was a judgment Humboldt never revised. Sixteen years later he responded dismissively to a query from Wilhelm about the relations between Quechua language and Incan social structure.

Without doubt, the Incan government was kinder and ruled more by law than the despotism of the Mexican Sultanate, but these states that have only a civilization "en masse," where individuals are nothing, arrest without doubt the progress of the human species even more than the most bloody of despotisms. The worst is the stupidity of a convent, despotism at least sometimes forces a reaction. (LA, 296)

Even as he condemned de Pauw and Buffon for unfounded theorizing, Humboldt's explanation for the deficiency he saw in American arts and social structures was not far from many of their conclusions. Buffon and de Pauw might have been wrong to think the American continent had recently emerged from the sea, but they were right to think that culture was retarded in the Americas because America was separated from the civilizing influence of Europe, and because the "wild and agitated" state of nature in the Americas was a brake on progress just as it had been in Eastern Asia. It was to make this point, Humboldt told his readers, that he included scenes from nature in his *Atlas* along with pictures of carvings and pyramids, illustrating the crucial difference between "nature laughing or savage."

One thing Humboldt never doubted. Regardless of differences between the "savage" Indians of the Orinoco, the engineering Incas of the Andes, and the warlike Aztec of Mexico, native Americans shared the same physical and mental racial traits.

> The nations of America, with the exception of those living in the polar circle, form a single race characterized by the shape of the skull, the color of the skin, the extreme scarcity of beard and straight limp hair. The American race has rapports that are very visible with Mongoloid peoples. (VC I, 21)

American types might differ among themselves as did "Caucasian" Arabs, Slavs, and Persians, but in the Inca and Aztec Humboldt saw, or thought he saw, characteristics he also saw in "savages" of the Orinoco: "a mournful, somber aspect that contrasts with the arts and the sweet gentle fictions of the peoples of Greece" (VC I, 42). Again Humboldt settled on what he called "middle ground." He would not follow theorists who, on the basis of a few examples, argued that colonists from Egypt or China established colonies and were responsible for an art inferior but "not unworthy of notice." Nor would he follow others who presented facts without any proof. What he presented in his *Atlas*, he said, were "analogies," important "historically" in that they might eventually turn out to indicate contact between some Asian culture and the Americas.

As Humboldt puzzled over Aztec codices in the Vatican library, travel in Europe was becoming more and more difficult. Britain and Russia signed a treaty vowing to drive Napoleon out of the Netherlands. Switzerland, Austria, and Sweden joined in. In mid-July 1805 as Humboldt and Gay-Lussac rushed down from Rome to Naples to watch an eruption of Vesuvius, battle lines were drawn up. As they lingered in the warmth of Italy, Austria challenged Napoleon in Bavaria and was quickly defeated. Wilhelm wrote from Rome more and more insistent. Humboldt must return to Berlin. He must renew his allegiance to Prussia. In October as Humboldt and Gay-Lussac made their way back across the Alps to Berlin, Napoleon held court in Vienna. Humboldt wrote to Spener, a Berlin editor with whom he hoped to do business. His plan had been to come to Berlin by way of Vienna and Fribourg, which was now impossible due to the "war of the maharajas in Europe." Instead they would have to go by Heidelberg and Cassel, staying only a few days in Göttingen, if the Russians advancing on

Hanover with the British would allow even that (LA, 200). Arrived in Berlin in mid-November they found the city in crisis. The king, Frederick William, wavered, hoping to hold on to Prussian territory, vacillating between a faction that called for war and another that urged caution. No one could think that peace between Prussia and France could last much longer.

In Berlin, Humboldt was welcomed as a national hero. He was invited to court. He gave lectures at the Berlin Academy. None of it made him happy. Christmas Eve of 1805, he wrote to Georges Cuvier at the Muséum in Paris in despair. He was suffering from the cold. He had a painful skin condition. Again he quoted Pliny, this time from the elder Pliny's *Natural History*—Berlin was a *"pars mundi damnata a rerum natura,"* a part of the world damned by nature. He could count on Cuvier to remember Pliny's grim description of Nordic climates: "snow continually falling . . . plunged in dense darkness, and occupied only by the work of frost and the chilly lurking-places of the north wind."[5] Nor was the scientific climate in Berlin much better:

> But alas! My worthy and respectable friend, what can I say to you of the impression made by this literary world, this Academy, after having lived so long in Paris and near you? It is a passage from life to death. What a public, what a lack of interest, what sad and boring taciturnity! . . . There are only three men here who have any lively interest in the progress of human knowledge, Klaproth, Tralles, and Willdenow.[6]

Especially irritating to Humboldt was Prussian antipathy to anything French, which meant that "you don't dare to say outside what you are thinking inside." "Meanwhile," he quipped to Cuvier, "to console me, I have been made chamberlain" (LA, 201–202).

Chamberlain to the king, advisor, hand-holder, comforter, courtier with no real power: the post and its many responsibilities would now constrain Humboldt's movements and activities for the rest of his life, involving him in endless diplomatic, ceremonial, and social duties. There would be negotiations with the French, escorting crown princes, entertaining at court, reading the king to sleep at night, entertaining visiting dignitaries, and in 1814 welcoming a conquering Prussian army into Paris. Why did he accept? As he put it in his letter to Cuvier: "Would I not be ungrateful if I dared to complain personally? The King has showered me with kindness and marks of interest." No matter disclaimers, such a mark of royal interest was flattering, and much as he might protest that he was "too much honored," honor was something Humboldt found it hard to resist even as he chafed against it. He would not be deterred from his work, he told Curvier. Could Cuvier look over the descriptions for the *Observations on Zoology* and correct anything he found wrong before it went to print? Just go ahead and make changes, he told Cuvier, no need to consult. If there was something Cuvier needed to ask, he should communicate with Bonpland. And could he talk to Schöll, the Paris publisher, who was slowing up publication. "You know what interest it must have for him, for me, and also for the public, to hasten the publication of my works. . . . I cannot believe that, given the interest with which the public honors me, a bookseller could take risks with my work" (LA, 202).

At Christmas writing to Bonpland in Paris Humboldt was no more cheerful. He was in pain from rheumatism, sick from fever, and had a skin rash. Bonpland should continue to praise the Spanish botanists to ease difficulties there. Humboldt added a postscript that must have renewed Bonpland's concerns about the collections. He was working with Willdenow on their plants, said Humboldt, identifying new species. Specimens were lacking. Bonpland must send on Humboldt's share of the plants. Better still, bring them himself. It was Humboldt at his most seductive. He would make Bonpland happy. They would live and work together (HCH, 24–25). A little more than a week later a worried Humboldt wrote again in answer to a letter from Bonpland. Bonpland should not talk about leaving Europe, He should think about his reputation and about the great ensemble of publications that was to establish their fame. He was sure that Bonpland could not have forgotten him given all they had been to each other in so many years of travel. Yes, "a man cannot be held hostage to a book," but Bonpland must not think of leaving before their great work is finished. He had to come to Berlin, work with Willdenow, only then leave Europe if he must.

Plants were hardly the most pressing thing on Humboldt's mind. Meeting British diplomats in Berlin, he was beginning to see the importance of another of his projected publications, the expanded and further researched version of the political and economic report he prepared in Mexico City for the viceroy of New Spain and passed on to Jefferson in Washington. In January of 1806 he wrote to Pictet, at work in Geneva recruiting English translators and writing a preface for a London edition of what Humboldt now was calling his "Mexican statistics." It is going too slowly, Humboldt wrote; Pictet should get someone else to do the translating, leaving himself free to make corrections. And Pictet should just go ahead and use his own judgment about any notes to be added on pronunciation and spelling. He had great hopes for this publication, he told Pictet, now that he saw how his research on Mexican mining turned the heads of British diplomats in Berlin. Longmans in London asked him to consult some current works to be sure of his facts. Did they not realize he had read the books before they ever even heard of them? No French publisher would have treated him this way. Did they think he was a drapery maker out to pass off someone else's designs as his own? (LA, 206)

In one thing Humboldt was not mistaken. There was interest in England and in the United States in his *Political Essay on the Kingdom of New Spain* with its accompanying *Atlas* of maps and diagrams and its frontispiece celebrating the gods of industry and commerce. In Berlin, socializing with British diplomats, he began to see, as he described it to Pictet, that the interest shown by the British might be "very useful for the sale of my works" (LA, 205). More important, he now understood and was ready to deliver what was wanted: not "what imagination and science might produce" but rather tables of figures and balance sheets showing possible profits. And this he was ready to produce, all they could ever want and more. "I hope that every English soul will rejoice at so many piasters" (LA, 207). Given the statistics he could give them on mines, the exportation of silver, trade, and what the maps and land profiles would furnish, his book on Mexico would be a very "piquant" work. This would be no "general physics" or little travelers' tales. It would be "a work written with great precision, for the businessman and politician" (LA, 208). As such, timing was essential, especially given that the Spanish had a copy of his preliminary report and might publish before him. As a result, he was working very hard, "translating European style" with constant reference to commercially useful fact. And no, he would not agree with the English for 150 livres per volume. He would be ruined if he did. And still he has heard nothing from Schöll in Paris and cannot see why they are so slow.

Publicity was much on Humboldt's mind. He asked Pictet: Could Pictet write a biography of him for promotion, only not make it a eulogy, because "I am always so much honored that it irritates me." In it could Pictet try to correct the charge always made against him that he occupied himself with too many things at one time—"Can you reproach a man for having the desire to know and to embrace all that surrounds him?" Most important, he told Pictet, would be to emphasize the transcendent vision of his new "philosophical" science—"To have the general view, to conceive the liaison of all phenomena, that liaison we call Nature, it is necessary to first know the parts, and then reunite them together organically under a single point of view." But also important at the same time would be to take note of the variety of his sources—"I have lived with almost all the celebrated people of Europe, I have been enthused by their works and they have communicated to me their tastes" (LA, 209). As material for the biography, Humboldt sent to Pictet a self-written draft, "My Confessions," to use as if the information came from Pictet's own knowledge and research. In it Humboldt reviewed at length his early life and education, his memoirs on underground flora and galvanism, his meeting with Bonpland—"one of the great good fortunes of my life"—the success of his voyage, his return to Paris, the projected slate of publications from the voyage. At the end came a strange moment of self-revelation:

> Unquiet, agitated, never taking pleasure in anything I have accomplished, I am only happy when I am undertaking something new and when I am doing three things at once. It is in this spirit of moral inquietude, result of a nomadic life, that one must look for the principle causes of the grand imperfections of my [character]. I would be more useful for the things and the deeds I have inspired, for the ideas I have given birth to in others, than for the works I published myself, Meanwhile I have not been lacking in good and great will or an appetite for work. In the hottest climates of the earth, I have drawn often 15 or 16 hours at a stretch. My health has not suffered and I am preparing for a trip to Asia after publishing the results of my voyage to America.

Immediately, what might be read as critical self-reflection and a plea for understanding and sympathy dissolved into a mix of bravado and ironic self-ridicule.

> Do you want to follow my life at this moment? Then you might add that I have traversed all of Italy, that I have had the pleasure of seeing in fifteen months the cities of Mexico City, Philadelphia, Paris, and Rome, that Vesuvius has offered up to us its festival. But do not say this: returned to my country, I was made . . . Chamberlain!

In the margin Humboldt added one of his many afterthoughts: "But say at the end something nice about the King, who, in truth, has honored me much" (LA, 243).

By the spring of 1806, opinion in Prussia turned sharply against France and Frenchmen. Gay-Lussac's leave from the École Polytechnique was canceled and he went back to Paris. Always grateful and generous with intimate friends,

Humboldt wrote to Cuvier, now secretary of the Institut de France. Could he see that Gay-Lussac was elected to the open post of physics at the Institut? He praised Gay-Lussac's abilities and "how well he directed me in my atmospheric observations." He himself was working hard on his *Mexican Atlas*, he told Cuvier, and an architect in Berlin, Friedrich Friesen, was drawing up maps and land mass outlines.

In March, Humboldt wrote to Bonpland acknowledging the arrival of a case of plants from Paris, again urging Bonpland to come to Berlin. He and Willdenow were making "abbreviated descriptions" of all the plants, he wrote. If Bonpland would come in the fall and work with them, they could travel back to Paris together. He now could see, he wrote, that botanical work was not that difficult. Separating out and describing new species did not need to take much time. What was important was not to get upset, to make things agreeable. Yes, one should not be a slave to a book, but still, he reminded Bonpland, there were things he needed to do in Paris: money problems with the publisher Schöll, who was having financial difficulties, costs, delays, perhaps finding a new publisher. But when he got to Berlin Bonpland would see how much easier Willdenow made the work. Willdenow had looked at all the plants, seen how many of them were new: out of 40 as many as 25 might be new (HCH, 32). Then abruptly it was back to Schöll and a long list of questions Bonpland was to raise with them and resolve, but resolve discreetly, without letting the public know there was any problem with publishing. And it was back again to plants needed in Berlin and the method by which they should be sent. Bonpland must let him know when the next case leaves for Berlin. And again that sore spot of Cavanilles. Willdenow, said Humboldt, had confirmed it. Cavanilles made mistakes in his description of *Bonplandia*. Bonpland had the better plant. He and Willdenow had also named other plants for later installments of *Plantes équinoxiales*. He hoped that Bonpland would not be angry: "You know that all is common between us" (HCH, 33).

Not surprisingly, by the beginning of April Humboldt was responding to what must have been letters of protest from Bonpland in Paris:

> Calm yourself about the *Bonplandia*. There is not a Prince of Botany that has a more respectable genus. And I wager it is not a *Quassia*. With this you will have the air of correcting the genus of a celebrated botanist and the fault falls on him. Cavanilles's *Bonplandia* has flowered here. It is a new genus that we want to call *Caldesia grintlorn*. Abandon to Caldes this cursed little plant and believe me, your plant has better credentials. (HCH, 35)

Again he urged Bonpland: Come to Berlin to work with Willdenow.

How these onslaughts of mingled affection, longing, recrimination, and instruction were received by Bonpland in Paris we know only from Humboldt's responses. Certainly Bonpland was in no way eager to come to Berlin. He was working with his own journals made in the field and fresh memories of living plants. He had immediate access to the rich collections of the Jussieus, Desfontaines, Lamarck, and others at the Muséum. Also troubling would have been the form that botanical work seemed to be taking in Berlin: a list in Latin of supposed new species discovered on their voyage with abbreviated descriptions. But beside all this there was the fact of Humboldt's unhappiness, and the letters of entreaty that continued to arrive from Berlin, alternately affectionate, manic, scattered, demanding. In May of 1806:

> I am returning from a long herborizing with M. Willdenow and
> I am so weary I will not be with you for long: but long enough
> to repeat to you without ceasing how much your letters give me
> pleasure, how much my soul is occupied with you day and night.
> Yes, my good friend, it is no small thing to have passed seven
> years together, to have had together an ensemble of great joys and
> braved great dangers. It is a consolation to me to know you are
> in Paris, because day to day I know more what it is to not be in
> Paris, when at the same time one is condemned to live in this
> wretched Europe. (HCH, 35)

Always there was talk of money, how much might be made from the Mexican statistics, and always the same plea. Bonpland must come and stay in Berlin for three or four months. Willdenow was "at least as amiable as Desfontaines." He has a herbarium of 15,000 to 16,000 plants all classified, knows more species than anyone else, Bonpland can spend all day with him. Yes, Willdenow made mistakes, but no one has worked on more species. But then came a passage guaranteed to have an effect on Bonpland very different than the one Humboldt intended:

> I begin to see (what I used to often doubt) that short descriptions
> of all our species can be achieved in six months. It requires only,
> dear Bonpland, that you send to us soon the rest of my share of
> the herbarium. Have it leave as soon as possible. I am preparing
> everything here with Willdenow. . . . In our collections for every
> 295 plants collected, there are 195 new as you can see from the

enclosed papers that I ask you to conserve carefully. It is certain that we have 2,000 new species. (HCH, 37)

Humboldt went on to spell out the method they would use. They would separate out their plants from those in Willdenow's collections. To each specimen they would attach a three- or four-word "diagnostic phrase." With the addition of eight ten lines more for each specimen, they would soon have several volumes of new species that "will contribute more to our glory." "The truth will be saved for science and we would have shown what we have done" (HCH, 38). Bonpland would come to Berlin. They would work together. Bonpland would finish the drawings there, and they would go back to Paris, together perhaps with Willdenow. In the meantime Bonpland should finish the last three installments of *Plantes éqinoxiales* and the beginning installments of the *Melastomacées*. At the end came an attempt to lighten the tone: Would he have to go and bring Bonpland back to Berlin himself? But of course that was impossible:

> I fear that I could not leave from here so soon. I cannot remain alone here. Since Gay-Lussac left, this country is a hell for me. (HCH, 39)

And it was back to money, bits and pieces of publishing business, lighthearted banter, regards sent to Cuvier and Desfontaines.

In June came renewed and sharper pleading from Humboldt for plants to be sent so work on the list of new species could continue. He, Humboldt, would pay the shipping if necessary. He deserves better than this delay. He asks only for doubles. His patience is fraying. When exactly will the rest of *Plantes équinoxiales* and the *Melastomacées* volumes be published? In August came more complaints, No letters were arriving from Bonpland. Why does he not write? By September, Humboldt was conciliatory. He will accept less, maybe three volumes of *Plantes* and one of *Melastomacées*. He too is anxious to leave Europe. If Bonpland comes to Berlin that winter they can finish all the botany works, *Plantes*, *Melastomacées*, *New Genera*, and be gone. Bonpland must 1) bring all the promised plant doubles to Berlin, 2) bring all his manuscripts and journals, and 3) bring all the plants of which he has only one copy to use and take back with him when he leaves. Meanwhile he must finish all installments of the other publications. Yes, the war in Europe was making travel difficult, but the fighting may soon die down.

For a time no letters at all arrived in Berlin from Bonpland in Paris. Perhaps they were written and lost, given the fighting; perhaps they were not

written at all. When a letter finally arrived along with some completed installments, Humboldt was ecstatic.

> We are, dear and tender friend, like people who lose each other
> from view and then find each other again. I must begin by saying
> that I love you so tenderly and so much, if you did not write for
> four years, it would be inconceivable for me to complain about
> you with any bitterness. (HCH, 46)

It was September 14, his birthday, said Humboldt; he was feeling sentimen-
tal. He was sending money, enough to pay for dinners out for Bonpland and
friends. He and Willdenow were happy with the three installments of *Plantes*
and the first volume of *Melastomacées* that they had received. All very correct.
The melastomes superb. In a letter to Bonpland a month later at the beginning
of October, business details proliferated along with an additional request: The
new installments were admirable, but in the published text could Bonpland put
notes in a few places saying that Humboldt did the drawing for the engraving
in the field—"such a remark will cost you little" (HCH, 50).

Meanwhile hostilities in Europe showed no sign of abating. In August
Frederick William rashly joined an alliance with Russia against France. If he
had joined with Britain and Russia the year before, such an alliance might have
had a chance. With only defeated Russia as ally, the Prussian military was no
match for Napoleon's army. It was no time for travel. Bonpland would have
to stay in Paris. On October 14, Napoleon defeated the Prussian army at Jena
and destroyed what was left of it at Auerstedt. On October 27, 1806, Napoleon and his army marched triumphantly into Berlin. In the depth of despair
Humboldt wrote to Gérard in Paris. Since he left Italy, since Gay-Lussac left
Berlin, he is living in a "moral desert." The "erasure of Prussia's independence"
makes him wish he was back in the forests of the Orinoco. After ten years
of happiness, he has now been made to share the "miseries of my country."
He will get on with his work, but he does not work well alone. "I feel each
and every day that one only works well there where others around you are
working better" (LA, 217).

For consolation that winter Humboldt found a new collaborator, Jabbo
Oltmanns, an obliging and talented young mathematician and astronomer who
agreed to help him with his observations. Humboldt praised him in a letter to
von Zach, director of the Observatory in Genoa. Oltmanns was an "astonishing
young man," he told Zach, modest and with great powers of perseverance,
and even better, with a faculty for pure mathematics. Oltmanns was helping

him not only with observations but with the mathematical equations that made scientific sense of those observations. Leaving plants to Willdenow and the streets to the French, throughout the long, cold, and humiliating winter of 1806–1807 under French occupation, Humboldt and Oltmanns worked through the night in a rigged-up observatory, watching the stars and making readings for Humboldt's *Observations on Astronomy*. They looked for variations in geomagnetism, watched the needle move depending on latitude and over time, and then also in sudden extreme variations that Humboldt found both exciting and mysterious. The observations, arranged and interpreted by Oltmanns along with some measurements made by Humboldt in his travels would be ready for publication once he returned to Paris: *Recueil d'observations astronomiques, d'opérations trigonométriques et de mesures barométriques* (1808), with Humboldt listed as author, but "edited and calculated by Jabbo Oltmanns."

For additional consolation that winter, Humboldt turned to the writing of a popular work, *Aspects of Nature*, written this time not in French but in German.[7] Combining a Schiller-like aesthetics of the sublime and a Goethian passion for nature with touches of spiritualism from the "Rhodian genius," Humboldt offered to demoralized and humiliated Prussians a way to ease the misery of their present situation. As he put it in his Preface,

> To minds oppressed with the cares or the sorrows of life, the soothing influence of the contemplation of Nature is particularly precious; and to such these pages are more especially dedicated. May they, "escaping from the stormy waves of life," follow me in spirit with willing steps to the recesses of the primeval forest, over the boundless surface of the steppes, and to the highest ridges of the Andes. (AN, vi)

In *Aspects of Nature* Humboldt took his readers on a virtual tour, away from "civilized" coastlines with their commercial cities and cultivated fields into "savage" wilderness. The opening chapter, "Steppes and Deserts," transported them to inland rivers where the primitive Guarani "live in the trees like apes" and depend on one species of palm tree for all their physical needs:

> Thus in the lowest stage of man's intellectual development, we find the existence of an entire people bound up with that of a single

tree; like the insect which lives exclusively on a single part of a particular flower. (AN, 36)

He took them to where "massive leaden-coloured granite rocks narrow the bed of the foaming rivers. Mountains and forests resound with he thunder of the falling waters, with the roar of the tiger-like jaguar, and with the melancholy rain-announcing howlings of the bearded apes" (AN, 41). He showed them tribes of men, some "nomadic, wholly unacquainted with agriculture, and using ants, gums, and earth as food." He showed them man, ever armed against man, "drink with unnatural thirst the blood of their enemies; others apparently weaponless and yet prepared for murder kill with a poisoned thumb-nail" (AN, 41). He took them higher up, to view the great patterns of nature, the physiognomy of vegetation, zones of color and texture etched on the side of Chimborazo, and higher still to celestial orbs moving in undisturbed harmony. Not only did he offer "mental enjoyment of the highest order'" but also insight into the "history of man and his civilization." He showed how climate affects vegetation, and how national character and the grave or gay dispositions of men depend on climatic influences. If Indians were "gloomy" and Asians "despotic," readers could see how a small region between the Euphrates and the Aegean had been able to attain a very different "amenity of manners and delicacy of sentiment." He would allow those not so blessed by climate, those who did not inherit the learning of Greece and Rome, those who lived in northern snow and ice, to read works like his, look at paintings inspired by such works, and in thought achieve something of the manners and the sentiment of more favored lands.

Certainly in Berlin that winter escape was welcome. French officers rode arrogantly through the streets. Food was scarce. Humiliating deference was required when dealing with French officials. By spring of 1807 what little was left of the Prussian army had faded away. At Tilsit, Napoleon imposed harsh terms on Prussia and moved his army on, leaving an occupying force in charge in Berlin. Humboldt renewed his pleas to Bonpland. He was miserable, he wrote the day after Christmas 1806. His country was in ruins.

Come, come, dear Bonpland, as soon as you can. Stay until spring with me, in a little garden two steps from M. Willdenow. I will return you to France. You will live with me. You will make a great work of 7,000 species. Here you will succeed in making yourself a great botanist. M. Willdenow has one of the greatest herbaria in the world. You will see what he has made of the diagnosis of your plants in the last volume. He has already prepared more than

800 of our new species that I have named with him and which
I will give you in catalog form. I don't doubt you will retouch
certain species. No great harm. You can discuss it at your leisure.
But think! 800 new species only among the plants we have here
at Berlin. (HCH, 50–51)

And on and on with more instructions. A check due from Berthollet would
help pay for the trip. He should bring with him all that he needs to finish the
manuscripts for Schöll. And bring the plant doubles promised to M. Willdenow.

With the war over at least for the moment, Bonpland no longer had
an excuse for delay. Reluctantly he packed up his collections and headed east,
stopped at roadblocks so his papers could be checked and his crates of plants
opened and examined for contraband. In Berlin the old intimacy of travel was
gone. He found Humboldt short of money, constantly called on to mediate
between the court and French officials, writing so obsessively by day that his
rheumatic right arm was partially paralyzed, staying up all night recording
variations in earth magnetism with Oltmanns. Bonpland was left with Willdenow. For five weeks they worked together, but Berlin was hardly welcoming to
visiting Frenchmen. Regardless of the efforts of a few of Humboldt's friends,
the intellectual community gave Bonpland a chilly reception. A lecture at the
Society of Friends of Nature was coldly received. The rooms where he and
Willdenow worked were poorly heated. Willdenow had lent out bits and pieces
of Humboldt's herbarium to other botanists, resulting in more confusion in
naming. Alien plants were mixed in with the herbarium from the voyage.
Plants were missing. Nor did abbreviated descriptions and a catalog of hastily
named new species and genera hold much appeal for Bonpland. The plan was
to stay until spring and return with Humboldt to Paris. When an opportunity
for escape materialized, Bonpland took it. A French official stationed in Berlin
was traveling back to Paris with dispatches. Could Bonpland travel with him?
The answer was yes. Working through two long days and nights, Bonpland
packed up his 10,000 plants in nine cases, left some plants and manuscripts
for Willdenow, and took his collections back to Paris. Arriving exhausted at his
Paris apartment at the beginning of November 1807 after nine days and nights
on the road with no rest stops, Bonpland wrote a quick note to his father:

I am going to jump into a delicious bath, where I will rub myself
down vigorously, I will eat a good meal because I hardly ate all the
long trip, go to bed and hope to recover from the nine nights I just
passed. . . . I embrace you with all my heart, your son. (AB, 18)

10

Botany on Demand

Two months later, in January of 1808, Humboldt was allowed to return to Paris. As a result of the peace treaty signed at Tilsit, Prussia had lost half the territory it controlled, including a large portion of Poland. In addition Napoleon had imposed a crushing debt of war reparations. When King Frederick William sent his brother Prince Wilhelm to Paris to try to negotiate better terms, who better to go with him than Humboldt, the chamberlain with so many friends in Paris? Once back in Paris, Humboldt fulfilled his royal duties, going with the prince each day to the Tuileries for meetings with French officials, escorting him to the theater in the evening, and introducing him in fashionable salons. Mornings and nights he was back with Gay-Lussac, poor, but happy. He wrote a note to Pictet in Geneva:

> I pass my days at the École Polytechnique and Tuileries. I work at the École, I sleep there, I am there every night and every morning. I live in the same room as Gay-Lussac. This is my best friend whose conversation everyday makes me better and more active. We stimulate each other reciprocally. I see that after having lost everything, I can still be independent on forty sous a day. (LA, 248–249)

With income from family estates diminished due to Prussia's loss of territory in Poland, money was much on Humboldt's mind, including profit from his publications. The most likely source for that profit was the "Mexican statistics," and Pictet in Geneva with his many contacts in London and New York was a valuable ally in mapping out a strategy. A few days later, Humboldt wrote to Pictet again, this time getting back to business—"I present myself to you as humble writer"—and enclosing installments of the *Political Essay*. Could Pictet check over the sections on customs, volcanoes, the look of the country, and also sections on "savages?" And he was also sending on installments of the

175

Astronomy—"Never has such a great number of observations been calculated with more intelligence and after such a uniform method. It is the merit of M. Oltmanns" (LA, 249).

Two months later Humboldt wrote to Pictet to say that the first installments of his "statistics" were at the printers. In addition Schöll was publishing abridged volumes of *Tableaux de la nature*, a French translation of *Aspects of Nature*—"It looks like it will make a fortune." But he would have to ask M. Bonpland for the bumblebees that Pictet requested—"The insects he collected are his alone." Along with the flurry of publishing, happiness at being back in Paris seemed to all but take Humboldt's breath away:

> I live always between the soda and the potassium hydroxide, between
> Thénard and Gay-Lussac. Also the ammoniacal M. Berthollet visits
> us sometimes; we believe ourselves all hydrogenated. (LA, 252)

In the end, Napoleon remained unmoved by the Prince's entreaties. Prussia would have to pay for its defiance or more of its territory would be taken. In the autumn of 1808, when the prince was called home with nothing accomplished, Humboldt begged the king for permission to stay on. How else could he finish his great work, work that would bring renown to Prussia? The king demanded terms. Humboldt was not to forget he was Prussian. He was to be on call to promote Prussian interests in Paris and elsewhere. He had to return periodically to Berlin. Humboldt agreed to it all and settled down for the winter. He was watched by Napoleon's secret police. His correspondence was intercepted. When he went away for a few days his apartment was searched. His letters were opened and mined for useful bits of incriminating information. Neither gifts nor carefully worded compliments would ever ingratiate him with Napoleon, who continued at best indifferent and at worst hostile to any overture. None of it mattered, given his happiness to be back in Paris and given the growing interest in his *Political Essay* both in Britain and in the United States.

As soon as the first installment was printed, Humboldt sent off a copy to Jefferson in Washington. Getting no response and fearing it had not arrived, he sent another, this time managing at some cost to the courier to get it into the diplomatic pouch. For good measure he attached a flattering note. Jefferson, he wrote, would find his name cited in the text "with that enthusiasm it has always inspired with friends of humanity" (May 30, 1808).[1] When a note of thanks and acknowledgment arrived from Jefferson, Humboldt was even more effusive, sending on two more installments of the *Political Essay* and three of his *Astronomy* and begging Jefferson to "accept these trifles with indulgence." He also added an apology. He was sorry to have said the things he did about slavery in the United States in the first installment. Now that he understands that the United States Congress is taking steps toward slavery's abolition, he regrets them. He had been carried away, perhaps not so reprehensible given the subject. In new installments, he assured Jefferson, he had revised what he said about slavery in both a note and a supplement. Two years later a fifth installment of the *Political Essay* crossed the Atlantic addressed to Jefferson "as a feeble mark of my profound and respectful veneration"and again with compliments. He, Humboldt, had to write under adverse circumstances due to surveillance from secret police, whereas Jefferson could write "surrounded by citizens who are hard-working, enterprising, and worthy of the liberty that you have conquered and preserved for them" (September 23, 1810).

Humboldt was right to tread carefully around the subject of slavery. Jefferson himself owned slaves, and was ambivalent on many issues surrounding its abolition.[2] With abolition gaining momentum in the North and southern slave owners looking to migrate into parts of New Spain, Humboldt's "statistics" and maps might help to show the way and so ease some of the tension. As for the British, they had other interests. There was great economic potential in the large sweep of territory that was New Spain. The soil was fertile and could support a working population. The climate was varied. Rich mineral deposits were located in temperate areas more accessible than the remote mines of Peru. In his *Essay* Humboldt was precise. With the use of modern mining techniques, Mexican output of precious metals could increase threefold.[3] Spain's hold on her colonial empire was weakening. Napoleon had forced the Spanish sovereign to whom Humboldt dedicated the *Political Essay* to abdicate. French armies occupied a large part of Spain. Independence movements were strengthening in Spanish colonies, making the prospect of profitable investment in an independent Mexico more and more enticing. The *Atlas* that accompanied Humboldt's *Essay* with its frontispiece picturing the gods of commerce and industry mapped the terrain on which roads could be built, mines dug, and land cleared for plantations.

In his "Geographical Introduction" to the *Atlas* Humboldt directed readers' attention not only to profits to be made by individuals and firms, but to larger global commercial currents analogous to those mapped by his meteorological and astronomical observations. He wrote to Conrad Malte-Brun, a Danish geographer working in Paris. Could Malte-Brun send him a map of Russia?

He was working, he said, on a "great map," not just of a country or region, but of the flow of precious metals and money around the globe from the Americas to Europe and Asia. For this he needed numbers, exportations from Russia to China, from Europe to Asia, Egypt, Asia Minor, India, China, so as to plot what he called the "voyages of silver."[4] The quantity of gold and silver now coming from the New World was more than nine-tenths the total world output of precious metals, and his *Essay* presented data on that output more precise than anything in the writings of Adam Smith, Robertson, or Raynal. In addition, he included calculations of the accumulation of precious metals in South and South East Asia. It all began, wrote Humboldt, with a vision he had and a little map he drew at sea in 1804 on his way back from Philadelphia to France. Unlike the east-to-west flow of "global currents of ocean, atmosphere and of the civilization of our species," the flow of precious metals goes the other way, from west to east. If civilization moved west—from Greece and Rome, to Europe, and finally to the Americas—precious metals moved back the other way from the Americas to Europe, where they were accumulating for the most part in Northern Europe.[5] For the British this was welcome news.

When renewed insurgency challenged Spanish Royalists in Mexico, Humboldt sent Jefferson additional information on the region, showing no sign of disagreeing with questions addressed to him by Jefferson: Could Mexicans govern themselves? Could they ever rise above bigotry, the shackles of the priesthood, rank and wealth? Could they ever have a true Republic with majority rule and free enterprise? If Jefferson contemplated the annexation of Texas, if British bankers were looking for quick profits, Humboldt did not see the use of his "statistics" for these purposes any of his concern. What motivated him, as he explained at length in the introduction to his *Atlas*, what guided him in all that had to do with his voyage to the New World, was simply "the desire of exactitude and the love of truth." What was done with that exactitude and that truth was another matter. When Mexico achieved its independence and excerpts from Humboldt's *Political Essay* and copies of his maps were used to entice British investors into what became known as the "Mexican Silver Bubble," Humboldt disclaimed responsibility. Asked to be on the board of directors, he declined, citing his "disinclination for public affairs." Years later, when John Stephens, the discoverer of the Mayan ruins, visited Humboldt in his lodgings at the king's palace at Sans Souci, he found Humboldt with the king and the king's military council, poring over Humboldt's maps of New Spain, admiring the campaigns of Zachary Taylor defending the new slave-owning state of Texas.[6]

Sales increased along with Humboldt's confidence. A letter to Pictet in December of 1810 was triumphant:

I am becoming a famous man and daily sense that few others have gotten there with so little cost. I have been doing singularly well these last two months and I have taken a great crack at my work, I say crack because in these things it is a question more of the arm than the head. My work on Mexico is toward the end. You remember the English bookseller that did not want my astronomy because it would be no more than some reheated "Mexican-guide," he is ecstatic over the Mexican statistics, which he regards as the philosopher's stone. Ah indeed! In these last folders, his eyes will be ravished by so many numbers, and all about silver. (LA, 259)

The *Political Essay*, with its frontispiece image was, just as he hoped, a money-maker, going through several English editions as well as editions in Spanish and French. Even better were sales of abridged versions and excerpts in pamphlet form.

At first, given Humboldt's happiness to be back in Paris, his renewed intimacy with Gay-Lussac, and excitement over the "Mexican statistics," few demands were made on Bonpland, who continued to work at his own pace writing commentaries for the second volume of *Plantes équinoxiales*. If the opening plate in the first volume had been the wax palm, also interesting was the plant Bonpland choose as frontispiece for the second, a new genus he called *Culcitium*, the "bedding plant." In *Plantes équinoxiales* he described two species, one found on the slopes of Pichincha near Quito and another on several Peruvian mountains, including Hualgayoc, famous for its silver mines. Here was a different kind of treasure, not precious metal, but a plant, not only striking-looking for its whiteness, but prized for its ability to save the lives and limbs of travelers stranded at high altitudes. All parts of the plant were covered with a fluffy down, and from that down it was possible to make a warm bed. In his commentary, Bonpland explained the process at some length. Leaves and stems were cut and pressed down flat, then came a layer of the downy substance that covers all parts of the leaves, and then another layer of each made a soft enveloping mattress. "The traveler with the help of this bed can rest from his fatigues, and is exempt from the fear of waking up with frozen feet" (PE II, 3).

Along with lengthy botanical descriptions, Bonpland's commentaries cited endless such uses of plant products. *Espeletia grandiflora*, gathered around

Santa Fe with its large yellow daisy-like flowers, not only was beautiful but exuded a resin used by local printers as an additive to ink making it more permanent. *Myristica otaba* was the source of a healing salve. *Mikania guaco*, to which he was introduced by the "celebrated Mutis," had medical properties unacknowledged by European botanists, although it was cited many times by Spanish botanists as a superior remedy for venomous snake bites both ingested and as a poultice. He watched the low shrub *Menodora helianthemoides* eaten eagerly by sheep, mules, and cattle on the high plains; it might be useful as a perennial forage plant that would not deplete grasslands and prairies. *Andromachia igniaria* he named after Nero's physician Andromachus; its widespread use as a styptic had been taught to the Spanish by Peruvian natives. Another South American product, ipecacuanha, was widely marketed in Europe as an emetic. Bonpland found, identified, and described the plant from which it came, but raised questions about its reputed medical value. And then there were the South American oaks. In volume 2 of *Plantes*, Bonpland identified and described twenty-five new species, many of which might be naturalized in France for shade, beauty, and food for wildlife.

But even with a second volume of *Plantes 'équinoxiales* under way, as excitement over the "Mexican statistics" abated, Humboldt began to complain again about slow progress on the botanical publications. He knew better than to accuse Bonpland of sloth. Here was a man who for five years had been a tireless companion in difficult situations. Courageous, learned, zealous in pursuit of rare plants, blessed with equanimity in danger and good cheer in hardship, no one could have been a more diligent worker. Too many times he watched Bonpland probe with the utmost of care into leaf mold, pull out gently from the debris a tiny bloom, lay it on the palm of his hand like a fragile jewel while with the other he reached into his pocket for drying paper, gently lay the paper on a board, place a small-petaled flower in the middle, and fold over it tenderly so damp jungle air would not mar a perfect remnant of living form. But could he not hurry up? Sixty thousand individual specimens gathered in the midst of discomfort, biting insects, fevers, the danger, endless sleepless nights lying in a damp hammock listening to the howls of jaguars and monkeys, and still only one volume was completely finished. Botanical publication might not be a money-maker like Mexican statistics, but it was needed to give scientific credence and prestige to his other works. Plants they discovered might be published by others, and he who publishes first gets the credit. Travelers returned home to fame; years, months, even weeks later they were forgotten in the wake of other travelers returning from exotic locations. They had been back now for five years. The romance of their explorations in the interior of South America was fading. Rivals were on the scene. Certainly he, Humboldt, had done his part, and he had given Bonpland due credit for past and future contributions, as in the preface he wrote for *Plantes équinoxiales*:

> Although *Plantes équinoxiales*, like all the works from my expedition, bears both the name of M. Bonpland and my own, it does not necessarily mean that we had an equal part in that work. M. Bonpland has not only written it himself from our manuscripts, but to him also is due the greatest part of the botanical work. United by ties of most tender attachment, we have shared all the sufferings and the dangers of this undertaking. We have herbalized together for more than six years. The plants were collected by both of us, and in spite of my astrological work and geological researches, I did a great number of drawings in place, but hardly a ninth of the plants were described by me. It is M. Bonpland who with the greatest of devotion, in the midst of the fatigues of a painful travel and often at the expense of his sleep, has prepared and dried himself alone near to sixty thousand specimens of plants. . . . If some day my enterprise is looked on as interesting for the progress of botany, that success must almost entirely be attributed to the active zeal of M. Bonpland. (PE I, vii)

As Humboldt saw it, he kept his word, affixing Bonpland's name even to his own *Personal Narrative* of their voyage. It was their agreement. All the works that came from the expedition would appear under both their names. And the financial proceeds, such as they were, would be shared, with Humboldt acknowledging that Bonpland had been essential to discoveries that supported and gave credence to his popular works. And there was another consideration. Given the hostile relations between France and Prussia, given Napoleon's total rebuff of Humboldt's request for funding for a new expedition, it was useful, perhaps even necessary, to have a French citizen as coauthor.

Neither sloth nor incompetence was keeping Bonpland from turning out botanical copy. For him the aim of their expedition had never been publication, but rather plants, many of which were now alive and growing in Empress Josephine's gardens and greenhouses. As he worked on installments for the second volume of *Plantes*, more and more he was out at Malmaison, giving advice and overseeing cultivation. Josephine's popularity and charm had brought plants to Malmaison from all the world. Even the British refused to look on her as an enemy. When a French ship was captured at sea, botanical shipments for Malmaison were taken back to England, readdressed, and sent on to Paris. Josephine's standing order with the premier nursery in England, Lee and Kennedy, was honored even during war years, with plants arriving by special arrangement. Seeds and plants found their way to Malmaison from the Canary Islands, from India, China, and Japan, from the eastern seaboard of North America, from French Guyana and Suriname, from the Cape of Good Hope and South Africa. Much of what survived from Nicolas Baudin's expedition to Australia and the Pacific found a home at Malmaison, which under Josephine's proprietorship was now a research facility for the study of new plants, a model farm, a working laboratory for plant cultivation, an atelier for floral art, and, with Bonpland's active involvement, a proving ground for naturalization and distribution.

There is no sign that Humboldt resisted Bonpland's involvement at Malmaison. In publishing, contacts and sponsors in high places were an asset. Nor had he raised any objection when Malmaison's official botanist, Ventenat, died in the summer of 1808 and Josephine named Bonpland as his replacement. A coauthor with a royal insignia had to be an asset. Even the more important appointment Bonpland announced to his family at the end of 1808 might have seemed to Humboldt an honor more ceremonial than time-consuming, although Bonpland's letter to his family announcing the appointment suggested considerably more in the way of commitment:

> I have, it is true, been named by the Empress as her botanist and charged with the job of describing the plants of Malmaison, as M. Ventenat did before his death. However, to this title—of little profit but much honor—has now been joined to another, no less honorable but with the advantage of greater profit: Her majesty the Empress has given me, after a very short time, a great mark of her confidence. She has named me intendant of her domain at Malmaison and adjoining properties. (AB, 21)[7]

It had been a painful year for the Empress. Napoleon might consider himself master of Europe, but in Paris there was hostile grumbling. Would war with all its death and suffering never end? Was there to be an eternal parade of maimed and wounded veterans returning home, and an eternal conscription of ever younger and now older men? Would there be no one left to tend the fields? No farmers to provide food for the cities? Were the victories announced really that decisive? Were Napoleon's attempts at royal protocol more ridiculous than impressive? The national legislature met for only a few weeks that year. The Council sat silently listening to the emperor orate. Police spies were everywhere looking for signs of treason. Rumors and jokes made the rounds. The Emperor had no heir. Could the master of Europe be impotent? If he died in battle, who would rule after him? Napoleon's advisors became increasingly adamant. He had to have an heir, and if Josephine, who had two children from her previous marriage, was no longer able to provide one, he must divorce her and arrange marriage with a fertile royal princess. Meanwhile Napoleon was making Josephine's life miserable, one moment clutching her to him, another pushing her away. More and more out at Malmaison, checking on his seedlings and cuttings, Bonpland encountered a subdued and sometimes tearful Josephine, wandering among her flowers, wrapped in a voluminous Indian shawl, brightening at the prospect of talking about plants. Unlike the reserved and aristocratic Ventenat, Bonpland was ready with comradely instruction. Friends and dignitaries arriving to tour the garden and greenhouses began to comment on Josephine's newly acquired knowledge of botanical Latin.

Meanwhile, Napoleon vacillated, torturing Josephine with contempt and abuse one moment only to storm into her bedroom and embrace her the next. A brief moment of reconciliation came in Spain when he summoned Josephine to come and help him lure the Spanish royal family into abdication, but even in Spain French power was fraying. There were desertions and insubordination in the army. The Austrians were rearming. Josephine was seldom at Malmaison the summer and fall of 1808 as she weathered the changing moods of the Emperor at Fontainebleau and St. Cloud. When Ventenat died, it had been just one more misery. For a long time there had been no effective oversight of gardens and greenhouses at Malmaison, as director after director was dismissed when Napoleon flew into a rage at expenditures made on plants and gardens. Taking on the job of director in January of 1809 would be no easy task as Bonpland fended off attempts by Napoleon to fire him, restrained ineptitude and corruption in the staff, traveled to Vienna, Schönbrunn, and Geneva to pick up plants, inspected flocks of Merino sheep, and thinned overgrown woodlots. Many of the plants received from correspondents and travelers abroad languished in greenhouse storerooms. Many planted under glass never bloomed. Others simply disappeared. Seeds rotted in unlabeled jars. Plants died before they could be repotted or were sold off by gardeners under the table. To find the parentage of a "pretty" *Sida pulchella* with strongly scented flowers planted from unidentified seeds, Bonpland solicited advice from nurserymen friends, and could only guess that the seeds had probably come from Australia via Baudin. The seeds of *Chorizema ilicifolium*, with glossy holly-like leaves, lay dormant until Bonpland planted them in the greenhouse in 1811, adding a useful foliage plant to Josephine's collection. *Melaleuca chlorantha*, a Baudin offering with honey-like sap, did poorly before his arrival but flowered for the first time a year later. Tender magnolias that had refused to set seed were loaned out to nurseries in warmer climates. Half-hardy magnolias, placed in sheltered, well-watered corners, survived and set seed.

That first year of Bonpland's tenure as director at Malmaison, the writing of botanical descriptions and commentary for *Plantes équinoxiales* slowed. Bonpland and Humboldt met occasionally and exchanged notes, as here from Humboldt in the fall of 1809:

> I am sorry not to have seen you, dear Bonpland. I arrived an instant after you. I was even more sorry not to have lunch with you. It was not the dog of time that kept me but the booksellers. The first volume of the work on the monuments will appear on December 15. I will send to you a copy decent enough to offer *in your name* to Her Majesty the Empress. . . . Let me know how many copies you want of the statistics and the zoology. (AB, 226)[8]

If an influential aristocrat was looking for a plant, Humboldt would call on Bonpland to provide it from Malmaison:

> I must ask you right away, dear Bonpland, to give me some outdoor shrubs for M.de Chateaubriand. Madame de Grollier is persecuting me for them, and I have a thousand reasons not to displease her. I have lost the list she gave me. It was that rubbish she asked for, the *Mélia azedarach*? the *Broussonnettia*? It makes absolutely no difference what you give: no one will examine them when they arrive, it is only that they be given. (AB, 226–227)

It was not the kind of request that Bonpland felt comfortable honoring, especially when he was trying to curb such skimming among the staff, but for Humboldt favors were part of the business of publishing. Humboldt closed his note with a compliment: "You bring me great pleasure. Her Majesty the Empress has spoken much to me about you and with great affection."

At the end of 1809, after successful negotiations with the Austrian emperor in regard to the Emperor's eighteen-year-old daughter, Napoleon made his decision. Josephine was summoned, told with much drama that she would be divorced, and returned to Malmaison a shadow of her old self. She was to be Dowager Empress and live in seclusion. Malmaison remained her property and she was given an allowance to buy plants. For the moment, to be out of the way of the upcoming royal wedding between Napoleon and an Austrian princess, she would have to leave Paris and take up residence in a run-down chateau in the woods of Navarre. Now added to Bonpland's responsibilities at Malmaison were neglected grounds and greenhouses to be restored at Navarre. When he could, Bonpland worked on remaining plates for the second volume of *Plantes équinoxiales* and for two additional volumes reordering the *Melastomacées*, writing to Humboldt now and then for added information for his commentaries.

In the fall of 1810, as work on the Mexican "statistics" came to an end and with Willdenow on his way to Paris, Humboldt's patience came to an end. He wrote to Bonpland the letter cited and recited by Humboldt's biographers as proof of Bonpland's incompetence and laziness:

> You have not written me a word about botany. I beg you to push
> on to the end, for since the departure of Madame Cauvin, I have
> not seen more than a half page of manuscript. I am determined
> not to throw away the results of our expedition and if in eight
> months there appear only ten plates—that is to say what any
> botanist in Europe could finish in fifteen days—there is no reason
> why volume 2 of *Plantes équinoxiales* would finish in three years.
> Meanwhile, there is the fact that M. Sterne has said that he does
> not want to print the *Species* before the second volume of *Plantes*
> is finished. I beg you once again, my dear Bonpland, to carry on
> to the end a project that is of such importance for the sciences,
> for your moral reputation, and for the agreements you yourself
> contracted with me in 1798. I beg you to send the manuscript,
> for as to assurances you have made on your own, you know that
> they in no way advance this affair. I am having to make these pleas
> to you, because I am about to pay M. Willdenow 3,000 francs
> in advance for the *Species* and because the public, believing that
> for 2 years you have not occupied yourself anymore with science,
> would not want a new work of botany before the first is finished.
> M. Willdenow is on the way here, at least so I suppose; I know
> for sure only one thing, that money is to be paid out in Berlin.
> I hope to see you soon here, my dear Bonpland. I embrace you
> heart and soul, and I know that within a month, if you love me
> a bit, you will do what I ask. (LA, 257–258)

Most disturbing to Bonpland as he read Humboldt's letter might have been the charge that he had not fulfilled promises made when they set off together on their travels in 1798. Through it all—Humboldt's giving away of his plants to Willdenow, Humboldt turning over work on the classifying and naming plants to Willdenow, Humboldt's insistence that he work with Willdenow—much of the work of publishing and corresponding had been left to Bonpland, with Bonpland trying as best he could to clear time and space for work with the plants he collected. Although money was at times a problem for Humboldt, it was even more a problem for Bonpland. The pension awarded him by the Muséum was enough for bare survival, but the post of director at Malmaison gave him a degree of ease and freedom. Also important was deepening commitment to Josephine as a friend and partner in the cultivation and naturalization of beautiful and useful plants.

Leaving aside the assertion that a competent European botanist could prepare twelve finished botanical plates for publication in fifteen days along with detailed descriptions and commentary on history and uses, an intendant charged with directing two large establishments might have been excused for taking somewhat longer. Also unacknowledged in Humboldt's letter was the public and personal tragedy suffered by the woman with whom Bonpland was now closely involved both professionally and as a friend. Exiled to a damp, chilly, abandoned chateau at Navarre, watched closely by Napoleon for any hint of scandal or excess, Josephine struggled to put together a life for herself and her children, and gardens were one of her few consolations. In that year of ten plates, Bonpland traveled constantly back and forth from Navarre to Malmaison, maintaining plantings, forests, and glass houses at Malmaison at the same time as he did what he could to restore the neglected grounds at Navarre. That any plates were finished under such circumstances might seem remarkable.

But the conflict with Humboldt went deeper than time management. Of much greater concern to Humboldt than commentary on the uses or history of plants was the multi-volume catalog in scientific Latin of new genera and species that was to document the botanical importance of his voyage and provide scientific support for his "geography of plants." As he wrote his accusatory letter to Bonpland in September of 1810, a good portion of Humboldt's publishing vision had materialized. The *Geography of Plants* was out with its accompanying *Tableau physique* of isothermal zones on the slopes of Chimborazo, as were the collection of astronomical observations correlated and calculated by Oltmanns and a collection of zoological observations in two volumes with contributions by Cuvier and Latreille. A mass-market abridged version of the pictorial *Atlas*, *Views of the Cordilleras*, was now on sale with its dramatic Andean scenes and Aztec manuscripts. *Ansichten der Natur* (*Aspects of Nature*) was a best-seller in

Berlin and elsewhere with its uplifting message of consolation and pleasure in the contemplation of nature in times of trouble. The "Mexican statistics"—*Political Essay on the Kingdom of New Spain*—with accompanying maps and diagrams were selling well in French and English. A *Personal Narrative* of the voyage was in process. Certainly Bonpland was lagging behind. Thirty-some volumes were to have been finished in two or three years, at which time Humboldt planned to be off to Asia on a new and grander expedition.

Had there been a bargain? Had Bonpland agreed to years of taxonomic work writing up thousands of Latin descriptions of supposed new species? Should he have refused the job of botanist at Malmaison and, soon after, the post of intendant? Or was it Humboldt who had not kept his part of the agreement, who from the beginning turned over plants Bonpland collected and described to Willdenow in the same way he turned over his atmospheric or astronomical observations to Gay-Lussac and Oltmanns to correlate and calculate? One thing is clear: If Bonpland lagged behind, it was not because his abilities in botany proved unsatisfactory. It was because his botanical abilities were in demand, tending and cultivating new plants at Malmaison, naturalizing foreign species in gardens and woodlands, cultivating hundreds of exotic heathers in the damp climate of Navarre, writing descriptions and comments for the second volume of *Plantes équinoxiales*, reordering the family of Melastomataceae for the two-volume *Monographie des melastomacées*, to say nothing of eventually writing and publishing *Rare Plants Cultivated at Malmaison and Navarre* as tribute to Josephine and her flowers.

In all these works, as in his botanical field journals, Bonpland innovated, adding to scientific descriptions of each plant's physiology wide-ranging commentary on the history, habitats, and uses of plants, implementing a view of natural science promoted by professors at the Jardin and Muséum in the early idealistic days of the French Revolution. The new botanist would have a grasp not only of identifiable plant parts but of geology and the composition of soils and rocks. They would know geography, understand climates and land masses. They would foster mutually advantageous relations between plants and peoples, farmers and legislators. Botany would be a science useful for propagation, grafting, and hybridization. Botanists would do more than collect curious plants; they would describe the organs of plants and vital plant functions of absorption, transpiration, rising of sap, dormancy, flowering, fruiting. Their work would not only be technically proficient, but would involve "a feeling for the organism," an ability to relate to plants as organized bodies with lives and a vegetal sensation and motive force of their own. In Bonpland's writings such moments of seeing and responding to plants as living beings in distinct habitats constantly surface: *Matisia cordata*, growing in a warm humid valley, its fruit tasting like apricots. *Marathrum foeniculaceum*, perched high up on its dangerous 195-foot cliff. *Mimosa obtusifolia* deep in the Orinoco forest, the deep violet hue of its flowers against the blue sky, "agreeably charming the eye" at the same time as its wood was useful for making the paddles for native canoes. Pure white *Passifora glauca* on Mount Quindío, in flower in October. Orchids so multiple and varied, with as many genera as species. *Bignonia chica*, source of a dye that might be of great use to European dyers and artists. *Geoffroya superba* from the banks of the Amazon, a magnificent tree with its thick trunk, spreading branches, bright green leaves, covered all over with yellow flowers, providing not only wood for construction but fruits and nuts eaten avidly by parrots and monkeys.

In March of 1811, the long-awaited royal heir was born to Napoleon and christened the "King of Rome." A fragile peace still prevailed in Europe. In Paris Humboldt concentrated on the business of publication, still talking about a new expedition, still complaining about the slowness of botanists, editors, translators, and printers, still discontented. At the Institut de France the mathematician Biot claimed to be able to do a better version of tables of Humboldt's hypsometric observations than Oltmanns's, and Humboldt bristled. "You can see that the sciences do not gain much from such a merry-go-round," he wrote to Pictet (LA, 263). It was hardly his only complaint. His writing, he told Pictet, was in a very "anemic state." He had to correct various mistakes. He had been mistreated by John Black, translator of an English edition of his *Political Essay*, who seemed to be a "bitter ass" and who made notes questioning aspects of the text, including his use of Blumenbach's term "Caucasian race." A year later, still at work on his publications with no end in sight, and with Bonpland still not turning out copy with sufficient speed, he complained about the arguing that went on at the Institut de France between mathematicians like Simeon Poisson and Pierre-Simon Girard. To the botanist Augustin de Candolle, who had provided some botanical material for his geography of plants, Humboldt wrote with ironic distaste: "All the passions have been at play and I regretted that the spectacle had been of such short duration. Since the Institut no longer occupies itself with moral theory, the members are reduced to simple practique." He added, "I work always on this endless 'voyage,' which bores me furiously" (LA, 266). Always on his mind was getting advance copies into the hands of those who could promote his books and gain backing for the remaining writings from the voyage. Much of the income from the family's Polish estates had been restored, but money was still short. The "Mexican statistics" were selling well, but there were few subscribers for the complete series of twenty to thirty volumes of his *Voyage*. Nor was there any chance that profits from publications would ever cover the expense of four years of travel and the costs of production. To Jomard, editor of Napoleon's *Voyage to Egypt*, he wrote promising to send a copy of his *Atlas pittoresque* and hoping for some publicity. To editors of journals he wrote requesting that they announce upcoming installments or volumes to keep the public aware of future publications. Always there were deadlines to meet as new installments went to press. In July of 1812 came a final blow. Willdenow arrived in Paris to work on the multiple volumes of *New Genera and Species*, immediately fell ill, returned to Prussia, and died, leaving a twenty-four-year-old assistant, Carl Kunth, to finish work on the plants.

Kunth, the nephew of Gottlob Kunth, manager of the Humboldt estates, was one of Humboldt's protégés. When Gottlob was made supervisor of the Humboldt household, Carl had been sent to live with his uncle and profit from the family's improved status. Gottlob found Carl a job as merchant's clerk, but when Humboldt returned to Berlin in 1806, he took the young man under his wing, arranging for him to take classes in botany at the University of Berlin with Willdenow. Carl, who had gone on to become Willdenow's assistant, was now given the task of finishing Humboldt's botanical works. In December Humboldt wrote to a friend apologizing for missing a social gathering the night before:

> In a few days I have to prepare three cahiers of zoology and of plants. I am overloaded with proofs. I work in a remote quarter. The death of Willdenow has put me in another bind. My absolute disappearance these days is only for that. (LA, 268–269)

As for Bonpland, he also had even more to distract him. With the royal marriage consecrated and the birth of an heir, Josephine had been given permission to return to Malmaison. There were repairs and improvements to be organized and carried out. Also Bonpland had new responsibilities. A matchmaker of people as well as of flowers, Josephine always took vicarious delight in the romantic affairs of others. She was notorious for finding husbands and supplying dowries for young girls who might not otherwise marry. Adeline was a special case. Josephine met her briefly when Adeline was a child, and when the girl appeared at Malmaison with a baby in her arms, she had a story to tell bound to engage

Josephine's sympathies. At seventeen, Adeline had been forced into an arranged marriage with an abusive nobleman eleven years her senior. A first child was born dead, and a second was conceived. To escape before a second child was born, Adeline fled to a convent, where she gave birth to a girl, Emma. Now, pursued by a vengeful husband who was threatening to take the child away, Adeline sought refuge and protection with Josephine at Malmaison. Josephine took her in. She placed the child with a nurse. She enlisted the help of friends with legal connections to try to get Adeline a divorce. She invited Adeline to stay at Navarre and at Malmaison. Most important, she introduced Adeline to Bonpland. Who better to be the girl's protector than reliable, kind, and single Bonpland? As a result Bonpland how had not only himself and plants to care for but a family.

A first thought had been to shelter Adeline and the baby Emma with his family in La Rochelle until a divorce was obtained and they could marry. When his family refused to meet, much less shelter, a woman who left her husband and was involved with another man, Bonpland defied them. He wrote to his sister Olive:

> Many people see others but do not see themselves. My so-called escapade is of little consequence to the public, and if people knew, as you do now, the situation of Madame B, they could only respect it. This woman, as I told you at Chauvins before she arrived there, is a rare example of tyranny and vexation. When a woman seventeen and a half years old throws herself into a convent and puts herself under the protection of the law in order to extract herself from a position sought after by most women in order to live with privation and chagrin, she is not contemptible and deserves a better fate. And if, in this state of misery, she is presented with a man who obliges her without ulterior purpose, is it not permitted to her to attach herself to him and share her pain with him, and to take joy in the hope that she might one day share with him the happiness he is in a position to expect? (AB, 56–57)

For Bonpland more was involved than a casual love affair. There was honor and principle. There was the courage of a woman who refused to submit to abuse and had acted in her own behalf. In comparison, his brother's haughty refusal to accept Adeline as a patient and his sister Olive's worries about appearances were petty and abhorrent. Retreat to the French countryside would no longer be an option, but at the same time life in Paris was proving more and more intolerable.

A long manic letter of defense and recrimination written by Humboldt to Bonpland early in 1813 provides some insight into complaints that Bonpland now began to voice more forcibly about the use of their collections. He wanted to talk, wrote Humboldt, not quarrel. No doubt it was misunderstanding that had caused the difficulty between them. Of course the botanical work belonged to Bonpland. Of course, as a man of honor, Bonpland would continue work on the plants. He was hurt by Bonpland's reproaches, could prove that never in his correspondence had he taken a peremptory tone.

> Since the year 1798 to this day I have had only two things in view: the sciences and the obligations your goodness has imposed on me. I address myself to your heart: you will judge whether I have ever wished to take away your work, snatch from you by vile ruses what is due you or force you to consent to arrangements that could diminish your merit in the eyes of the public. (HCH, 58)

On and on, Humboldt wrote, page after page, in a torrent of incoherent anguish and complaint. He might have chosen an etymologist or a mineralogist to go with him to South America, but he chose instead a botanist because he was so much drawn to botany. Constantly he mentioned Bonpland's name to important people he dealt with; always he added Bonpland's name to publications. If his own name was everywhere, so was Bonpland's. Was he not owed some gratitude? Bonpland had received a government pension even though his travels were not funded by any government. It was Humboldt who introduced Bonpland to Josephine and it was because of his voyage that Bonpland had been given the post as intendant. Yes, he went off to Italy with Gay-Lussac, leaving Bonpland behind to take care of publishing business, but he needed to learn about chemistry. As for Bonpland's trip to Berlin and Bonpland's complaints the about the state of the botanical collections there, Humboldt protested. Was not a third of the plants collected his, 'Humboldt's, to do with as he liked, especially as he had ceded to Bonpland the remaining two thirds? "Two thirds remained for you because I thought that an herbier destined for the government and for which I solicited a pension which you enjoy, might better be seen as belonging to you rather than to me" (HCH, 59). Had some evil spirit suddenly invaded Bonpland's consciousness causing him to suddenly see his best friend and protector as "a great devil?" (HCH, 63).

In fact, Bonpland's complaints were of long standing. First had come the sending of plant specimens to Willdenow in Berlin, supposedly for safekeeping, but with the proviso, perhaps unknown to Bonpland, that Willdenow could name and publish plants, only "not many and not all." Then there was Humboldt's decision to leave Bonpland behind in Paris to work on publishing while he went to Italy with Gay-Lussac, and Bonpland's discovery of the misuse of the plant name *Bonplandia* with its insult to Cavanilles. Most troubling of all was the realization that in Berlin Humboldt turned their collections over to Willdenow, and Bonpland's discovery of the disordered state of plant specimens and manuscripts in Berlin with labels missing, random notes made in journals, plants lent out to other botanists, and confusion in naming. Then came another blow. When Willdenow died and Kunth came to Paris to take up work on the plants, Kunth left part of the herbarium and some of Bonpland's journal manuscripts behind in Berlin, and Kunth and Humboldt went on with the work without them. Through it all Bonpland tried to make the best of a bad situation, more and more ceding the listing of new species to Willdenow and Kunth.

Then came a breaking point. In the summer of 1813, when Bonpland returned from a trip to nurseries in the south of France, he found that while he was gone Humboldt and Kunth had published on their own an installment of his *Plantes équinoxiales*. In it Humboldt had renamed one of Bonpland's plants *Kunthia montana* "in honor of M. Charles Kunth, distinguished author of a new Flore of Berlin" (PE II, 131).[9] To make it worse, the plant, caña de la vibora, cane of the viper, whose sugary sap was used by natives as an antivenom, was of special interest, as Bonpland made clear in his commentary:

> One is astonished at the sagacity of natives who figured out that the stem of a smallish palm contained a powerful antidote. As travelers make known to us new species of that grand family of palms, of which one hardly yet as described a tenth part, physicians will abandon the prejudice that nature has only disposed in plants of this group saps that are watery and insipid. (PE II, 130)

Bonpland had no problem with naming a plant after Kunth, but to arbitrarily rename a plant so casually and without consultation was one small thing too many. Humboldt pleaded innocence. He had chosen for his tribute to Kunth a plant he himself had described and drawn and simply changed the rather long-winded "*Willd. thanatophyga*" to something simpler. To have named a plant after Kunth, "was that so evil?" Furthermore, he had asked Bonpland if it was all right if publication of the installment go on while Bonpland was away in Province, and Bonpland had not said explicitly that no editing or renaming was to be done (HCH, 64).

Through all of his outpouring of outrage and hurt that his friend and companion of so many years seemed to have turned against him, Humboldt made one repeated defense: Bonpland had agreed to everything. He asked Bonpland, Should Kunth come? Bonpland said yes. On the occasion of Josephine's divorce Bonpland himself remarked once that he himself "regretted" not leaving both plants and manuscripts in Berlin for Willdenow to deal with (HCH, 60). When Humboldt asked if it was all right for Kunth to come to Paris, Bonpland "said with a laugh," how could Humboldt doubt that he would give permission for Kunth to come and bring back his plants and manuscripts (HCH, 63)? Had Humboldt simply chosen to miss the irony? Did he simply hear what he wanted to hear? Or was it, as Humboldt argued, Bonpland who was at fault, Bonpland who should have made his complaints clear? Occupied at Malmaison and Navarre, deeply concerned with the plight of Josephine, caring for living plants, gardens, wife and child, time and again Bonpland had avoided outright quarrel, had simply continued on with the botanical work as best he could As Humboldt saw it, what happened was simple. Bonpland had given up on "science." As Humboldt put it: "You complain that your names are seldom seen, but you forget that it is your own occupations that force you to believe yourself a stranger to all dealings with people who occupy themselves with the sciences" (HCH, 64). In other words, Bonpland was too busy naturalizing, propagating, and studying plants to work with "scientists" like himself and Kunth compiling a list of Latin names and abbreviated descriptions of "new genera and species" collected on their voyage.

11

Taking Leave

It was becoming harder and harder for Bonpland to imagine remaining in Paris. First there had been return to a city full of secret police, gaudy theater productions, and looted wealth. Then came disagreements with his family over Adeline and with Humboldt over botanical publications. Working on plants in his apartment in Paris and in his quarters at Malmaison, caring for Adeline and baby Emma, who now considered him to be her father, there was little to keep Bonpland in place. As he wrote his letter to Olive in the summer of 1813, with a new European alliance forming against Napoleon, it was hard to think of remaining even in France. One possibility had been return to La Rochelle, settle down to family life as he once joked with Olive, but his family's rejection of Adeline had taken away any thought of that provincial dream. Certainly Bonpland had no desire to join Humboldt on a new expedition to Tibet or China. More and more he thought how much he might have accomplished on their travels if he had not had to move so quickly from one location to another, climb so many mountains, travel with so much baggage, but had stayed in one place for a time like Mutis, Cervantes, and Caldas.

If he had a country estate, Bonpland wrote to Olive, a bit of orchard, some timber to manage, some fields to plant, if he had an independent income to support his botanical projects then he might stay in France. As the intendant of Malmaison and Navarre, as the author of *Plantes équinoxiales*, as Humboldt's travel companion, there was no horticultural establishment where he would not be welcome, no garden where he would not find confederates, no rare hothouse plants he might not propagate. He could work in Paris at the Jardin or take a chair at one of Europe's natural history museums. But he had had enough of museums and aristocratic gardens, and enough of deference to authorities whose only claim to superiority was an accident of birth or willingness to curry favor. In short, he had little desire to "howl with the wolves, bite with the dogs" among the fashionable elites. Ten years watching

195

Europeans kill each other, destroying both land and plants, left him with little sympathy for anyof Europe's warring factions, not with resurgent monarchists or with Napoleon's state-run bureaucracy, not with Humboldt's cautious liberalism, or even with the fervent republicanism of Humboldt's friend Arago. It was impossible to think that any progressive system of government would be forthcoming very soon in Europe.

Napoleon's Grande Armée limped back from defeat in Russia. Prussia joined with Russia, Austria, and Britain in a powerful new coalition. Napoleon and his forces were driven back to the borders of France. A peace treaty was proposed and rejected. In March 1814, victorious Prussian and Russian armies marched through the Arc de Triomphe and occupied Paris. The war was over, at least for the moment. The French monarchy was restored to power. In Paris Humboldt was busy in his role as chamberlain, mediating between the conquering Prussians and the defeated French. At Cuvier's request he intervened when a Prussian general tried to lodge troops in the Muséum. He arranged transport so feed could be brought to animals in the Jardin's zoo. He greeted arriving dignitaries, among them Metternich and Humboldt's brother Wilhelm. He served as aide to the Prussian king, taking him to museums and monuments, escorting him to the theater at night. When the king was sick or out of sorts, he read aloud to put him to sleep at night. There was recompense. The king had promised to donate funds for a new voyage to Asia and gave him a sum of money to offset some of the cost of the South American publications. A stipend was allowed for living expenses in Paris. In June he accompanied the king, Metternich, and his brother Wilhelm on a state visit to London, which gave him an opportunity to lobby for permission to visit British territories in Asia. This time, he told officials at the East India Company, it would be a real expedition, not with one botanist assistant but with a team of experienced scientists. He would go to Persia, to the mountains of Tibet; he would trek across the Himalayas to the River Ganges, and across the whole of India to Ceylon and then on to Java. He would sail the Pacific to America and from there back to Europe. No previous voyage had ever gone so far or covered so great a portion of the earth. His aim would be to study everything: altitude, barometric readings, geomagnetism, rocks, plants, and animal life in all kind of terrains—steppes, deserts, mountains. Wilhelm, now in London serving as ambassador from Prussia, described his brother's restless ambitions in a letter to his wife, Caroline:

> You know him and his ideas well enough. They can't be ours, much
> as I love him. It's truly comical when we are together sometimes. I

let him prattle on to his heart's content. What's the use of quarreling when our ideas are so different? Alexander is not only a unique and unusual academic with very broad views, he's such a good character as well, so soft, so helpful, so self-sacrificing. But he lacks inward peace and satisfaction. Because he doesn't understand people, though he lives with them so closely. (Botting, 220)

To Alexander's disappointment the British would have none of it. He was received politely. They would see, would let him know, etc. In the end no permission to enter British territory was ever forthcoming. There was one bright spot: For the moment, the King Frederick William had agreed to let him stay on in Paris to finish his *Voyage*, on the understanding that he would be on call for diplomatic duties and would return to Berlin at soon as publication was finished.

If the presence of royalist troops in Paris kept Humboldt busy that spring of 1814, Bonpland was equally occupied at Malmaison. In the turmoil of rival factions with decisions being made as to the fate of Napoleon and the form of the future French government, Josephine, with friends in all camps, was a pivotal figure. Metternich and Tsar Alexander sent messengers to Navarre, where she had weathered the invasion. They reassured her. She was admired by all. Her gardens at Malmaison were well known. Would she come back to Paris and help smooth the transition? Act as a hostess at Malmaison? Bring various factions together? Josephine agreed, and that spring Malmaison was a meeting place for dignitaries. The Tsar visited regularly, promising that she and her family would be given an income. Foreign visitors were given tours around the menagerie, greenhouses, and gardens. Frederick William visited. Russian grand dukes and British generals came to admire Josephine's flowers. But the happy days of return to Malmaison were few. On a chilly day in mid-May, she went driving with the tsar in an open carriage and caught a cold. A week later, sick and feverish, she insisted on coming down to attend a dinner given in honor of the tsar and Frederick William. She opened the ball that followed. Later, with the sweet smell of lilacs and lily of the valley coming in through the open doors, she took a cooling stroll in the grounds with the tsar. Five days later she was dead of pneumonia and a weakened heart.

Bonpland had consoled and befriended Josephine throughout the painful time of her divorce from Napoleon, her banishment to Navarre, and the birth of Napoleon's heir. He cultivated the flowers she loved and facilitated her many projects. He coached her in botanical nomenclature and took under his wing her young protégé Adeline. After the divorce, he saw her saddened and tormented on the few occasions when Napoleon visited Malmaison. He watched her drawn into the rush of festivity and display that followed Napoleon's defeat. He consulted with her doctor during her last illness and sat and held her hand the day before she died. Now she was gone and a last tie that might have kept him in France was broken.

At first there was too much to do to think about the future. Not only was the managing and accounting of Josephine's estate left to him as director to arrange, there was Adeline and now-five-year-old Emma to think of. With Josephine gone and Adeline's husband still threatening to take Emma away, Bonpland had to find them a safe place to live, and it was unlikely to be in France. In July, a little more than a month after Josephine's death, Bonpland sat down to write a conciliatory letter to his brother announcing a decision: "We both complain about the long silence between us; we both have committed wrongs; I admit my own, let us break this long silence." Could Michel, he asked, give him some idea as to his share of the proceeds from their father's estate so he could know what he can count on and what he might be able to do in the future?

> I have decided, my friend, to go to America in the spring if the
> colonies become calm and livable. I prefer the Spanish colonies, but
> at the moment they are in combustion. But now that the state of
> war in Europe has ceased, it might well be that it will end there
> also, although it remains to know whether it will be now or not
> for some years. (AB, 63)

He had been offered a post in Cayenne, he told his brother, but he would have had to leave in September, impossible given that he first has to finish *Rare Plants Cultivated at Malmaison and Navarre* in honor of Josephine's garden, the last installments of *Plantes équinoxiales*, and the *Monographie des melastomacées*. These will take him the winter, after which, when a suitable proposal arrives, he will take it:

> If I succeed in my projects, after eight or ten years, I will be free
> of any kind of need, and can live any way that seems good to me
> and as I wish, whereas if I remain in Europe I will surely vegetate
> all my life. So, if I must vegetate, I want to see America again.
> (AB, 63–64)

Michel's response was cool and curt. He understood the events that led to his brother's decision, but it was a bad decision. The roads would not be safe in the colonies. Rebellion there was destroying any natural resources that those countries might have.

> I can see no way in any America to make an "honorable" living. It's not enough to say "I am going to America." It is necessary to know what one will do there. What will you do? I ask you. (ABH, 167)

For the sober Michel it was a brother's final desertion, not only of himself but of common sense. The Bonpland-Goujauds were "good plants," landowners with ancestral ties to the land. A future had been laid out for them, the two of them together, part of the medical and scientific leadership of La Rochelle, working together. Now his brother was throwing that future away. Judging from his introduction to the first volumes of his *Personal Narrative* now appearing in print, Humboldt would have agreed. It was a bad time to consider travel to South America, let alone emigration:

> Internal feuds are inevitable in regions where civilization has not taken root and where, thanks to the climate, forests soon cover all cleared land if agriculture is abandoned. I fear that for many years no foreign traveler will be able to cross those countries I visited. (PN, 13)

Writing to his sister the same day as he wrote to Michel, Bonpland spoke more openly of his situation. The inventory of Josephine's estate was finished, he told her. He was able to take a breath. He would finish his old projects, and in the spring he would decide what to do, whether to stay in Europe or go to America. Josephine's death, he said, "came like a stroke of lightning [and] changed my life . . . it is a sadness not to be talked about because to speak opens wounds that are not yet scarred over" (AB, 64). Eugene, Josephine's son and heir, had asked him to stay on at a reduced salary, but the position offered little hope for the future and would mean he could not work for himself. After same brotherly advice on family matters, he made clear to Olive the probability that he would return to America:

> Next spring I will have put together what resources I can, and it will be very probable that I will put my eggs in one basket, to become property owner in America. However crazy this project may seem to you, it is not really. If I remain in Europe my existence is all mapped out, and without being beautiful it is nonetheless not bad, provided that is if I go on foot, eat bread, beef, roasts, and

vegetables and I don't move from where I am. All that, you know, would not suit me very well. It is necessary to have nothing with which to reproach myself, and to try my fortune. (AB, 65)

"What I might have done!" "What I might have seen and accomplished." "If only I had not taken the easy path!" Such regrets were not for Bonpland. But it was no easy task to decide where to go, as Spain's American empire continued to implode. Whatever grumbling had gone on among Creole settlers against colonial authorities, those authorities had at their backs the consecrated authority of the Spanish crown. Now, with that authority in question in the wake of Napoleon's invasion of Spain, armed rebellion was gaining ground. A junta took over in Buenos Aires. Francia declared independence in Paraguay. Miranda and Bolivar were leading revolutionary armies to victories against royalist forces in New Grenada.

At first Caracas seemed promising as Bolivar surged back after defeat in the fall of 1812, declared himself "El Libertador," and announced a free and united South America. When Humboldt and Bonpland met Bolivar briefly in Paris in 1804, Humboldt had dismissed Bolivar's dreams of independence in South America as frivolous. Bonpland, on the other hand, listened with interest, as Humboldt later recalled:

I admit that I was wrong then, when I judged [Bolivar] to be a man immature, incapable of an enterprising undertaking fruitful enough to result in any glorious finish. It seemed to me, after the study I had made of various sectors of American society, that if a man capable of making a revolution could rise up in some place or other, it was in New Spain, which had given those indications at the end of the last century and whose tendencies were not unknown. My companion, Bonpland, was wiser than me, because from the beginning he judged Bolivar favorably and even encouraged him in my presence. I remember Bonpland wrote to me one morning telling me that Bolivar had made him party to some of the projects he was nurturing in regard to the independence of Venezuela, and that he would not be surprised if they turned out well because he had of his young friend the most favorable opinion. It seemed to me then that Bonpland was as crazy as Bolivar. But the one who was crazy was not him but me. I came very late to understand my mistake regarding a Great Man whose acts I admire, whose friendship gives me honor, whose glory belongs to the world. (Minguet, 118–119)[1]

But now in the summer of 1814, after early successes, the Bolivarian revolution had stalled with victories by royalist forces, rebelling Indians, and a competing revolutionary group in Bogotá. In the meantime, Bonpland had to find somewhere that Adeline and Emma could live in safety until a decision was made. He settled on London, where he was in close contact with Francisco Zea, a Columbian botanist with ties to the revolution in New Grenada.

The two men had much in common. As a young man Zea worked with Mutis at the Botanical Expedition in Bogotá. Under the pseudonym Hebephilo he wrote tracts urging young people to study natural history and celebrate their native traditions. Arrested by Spanish authorities in 1795 for publishing a translation of the French revolution's Declaration of Human Rights, Zea was sent to prison in Spain. Released in 1799, he was refused permission to return to South America and went to France, where he met Bonpland and professors at the Jardin and Muséum. Allowed to return to Spain, Zea worked with Cavanilles at the Royal Botanical Garden in Madrid, and at Cavanilles's death took over the directorship. His inaugural lecture—"The Merit and the Utility of Botany"—proposed a "Project of Reorganization of the Botanical Expedition in Bogotá" emphasizing the social role of botanical knowledge. Discoveries in botany, he argued, should not be limited to the finding and naming of new species; they should be of use in agriculture, economics, and the arts. Botanical science should include not only classification and studies of plant physiology, but experimental farms and scientific agriculture. This was science as it was taught at the Muséum in Paris, science the aim of which was to make the world a better place not only for wealthy Europeans, but for cultivators and artisans.

Zea was briefly made minister of the interior during the French occupation, but when Napoleon was defeated and the monarchy was restored, his property was seized. Again he was expelled from Spain. Now, living in London, in close contact with Bolivar, he was waiting for the chance to return to South America and continue the revolution in both politics and the sciences. There had been trouble in Bogotá after Mutis's death, Zea told Bonpland. Struggle over the leadership was bringing research to a halt. New talent was needed. Would Bonpland go, take up the reins, solve problems, see that work continues?[2] It must have been tempting, but royalists were back in control in Caracas. There was no operative national government. The countryside was in revolt. Bonpland had no desire to go from one war zone into another. No decision was made. Zea and his wife welcomed Bonpland and his new family in London, helped him find a place for Adeline and Emma to stay, and promised to look after them while Bonpland went back to Paris to settle his affairs, one of which was Humboldt's *New Genera and Species*.

At Malmaison a letter from Humboldt was waiting for him. A first installment of *New Genera* was ready to go to the printers, wrote Humboldt. All that
was needed was Bonpland's agreement. Bonpland should visit the publisher
Schöll and establish that the work was his property. Second, he should register
his agreement that his name was on the title. Third, they needed his approval
of their plan to suppress all references to B, K, or H and use only references
to numbers in Bonpland's journals, which, if Bonpland agreed, would then
be deposited at the Jardin des Plantes. Fourth and last, said Humboldt, he
needed Bonpland's approval of a preface that he, Humboldt, would write in
Latin, in which he would say that Bonpland wanted to leave Europe and out
of friendship had ceded the writing of *New Species* to M. Kunth. Humboldt
would then go on in the preface to describe the botanical journals, the analytic
drawings made by both of them, ending with remarks on the geography of
plants and the meaning of a frontispiece picturing the heights of trees, snow
lines, and vegetation zones.

Bonpland answered with chilly precision:

> Far from being opposed to the early publication of *Species*, I am in
> accord with you and M. Kunth that it appear as soon as possible.
> I don't know why you would think that I have any fears on the
> subject, since I believe that I have neglected nothing of what you
> wished me to do after our last most agreeable visit on the subject,
> and I will respond frankly to all the issues you bring up in your
> letter. (AB, 66)

First the question of author. The work on new species and genera, wrote
Bonpland, had been given to Kunth and should be published under his
name. Kunth had at his disposal all the plants and all the manuscripts, and
he would write the work as he intended just as Bonpland was writing *Plantes
équinoxiales* as he, Bonpland, intended. If Bonpland or Humboldt were writing
New Genera and Species, they would add to their descriptions written in place
new understanding acquired from studying other authors or from comparing
plants in other collections. But they were not writing it, and for this reason,
said Bonpland, he disagreed with the addition of "notas adjecit."

> The result, in my view, could be to establish a certain rivalry between
> the propriety of your observations, Kunth's, and my own, which
> would be disagreeable. Kunth writes the work, he takes all our
> descriptions, all the names that we have been able to give on the

voyage, and he arranges them in his own manner and he publishes according to his understanding. (AB, 66–67)

A complete set of doubles was at the Jardin, He would make sure a corrected copy of his descriptions was deposited there also. In short, Bonpland no longer wished to be identified with the work except as collector of the plants catalogued and author of the descriptions that Kunth used as his source material.

Second was the question of citations. Bonpland disagreed with Humboldt's suggestion that references to Bonpland, Humboldt, or Kunth be deleted and references to numbers in Bonpland's botanical journals be substituted. Instead references should be to individuals and not to the journals. Bonpland:

> In this regard we would follow what Desfontaines has done and other botanist authors, that is to say we keep our manuscripts for ourselves because they are more useful to us than they would be to anyone else and we, reading the descriptions, can relate to them in a way no one else can. (AB, 67)

Not only, wrote Bonpland, did he not want to be credited as author, or have his journal numbers referenced, he disavowed any property right in the work or claim to any proceeds from it. Humboldt had urged him to go to Schöll and make it clear that the work was his. No, said Bonpland, it was kind of Humboldt to offer, but perhaps Humboldt had forgotten some things. First, Humboldt had already advanced a good amount of money for the making of plates and engravings and other printing services. Second, Humboldt would need to be reimbursed for money given to Willdenow, which came to, as Humboldt already told him, as much as 6,000 francs. In addition Kunth would need recompense for his work. "After these reflections, my friend," Bonpland concluded, "you must see that I am not making any sacrifice of money in renouncing any benefit from this work, although it certainly might not have been the same if we had not experienced obstacles." In short, if there had not been such urgency to get into print, if such damage had not been done to the collections sent to Berlin, if Willdenow had not died, it might have been possible to make the endeavor worthwhile. As it was, Bonpland asked only that a number of copies be given or sent to him in case he left France before the work was published. There was one last stipulation:

> I find very good the plan for the preface, only I believe it suitable and conforming to the truth to say not that it was after my plan

to leave Europe, but rather (what is sure) after your insistence, that
I give up the right, which I have and which you accorded to me,
to write the Flora. (AB, 67–68)

Humboldt's reply was immediate and conciliatory. He agreed to all Bonpland's demands except for the question of ownership of the work and profits, which he insisted would remain Bonpland's. Kunth's name would appear on the title page with only "*in ordinem digressit.*" There would be no citations to the numbers in Bonpland's botanical journals. Again came a rush of self-defense. On the question of references to numbers in the journals, he wrote, Bonpland might well reconsider. It never "entered his mind" that Bonpland would give up the journals; he only wanted to give ample notice to the public of the work done by Bonpland and show that descriptions had been written on location mostly by Bonpland. And yes, in the preface he would say only what Bonpland approved, would not mention Bonpland's upcoming voyage, would say only that Bonpland ceded his right in response to his Humboldt's insistence that he turn the work over to Kunth. In the preface he would say about Willdenow and Kunth only what Bonpland approved, "I hardly think that there can be much to risk since I am talking before the public about those I love." (HCH, 66–67)

Humboldt had other things on his mind. The projected list of volumes of publications from the voyage was now two thirds complete, but sales lagged. He wrote to Aimé Martin at the *Journal des débats* in November of 1814. Could they remember to add Bonpland's name as coauthor, and to make clear to readers which of the works were finished and available for sale: the *Geography of Plants*, the *Political Essay on New Spain*, *Observations on Astronomy*, *Observations on Zoology and Anatomy*, and *Plantes équinoxiales*. All that remained was his *Personal Narrative* in three volumes, and the second volumes of the zoology, the *Melastomacées*, and *New Genera and Species* (LA, 269–270). Again he reiterated, although the zoology and botanical works were important, they were only an auxiliary to the larger vision presented in his "grand tableau" of the relation between vegetation and climate in the *Geography of Plants*. This, as Humboldt saw it, was his great discovery. But now a recent incident was putting that discovery under a cloud.

At one of the gatherings of scientists at Arcueil, Humboldt heard something that shocked him. The speaker was the botanist Augustin de Candolle, who had cited Humboldt in his survey of the history of "geography of plants" as "the first writer to have treated the subject in a systematic matter." But now, as Humboldt sat half-listening to Candolle's talk at Arcueil, he heard something that gave him a "deep pang," as he described his reaction a few days later in an agitated letter to Candolle. Among those who contributed to the geography of plants, Candolle mentioned the geographer Giraud-Soulavie, and also "Strohmayer," whose work appeared before Humboldt's. Then, when he came to Humboldt, he said "enfin M. Humboldt." "Enfin!" "finally" as if he Humboldt was only one in a series, following after others, as if he had not discovered something totally new, seen a truth of nature never before revealed, but just continued on with work already under way. As Humboldt put it in a second letter to Candolle written the next day:

> Alas!, I who flattered myself, now having executed only a project along with others, I who believed that I had produced the first map and the first single work based on exact measurements of height and average temperature. I armed myself at Passy with Strohmayer's dissertation. I want to beg you to give me back my life. I have not been able to see you alone and am forced to leave this enduring monument to my vanity and the pettiness of my character. (CI I, 198)

Yes, Humboldt continued, Candolle cited his work on the geography of plants, but the "history" he gave to the subject made it seem as if his, Humboldt's, work was simply a sequel to what had gone before. He was made sick because of it, he told Candolle, and it left an impression on his friends who were at the gathering. He challenged Candolle. Is this the "historical truth"? Look at Strohmayer; see if his book contains one number, or measurement, see if it is not just a "mass of citations." Yes, Giraud-Soulavie had done important work and also Strohmayer. Yes, Strohmayer had developed some ideas taken from his, Humboldt's, *Florae Fribergensis* on the migration of plants. But was it not he, Humboldt, who published the *first* botanical map and the *first* work based on actual measurements and observations of temperature, who revealed the underlying truth of it all?

Particularly irking for Candolle might have been Humboldt's misspelling of Stromeyer's name, which indicated, not only, as Humboldt himself admitted, that Humboldt had not known of Stromeyer's work when he had published his *Geography of Plants*, but that after he heard it mentioned by Candolle at Arcueil he had not actually bothered, as he had claimed, to "arm himself" with it. Always one to take the high road, Candolle smoothed the quarrel over, making cosmetic changes to his entry "Geography of Plants" for the forthcoming *Dictionary of the Natural Sciences*, changing the wording to say that Stromeyer's contribution had been to lay out the scope of a geography of plants, and adding some stronger language when mentioning Humboldt.[3] The "enfin" remained but on the next page with reference to *New Genera and Species*, with Candolle perhaps hoping that Humboldt would not read that far. For Humboldt the "quarrel" continued to rankle, and he was hard at work on a response to be read at the Institut so as to put on record and make public his complaint.

More than embarrassment at not having mentioned a previous source, and more than a claim to be "first" or "only," was at the heart of this squabble, as Candolle went on to make clear in his entry "Geography of Plants" for the *Dictionary* as well as in the preface to his authoritative five volume revision of Lamarck's *Flore française*. Scientific findings are conditional and subject to observed fact. Far from showing global bands of similar vegetation, the growing body of botanical field surveys around the globe showed that in isothermal zones with exactly the same "external factors" of climate and altitude were found different species of plants native to particular geographical locales. As Candolle put it in his entry for the *Dictionary*:

> It is not difficult to find two places in the United States and in Europe, or in tropical America and Africa which present exactly the same circumstances, average temperatures, same elevation, same soil, an equal amount of humidity, while almost all, perhaps all the plants would be different in comparable localities. One might find a certain analogy of aspect and even of structure between the plants of these two supposed localities, but they would be in several different species. It seems then that other circumstances than those which today determine stations have influence on habitations.[4]

In short, Humboldt had failed to make a vital distinction between what Candolle termed "station" and "habitation." A station is defined by external factors—temperature, altitude, soil, water, climate—that determine conditions under which particular plants can survive and grow. Habitations are specific geographical locales, regions set off from other regions by oceans, mountain ranges, deserts with their own regional climate and history. Although a rational creator might place the same plants in similar "stations," plant surveys showed something very different. Barring seeds sown by travelers, plants in one bounded region of habitation differed from those in another similar climate zone. Humboldt's "analogies of aspect" (the similar look of certain kinds of vegetation) and "analogies of structure" (the roughly similar form of plant parts) might be useful for landscape painters and creative artists, but they were not botanical science. When someone said he found a European-type plant in some far off untraveled place, said Candolle, the report was usually wrong:

> The first travelers always believed they found in faraway places plants from their homeland, and it pleased them to give them their names, but as soon as they brought back specimens to Europe, for most the illusion dissipated. If when looking at dry specimens any doubt remained, cultivation in gardens helped to remove it.[5]

In America few indigenous species were common to Europe and even fewer to other regions of the world. The conclusion was inescapable: there were botanical regions with natural boundaries and their own native species. Species competed within a region in "perpetual struggle" for resources. To think that climate and kinds of plants lined up in some regular way, said Candolle, "retarded progress in science, and kept it from achieving exactitude." Good colleague that he was, Candolle added after his own entry a rejoinder from Humboldt, "On the Laws that are Observed Among the Distribution of Vegetal Forms." No, insisted Humboldt, the isothermal lines marked on his *Tableau* might have to wiggle and vary depending whether they passed over land, or ocean, or a coast line but this did not mean that his geography of plants was ill-founded.

As a scientist Candolle went where the facts took him. If he refrained from discussing the controversial question of the origin of species it was not out of prudence but because he had not yet come up with a coherent answer. Why were particular plants native to a particular region? Candolle rejected both Willdenow's fanciful theory of "mountain origin" and also Lamarck's unsubstantiated claim that individuals pass on to their offspring acquired characteristics. Only dedicated field work and careful study of species difference would decide the question. In Darwin's historical introduction to the *Origin of Species* there would be many references to Candolle and to Candolle's son, Alphonse, who carried on his father's statistical surveys and studies of native plants after his father's death, but none to Humboldt.[6]

While Humboldt sparred with Candolle over the geography of plants, no decision had yet been made as to where Bonpland would settle his family. In

December of 1814, faced with opposition in Bogotá and Quito, Bolivar fled to Jamaica and then to the newly independent republic of Haiti, where he was lobbying for arms and troops to make a renewed onslaught on the mainland. But Bolivar was not the only South American revolutionary recruiting scientists in Europe. The unfailingly optimistic and volatile Mariano Sarratea was in London as ambassador for a new government in Buenos Aires, capital of the old Spanish viceroyalty of La Plata. There prospects seemed more promising. After the May revolution of 1810, the Spanish viceroy was expelled. With Napoleon's troops occupying Spain, provisional independence was declared for at least as long as Napoleon was in power. After two military juntas, and several ruling "triumvirates," at the end of 1813 a director was named. Plans were made for a constituent conference to be held with representatives from each of the Argentine provinces, who would meet and decide on a form of government. British and French traders were now doing business in Buenos Aires, said Sarratea. He was confident that both England and France would give the new government recognition and support. If Bonpland came to Buenos Aires, he would find a warm welcome. The newly independent South American states needed not only political recognition and arms to defend themselves, but intelligence and scientific expertise. Plans were being made in Buenos Aires for a natural history museum and a botanical garden, both of which Bonpland could establish and oversee. When the university opened he might organize a department of botany. Under the auspices of a progressive government informed by enlightened men like Sarratea and Bernardo Rivadavia, possibilities seemed endless.

Meanwhile there was much to do in London to prepare for such a move. Bonpland visited Kew Gardens and the Kensington nursery of Lee and Kennedy, choosing stock to take with him to Buenos Aires. He collected books to begin a science library. He met with Robert Brown, director of the library of Joseph Banks, and had dinner with Banks, ignoring Banks's counsel that he should give up any thought of going back to South America. He spent days in the botanical archives of the East India Company looking at herbaria, noting in his commentaries in *Rare Plants* that the British East Indies Archives contain "all the plants from China we cultivate, and judging from these documents, some of these plants do better in our climate than in their native country." Hopefully the same would be true in La Plata.

Money matters in La Rochelle were pending. He was waiting for Michel to send his share of proceeds from the sale of the ramshackle cottage in which he and Adeline were supposed to stay on their abortive visit. Funds were still due him, both from his father's estate and a sum of money left him by Josephine in her will. He was working hard to finish not only the *Monographie des melastomacées*, but also *Rare Plants Cultivated at Malmaison and Navarre*. Spring found him still at Malmaison, waiting for peace to come to South America and final assurance that a position would be forthcoming in Buenos Aires that would provide him with an income and a home for Adeline and Emma. It could only strengthen his resolve to be gone when in March of 1815, a visitor arrived at Malmaison. Napoleon escaped from the British on Elba, marched a pick-up army across France to Paris, and immediately came to Malmaison to mourn his lost Josephine. Several months later he was back waiting to hear his fate after his last defeat at Waterloo.

Writing to Olive that same month, Bonpland was working hard to complete his obligations and be gone. Yes, he would like to come to see the family in La Rochelle before he left, he told her, but did not know if it would be possible: "We can't do everything we want in this life." She should not worry. The only real danger was the sea, and lots of ships come and go. As for war, who was to say that peace was any more likely in Europe?

> War is less the order of the day in these countries—at least where
> I will be going—than in our so civilized Europe, where kings prey
> on peoples to assure their dynasty, and where the French are feeble
> and pusillanimous enough to cut each other's throats. Believe me, I
> assure you that it is much more agreeable to live in the midst of a
> people who are less "civilized" than we are here in France. (AB, 69)

Was Europe really so civilized? Where "kings prey on peoples"? Where Frenchmen are ready to tear each other apart on the slightest pretext? He and Humboldt spent months wandering the vast empty llanos and sailing down the wide Orinoco without being murdered or assaulted. In America one might begin again, cultivate different kinds of relationship with land and plants, not as seigniorial master, not as a colonist extracting profit or exploiter of slave labor, but as part of what might become a new kind of human community.

In August 1815 proofs for *Rare Plants Cultivated at Malmaison and Navarre* went to Delile for correction. In November he wrote to Olive that he was only waiting for the final settlement of Josephine's estate and the sum of money Josephine left him in her will to be on his way. From January to March of 1816 he was in London, visiting nurseries for planting stock to take with him. In March he was back in Paris, putting his papers in order, packing up his herbarium and manuscripts, as well as crates of books for libraries at the new botanical garden and university. To Olive went a last goodbye and some lighthearted advice. Her husband, Gallocheau, had gotten a judgeship he wanted with some help from Bonpland. Olive was unhappy that she would have to move from their country house to a nearby town. What would he do if he were her? He would spend the summer season in the country and the winter in town, Bonpland told her. He would get the mayors of each place to fix up the roads, so that Gallocheau could come home after long days in court to rest from "the kind of wrangling that merits desertion." Given what he was about to face, Olive's fears and worries were hard to take seriously. As for seeing the family before he left, it would not be possible. One cannot always do what one wants. He had to finish work at Malmaison, go back and forth from Paris to London, and prepare for the voyage. He hoped to come back one day. They still had many years to live. He will think of her always.

In July renewed urging came from Rivadavia, who was now back in Buenos Aires. The congress of the Argentine provinces met at Tucumán. War with the royalists was over. A supreme director of a United Provinces of the Río de la Plata, Juan Martín Pueyrredón, had been appointed. Artigas, the renegade caudillo commanding a militia in Uruguay, walked out of the congress, as did Ramírez from Entre Ríos and López from Santa Fe. Still Sarratea gave his assurance. In Buenos Aires Bonpland would be a minister of state. He would have funds to create a botanical garden. He would design courses in botany at a new university. Allied with a progressive government, he would accomplish something greater than any museum collection of flora and fauna, greater than any aristocratic pleasure garden, greater than luxury folio publications. There would be no more carrying spoils away to Europe, no more exploitation of native labor so that a few Europeans became rich. Cultivation and production in a free America would be for the benefit of Americans, native and naturalized.

At the end of October Bonpland met Adeline and Emma at La Havre to supervise the loading of their belongings into the hold of the brig *Saint-Victor* bound for Buenos Aires. His journal shows him in perpetual motion. Packing was done, redone, with crates placed in various holds of the ship. Last letters went to friends and colleagues: to Rivadavia, Humboldt, Kunth, Delile, and the publisher Schöll, settling affairs and setting up future contacts (MNHN, ms 212). There was one last incident. At the last moment, a desperate Kunth arrived at the dock with a letter from Humboldt. It seemed the Muséum's collection was incomplete. Plants had been mislaid and mishandled. Could Bonpland give them some of his plant specimens?

Kunth returned to Paris without the missing plants but with a last letter from Bonpland to his friend Humboldt: "I was happy to see Kunth, and to have had a renewed mark of your friendship, I would have been happy to return him arms full of plants" (AB, 75). Unfortunately, explained Bonpland, plant specimens were now buried deep in the hold of the ship. He regretted that he had not taken care when he packed them to see if doubles were mixed in, but since no notice had been given it had not been necessary to do so. Kunth gave him a detailed list of what was missing. When he arrived in Buenos Aires he would go through his collection and try to supply them. Although he did have access to the *Rhexia* and *Melastoma*, he would need them himself to complete the last installments of the *Monographie des melastomacées*. Later he would send on both the manuscript for the *Monographie* and the doubles wanted by Kunth so that the Muséum collection would be complete. Yes, Bonpland wrote to his old comrade, he regretted not seeing him in the last moments of leaving Europe:

> Still in spite of all the pleasure I would have in embracing you, it is better you did not make the trip to Le Havre. I dislike, as you know, nothing more than these moments of goodbye, all the more so when they are so real. (AB, 76–77)

He assured Humboldt: He would continue with the work they took on when they left for the New World. He would help as much as he could with the collections. He would devote himself to natural history and agriculture and see what would come of it. Perhaps someday he would come back:

> The closer the moment of leaving France comes, the more I experience regrets, still I have the firm intention of returning as soon as it will be useful to my interests, that is to say, as soon as I have put together enough to live tranquilly with my work and have the free disposal of my time. If I do not succeed, I will remain there buried on some hill or in some pretty valley. (AB, 77)

He reassured Humboldt: He had talked for a long time with young Kunth about the work on *Rhexis* and *Melastoma*. He explained to him again what had been agreed. He explained to him how to settle bills with the binder, and about money that Schöll would owe to him when he turned in the first installments. Kunth left reassured. Early the next morning, the ship sailed for South America.

PART IV

WORLDS APART

PART IV

WORLDS APART

12

A Lost Friend

In Paris Humboldt's life continued on much as before. He completed a second volume of his *Personal Narrative*. He researched historical and scientific material for a third volume. He visited London again, this time with the young physicist Francois Arago. Still no permission to enter British colonial territories was forthcoming. A year later he was back in London working contacts including the prince regent, but to no avail. London was not a place he enjoyed being. He never won the acclaim there he had in Germany and Paris. The British were stiff and unaccommodating. Reviews of his publications were not always positive. John Barrow, co-founder of the Royal Geographical Society and secretary to the Admiralty, had good things to say about his literary style and his ability to involve the reader, but Barrow's comments in the *Quarterly Review* were mostly negative. Many of Humboldt's notes and data, he said, were unrelated to the voyage; there was little or no original material, mistakes in oceanography and geology, too much theorizing from poorly digested second-hand sources, and the geography of plants was not based on actual plant surveys.[1]

Even Paris was not the same. His friend Arago was now secretary at the Observatory, busy with magnetic and astronomical researches, and married with a wife and children. After one blissful year in 1810 when Humboldt shared Arago's bachelor quarters at the Observatory, Arago had little time available. Arago was unfailingly cordial and always grateful for Humboldt's interest, but often, in the press of research and family obligations, he failed to respond to Humboldt's notes. Work on volumes for the *Voyage* dragged on, especially the botanical volumes, with Kunth working slower than Humboldt expected. At the beginning of 1818 Humboldt took advantage of an acquaintance traveling to Buenos Aires to send a letter to Bonpland. Why, wrote Humboldt, had Bonpland not written to him? He had written to everyone else, but to him, Humboldt, had come only one short note introducing a friend who was visiting

Paris, but nothing about his work in Buenos Aires, no news, nothing about whether he was happy or how he was being treated:

> This is not a reproach, my excellent friend, that one note itself says that you have written other letters. Perhaps they never arrived, just because they had my address on them—there are so many people who think they are paid to read the letters of others. It does not occur to me that you could forget me, but it is a hardship for me not to have your letters. (LA, 272)

And Humboldt had good news. Bonpland had been elected to the Institut de France. There was a rival candidate, but in the end the vote went his way with Jussieu, Arago, himself, and all of Bonpland's other friends rallying around his candidacy. More important, could Bonpland send the missing plants that Kunth was supposed to have had within a year?

Botany had become drudgery, as Humboldt indicated in a letter to Candolle from London, where he was trying once again to promote an expedition to Asia.

> I am happy enough to see the end of this interminable oeuvre. In a few days the second volume will be finished. I am printing at the same time and at my own expense a fourth volume, of composite flowers. . . . M. Schöll has already begun a third volume, and I will still do the fifth, so then it will be done. It has needed some courage to achieve a work of botany that cost 180,000 francs to put together. (LA, 275–276)

In London, he told Candolle, he had a chance to see a copy of Candolle's revised edition of Lamarck's *Flore française*, but could look only briefly at the preface. Would it be possible to get some sort of synopsis?—"You have done a work both excellent and useful, and it would be a work of charity." Humboldt enclosed with his letter copies of three installments of Kunth's *New Genera and Species*, asking Candolle to be indulgent. "In a work of such breadth all cannot be done with the same care."

Candolle might have breathed a sigh of relief that Humboldt had not read any further in his *Flora*, initiating more protest. In his *Autobiography* Candolle reflected briefly on what he called their "quarrel." Humboldt, he said, came to the meetings at Arcueil occasionally and added much "energy and interest." But Humboldt never forgave him for saying that others before him had studied the geography of plants, even though out of courtesy Candolle had overstated rather than understated Humboldt's contribution to the field. As Candolle put it, Humboldt "affected to pass himself off as the creator of a science of botanical geography, to which he has added a few facts and exaggerated a true theory so much as to render it false" (Candolle, *Memoires*, 167). In many ways, it was a similar disagreement that had driven Humboldt and Bonpland apart. Botanical research as it was understood by both Candolle and Bonpland was not data for a theory of Nature. Candolle's biogeography mapped systematic ways in which plants struggle for existence, spread, compete, and become extinct in particular regions. Like Bonpland, he studied the chemical productions of plants and how those productions were put to use in human life. He mapped circadian rhythms of leaf movements in response to light and seasonal changes, an understanding of great use in agriculture. In such studies, more important than instrument readings and numerical correlations of "external factors" was patient methodical observation of living organisms in relation to their environments.

Another of Humboldt's frontispiece engravings, chosen by him for the German edition of his *Geography of Plants*, expresses a very different view of nature and science. Again Humboldt looked to the Greeks for inspiration, this time not to Athena and Hermes, gods of industry and commerce, but to Artemis, goddess of nature, and Apollo, god of reason and poetry. In Humboldt's frontispiece, Nature, pictured in the guise of the cult statue of Artemis at Ephesus, stands stiff and lifeless. Multiple breasts hang down from her chest like globes of over-ripe fruit. Her arms outstretch like a doll's. Her legs are tight bound by bands of carved bas-relief animals. Standing beside her, gloriously naked except for the perfunctory fig leaf, a handsome young Apollo lifts from her rigid shoulders a covering of heavy fabric.[2] At the bottom of the plate a small graven tablet commemorates Goethe's "Metamorphoses of Plants." There was some precedent among naturalists for identifying Nature with the Ephesus Artemis. In a frontispiece to Linnaeus's *Fauna of Scandinavia*, she rises triumphantly out of a leafy forest glade surrounded by small animals and birds. Georg Forster in *Views of the Lower Rhine* put her on a pedestal with a reverent naturalist kneeling at her feet. Humboldt's scientist is more bold. Neither Linnaeus's quiet hidden wilderness observer, nor Forster's respectful worshiper, but imbued with the magic of poetry and the force of reason, he lifts away the veil of appearance to reveal what Goethe had called "the secret law," "the sacred mystery," the "foreshadowed pattern" behind the complex transformations of organic life.

Meanwhile, working under Humboldt's supervision in Paris, Kunth was struggling on, dealing with confusion caused by Willdenow's heirs and misleading bits and pieces of description passed on in Willdenow's notes. Labels had been removed and manuscripts lost. In Berlin plants were lent out to other researchers and named indiscriminately. Humboldt wrote with growing irritation to Wilhelm, now retired from public service and living at Schloss Tegel, the family estate:

> Kunth is with the angels if not still in Purgatory. Look at the letter that has done him in. He did not write it to be printed. But in any case, the fact is true and the complaint is just. We have added to the third volume of *New Genera* a similar complaint against Schlechtendal, who, without my permission, gave my plants with bad descriptions to MM. Römer and Schultes, who published my *Species*. The result is that the same plants are published with different names. Say nothing about this last complaint that brings up some of Willdenow's blunders if no one yet has seen it at the Academy. (LA, 279).

In addition to confusion and complaints, there was the interminable expense of it all. With little chance of finding a market for descriptions of plants in Latin, as Bonpland predicted all the cost of botanical publishing fell on Humboldt. Nor was Humboldt happy with his publisher Schöll, who hired cheap colorists to make expensive "hand-colored" versions of *New Genera*. He was sending on the latest volume, Alexander told Wilhelm, but it would not be the colored version. The painters, unprepared for the job, were "abominable." It had been a put-up job by Schöll to sell some high-priced copies (LA, 280).

Costs continued to mount. Writing to the Prussian minister of finance, frustration and anger broke through Humboldt's usual diplomatic politesse.

> I would never have believed myself authorized myself to address myself to his Majesty the King, to ask him to buy some of the completed series of my works or to give me a subvention, in spite of any hope that I might have had of the success of such a request, for I am a complete stranger to the sale of my works and their sale can gain for me no pecuniary advantage. (LA, 281)

Forced to hawk his work, as if he was selling shirts! And to his own head of state. This, when the governments of Russia, France, and Austria bought copies of the complete *Voyage* to distribute to libraries and schools. And this, when his aim had never been his own gain, but only "to advance the achievement of an enterprise that greatly exceeds in large expenditure all works of the same kind published at the expense of the author." He had, he said, one modest request. Might he be able to keep the small amount left of the advance he received of 24,000 francs, which was used, as was his own "small fortune," for botanical, geological, and geographical drawings and for typesetting and printing works? Might he perhaps be able to keep the little that was left for volume 5 of *New Genera*? If so, then all that would be lacking for the complete *Voyage* would be two or three more botanical volumes, a half volume of zoology, and two more volumes of his *Personal Narrative*, and since other governments had subscribed to the whole series, might it be possible to think his own government might do so as well? Had not the previous minister of finance once talked about raising his subsidy, although he is not asking for that now since he was given a promise of money for his next expedition? After a long itemized list of expenditures, Humboldt ended with an apology:

> Your Excellency will certainly pardon these explications and these hopes, knowing me to be completely distanced from the sale of my books, without any pecuniary interest and only desiring the completion and the popularization of these books. (LA, 283)

As usual he could not resist a postscript. He heard the government had given one Prof. Klaproth more than 40,000 francs for works including a Chinese vocabulary and maps of Tibet!

At the beginning of 1821 he wrote to Wilhelm. The last volume of *Genera* and a volume on mimosas were almost finished. He had not money enough to keep Kunth in Paris any longer, given that he was now forced to live on only 625 francs a month—"I must from time to time refresh myself and pay my debts." As a result, he was sending Kunth back to Berlin and urged Wilhelm to befriend him. In any case, he added, he himself would be leaving very soon for the Orient. A few months later he wrote again. He was working on *Zoology*. They had a living electric eel on which to experiment, but it died from being constantly tormented. Still, the Academy approved his observations (LA, 284–285).

If botanical and zoological publication were a burden, the Mexican "statistics" continued to be a success due to developments in South America. The federal republican government of a newly independent Mexico was looking to develop mineral resources and had issued a call for expert advice. In Bogotá Bolivar had succeeded in defeating both monarchists and rival revolutionaries and was founding a national school of mining. Bonpland's friend Francisco Zea was back in Paris as Bolivar's agent looking for scientific talent, and Humboldt was invited to interview the two young graduates from the School of Mining at Saint-Étienne recruited by Zea. One of them, Mariano Rivera, had announced his plan to follow in Humboldt's footsteps and update his observations. The other, a young mineralogist named Jean-Baptiste Boussingault, turned out to be even more interesting. In his *Memoires*, Boussingault recalled his first interview with Humboldt:

> Humboldt first wanted to meet me (look me over). He talked a
> lot and well. I listened to him like pupil listens to a teacher, and
> he was pleased, as he put it, to recognize in me "the great art of
> listening." He showed for me even then the lively friendship that
> he would maintain for me until his death. (Boussingault, 179)

"Looking me over" quickly led to more. Not only did Humboldt hand over to the twenty-one-year-old Boussingault "precious relics" in the form of measuring instruments he himself carried to South America twenty years before; as Boussingault put it, "he insisted on teaching me the use of these instruments and made a date to do so." Boussingault spent a day in Humboldt's apartment measuring angles and declensions out the window while Humboldt marked numbers down on a large pine work table he used as a scratch pad. Boussingault:

> Humboldt was fifty-five, gray haired, and with mobile features. He
> dressed just as he had at the time of Directory in a formal suit,
> shirt, top hat, cravat, and a kind of soft boots found nowhere else
> in Paris. He did not use paper to make notes, but wrote on his
> long pine work table. When the table, covered with numerical
> calculation and logarithms became too full, Humboldt called in a
> carpenter to plane it down. (Boussingault, 179)

Meeting this attractive young mining engineer about to leave for Mexico and Bogotá, an idea began to take shape in Humboldt's mind. He had once been warmly welcomed and honored in Mexico. Given his Mexican statistics, certainly he would be welcome again. He might found an institute there, assemble around him a society of young scientists. When Boussingault finished his stint as professor at Bolivar's school of mines, he could come to join him. They could work together.

In Paris Humboldt worked diligently on the young man's behalf, sending him a stream of instructions and encouragement. He wrote letters of introduction for Boussingault to take with him, including one to Bolivar, with whom he had had no contact since a brief meeting in Rome in 1806. Just as Boussingault was about to leave for London and the trip to South America, Humboldt wrote with excitement. He had just received a letter from Bolivar, introducing a Mr. Bollman who was coming to Paris. In the letter Bolivar referred to Humboldt as "the man who with his eyes dragged America out of ignorance and with his pen painted it as beautiful as its own nature." Now that he was sure a letter from him would be well received, he would write to Bolivar directly. There was a last nostalgic dinner in Paris with Humboldt, Arago, and Gay-Lussac. The day before he left, Boussingault sent a polite note to Humboldt thanking him for all his help, to which Humboldt immediately and impetuously replied:

> My dear friend. If you do not marry at Bogotá, which could happen because you are young, spiritual, and amiable—and I would not have the courage to blame you for it—you will pass many long years with me under my roof. This is my hope. If I had not been depicted in your eyes as a man so little accessible I would have had the happiness to know you *five months sooner*. We could have planned our projects together at length. It is useless to complain about what is done. One must think only about what one can draw on for the future. Only death now can change my plans. I am fifty-two and have a very young spirit. I am fixed in my determination to leave Europe and live in the tropics in Spanish America in a place where I left so many memories, and where institutions are in harmony with my desires. (LA, 291)

He "trembled," Humboldt wrote, to set a date when he would come. He still had publishing to arrange, but most probably in fifteen to eighteen months "I will be ready to receive you." He would go to Mexico. He would establish residence there. Funds promised him by the king were for travel to the East Indies, but he would go there too. He would go from Acapulco to the Philippines for a year, then back to Mexico, and if things worked out there, he could come south to be near to Boussingault, where "I hope we will be reunited." In the meantime, said Humboldt, he was off with the King to a conference of European monarchs at Verona. After that it would be on to Naples and Vesuvius—something of a bother—but it would take only a month and he could not refuse "this very public witnessing of the King's favor, important for my family and the political situation of my brother."

None of it, he assured Boussingault, would change his plan to be reunited with him in South America.

A last polite restrained goodbye came from Boussingault in London, to which Humboldt immediately replied, enclosing the proofs of his *Memoire on Geognosy* and hoping that his letter would arrive before Boussingault left: "How could you ever fear to use too much familiarity with me? You know how much I am attached to you for life." Boussingault should feel free, he said, to revise or edit his *Geognosy*. His aim was to cover everything, and there were often mistakes in the parts. Never should Boussingault let fear of offending stand in the way of correcting his mistakes:

> If my work has some merit, it is in the ensemble of views which embrace the formation of the two hemispheres. It is the first attempt in this genre, but a work which embraces all may not be in harmony with each. That is natural, and the more you distance yourself one day from my ideas of today, the more I will conclude, my dear Boussingault, that you have consulted nature, and seen with your own eyes. So do not let yourself, please, be influenced by my "rock layerings." Call "above" all that I call "below." This is truly the way to discover the truth. (LA, 293)

It was Humboldt at his most charming, humble, engaging, and passionate best, eager to help a young man make his way in the world, hoping against hope that something more might come of it.

Humboldt accompanied the king to the Congress of Verona that fall with new vigor in his step and even less interest than usual in diplomatic maneuvering. When he wrote to Wilhelm from Verona, it was not about Greek independence, Austria's occupation of Italy, or French intervention in Spain, but about his new plans for Mexico:

> I have a grand project for a grand central establishment of the sciences in Mexico, for all of free America. The Emperor of Mexico, whom I know personally, is going to step down. There will be a republican government. The idea of ending my days in a manner that is most agreeable and most useful for the sciences in a part of the world where I am particularly cherished and where all gives me hope for a happy existence. This is a way to not die without glory, to gather around me many educated people and to enjoy that independence of opinion and sentiment which is necessary to my happiness. (LA, 294–295)

Humboldt went on to describe the details. He and his scientists would explore all of South and Central America, there would be a "short" trip to India and the Philippines, which are "states virtually federated with Mexico." His Mexican statistics were paying off. An investment fund was being put together in France of four to five million to renovate Mexico's mines. Of course, he himself would have no monetary interest in such a fund, but money would be available to employ scientists like Boussingault, and he was sure that the directors of the fund would follow his advice whenever he was ready to give it. He ended with a characteristic moment of doubt. Wilhelm would probably laugh at this project, but it was not only in France that there was a rush to profit from the mineral wealth of Mexico on the basis of his statistics. An even larger investment fund was being put together in London.

In Verona, as European statesmen quarreled over what to do about the growing tide of revolution in Spain and Greece, Humboldt avoided controversy. He had little interest in the maneuvering and bickering of diplomacy, but liked the sociality. Even more he enjoyed a sightseeing trip with the king to Venice and Vesuvius, which gave him another opportunity to look down into the crater of a volcano. After a nostalgic visit to Wilhelm at Schloss Tegel, he returned to Paris determined to finish the interminable *Voyage,* and be off to Mexico and reunited with Boussingault.

Two years later the dream was still with him. Humboldt wrote to Wilhelm:

> In Mexico, the federal republican government is a marvel. My intimate friend Mr. Alman is head of the ministry. The executive powers have had written to me in the name of the nation a letter of thanks for services I rendered in making known to the world the sources of their great internal wealth. There is no doubt that without my courage there would not now be above three million pounds sterling in England from the mines. Also to facilitate this action, the company had printed *Selections on Mexico from von Humboldt's Works* and announced that they would name me director, which, for good reasons I refused. It is a bizarre thing. To have exterior glory, one is always in the position of not being able to make a material profit from one's position. Virtue is very little useful in life. (LA, 297)

His statistics, he said, were comprehensive. He wrote not only of mineral wealth, but also of the degraded state of the mines, the complaints of the miners, the difficulty of access, the need to import food to feed workers. If those selling shares choose to ignore those parts of his *Essay* it was their responsibility. In any case, never would he lower himself to use his fame to make a profit.

Humboldt's fears were well-founded. The mining fund went bust. Investors lost life savings. He was blamed. No invitation would ever be forthcoming from the Mexican government to establish an institute. Boussingault returned to Paris after ten years in South America. Humboldt wrote to him from Potsdam, where he was attending the king. Boussingault should follow his example, said Humboldt. He must get elected to the Institut and publish his *Memoires* as Humboldt had his *Narrative*. Boussingault responded at first with deference and then not at all. He married, as Humboldt feared he would, studied agricultural science, and on a rural property owned by his wife established one of the first agricultural experimental stations researching soil and food chemistry.[3]

If Boussingault was gone from Humboldt's life, even more so was Bonpland. No plants and no letters were now arriving from Bonpland to Humboldt or to any of Bonpland's friends in Europe. First reports that he was in some sort of trouble in Paraguay were discounted. Humboldt was particularly skeptical of talk of abduction and murder. Knowing Bonpland as he did, said Humboldt, Bonpland had simply gone off to Paraguay of his own accord looking for plants. Humboldt sent a note to Bonpland addressed to Buenos Aires. What had decided him to take a trip to Paraguay? No answer came back, and inquiries made in Buenos Aires went nowhere. There were vague mentions of Paraguay, but no news of any kind now crossed the contested border between Argentina and Paraguay where José Gaspar Rodrígues de Francia, El Supremo, zealously defended Paraguay's right to territory ceded by treaty in 1811.[4] Garbled accounts of Bonpland's situation circulated. He was in jail. He had been captured and forced to serve as doctor in Francia's army. He had been beaten and starved to death. Finally there was certainty: Bonpland was alive and detained in Paraguay.

Humboldt, always ready to rally to the cause of a friend, immediately joined the effort to secure Bonpland's release. He and Cuvier drafted a letter to be sent to Francia from the Institut de France, also signed by Jussieu, Thouin, and Desfontaines, demanding that Bonpland be freed. A similar letter was written at the Muséum. Neither letter got any response from Francia, if indeed the letters ever reached him. Bolivar, now ruling over an independent Colombia, took stronger measures, writing his own letter to Francia:

> Since I was a youth I have had the honor of cultivating the friendship of Monsieur Bonpland and that of Monsieur Baron

de Humboldt, whose science did more good to America than all of the conquistadors. I now have knowledge that my great friend Monsieur Bonpland is being detained in Paraguay for reasons that are unknown. I suspect that some false information has been able to calumny this virtuous scholar and that the government over which Your Excellency presides has been taken in on the subject of this gentleman. (ABH, 180)

Bolivar claimed a special interest. He himself, he said, had been the reason for Bonpland coming to America. Although in the end Bonpland had gone to Argentina, Bonpland and his knowledge would be welcome in Colombia, "where I preside over the government by the will of the people." Although Bolivar honored Francia with the title of Excellency, it could hardly make up for his preemptory tone:

Deign to hear, Excellency, the outcry of four million Americans, liberated by the Army that I command, all of whom along with me beg for the clemency of Your Excellence, in homage to humanity, wisdom, and justice, in homage to Monsieur Bonpland. Monsieur Bonpland could swear to Your Excellency before leaving the territory that you govern that he will leave the provinces of the Río de la Plata, so as to in no way cause prejudice to the Province of Paraguay. As for myself, in the meantime I will wait with the anxiety of a friend and the respect of a disciple the day when I can march to the border of Paraguay to liberate this best of men and the most celebrated of voyagers. (ABH, 181)

In other words, Bolivar, a leader who headed a powerful army, was ready to march to the border of Paraguay. Given rumors that Bolivar would like an excuse to "liberate" Paraguay, given his announced ambition to unite all of the Northwestern Spanish colonies under one rule, given that everywhere in the wake of his victories and defeats, the countryside had been devastated and ruined, such threats could only provide Francia with all the more reason to distrust Bonpland and refuse any request for his release.

Many efforts were made. The naturalist Richard Grandsire, who met and admired Bonpland in Buenos Aires, managed to get as far as the border of Paraguay at Ytapua on the pretext of doing hydrographical studies, but was denied entry on the ground that hydrography was simply a ruse. After an abortive attempt to enter Paraguay from the north, Grandsire gave up with the vain hope that an official letter on Bonpland's behalf from the British consul in Buenos Aires might have some effect. Francia refused to accept the letter on the grounds that Bonpland was a French, not British, national, and Grandsire turned to Paris with no more than advice. What Francia wanted, said Grandsire, was recognition of Paraguayan independence, recognition that neither Buenos Aires nor any of the European powers had been willing to give. If a letter regarding Bonpland came directly from the French government or even from the French consul in Buenos Aires, Francia might be willing to negotiate.

Hard as Bonpland's friends worked to get the French government to intervene on Bonpland's behalf, all appeals failed. The letter that had been sent from the Institut was sufficient, they were told. Paraguay had been taken from Spain by force, and Francia could not be addressed as if he were head of a legitimate government. Bonpland, it seemed, was lost, perhaps dead, certainly a broken man. There was little that could be done.

Eventually a story was pieced together. On arrival in Buenos Aires, Bonpland settled down with Adeline and Emma, but with warring political factions in the city, rebellion up river, Francia's troops stationed on the border of Paraguay, and Brazil encroaching in the north, there was little thought of the promised museum or botanical garden. Bonpland was made chair of natural history but the promised salary never materialized, and the museum turned out to be one room in which a small natural history collection was stored. There was no provision for a botanical garden where Bonpland could plant out the stock he brought with him, or any buyer for the crates of books he had been encouraged to bring for a science library. Bonpland complained to a similarly disappointed friend in Rio:

> You, I, and I believe, many others, have been cruelly fooled in our hopes. I am the most to blame because I should have learned some lesson from what has occurred. But as we are now, the point is to get away with some honor. (To Joachim Lebreton, November 18, 1818)[5]

Bonpland's first thought had been for the fruit trees, grape vines, medicinal plants, and willow trees for baskets and fences he brought with him. He purchased on terms with his own funds a small property outside the city limits where he and his gardeners planted out saplings, roots, and cuttings, and managed to save at least a half of his stock. Back in the city, he and Adeline were immediately plunged into a hotbed of political intrigue, wrangling, gossip, pretention, and above all money-making. As Bonpland put it, "Everyone here is a merchant, you buy for two, you sell for four, and there are no other relations."[6] At some point, leaving Adeline and Emma to wait for him in Buenos Aires, Bonpland set out on an exploratory trip up river. Botanizing, prospecting—no one was quite sure which—along the border between the Argentine province of Corrientes and Paraguay, he had been arrested by a troop of Paraguayan soldiers, hit over the head, and carried away in chains, no one knew where. For all intents and purposes, Bonpland was dead and gone.

In 1826, Humboldt was ordered back to Berlin. There would be no expedition to the Orient. His *Voyage* was finished. His duties as chamberlain were at court. He could visit Paris for short periods of time every few years, but if his salary was to continue his residence would have to be Berlin and the royal palace of Sans Souci at Potsdam. It was a blow, but given his dependence on a stipend as chamberlain and his loyalty to the king, Humboldt had no choice but to obey. His arrival back in Berlin as a permanent resident was widely acclaimed. An article in the *Berliner Conversations for Poetry, Literature, and Critique* announced the return of a German hero, a scientist who did not simply calculate and measure like the small-minded French: "In the study of Nature, Herr von Humboldt has from the first directed his attention not so much to her phenomena as a conglomerate mass of objects, but rather to the deep meaning of her inner life." Prominent always was the image of Chimborazo: "He climbed the heights of natural philosophy with Schelling and Hegel without succumbing to bewildering empiricism."[7] But regardless of a warm welcome from the literati, in the streets Humboldt was a stranger. In Paris he was known everywhere. Waiters and cab drivers greeted him by name. And what good was it anyway to be praised in such company? To be compared to Schelling, who had never made an instrument measurement in his life, and to Hegel, who knew nothing about science.[8] And Chimborazo. How that image dogged him, recalling not his *Tableau* with its climate lines, but the memory of how unheroic had been the actual climb, the failure to reach the summit, the stumbling back down without measurements, with only Bonpland's mosses and flies. There were reputable Prussian scientists: Jabbo Oltmanns, who did the mathematical correlations for his *Observations on Astronomy*; Carl Friedrich Gauss at Göttingen, one of the great mathematicians of his age, with discoveries in number theory, geometry, and probability. But nothing in Berlin could compare to Paris, the Institut, the Observatory, the École Polytechnique, the young students filling the lecture halls. In Berlin scientists worked in isolation with none of the social adulation and publicity that Humboldt enjoyed in France. In short, he was marooned in a city where he had no desire to live, without the social life he enjoyed, and without the intimate friend he craved. But he had no choice. He needed the income. He would have to make the best of it.

What there was of intellectual life was hardly to his taste. Several years before, the poet and philosopher Frederick Schlegel had initiated a series of popular public lectures. The moralist Fichte debuted with his "Self-Posited Ego." Schleiermacher followed with "Christian Mediations." Afterwards came some lighter fare from Henrik Steffens, who abandoned lectures in anthropology at the University of Berlin for flights of scientific imagination. Now Schlegel was back in town and again at the podium, critiquing French physicists who failed to understand Nature as it was conceived by Schelling and Hegel. Immediately Humboldt was determined to right the wrong done to Parisian science. As a member of the Berlin Academy, it was his right to give lectures at the University, and when these proved a success, he announced his own series of public lectures for the winter of 1827–1828.

His fame preceded him. The lectures drew large audiences. At first he offered one a week, then by popular demand sometimes daily. Once in the space of only six months he gave more than sixty-six lectures. Much of the material had already been presented at informal gatherings and fashionable soirees in Paris, but never had he spoken to such large audiences. Topics followed one after another. First came a description of Nature in general terms, then the geological and geographical history of the earth with warnings against systems of natural philosophy not supported by fact or experiment. Science, he lectured his audience, was not some "short sweet saturnalia of a merely mental science of nature" as "local theorists" presented it, but offered real value. There was the beauty of nature to inspire poetry and landscape painting and the consolation of escape from trivial details of existence to a higher universal point of view. Audiences kept coming. Humboldt went back over old ground, covering subjects in more detail, citing name after name of scientists he knew and whose work he consulted, putting on exhibit the extent of his acquaintance and knowledge in all areas of science. Wilhelm wrote to Goethe in Jena: "Alexander is really a puissance and he has acquired a kind of fame by his lectures." But, as Wilhelm went on to remark, fame, no matter how eagerly sought, never seemed to sit very comfortably with his brother: "He is more than ever his former self, and still characterized by a kind of shyness, an unmistakable anxiety traceable in his manner when presenting himself before the public" (CB II, 121). There were moments when it all had to seem a failure. He was the great explorer, but only for a few short years. He had missed out on Napoleon's expedition to

Egypt and failed to join Baudin. The expedition to Asia that he talked about so much never materialized. The dream of Mexico faded. He was fifty-nine and feeling the effects of age.

Then, just when any possibility of a new expedition seemed to have vanished, a messenger arrived at his door. The Russian finance minister had some questions for him about precious metals. Was it possible to make coinage out of platinum? Was there reason to think there might be deposits of that precious metal in Russia's Asian territories? Might there be other valuable minerals there not yet exploited or discovered? Better still, would Humboldt be willing to lead an official survey of mines in the Urals for the tsar of Russia? It was hardly the grand voyage Humboldt once planned, but it was Asia, with the possibility of crossing Siberia all the way to China. Yes, answered Humboldt, but this time he would not pay for it out of his own pocket. He could manage a carriage for himself, his servant, and a geologist—Gustav Rose—to assist him in his observations and measurements. The rest would have to come from the tsar. The itinerary would have to extend all the way to the border with China, and he could leave only after finishing the course of lectures he was scheduled to give in Berlin. All the conditions were met, including the further addition of a naturalist, Christian Ehrenberg, to help with collecting. There was one proviso: It was to be a purely scientific trip. There could be no political critique or social commentary, no mention of serfs, or lower classes, or forms of government. Humboldt responded that he understood. A foreigner like himself, not speaking Russian, was bound to misunderstand and might spread false rumors.[9]

On April 29, 1829, two coaches set out from Berlin bound for Saint Petersburg. Humboldt rode in the first coach along with Rose, a mineralogist, and Ehrenberg, who carried a box of medicine in case Humboldt was taken ill. All were well wrapped up in furs and blankets against the early spring chill. A second carriage followed stacked high with luggage and instruments presided over by Humboldt's personal valet, Seifert. It was a hard, uncomfortable ride through cold and melting snow. Arrived in Saint Petersburg, Humboldt had dinner with the royal family, was charmed by the tsarina, and received a generous bill of credit to use on the trip. After several weeks of receptions and formalities, three coaches, purchased especially for the occasion, were ready to take him and his party on to Moscow. After a further round of festivities, the entourage headed east with a mounted escort of mining officials, local dignitaries, and armed guards.

Even in the comfort of the carriages, it was no easy trip. Unpaved roads churned with mud from spring melting. Accommodations were often primitive.

First came a long trek over open plains to the Volga River. Humboldt, dressed in his usual frock coat and flowing white scarf, would sometimes get out and walk by the coach to the amusement of his escort. At the Volga, a barge waited to take them up river to Kazan, a Moslem city where the inhabitants wore turbans. Then it was on to the Ural Mountains and the object of the journey, touring mines and prospecting for ores. After a month taking samples came a quick dash to the Chinese border through empty grassland, shut up in the coach, often having to wear face masks to protect against mosquitoes and an ongoing typhus epidemic. Arrived at the border at the end of August, Humboldt stood and gazed east into Asia. There was little to see there: several shelters, two Mongol guards under the command of a Chinaman in a silk gown, and a valley with grazing camels. Six months after leaving Berlin, he was back in Moscow for ceremonies even more elaborate then on the eve of his departure.

Invited to a special session of the Moscow Academy of Science, Humboldt prepared to give a talk on geomagnetic and meteorological phenomena, but found instead a parade of dignitaries and professors. Inside the hall he sat and listened to a long poem written for the occasion hailing him as "Humboldt the Prometheus of Our Days." In St. Petersburg it was much the same. Days were spent with the tsar and tsarina. He was given a sable cloak worth 5,000 rubles and a seven-foot-tall malachite vase. He had a chance to give his talk in response to an address in his honor at a special session of the Imperial Petersburg Academy of Science:

> Returned to my country after having traversed the icy crest of the Cordilleras and forests of the deep tropical regions, returned to an agitated Europe after having so long enjoyed the calm of nature and the imposing aspect of its wild fecundity, I have received from this illustrious Academy . . . (CI I, 286)

He was "unworthy," he went on, could hardly emulate the "eloquence" of the address that had just been made in his honor, but would say something about important discoveries made on this his second voyage:

> By a happy chain of events, in the course of a life both unquiet and sometimes laborious, I have been able to compare the gold-bearing regions of the Urals to those of New Grenada, rock layers of porphyry and trachyte in Mexico to those of the Altai, the plains (llanos) of the Orinoco to the steppes of southern Siberia. (CI I, 287)

Siberia is a vast land, he told his audience, ready for "the peaceful conquests of agriculture and the industrial arts, which enrich the people at the same time as they soften manners and progressively ameliorate the state of societies." Voyages like his own that reveal such possibilities were dependent on savants like themselves who supplied the instruments that made it possible for an explorer to "rise to the level of his century." Even more so did progress require "the support of magnanimous sovereigns like your own Tsar willing to fund such missions." There was much more to explorations like his own, concluded Humboldt, than simply meeting physical needs:

> The Western peoples have brought into the different parts of the world those forms of civilization, this development of human under-standing the origin of which goes back to the time of intellectual grandeur of Greece and the softening influence of Christianization. Divided by language and customs, by institutions political and religious, the enlightened peoples of our day—and this is one of the most beautiful results of modern civilization—form but one single family in that they have that great interest in the sciences, letters, and arts, in all that born from an interior source and from a depth of thought and sentiment, elevates man above the vulgar needs of society. (CI I, 298)

Still, at the end of a long talk, Humboldt did not neglect to make specific some of "vulgar needs" that government-funded expeditions like his own served. Astronomical instruments and calculations made it possible to precisely determine the location of ships at sea and the boundaries of newly annexed or pacified territories. Atmospheric studies of humidity and temperature patterns could be correlated with deforestation and the level of the water in lakes and rivers with an effect on agriculture. A global network of geomagnetic stations stretching around the earth could be established to assist mapping and navigation (CI I, 299). Little mention was made of the interests actually served on his trip to the Urals: deposits of platinum that might replace silver as a basis of currency, diverting more of the flow of wealth to Russia, or better still gold, or, as Humboldt promised the tsar, diamonds. Perhaps Humboldt was wary of making too specific a claim for increased yields. Newspapers that year of 1829 were beginning to blame him for the disastrous bubble in the sale of shares in Mexican mines marketed with so much reference to the optimistic predictions of yields in his *Political Essay on the Kingdom of New Spain*. In St. Petersburg his was a consoling message. The higher view that "elevates man above the vulgar needs of society" also leads to increases in national power and wealth.[10]

Back in Berlin, Humboldt read a memoir at the Royal Academy of Berlin on the scientific results of his trip—"Considerations on Mountain Systems and Volcanic Phenomena of the Asian Interior." A collection of miscellaneous writings was gotten together for publication in Paris, *Fragments de géologie et de climatologie asiatiques*. For the most part Humboldt left the scientific findings of the expedition to his two companions on the trip.[11]

In Berlin, Humboldt took back up his duties as chamberlain, administering to the physical and mental needs of Frederick William and his family. He accompanied the king to Warsaw for the opening of the Polish parliament. A few months later he personally escorted Frederick William's daughter, now tsarina of Russia, back to Russia after a visit to Prussia. He took an increasingly addled king to health spas. When the "July Revolution" of 1830 in Paris sent shock waves through royal courts, he traveled to Paris to observe and report back on the dangerously liberal monarchy of Louis Philippe. In Paris he saw little of Arago, now a delegate in a reconstituted and very active Chamber of Deputies, but found a new protégé to befriend and cultivate. Approached by a twenty-four-year-old Louis Agassiz, Humboldt invited the young man to dinner. "How much I learned in that one dinner," said Agassiz. Humboldt promised to sell Agassiz's work to a publisher, and when that failed, sent the young man money out of his own pocket.[12]

13

Warlords and Kings

Then suddenly, without warning, came news of that other friend, thought lost forever, dead or locked up in some Paraguayan dungeon. A letter was reprinted in European newspapers from Aimé Bonpland to Roguin, founder of a merchant firm in Buenos Aires.

São Borja, February 22, 1831

My dear old friend:

Convinced of the lively interest you have always taken in my lot, I have made haste to tell you of my departure from Paraguay. After a stay of twenty months at Itapúa, where I established and left behind a second agricultural enterprise, I left for the Paraná River after an official order of February 2. . . . To put an end to the funereal suppositions that you and all my friends must naturally have made during the nine years of my detention in Paraguay, I must tell you that I lived there a life as happy as possible for one deprived of all communication with his country, his family, and his friends. (AB, 80–81)

There had been more to Bonpland's trip up river than botanizing. Arriving in the city in the spring of 1817, he and Adeline were warmly welcomed by the French community, but there was little chance of leaving the "feuding monarchies" of Europe behind. As the Spanish empire disintegrated, England, France, and a now-independent United States competed for access to territory, raw materials, and markets for manufactured goods. Fearing that so-called "free trade" would lead to a British monopoly, French agents campaigned for a La Plata monarchy with a French royal at its head, perhaps the liberal "Duke of

233

Chartres" Louis Philippe. The British held back on recognizing independence, angling for favorable trade and investment deals. Inland, remnants of the Spanish army and groups of creole monarchists fought on, while in Buenos Aires a small cabal of Bonapartists from Napoleon's disbanded army plotted a coup. Meanwhile, upriver, local leaders resisted rule from the port city. A so-called unitarian constitution went into effect in 1819, and rebellion in the city forced Pueyrredón to resign as director and go into exile. For months there was no effective government. When Francisco Ramírez from Entre Ríos and Estanislao López from Santa Fe defeated a national army at Cepeda and declared a federation of independent provinces, Buenos Aires was in a state of crisis. If Rivadavia's university and botanical garden had ever been a possibility, there seemed little chance of it in any near future. Bonpland was ready to look elsewhere, and where better to look than the vast deltas, wetlands, and rivers of the Río de la Plata estuarial system, covering 3 million square kilometers of territory in Argentina, Brazil, Uruguay, and Paraguay?

Early in his stay in the city, he had begun to explore the delta, first the border island of Martín García at the mouth of the Uruguay River and then up into the Paraná Delta. He took a canoe through twisting channels between small islands, noting rich grazing lands, stands of willow and poplar, orange trees gone wild, heavy with fruit overhanging the banks. There in the wetlands he found an ever-changing world of water and shifting land, rich with birds, fish, and wildlife, far more valuable in his view that the tariffs and taxes so fought over in the city or the imported European products sold in city shops. Beyond the delta were the great rivers. The Paraná, flowing three thousand miles south from Corrientes and the border of Paraguay, and further back still from the highlands of Brazil and the famous Iguazu Falls. The Paraguay River, flowing south down to Corrientes from Asunción, where Bonpland's friend Roguin, director of a merchant house in Buenos Aires, kept an office. And the great Uruguay, with its rapids and waterfalls flowing through Rio Grande do Sul down a vast canyon and on to the coast and Montevideo. When an opportunity arose to accompany one of Roguin's agents on a trip upriver, Bonpland grasped at it. Perhaps upriver there would be somewhere he could settle his family and put his knowledge to work.

Nor after his capture had he been locked up in a dungeon in Paraguay. Instead he was given a piece of land to develop near the town of Santa María de Fe. There he set up a medical clinic, planted a diversity of crops, bred livestock, made remedies from native Paraguayan plants, and experimented with distilling local liquors, hiring at times as many as forty workers. But then abruptly, after eight years, he had been ordered to leave Paraguay for reasons that were never made clear, taking with him all his moveable belongings: livestock, tools, botanical and other collections, manuscripts, and any books he managed to acquire. Writing his letter to Roguin, he was on the Brazilian side of the Uruguay at the mission town of São Borja, waiting for his livestock and carts of baggage to cross the river. In short, Bonpland was very much alive and ready to resume work he began nine years before. He would explore the Jesuit missions on the Portuguese side of the Uruguay. He would go to Corrientes to recover what he could of his possessions there. He would come back to São Borja and settle his belongings in safekeeping. He would go downriver to Buenos Aires, try to locate Adeline and Emma, see about getting back his pension and retrieve what was left of his collections to send to the Muséum in Paris.

In regard to his treatment by Francia he was diplomatic. Apart from not being able to communicate outside the country, he had been given a degree of freedom. He was treated well by local officials. He lived pleasantly, practicing medicine and collecting and growing a variety of plants. He ran a distillery, a tannery and a forge, sold his products in the neighboring town and made a comfortable living. Most important, perhaps, he came to know what it was to work intimately with a piece of land. Unmentioned in his letter to Roguin was a less happy circumstance. In Paraguay, he shared his life and work with a partner, María Chirivé, an Indian woman with whom he had two young children, all of whom, on Francia's orders, he had to leave behind.[1]

Shown a copy of Bonpland's letter, Humboldt immediately wrote from Paris, posting the letter to Bonpland in Corrientes—"Afraid for such a long time as to your situation, sometimes even for your existence, my dear and excellent friend, I cannot describe to you the joy that seized me at the news of your deliverance." It had been so long, and there was much to tell, Humboldt's thoughts came quickly in a rush of disconnection. He had asked the French government to give the order to have Bonpland brought back to his country. He was in Paris for eight months on a diplomatic visit "made necessary by the agitation of all Europe." He celebrated his sixtieth year deep in Siberia. He traveled to the border of China. Soon he would be forced to return to Berlin.

I cannot wait to see you again, dear, dear Bonpland, to know what you have suffered. Now I do not know if I may soon be forced to go home in spite of the frightful cholera epidemic. At Tobolsk, just as at Berlin and Paris, everyone has been talking about you. (AB, 230)

Humboldt assured Bonpland: The President of the French Council said that there should be no problem getting back the arrears of his pension. In the meantime, always quick with financial help, Humboldt enclosed a letter of credit payable to financial agents in Buenos Aires:

> I am always very poor, but I thought that perhaps a miserable little sum of a thousand piasters could be useful. I flatter myself that in the end I will have your news direct. I have earned it by the affection and the gratitude I have for you. (AB, 230)

When Bonpland went to Corrientes in January to retrieve belongings left there, Humboldt's letter was waiting for him, and as soon as he arrived in Buenos Aires, he answered, posting the letter to Paris with thanks and a reciprocal outpouring of nostalgic affection and regret.

> Whatever steps I take, whatever the places in which I find myself, whatever may be the distance that separates us, my friend, I find everywhere new proofs of your generosity and especially your unalterable friendship. You know my heart better than anyone. . . . Dear Humboldt, how many times since 1816 you have been the principal object of my thoughts! How many memories of the past have tormented my soul, but I must also say, eased it. I have always wanted to satisfy your desires, and if one single time you have found in me any opposition, it was no more than momentary. I acceded all; I had to do it, and I will congratulate myself for it all my life. (ABH, 184–185)

Their disagreements over publication, the decision to give up work on *New Genera and Species*, his abandonment of Europe for a new life in America, Humboldt's rebuke in his 1818 letter: all struck a chord of regret. Nostalgia for their travels together on the Orinoco and in the high Andes remained strong just as it would throughout the rest of their two now very different lives. He was, Bonpland went on, in a flurry of activity. Although it might seem that he had been under an "unlucky star" for fifteen years, he would now like to think his fate will improve. He was taking up his work with great energy so as to return to his country as soon as possible.

It was a promise his friends would hear often in coming years, as Bonpland energetically pursued multiple projects in botany, agroforestry, and land management. He was waiting in the city, he went on in his letter to Humboldt, waiting for his collections to arrive from Paraguay and the missions. When they came he would organize them and send them on to the Muséum along with the collections made recently in Corrientes and São Borja. He will send plants to the Jardin, and rocks and mineral samples to the Muséum, both those collected recently and those he will collect on future excursions to Montevideo and other locations. For the moment, he is settled comfortably with their mutual friend Pedro de Angelis in Buenos Aires and has room to work on his collections, which were badly jumbled and disordered during his nine-year absence. As for return to France? Yes, but first he must visit the Portuguese missions and finish the surveys he began so many years before, and much else:

> The fertility of the soil and the richness of the vegetation are such in the Portuguese missions that I feel obliged to return there, and I think that even those who want so much to interest themselves in my prompt return to Europe will not disapprove of this voyage. It would be cruel to leave without enriching botany with such remarkable productions. (AB, 83)

As usual Bonpland could not resist giving examples. The roots of a new species of convolvulus seemed to have the same properties as salep, a hot beverage made from flour made of ground orchid bulbs being imported into Europe as a substitute for coffee or tea. Given the concern that its use was causing a depletion of stocks of wild orchids, finding a substitution from the common bindweed family might prove important. And the School of Medicine might want to do tests on a new genus of the Simaroubaceae family with a taste similar to quinine that he had used in his medical practice in Paraguay to treat stomach problems. Once its efficacy was established he would be able to arrange shipments back to Paris hospitals.

There were losses to face, not all of them easy or possible to retrieve. Much had been ruined or lost in his collections. Adeline and Emma were gone. Tired of waiting for him in Buenos Aires, Adeline went to Rio de Janeiro, where she petitioned the emperor on Bonpland's behalf, and then to France, to Lima, and was now untraceable according to inquiries made by Roguin. A few years later Bonpland would receive a loving but heart-breaking letter from Emma telling him of her suffering after his abduction and thanking him for all he had done for her:

> She whom you were happy to call your dear girl is always worthy of that name. She feels too much all that she owes to you, and the

memory of your kindness is deeply engraved on her heart. It would be so sweet someday to show you all her gratitude: And how not to love you, you so good, so generous, you who were for me more than a father, a benefactor, a friend. (ABH, 172)

Emma's sad story had a happy ending. After years in a convent where she was deposited by her mother, she was now in Paris happily married to a surgeon-dentist and with two children. The news, communicated by Emma, that Adeline had suddenly shown up in Paris no doubt tempered any inclination Bonpland might have had to accept Emma's invitation to come and live with her and her family so she could "embellish his old age." It had not been easy living with Adeline in Buenos Aires. Her impolitic involvement in political intrigues was one of the reasons for Bonpland's decision to explore upriver. And the story Emma told of Adeline's treatment of her after his disappearance could not have made the idea of reunion very appealing. Nor was Bonpland in any way ready to abandon America.

In Buenos Aires, another concern was his pension. Instructions had gone out from Paris to French diplomats and agents in Buenos Aires. They were to give Bonpland all aid and assistance and do whatever necessary to facilitate his repatriation, but regardless of Humboldt's assurances, restarting and getting back the arrears of the pension proved difficult. By French law, pensions were terminated if a "certificate of life" was not filed on schedule. Also by French law, there could be no restitution of arrears. But Bonpland was in no way destitute. He supported himself modestly in Paraguay. Much of his medical service was given free of charge or in exchange for local goods, but wealthy patients also came and paid for consultation. He made good profits with his French cakes and eau-de-vie. Produce from his gardens—by one diary entry, parsley, cabbage, melons, citrons, tomatoes, basil, cilantro fava beans, petits pois—sold well in local markets. Medicines made in his dispensary were in demand. He brought with him from Paraguay sufficient funds to buy a farmstead in São Borja, where he pastured his livestock and stored his books, tools, collections, and manuscripts. What he had in mind was hardly quiet retirement. It was to continue work barely begun when he was abducted and carried away to Paraguay, and for that funds were needed. Bonpland had not simply wandered into Paraguayan territory.

Back in 1821, exploring from the town of Corrientes along the upper Paraná, he came on ruins of the once-flourishing Jesuit missions of the Guarani Republic. Here he found remnants not only of churches, but of workshops and gardens, and, of even greater interest, groves of yerba, the tree whose leaves are used to prepare maté, the South America tea. He explored Candelaria, once administrative headquarters for a federation of mission towns that spanned Spanish and Portuguese territory. At the site of another mission, Santa Ana, he found salvageable buildings, pastures, groves of oranges growing freely in rich valley soil. With the support of Francisco Ramírez, who had declared himself head of an independent Republic of Entre Ríos, he met with the commander of the local Guarani militia, Artigas. With Artigas's help he organized work crews to begin to repair the damage done to yerba groves by twenty years of banditry and warfare. There were warnings. A Paraguayan fort directly across the river at Ytapua was manned by Francia's troops, Francia who closed Paraguay's borders to outsiders, who claimed territory on either side of the Paraná, who jealously guarded Paraguay's monopoly of yerba, "the Paraguayan herb." Bonpland ignored the warnings. As sure of the good scientific and social sense of his botanical ventures as Humboldt was sure of the cosmic truths of nature, Bonpland brushed danger aside. He would deal with the Paraguayans rationally, he would convince Francia that he meant no harm, show him that cooperation between European scientists and Paraguay was in the interest of all parties. What could be wrong with reviving deserted plantations and repairing the damage to valuable trees? With his teams of Indian workers, Bonpland went to work, clearing brush, shoring up buildings, and pruning trees.

He took trips, exploring neighboring forests, camping out at night, mapping terrain, and learning Guarani, a language rich in names for plants and animals. Even after years of brutal civil conflict, it was a land of wild beauty with marshes, small rivers, open savannah, and dense patches of jungle. Could a scientist be a threat to the powerful dictator of Paraguay? His motives were peaceful. With proper respectful negotiation they could collaborate. Why not a fruitful exchange of trade, botanical expeditions north into Paraguayan territory rumored to be exceptionally rich in plants? A first shipment of yerba was cut and dried, almost ready to go downriver in one of Roguin's ships. Other shipments might soon go up the Paraguay to Asunción. Why should Francia object? Bonpland was a scientist and a physician. He was in sympathy with Francia's defense of the poor and his closing of Paraguay's borders to bandits and warlords. Bonpland wrote a letter, addressing it to Francia by way of the commander at the fort at Ytapua. No answer came back, only the next day canoes on the river and soldiers who called out to him as he stood on shore. He had to leave immediately, they told him. Bonpland ignored the order. He would wait to hear from Francia himself. A week later a troop of armed men appeared at the landing near where Bonpland had his headquarters.

Bonpland's journal entry for December 8, 1821: "Toward eight in the morning the Paraguayans entered the village of Santa Ana with armed force, and we were treated as enemies." With those words Bonpland had disappeared. Now returned, he was determined to continue what he had only barely begun nine years before.

In Buenos Aires much had changed since he had left, and not necessarily for the better. In June of 1821, while Bonpland was exploring mission territory upriver, Bernardino Rivadavia had returned from Europe to become minister and then president of a new United Provinces of Argentina. Order was restored and Rivadavia announced far-reaching improvements. In the city there would be avenues and paved streets, sewage systems, schools, state houses, and universities just as in European capitals. How much these projects would improve prospects for the provinces upriver was unclear. Even more doubtful was the financing: large loans from London banks, much of which ended up in private hands, creating crippling debt that would not be paid off until the next century, giving the British a say in Argentine affairs not always beneficial. As Bonpland put it to his friend Adolphe Brunel, "Rivadavia seduced the country with theories of European order which were premature; the innovator wanted to improvise a European state with a people that he knew only a little and hardly accurately" (Brunel, 69).

It was not long before rebellion in the provinces and war with Brazil over territory on the east bank of the Uruguay brought down Rivadavia's unitarian government and forced Rivadavia into exile. Peace under rival federalists was short-lived, as was the presidency of the "unitarian" General Juan Lavalle, who attacked the capital and arrested and executed anyone suspected of federalist sympathies. While Bonpland waited in Itapúa for his final exit permit from Paraguay, Juan Manuel Rosas, cattle baron and Indian fighter, took Buenos Aires by storm, proclaiming himself "Restorer of the Laws" and supreme keeper of the peace. The city's residents, exhausted by years of violence and instability, made little protest. By the time Bonpland arrived back in the city, Rosas had a firm hold on power, supported by business interests and merchants, who quickly grasped the advantages of summary justice and a crony network of profiteers. Bonpland was celebrated as guest of honor at a banquet commemorating the Paris revolution of 1830. He offered a toast to Presidente Rosas. Otherwise he kept a prudent distance from city politics.

Immediately Bonpland went to work. Waiting for his crates of plant specimens to arrive from upriver, he began organizing what remained of his collections left in Buenos Aires for shipment to Paris and the Muséum. He also made an attempt to reinstate some of the projects he took on ten years before as "chair" of natural history. One was a survey of the flora and fauna of the Río de la Plata with commentary in Spanish and local names and uses, another a comprehensive plan for land use for the city and its environs. Already the urban sprawl of Buenos Aires was spreading upriver into the delta. Never would Bonpland forget his first impressions of the beauty and richness of wetland pastures and woodlands. In May he traveled upriver to the remnants of the agricultural colony founded by John and William Robertson at Monte Grande. In June he put together "Notes for Agricultural Establishment," a plan for land use in the province of Buenos Aires that could guide future settlement and development. Close in to the city would be a zone of intensive market farming to produce food for the city and products for export. Further out would come ranches for cattle raising with herd sizes calibrated to acreage and forage, and with special attention to dairy stock and merino sheep. Further out still would be managed forest for timber and other forest products.[2] Always, when time allowed, he continued to collect plants, insects, and birds.

That first summer back in Buenos Aires, Bonpland wrote letter after letter to Humboldt, addressing them to Paris, where he assumed Humboldt still lived, describing his many activities after so many years of silence. On the first of June, he followed his May 7 letter with an update. He had word that his shipments from upriver would arrive in eight days. As for returning to France, he told the French ministry what he must do before he can leave and how much he had already accomplished:

> I like to think that the government will look with pleasure on my determination to stay, since the principal object is to be useful to the sciences, to acquire additional material, and to recover what I have lost, at least a part. (AB, 84).

He is sending a second shipment of seed with ninety-two new species of plants to the Jardin in Paris—"I am not sending a separate shipment to you, since your relation with the Muséum is such that you can take what you want from them." But he will send seed to the botanical garden in Berlin if necessary. And he has a new project, collecting birds, which he fears are in danger given unrestricted marketing in the city of rare species:

> Everyone here is interested in birds, but I can see it is more a question of mercantile speculation than of science. Since I have birds from Paraguay and from this part of America, I think it a good idea to embalm and describe all that I can get. (AB, 85)

He has assembled a team of assistants, hired a young Frenchman to help with embalming bird specimens. He has located one of the gardeners he brought with him from Paris, who will go upriver with him to help collect living plants. Yerba is still on his mind. "I have much to say about the tea of Paraguay and the geography of this precious plant."

On and on he wrote in the old easy manner. There was still so much he wanted to explore—Patagonia, the Falklands, Chile, Tucumán—but he knows he must resist and perhaps be content with Brazil. He has so many questions to ask about publications in Europe, about Kunth's progress on the botanical work, about researchers like the botanist Augustin Saint-Hilaire, who he heard may be in Brazil. The long rambling letter ends with affection. "My famous friend, I see you every day more great, at every instant I admire you more."

On July 12 Bonpland profited from the departure of a French official for France to send with him yet another letter to Humboldt and some papers relevant to his pension, still assuming Humboldt was living in Paris. No word had yet come back from his old friend and he was worried, Bonpland said, about the cholera epidemic that Humboldt mentioned in his 1831 letter to Corrientes:

> I am slow, dear Humboldt, to know how this infernal cholera, which already has reached the harbor of Buenos Aires, has treated you. I don't really think it will get to you, because you have a great power of repulsive spirit for anything contrary to you. Meanwhile, the day that I see a written word from your hand will be, for me, a new day of happiness. (AB, 88)

His collections from upriver had almost been lost in a shipwreck—"Was this a return of my evil star?"—but finally they had arrived and he is opening and arranging them. He would soon return to the Portuguese missions where "spring awaits me." Meanwhile he has managed to get and read Saint-Hilaire's account of travels in Brazil:[3]

> One thing that gave me pleasure in this travel book was to find there Guarani names which justified the idea that I had formed of the immense extent of that nation and the great role they played on this continent before as well as after the conquest. I burn with impatience to see again the names we took down, or rather the words of diverse tribes or nations, as they should be called, that we knew on the Orinoco.[4]

Much as Bonpland enjoyed reading Saint-Hilaire's Guarani names, he was not so impressed with Saint-Hilaire's botanizing:

> I admire the assurance with which he announces the publication of the most interesting plants of Paraguay, where he has never been, and of which he could have gotten any clear idea only from Rengger and Longchamp who certainly would not have told him anything very precise. It is the fortunate voyager who sustains the old adage: "A good liar comes from afar." (AB, 89)[5]

Second-hand botany was hardly the most serious of Bonpland's complaints in Buenos Aires that summer as he waited for his collections to arrive from upriver. In the city, French and English agents intrigued and maneuvered to make profitable deals. Merchants and officials grew rich on the tariffs and duties charged on all commerce up and down the river. Provinces upriver were starved of development capital, flooded with expensive imported goods, unable to develop local industries and products beyond the export of rough cattle hides and salted meat. At the same time, upriver there was little unity. Bands of gaucho cowboys rallied around charismatic leaders. Demands were made, for free trade, a sharing of income from duties and taxes, a degree of protection for local industries. Each time, personal rivalries and a lack of competent command undermined any common front against the port and its stranglehold on commerce. Always the winner was Rosas, prototype for a long line of South American autocrats who would style themselves restorers of order and the personification of a national ethos:

> In effect this country, far from prospering, is going considerably downhill, with intrigues and parties which successively destroy each other, one after another. The government, such as it is, has the crazy pretention to duplicate our old governments in Europe. As a result, the South Americans prepare and hasten their fall which will be without remedy. (AB, 90)

To make matters worse, he told Humboldt, an incompetent French consul general and his scheming wife with ties to Rosas refused to allow a newly appointed French consul to enter the city:

> The government, to the great scandal of all of Buenos Aires that knows about such a pitiful intrigue, refuses to admit M. de la

Forest, who was named consul-general by the French government and chargé d'affairs in this republic. This has occupied the public much more than the cholera, which is again in the harbor, and is a cause of mourning for anyone who is French and for the sane mass of Americans. . . . As for the Americans, I am ashamed to say it, they are not truly yet worthy of being free and they will continue to make as many idiot mistakes as is necessary to bring about an advance in their education. (AB, 91)

It was a sad outburst for a man just returned from captivity and trying to make a new life for himself: a cholera epidemic barely held at bay, reckless military adventures, rival factions at each other's throats more out of ego and greed than principle. Most angering of all, the breakdown in French-Argentinean relations had resulted in a blockade of the port. Bonpland's shipment of cases for the Muséum in Paris still sat in the French consulate waiting to be sent.

Writing to Humboldt again in August, again addressing his letter to Paris, Bonpland still had no word from his friend since the first note and letter of credit waiting for him in Corrientes. Bonpland repeated his thanks for the advance of funds. In case his letters had been lost, he reviewed much of what he told Humboldt in previous letters. Again the Portuguese missions and yerba maté are on his mind. He wants to survey the rest of mission territory, assess what is left of the yerbas, increase his understanding of "Ilex, this tree from which Paraguayan tea is made," establish ways of drying and preparing the leaves other than those used by the Spanish, "who have followed blindly without making even the slightest changes." And he must finish collecting plants of the region. As for return to France:

I must tell you that I desire it as much as I fear it. Meanwhile I like to think that all my fears will dissipate when I see myself with collections that will offer me more advantages than those I would have had when I left Paraguay, and that I will have when I have gotten the little bit of information I lack on the agriculture of this country. (ABH, 193)

Not reassuring to anyone hoping for Bonpland's return to France would have been the rest of the letter. He wanted to explore not just the missions and Entre Ríos, but also Patagonia, Chile, and Bolivia, which might take one or two years. Nor did it seem that he would settle down to the business of publishing his works and securing his reputation:

An idea that suits me much when I think of Europe is the hope of
occupying myself practically with agriculture. During my detention
in Paraguay, I experienced with large-scale cultivation consolation
that I would like to mix with publications I would necessarily
occupy myself with after my return to France. (ABH, 194)

In other words, if there was "consolation" for Bonpland, it would not be in
clouds of literary celebrity with Humboldt, it would be on the ground, putting science and honorable enterprise to work. For Humboldt it had been so
clear. Travel in foreign lands was useful, both to establish a reputation and to
provide material for publication. Then one brought back what was discovered
to civilized Europe. But the "forms, the attitude of America," alluded to in
the first ecstatic letter to Michel from Bonpland in Cumaná were not so easily
transportable.

To make it worse, war between Buenos Aires and the breakaway province of Uruguay now threatened to prevent Bonpland's return up river to São
Borja. Afraid to remain any longer and be marooned in the city, Bonpland
took up the unfinished catalog and the commentaries he was writing for the
collections waiting at the French consulate and booked passage. Even then
there was trouble when contraband sabers were found on board the ship at the
dock. Rosas's troops were battling General Lavalle's unitarian forces upriver and
arms sales were forbidden. It was an order regularly circumvented by bribing
customs agents. In this case agents turned traitor and alerted the police. For
a moment it looked like Bonpland's "evil star" had returned, but after a delay
the situation was resolved. The ship was released, and Bonpland was on his
way upriver, giving his letter for Humboldt to a businessman about to leave
for France who would try to get it to Humboldt in Paris.

If Humboldt's image of his unfortunate friend did not match the reality of this
energetic man in motion, neither did Bonpland's image of Humboldt "every
day more great" quite match Humboldt in the 1830s and 1840s. Yes, he was
the famous traveler and author celebrated both in Europe and the Americas,
but he was not in Paris. He was either in cold damp Berlin or at the king's
palace at Potsdam, where regardless of the success of his public lectures and
writings his situation was more and more uncomfortable. The 1830 revolution
in Paris that deposed Charles X in favor of the constitutional monarchy of Louis
Philippe threw panic into royal courts in Germany and other parts of Europe.

For cautious liberals like Humboldt they were difficult times. Humboldt wrote to his friend François Guizot, who had served in the old House of Deputies in Paris and was now a minister in the new government.

> We count on the fact of your intellectual serenity, and on the fact that the political storm leaves you time to profit from the high sphere in which you are placed so as to advance the cultivation of good studies and deliver those studies from forms so contrary to the progress of public liberty. (CI II, 95)

As a moderate deputy, Guizot was pressed into drawing up a formal protest against Charles X's repressive "July Ordinances." Reluctantly he had supported the succession of Louis Philippe, but, distrusted by republicans like Humboldt's friend Arago, in the new administration he was given the minor post of minister of education. After offering to help a protégé of Guizot's in Berlin, and requests for aid for several of his own young friends in Paris, at the end of his letter Humboldt asked an additional favor:

> I was happy finally to have some news of my unfortunate friend M. Bonpland, and I would like it if it might be possible to get him . . . some kind of purely French decoration. (CI II, 95)

The next spring from Potsdam, Humboldt added to his letter of sympathy for a death in Guizot's family a thank you:

> I would like to tell also of my great gratitude in that you have deigned to remember my unfortunate friend, M. Bonpland in fulfilling the plea I made of you last autumn by making him a member of the Legion of Honor. This nomination gives me much satisfaction. I must fear for my travel companion that which arrives so easily in human affairs. When he had the fortune to be in the claws of Dr. Dictator, the republican tyrant from the banks of the Thames to the banks of the Obi, people asked me for news of him, pitying his fate. Drama fini: It's only a savant who traveled to collect some nice plants. One fears that he has been forgotten. (CI II, 106)

He also heard from some of Bonpland's friends, Humboldt added, that Guizot was helping in the effort to restore Bonpland's pension, the pension that had, Humboldt pointed out, been procured for Bonpland by him, Humboldt:

> M. Bonpland's pension of three thousand francs was based on the
> gift I made to the Jardin des plantes from the herbarium of my
> voyage. I deprived myself to be useful to my friend. I do not possess
> a shred of leaf, not a single souvenir of Chimborazo. (CI II, 107)

Humboldt continued to do what he could to further negotiations on Bonpland's pension, sending letters from Berlin and forwarding documents. Still there would often be that twinge of resentment. Had Bonpland's danger been overplayed, compared to what he was enduring in Europe? Did people remember it was he, Humboldt, who led the voyage that established Bonpland's reputation? Forced to curry favor at court to earn his pay and occasional cash tips on which he was financially dependent, with close friends Humboldt would more and more allow himself to descend from the high vantage of "truths of nature" to reveal a more vulnerable and petulant self.

Obliging the king, having to suppress any liberal sympathies, taking refuge in a "general theory of nature," he was not finding it easy to understand Bonpland's insistence on visiting ever-more-remote sites of deserted Jesuit missions, or why, for that matter, Bonpland had insisted on "collecting" so close to the border of a hostile Paraguay. Humboldt's impression of mission life in the highlands outside of Caracas had not been positive, nor had he been as interested as Bonpland in traces of Jesuit ingenuity or Guarani names. Even for Bonpland, the full significance of what the Jesuits had accomplished in their South American missions only gradually became clear. For Humboldt, it had to seem very far away. Distrusted by conservatives, who feared that as a Francophile and supposed liberal he might sway the court to the left, at the same time as he was repeatedly pressed into service as a loyal representative of the monarchy in diplomatic meetings and conferences convened to ward off the threat of French radicalism, Humboldt was often on unsure ground. Much as he might complain of stupidity and cruelty at the Prussian Court, he was even less approving of "radicals" in the new Council of Deputies in Paris. To close friends like Karl Varnhagen, he freely vented his frustration and contempt for politicians of all kinds:

> Believe me, dear friend, my wishes go as far as yours, but my hopes
> are very feeble. I have seen changes of government in France for
> forty years. They always fall by their own incapacity; the new ones
> give always the same promises, but they never keep them, and the
> march to ruin is renewed. I was personally acquainted with most of
> the men in power, some of them intimately; there were distinguished

well-meaning men among them; but they did not persevere; after a short time they were not better than their predecessors—nay, they became even greater rascals. (LHV, 24–25)

Forced to eat breakfast with the royal children, entertaining the royal family with stories of the Orinoco at lunch, accompanying the crown prince to meetings of "potentates" and their agents and ministers, swinging back and forth like a "pendulum" between Berlin and Potsdam, trying to keep the wavering and often befuddled king informed and focused, Humboldt was hard pressed. As he himself so often reiterated, politics had never been his interest, and yet it was on politics that he was forced to rely, dependent on his salary as chamberlain and committed to the king.

There was one consolation. Traveling between royal residences, answering letters from fans and favorites, promoting his project of establishing a chain of observation stations circling the globe, keeping up with duties at court, writing late into the night, he was beginning what was to be his crowning achievement, a multi-volume work he would call simply *Cosmos*. He described the project in a letter to Varnhagen:

> I have the extravagant idea of describing in one and the same work the whole material world—all that we know to-day of celestial bodies and of life upon the earth—from the nebular stars to the mosses on the granite rocks—and to make this work instructive to the mind, and at the same time attractive, by its vivid language. Every great and sparkling idea must be noticed, side by side with its attendant facts. The work shall represent an epoch of the intellectual development of mankind in their knowledge of nature. (LHV, 35–36)

Sure that his vision was unique and like no other, using material from his Berlin lectures enlarged and augmented with additions from many secondary sources, and with his faithful friend Varnhagen as sounding board, reading and editing drafts and making suggestions, Humboldt began work on a first introductory volume. This would be no purely "metaphysical" approach to nature without basis in fact or scientific observation like the "Naturphilosophie" of Schelling. Certainly he would not mimic speculative writings like those of the Hegelians. More and more he was finding the reverence given to Hegel, who died in the 1831 cholera epidemic, an affront.

For a time work was interrupted by personal loss. In the spring of 1835 Humboldt's brother Wilhelm died after a long illness. "I never thought my old eyes had so many tears," Humboldt wrote to Varnhagen a few days later (LHV, 42). That winter in Berlin, helping to publish a posthumous collection of his brother's writings, he was oppressed by what he saw as overblown and insincere expressions of sympathy. In reference to a preface Varnhagen was providing for the collection, he wrote, "You are the only one in this harmony-barren, genius-deserted city who possesses a harmony of style and a sense of moderation in the utterance of painful sentiments" (LHV, 46). Nor was there any let-up of his duties at a court festering with anger against the French, who had betrayed the principle of hereditary rule and the "legitimacy" of monarchy. On one occasion French royals were coming to visit. Varnhagen recorded in his diary that Humboldt was in a tumult. It was Humboldt's job to see that the visitors were received with civility but at the same time roundly insulted. Hardly an easy task.

What was left of Humboldt's family continued to disappear. Caroline, his brother's wife, died. Wilhelm's eldest daughter died in 1837. Wilhelm's other daughter moved away to Posen, where her husband was stationed. No one was left at the family estate except graves, complained Humboldt; "my last family tie is severed." On his birthday in September 1835, he wrote to Bonpland telling of his sorrow at his brother's death. No answer came back. Bonpland had also deserted him. Days were busy. There were duties at court and letters to write promoting his idea of a global network of magnetic measuring stations. The Russians had more or less signed on, but the great challenge was England with its vast empire, England where he was not quite the celebrity that he was in Paris or Berlin. Their science, he thought, was too pragmatic, too utilitarian. Even the English language was lacking, a language of practical men without the resonance and depth of German. Late at night, he returned to the consolation of *Cosmos*.

Finally word reached him from Bonpland. Even when addressed to the right city, transatlantic correspondence was slow and uncertain with many letters lost or misdirected. Bonpland had not received Humboldt's letter about his brother's death until a year after it was sent and immediately responded. But when Bonpland's answering letter finally arrived in 1837, judging from Humboldt's jottings between the lines, it provided little comfort. Here with Humboldt's handwritten annotations in bold:

How greatly have I been grieved by your letter, dear Humboldt! Let me mourn with you and with your illustrious famous family the loss of the elder of the Humboldts. . . . I was not aware before of the precise date of your birthday; [**September 14, 1769—I am** antediluvian] now that I know it, I shall find a fresh occasion for specially calling you to remembrance. This year I shall certainly celebrate the day . . . sixty-six years are nothing dear Humboldt, [they are a good deal when one is unhappy!] Dr. Francia is now in his eighty-fifth year, [to what an age these tyrants live!] he is very active and vigorous and rides on horseback every day. I was born, as you know, on August 23, 1773. Before I was attacked by the two severe illnesses, from which I am now convalescent, I used to ride full gallop a distance of twelve or fifteen, and sometimes even thirty leagues a day; when my health is re-established, I must limit myself to eight or ten leagues a day. As long as one is happy, one is always young. Anxiety and grief age us, undermine our health, and at length kill us. I always imagine you are very happy; I am sure you ought to be, surrounded as you are by earthly splendor, [!!] and covered with renown, [!!] which is daily on the increase. You ought to live a century and then you will enter upon a second life which will be eternal. [a grand prospect that, forsooth!] (CB II, 196–197)

Conflicting currents of thought and feeling flow back and forth in this epistolary dialogue across space and time, misconceptions made even more painful in that they are between friends with every reason to think they know each other well. Bonpland's Humboldt sits surrounded by luxury, basking in the bright light of eternal fame. True enough. But passing up the Uruguay River into a vast river land, Bonpland could hardly have guessed how fame could sour. The Humboldt Bonpland knew in Paris was out every night at the fashionable salons, entertaining with his erudition and his stories of adventures on the Orinoco, admired, inspiring, heroic in his output of published work. None of that had changed. What changed was the sense that it was not enough, nor could anything be enough when, as Humboldt's jottings between the lines indicate, one is alone and unhappy. The life that Bonpland described—riding long distances on horseback, tending patients, collecting plants in remote regions, working with local officials—had to seem no more than distant folly. And why would Bonpland go on and on about Francia, the dictator who had locked him up? The answer, of course, might not have made much sense to Humboldt stranded in Berlin. Bonpland was watching Francia because he was waiting for him to die, at which point he could travel back up the Paraguay River and collect the plants that Saint-Hilaire knew only by hearsay, perhaps even find his lost partner María and the children he had been forced to leave behind.

Back in Berlin, Humboldt's notes to Varnhagen were peppered with insults: "This intellectually desolated city"; "Fortunately, people in the great French world are entirely free from the paltry gossip and fault-finding that rule in Berlin and Potsdam, where they subsist for months, in thoughtlessness, upon the self-created phantasy of a weak imagination" (LHV, 49, 57). More than ever he was contemptuous of what passed for intellectual life in Berlin, with Hegel's followers divided now into opposing camps, both constantly proclaiming the genius of Hegel and his "Philosophy of History." When Varnhagen, who had been a friend of Hegel's, sent Humboldt some of his own "Hegelian" commentaries on history as "molded by a man of genius," Humboldt forced himself to be gracious—"You have prepared for me a delightful pleasure"— before lapsing into thinly veiled parody:

> In the approaching millennium everything will be simplified—the individual life of nations is preserved, in spite of warlike expeditions over continents. Since the great epoch of Columbus and Gama, who made one part, one side of this planet known to the other, that fluctuating element, the ocean, has established the omnipresence of one kind of civilization (that of Western Europe). Its influence breaks through the rigid barriers of continents, and establishes new customs, new faith, new wants of life even in the most unorganised parts of the earth. The South Sea Islands are already Protestant parishes;—a floating battery, a single vessel of war, changes the fate of Chili. . . . (LHV, 56–57)[6]

The World Spirit working its way, an irresistible current that no individual could control, Humboldt with all his talk of civilization making its way inland from the coasts of America found much in the Hegelian mode to parody. Days later he sent a note of thanks to Varnhagen for a gift of a copy of Hegel's *Philosophy of History,* promising to read it:

> The historical studies of Hegel will interest me particularly, because, until now I nourished a wild prejudice against the idea that each nation individually is bound to represent an idea. In order that the predilection of the philosopher may be fulfilled I shall nevertheless read it attentively, and gladly abandon my prejudice. (LHV, 58)

Two weeks later, off for his regular visit to the spa with the crown prince, he wrote to Varnhagen that he was taking two books with him—Varnhagen's biography of Sophie Charlotte and Hegel's *Philosophy of History*—noting that his own taste tended rather to the first than to the second:

> I shall certainly find a torrent of ideas in that Hegel, whom his editor, Gans, in so masterly a manner has not deprived of his great individuality; but a man who is as I am, like an insect, inseparable from the earth and its natural variations, feels himself uneasy and constrained at an abstract assertion of totally unfounded facts and views on America and the Indian world. (LHV, 59)

Catching himself, he added in deference to Varnhagen, "At the same time I appreciate what is grand in the conception of Hegel"—but as usual could not resist a postscript:

> I have badly arranged my life; I do every thing for becoming prematurely stupid. I would gladly abandon "the European beef," which Hegel's phantasy presents as so much better than the American, and I could almost wish to live near the weak inanimate crocodiles (which, alas! measure 25 feet). (LHV, 60)[7]

Varnhagen, editing and criticizing the first drafts of *Cosmos,* continued to urge Humboldt to temper his language in relation to Hegel. Years before, when Varnhagen passed on to Humboldt Hegel's complaint that Humboldt had publically maligned him in his lectures, Humboldt had shrewdly sent on to Varnhagen notes for the wrong lecture, insisting that nothing said there could be construed as being against "philosophy" or Hegel. Now again Humboldt dodged the question. Yes, he included in a draft of a first volume of *Cosmos* passages from his lectures that ridiculed some systems of natural philosophy as "gay Saturnalia." But he was not referring to Hegel but rather to Steffens's flights of fancy in his public lectures. And, he assured Varnhagen, to make it clear he added a "positive" declaration to that effect (LHV, 101).

Varnhagen was not satisfied. Should Humboldt not give actual examples, actually cite Steffens, to make it clear he was not ridiculing Hegel? Humboldt was losing patience. The examples he mentioned were not from Steffens himself, he said, but from Steffens's followers, and anyway Steffens was so puffed up with his own importance he would take it as a compliment not to be mentioned. No, he stood on principle. "We ought in writing show the same courage as in speaking" (LHV, 107). In *Cosmos* the condemnation of pseudo-scientific "Saturnalia" remained, with Humboldt following in the next passage with a quote from Hegel carefully chosen to seem to support Humboldt's point of view.[8] Writing to a friend, Humboldt explained his strategy. With Hegel he thought it best to be magnanimous and appear not to cast blame on either him or Schelling for what was made of their philosophy by others. At the same time nowhere did he say he admired either of them, but rather used "forbearance towards the departed Hegel" and a transparent artifice of goodwill towards Schelling (CB II, 122). Always the diplomat, impatient with critique, cavalier with the truth, concerned above all for his own image, it was not Humboldt at his best. Quoting Humboldt's letter in the *Commemorative Biography* written after Humboldt's death, Alfred Dove could not help but anticipate a reader's reaction:

> What an inextricable entanglement, will the reader exclaim, of intrepid boldness in regard to the truth of facts, and paltry circumspection in the matter of personal relationships, what a mixture of noble veneration displayed in the exercise of lenient indulgence towards the dead, and of unworthy malice, wounding where it flattered, towards the living! (CB II, 122)

Meanwhile, far away from such literary squabbles, Bonpland was in rapid motion, continuing his travels in Corrientes and Misiones, returning periodically to São Borja for supplies and to check on his livestock and plantings. If in Buenos Aires he eagerly consumed new scientific publications in his friend de Ángelis's library, even more he now reveled in a new freedom to explore wetlands, forests, and grasslands.[9] The fall of 1834 he sent to Mirbel, director of the Muséum in Paris, another shipment of seeds, apologizing that he had been able to send so few species. The year had been dry and there was little vegetation; still, some of the seeds he was sending were of particular interest. "Yati," a palm from the coconut genus: its leaves were used locally for a thatch on roofs that lasted more than ten years without repair. And there were fruits from other forest trees, one species with wood hard as ebony used for furniture making, one with a red color, and another so black that it was used to make a black dye. A species of *Convolvulus* was important for soap makers because its cinders continued a rich amount of potassium. Its Guarani name, "mandiyuna," meant "like cotton" because around the seed was a puffy substance resembling cotton. Once again he noted the botanical resources of the Guarani. "The Guarani language is very rich; they extended very far, and one could make a good estimate of the extent of this ancient American nation" (AB, 95). Perhaps most interesting of all was the last of Bonpland's offerings to the Muséum, seeds of a giant water plant growing in the shallow lakes and marshes around Corrientes that he first discovered and described in 1820 traveling up the Paraná from Buenos Aires.

Back then, standing on shipboard, watching along the banks, he spotted what appeared to be huge green meter-wide floating platters. Taking a small canoe to explore, he came upon tall stems springing up out of the muddy bottom, flowers opening with snow white petals deep rose red at the center attracting swarms of insects. There had been no time then to search for seeds or to further investigate, but in Corrientes he inquired, and learned the plant's local name and the use made of its seeds:

> It is a new species of *Nelumbium* that recalls the banks of the Nile. But this plant is native to the province of Corrientes and found there only in very few places. It likes and is found only in coves formed by the Paraná and other neighboring rivers; never is it found where the water current is strong. The stem is armed with thorns of which the prick is very venomous, its leaves extending on the surface of the water are twenty-four to thirty inches in diameter and resemble in form those rounded platters on which coffee is served. . . . Here one gives to this plant the name *maize of the water*, because its seeds resemble maize and serve the same purpose. The flour that comes from maize of the water is much superior in quality to that of white maize, which is the best of all the varieties of maize known here. (AB, 95)

Now, he told Mirbel, he has had an opportunity to study the plant closely and has seen it flower and seed. He will be able to send ripe seeds on to Paris for possible cultivation. The plant likes specific conditions, warned Bonpland. If Mirbel plants it at the Jardin, he must be sure that the water is changed regularly and never has too much of a current.

Bonpland added to his letter to Mirbel a postscript on maté, that plant on his mind since his first explorations on Martín García:

> I have a great interest to know if the plant maté, the "herb of Paraguay," is in France. M. de Saint-Hilaire has seen it in the province of San Pedro and, I have no doubt, has made known to you this

interesting plant in all its aspects. It is hard work to cultivate the plant. (AB, 96)

Here Bonpland left much unsaid. His had been the first botanical description of yerba, sent to the Jardin after he found a lone specimen on the island of Martín García in 1818, a description that he updated from Candelaria when he had a chance to examine the fruits in 1821. On his return from Paraguay in 1831, he found that his description and the name he gave the plant, *Ilex theaezans* or "the tea ilex," had been replaced by Saint-Hilaire's misleading *Ilex paraguayensis*. What disturbed Bonpland was not the lack of attribution, or even the fact that Saint-Hilaire based his description on a single specimen and had never been in Paraguay; it was inaccurate naming and description of an important plant. As he knew from explorations in the missions and in Brazil, Paraguay was in no way the only place where yerba grew naturally, nor was there only one species of yerba. Furthermore, from his study of the Jesuits and his research in the missions, it was clear that the species of yerba used to fabricate maté made a great difference in the quality of the product. This was the kind of knowledge that had made the Jesuit maté superior, sought after, and more expensive than forest yerba. This was the discovery that might curtail the indiscriminate and murderous cutting of wild yerba. This was the knowledge that had supported the communal life of the missions and their legendary arts and music. Saint-Hilaire and other botanists noted uses made of plants like yerba, but more as ethnological curiosity than practical knowledge. From the standpoint of the well-being of the mission territories, accurate knowledge of such an important local product was essential. Why could maté not be cultivated and fabricated with the same finesse and intelligence as the Chinese did tea, or the French wine? Surveys should be made and study not only of different species but of different varieties and terrains. For Bonpland, botany was practical science necessary if the world was to be made a better place. To the last years of his life Bonpland would work to correct the false impression given by the misleading name chosen by Saint-Hilaire, as here late in life in a letter to his friend and agent Delessert in Paris:

Ilex paraguayensis, or *Ilex theaezans*, as it would be more accurate to call it, does not exist as a sole plant, and is not found only in Paraguay. I have in my herbier three new species of *Ilex* and with all of them maté is made, or rather the herb regularly called maté. (AB, 179)

Back in Buenos Aires again in December to turn in his certificate of life, still hoping for a resumption of his pension, Bonpland waited for a response, more and more fearful that the pension was a lost cause. Although letters from Mirbel, director at the Muséum, indicated that the twenty-five cases of natural history objects that he sent in 1832 had arrived, he still had no official acknowledgement of the arrival of the numbered catalog and commentary he sent on from São Borja. Without it, the contents of the cases might be all but useless. And still there was no sign from Humboldt that he was receiving Bonpland's letters.

A letter waiting for him in Buenos Aires from a boyhood friend in La Rochelle helped close for a moment the widening distance between him and Europe. Immediately Bonpland responded:

> How many events have passed, my dear good friend, since we saw
> each other the last time in our Rochelle! What changes of fortune
> I have experienced! What losses I have had, my dear Gigaux! You
> have been more prudent, wiser, and happier than I am. You have
> passed this long series of years in a tranquil manner, seeing each
> day your fortune, family, and happiness grow. So different from you,
> I have experienced many losses and have had many torments. But
> in the midst of so much trouble, my old friend, I am still green
> and I do not despair of comparing my forces with yours. (AB, 99)

Schoolboys sparring with swords, horseback rides on the cliffs, carefree life in the French countryside: images of a lost provincial past flicker in the increasingly toxic intrigue-ridden atmosphere of Buenos Aires with Rosas's secret police lurking in the shadows.

> It is not the épée or fleuret that I want to draw out of its sheath,
> it is not a game on foot or horseback I want, it is the happiness
> of seeing you that I am so ambitious for, to embrace you, to offer
> my respects to Mme. Gigaux, to your family, to see, to know your
> numerous offspring, to talk with you, to remember with you the
> superb Rue des Noyers, Madame Le Sage, those little one cent
> pastries, etc., etc. Ah! dear Gigaux, how far away are those happy
> days of our youth! (AB, 99–100)

As always came that promise to return, to tell his "stories" in person, but in the meantime he is in regular communication with his brother, who can tell Gigaux all that he has been doing. In a letter to Olive a few days later, he compares his situation with that of her and their brother in La Rochelle, and ends with a nostalgic walk from room to room in the house where they both grew up.

Humboldt was still on his mind. He wrote to him once again, enclosing catalogs of the contents of two cases of rock specimens he sent to Paris in 1832, and of the collection just arrived from São Borja he is about to send to the Muséum. He was thinking of him, he told Humboldt, when he included in the rock catalog not only preliminary identifications but exact locations—"I would very much like for you to look at the rocks along with the catalog and in that way you will have an idea of the geology of the country I am traveling" (AB, 98). It would be as if they were traveling and working together again. His collection was more complete than others available and might even be the basis of a joint work on the geology of the area. Humboldt could publish whatever from it he wished, and if not, the scientists at the Muséum could do the same. They would be partners still.

In January with still no word from the Muséum in Paris, Bonpland took action, sending a long and detailed inventory of and commentary on plants, useful barks and roots, birds, rocks, and fossils in the twenty-five cases already sent (AB, 103–113). Of greatest importance, he said, were the 3,000 new species of plants collected between 1830 and 1832 in Paraguay, Misiones, Corrientes, Entre Ríos, and Buenos Aires. It was only a third of what he had collected during that period because for some plants he had only one copy. But, he told the Muséum, as he continued to collect he hoped to send on more so they would have a comprehensive floristic survey of plants of the region. Again he called attention to his method. Each plant specimen was individually described and indexed to botanical journals that he kept in his possession. Each plant specimen had a label with a number, the common Spanish or Guarani name, and the scientific name. Inquiries about a species could then be made to him by number or name. As a result, he would be able to supply information that cannot be gotten from a dry specimens alone, but only from someone who has seen the living plants, has described them newly gathered, and who, informed about the locale, has questioned local inhabitants about their properties and utility.

In addition to the La Plata collection, Bonpland singled out two other groups of plants in the cases sent. One was doubles from his collection of plants collected with Humboldt to fulfill that old promise to replace those that had been damaged or lost in the Muséum collection. Second, he sent plants from his general collection that had been damaged during his detention in Paraguay, some of which might be restored at the Muséum and be of use.

Other cases contained rocks collected earlier with Humboldt in Peru and Mexico—incomplete because some were taken from the collection while he was in Paraguay but possibly of interest because they could be cross-referenced with Humboldt's geological publications. Also there were birds—153 new species. Animals—the viscacha, a rabbit-like rodent not well known, four embalmed, two skeletons, and a skull for Cuvier's studies in comparative anatomy. Fossil shells, a mammoth bone and fossil tooth. Barks for tanning—in particular a new species he thought might revolutionize the tanning process; medical plants—including the root of a new species of *Convolvulus* used as a purgative that was better than the Mexican jalap and with a pleasant rose-like odor, and "Rayz del Guaycuru," a remedy sold in Buenos Aires pharmacies for all sorts of maladies, which he was convinced might have no efficacy at all. Again Bonpland called on Muséum chemists to run trials for chemical qualities and efficacy. To aid in such trials he included in his inventory detailed descriptions of how each extract or plant product was fabricated in local practice and results from his own experiments. Only in this way could it be established which plant substances were truly of use.

This time, to try to insure that shipments would get into competent hands, he sent separate commentaries to specific professors. To Antoine Jussieu's son, Adrien, now in charge of the Muséum's herbiers, he wrote explaining his method of numbering indexed to the botanical journals, urging Jussieu to address any questions about a plant to him, and to publish anything of interest whether for novelty, usefulness, or locality. To Constant Duméril, professor of zoology at the Muséum, went a mini-treatise on what was known of extinct species in the region of Corrientes and Entre Ríos, based on current South American studies and on his own exploration and findings of bones and fossil shells. To the doctors at the Faculty of Medicine went a letter calling their notice to medicinal plants included in his shipments to the Muséum and asking that patient trials be run.

Still in Buenos Aires in March, still waiting for news of his pension, he wrote again to Humboldt. His already long stay in the city had been prolonged, he said. He is trying to use the time productively, although he is worried about his shipments. Even worse is endless negotiation for the pension. In this regard he is losing patience. He has offers of employment from the government in Buenos Aires, but more to his taste is another kind of project upriver, "an agricultural society" raising merino sheep, mules, cattle, and mixed crops. He is only waiting for favorable winds to go back, and in the meantime he has made friends with the British Ambassador, "who gives good dinners and like all rich Anglaise has excellent wines." Bonpland ended his letter with affection and concern for an old friend:

> I await with impatience some lines from you that will let me know that as always you are in good health. That unfortunate Berlin climate saddens me. Instead of seeing you warming yourself in those boxes of Prussian pine in front of one of those high ceramic stoves whose whiteness fatigues the eyes and whose heat draws all the moisture from the air, I would like to see you breathe the fresh and healthy air of the orange groves of the missions. The orange trees bear constantly two, often three, and even four kinds of fruits.

Again come memories of their travel together:

> We enjoy here the same temperature that we found at Ibagué before going on to the Cordillera. At each moment I recall how you admired the orange groves of Hiers, and the palms of the coast at Cullera and of Valencia. I am convinced that one must when aged live in temperate climates, and that the cold regions are contrary to old age. Goodbye, my illustrious friend. Keep your health as I keep mine, and think always of your old and your most faithful friend. (AB, 124)

Finally in July of 1837 came good news. Delessert, his friend and banker in Paris who worked so hard on his behalf, wrote to say that both the resumption of the pension and payment of arrears had been approved. That September, with funds in hand, Bonpland made a formal proposal to his friend, the governor of Corrientes, Pedro Ferré, for a large land grant along the Uruguay.[10] His plans were ambitious. He would breed sheep, crossing Spanish merinos with local varieties, and raise oxen, horses, and cross-bred mules. He would establish orchards and fields. He would plant fruit trees, vineyards, and yerba. He would grow a variety of vegetables and cultivate exotic and medicinal plants. He would create a "new Malmaison," free of meddling Napoleons, devoted to beauty, productivity, and the public good. In February 1838 a formal decree came down from the provincial government. Based on his surveys, plans, and scientific expertise, the land was his to develop. Immediately Bonpland went to work, hiring workers, building sheds, riding the land, driving off squatters, rounding up herds of wild horses, fencing in corrals and pastures, planting a garden not unlike the one described by Bernadin de Saint-Pierre in passages read out by Humboldt as they sailed up the Orinoco:

> They dug up young saplings of citrons, oranges, and tamarinds whose crown is such a beautiful green, and others whose fruit is full of a sugary cream that has the perfume of orange flower water. He planted grown trees around the property. He sowed the seeds of shrubs that, already in their second year, had flowers and fruit. He planted papaya with its branchless column of a trunk bristling with green melons and large-leaved crown like a fig tree; he planted pepins, noyaux de badamiers, mangos, avocadoes, guavas, jaques, and jameroses. (Bernadin de Saint-Pierre, 100–101)

A literary fantasy, but now perhaps it might be made real. Not in Europe, where every plot was owned and fought over, but in a new world where local inhabitants and progressive researchers created new kinds of relations between plant and human communities, practiced an agriculture that did not clear forests, grow one exportable cash crop, or require servile labor, but developed products native to a particular terrain and climate. One could work with new species and varieties, experiment with the selective breeding of livestock, create an alliance of plants, animals, and humans, benefiting both in an ensemble of complementary activities, animals for farm work and fertilizer, crops to feed animals and people, medicines, stimulants, forest habitats for wild game and timber for furniture-making. There was no end to the affinities, no end to reciprocities and opportunities that might be possible in this new life on the land.

The vision had been with Bonpland for a long time. Glimmers came as he worked in his grandfather's vineyards in La Rochelle and did restoration and naturalization at Malmaison, returned all the stronger fleeing the toxic politics of Buenos Aires and touring the remains of Jesuit missions along the Paraná, made material in Paraguay when he was forced to make a living on a piece of land. Now it might be realized freely, scientifically, the culmination of years of study in Paris, field work collecting plants, breeding merinos at Malmaison, not at the direction of a distracted empress or threatened by a volatile dictator. With support from a progressive friendly provincial government, private initiative and public good might come together in fruitful responsible life on the land.

14

Cosmos and Microcosm

Back in Berlin and in his apartments in the grounds of the palace at Sans Souci, the vision that was absorbing Humboldt's energies transcended any such local, regional, or even national interests. It was all that exists, not only all the living world but all of the physical earth and the celestial world of comets, planets, sun, and distant stars. This he made clear in a preface to the collection of writings from his trip to Siberia, published in 1843. His writing, he warned readers, would not offer the same interest as a travel book, nor would it be about one place or region. When he wrote about Asian mountains and isothermal lines, it was not to describe a particular place but "to signal imperishable traits by which nature is pleased to diversify soil, climate, and productions." The approach, he told readers, represented a new era in thinking:

> In each era a new direction of thought penetrates the spirit. It is
> by the coming together of diverse branches of the physical sciences
> so as to fertilize each other mutually, it is by the art of collecting
> the largest number of facts, to grasp them, and to rise up by way
> of general ideas, that one can inspire an interest that one would
> not, perhaps unjustly, accord in the same degree to special studies.
> (*Asie centrale*, xii)

"Unjustly" or not, writing the preface to *Cosmos* a year later, there was no sign that he had reconsidered.

To express the scope of what was to follow, Humboldt turned again to the Greeks, this time not to Greek gods but to Greek philosophers. His subject, he wrote, would be "το παν," "the all," nothing less than "what is," a reality that even as it is subject to change and motion, birth and destruction, is somehow one and unchangeable.[1] This new work, Humboldt emphasized, would be written not in French but in German, a language that unlike pragmatic English or analytic French lends itself to holistic vision:

> Proud of a country that seeks to concentrate her strength in intel-
> lectual unity, the writer recalls with delight the advantages he has
> enjoyed in being permitted to express his thoughts in his native
> language; and truly happy is he who, in attempting to give a lucid
> exposition of the great phenomena of the universe, is able to draw
> from the depths of a language, which, through the free exercise of
> thought, and by the effusions of creative fancy, has for centuries
> past exercised so powerful an influence over the destinies of man.
> (CO I, 56)

The publisher's preface to a new German translation of Humboldt's *Personal Narrative,* published about the same time, similarly emphasized the Germanic quality of Humboldt's thought:

> This outstanding work can rightly be called one of the most beau-
> tiful monuments of the German mind, and every German who is
> familiar with it and knows how to appreciate it must wonder why
> it has not long ago been incorporated in an appropriate manner
> into German literature, to which, from its inmost depth, it belongs,
> in spite of its foreign guise. (quoted in Rupke, 26–27)

Much of the promotion of both books echoed Fichte's popular assertion of German exceptionalism in his "Addresses to the German Nation" during the humiliation of the French occupation. A "new era" was coming, Fichte proclaimed, led by a German intellectual elite capable of elevated thought. To that end German culture must remain intact, undisturbed by idioms and ideas from other languages and lesser cultures, including the French.

At the same time, Humboldt distinguished his cosmic "science" from "philosophy of nature" or "philosophy of history" as rival Hegelians conceived it. Closer, he said, were revelations experienced at Jena with Schiller and Goethe. *Cosmos* would be no mere "register of nature." He would probe deeper than physical fact to reveal a general harmony of form similar to Goethe's "primordial plant form" or to Schiller's joy and melancholy in communion with nature. Unlike Schiller, he would anchor insights in empirical fact gained from his own observations and measurements as well as those of other scientists. *Cosmos* would be more than a mere dictionary or "encyclopedia" of scientific knowledge. Instead he would bring together discoveries in a wide range of areas of research to reveal underlying interconnections between phenomena treated as distinct in different areas of science. He highlighted his own unique qualifications for such a task. Unlike other explorers, in his travels he had not stayed along the coasts, but had ventured inland. He viewed "the interior of two vast continents which represent the most striking contrasts manifested in the Alpine tropical landscapes of South America, and the dreary wastes of the steppes in Northern Asia. Travels, undertaken in districts such as these, could not fail to encourage the natural tendency of my mind toward a generalization of views" (CO I, 8). In 1845, a first volume of *Cosmos* was ready for printing, laying out the rationale and program for volumes to come.

Nature considered rationally, wrote Humboldt, has been the quest of mankind from the dawn of history and constitutes the progressive development of man's intellect:

> In considering the study of physical phenomena, not merely in its bearings on the material wants of life, but in its general influence on the intellectual advancement of mankind, we find its noblest and most important result to be a knowledge of the chain of connection, by which all natural forces are linked together and made mutually dependent upon each other; and it is the perception of these relations that exalts our views and ennobles our enjoyments. (CO I, 23)

Humboldt reviewed what he saw as the history of this intellectual achievement from primitive superstition, the beginnings of empirical investigation, and on to the "higher enjoyments" of a science unrelated to the "material wants of life." As in his address at St. Petersburg, he also added that by fortuitous coincidence this "enlargement of intellect" brings material benefits for nation states. At the same time, the aim of cosmic ecological vision was humanitarian in a greater sense than achieving national wealth or any utilitarian remedy for human ills. It brings a state of consciousness that transcends material pleasure and that compensates for the inevitable pains and miseries of human existence. Glimpsing the chain of cosmic connections "ennobles our enjoyments" by "force of mind" at the same time as it insures that the cosmic image of a harmoniously ordered whole is not empty fiction but is anchored in fact:

> Thus and thus alone, is it permitted to man, while mindful of the high destiny of his race, to comprehend nature, to lift the veil

that shrouds her phenomena, and, as it were, submit the results of observation to the test of reason and of intellect. (CO I, 24–25)

In *Cosmos*, the vegetation zones marked on Chimborazo and the Apollonian unveiling of nature pictured in the frontispiece to Humboldt's *Atlas* would merge. Readers would be taken up and away from physical involvement to a higher perspective "wholly independent of an intimate acquaintance with the physical phenomena presented to our view, or of the peculiar character of the region surrounding us" (CO I, 25).

There is no sign that Humboldt ever attempted to follow Kant into the maze of mind-bending antinomies generated when positing an ultimate reality or noumena beyond either human sensory perception or the formulas of modern mathematical science. At Jena he had been content to get Kant's thinking second-hand:

> [Wilhelm] is killing himself with study, has already read the whole of Kant's works, and lives and moves in his system. . . . I expect to learn a great deal from him, for I have no time at present to think of such subjects. I am so busily occupied with practical matters, that speculation must needs be laid on the shelf. (CB I, 59)

Although Humboldt was fond of pointing out to visitors a bust of Kant that presided over his desk in his study in Berlin, Kant is cited only twice in passing in the first volume of *Cosmos*, once in reference to a detail in Kant's work on astronomy and once more in regard to some random remarks of Kant on the Lisbon earthquake. Kant's monumental *Critiques* remained on the shelf, even though much of the thinking that had inspired Humboldt at Jena was a response to Kant's modernist dilemmas. If, in a modern scientific age, it is impossible to prove either rationally or empirically that God exists or that there is any divine purpose to the universe, if empirical knowledge is always contingent and provisional, if you can never think to know things in themselves but only human perceptions and ideas of things, how is it possible to penetrate to any ultimate reality? These were questions that inspired the circle at Jena. Humboldt simply ignored the problem. Nature is what the civilized man sees when he views and responds to nature's beauty. It is also what he measures, maps, records, and graphs with his instruments.

From this vision of the ultimate harmony of nature would come two kinds of enjoyment. First there would be the satisfaction of contemplating "laws that regulate the forces of the universe." Such contemplation can "exercise a soothing and strengthening influence on the weary spirit, calm the storm of passion, and soften the heart when shaken by sorrow." It brings enjoyment that overcomes the limits of physical existence in that it can be achieved anywhere, at home or in one's study reading works like his *Aspects of Nature*. A second kind of aesthetic pleasure comes from contemplating the physiognomy of landscape types as represented in painting and poetry. Here enjoyment is variable, ranging from the enlivening exuberant fertility of the tropics, to the melancholy dreary barrenness of the steppes, to the shivering sublimity of raging torrents and high mountain passes. Starry nights, deep mountain valleys, the steamy crater of Tenerife, lofty Chimborazo: all can arouse emotion, "opening a wide field to the creative powers of [man's] imagination" (CO I, 25–26).

In Berlin the first volume of *Cosmos* was received with enthusiastic acclaim. After a second volume on aesthetic pleasure, additional volumes were to follow on astronomy, meteorology, the earth sciences of geology and geography, and finally on that most difficult of subjects, living beings. In the last few pages of the first volume Humboldt gave a preview of what he might have to say in that last important volume. Always taking the high ground, dodging controversial questions of vitalism, spontaneous generation, the existence of the soul, and divine creation, Humboldt focused on themes from his *Geography of Plants*: the strong and beneficial influence exercised on the "feelings of mankind" when contemplating the "vegetable mantle with which the earth is decked" (CO I, 343), the specific distribution of plants in isothermal zones discernable to travelers like himself who "passed over vast tracts of land, and ascended lofty mountains" (CO I, 347). He ended with some remarks on the hotly debated question of human races: "The investigation of this problem will impart a nobler, and, if I may so express myself, more purely human interest to the closing pages of this section of my work" (CO I, 351). Again he cited Blumenbach's monogenetic origin of the races. Again he reiterated his opposition to slavery. No race is doomed to bondage. Every human is "designed for freedom." Again he noted important differences between peoples: "there are nations more susceptible of cultivation, more highly civilized, more ennobled by mental cultivation than others:"

> This is the ultimate and highest aim of society, identical with the direction implanted by nature in the mind of man toward the infinite extension of his existence. He regards the earth in all its limits, and the heavens as far as eyes can scan their bright and starry depths, as inwardly his own, given to him as the objects

of his contemplation, and as a field for the development of his energies. (CO I, 358)

There were moments of hesitation:

> When the human mind first attempts to subject to its control the world of physical phenomena, and strives by meditative contemplation to penetrate the rich luxuriance of living nature, and the mingled web of free and restricted natural forces, man feels himself raised to a height from whence, as he embraces the vast horizon, individual things blend together in varied groups, and appear as if shrouded in a vapory veil. (CO I, 79)

Again came back that vexed image of Chimborazo, seen from below rising majestically from the plain with snow line and vegetation lines clearly marked, but then again, from up near the peak all but blinded by mist and fog. One needs, wrote Humboldt, to resist being "overpowered by a sense of the stupendous richness and variety of the forms presented to us," to "dwell only on the consideration of masses either possessing actual magnitude, or borrowing its semblance from the associations awakened within the subjective sphere of ideas" (CO I, 79). Still, he admitted even in the first pages of that first volume, the noble view can have its blind spots:

> Accustomed to distant excursions, I may, perhaps, have erred in describing the path before us as more smooth and pleasant than it really is, for such is wont to be the practice of those who delight in guiding others to the summits of lofty mountains: they praise the view even when [a] great part of the distant plains lies hidden by clouds, knowing that this half-transparent vapory veil imparts to the scene a certain charm from the power exercised by the imagination over the domain of the senses. (CO I, 54–55)

Is it really possible to reduce the seemingly endless complexity and diversity of natural phenomena to the "unity of a principle?" Can experimental science based on observation of the external world ever achieve such completeness? Must not scientific generalization inevitably come to a point where a general law no longer applies or where one field of inquiry has no relation with another? This possibility even Humboldt himself had to admit:

> Experimental sciences, based on the observation of the external
> world, can not aspire to completeness; the nature of things, and
> the imperfection of our organs, are alike opposed to it. We shall
> never succeed in exhausting the immeasurable riches of nature;
> and no generation of men will ever have cause to boast of having
> comprehended the total aggregation of phenomena. (CO I, 73)

Still, wrote Humboldt, though it might not be possible to obtain a perfectly
clear view or "law of everything," it remained "the eternal and sublime aim of
all investigation of nature" (CO I, 75). One thing he made clear: The starting
point can never be a "subjective point of view of human interests. . . . The view
of nature ought to be grand and free, uninfluenced by motives of proximity,
social sympathy, or relative utility" (CO I, 83).

In Corrientes, with the French pressing for free trade on the rivers, Rosas ever
more ruthless in Buenos Aires, and Fructuoso Rivera declaring independence
in Uruguay, local human interests were very much on Bonpland's mind as he
began the work of fencing fields and planting gardens at the property on the
Uruguay he now called Santa Ana. Since Rosas's first term as governor in Buenos Aires, Bonpland's friend, Pedro Ferré, governor in Corrientes, had tried to
negotiate changes in federal policy that would lead to economic diversification
and development upriver. Customs income, he argued, should be nationalized,
shared by all the provinces, not kept for the sole benefit of Buenos Aires. There
should be free navigation on the rivers, allowing producers and merchants
upriver to trade directly with foreign buyers. Most important, there should
be protection for local textiles, leather goods, wines, teas, and liquors so as
to compete with imported goods and allow a mixed economy to develop in
place of the sole export of hides and salted meat. The argument found little
favor in Buenos Aires. Tariffs on imported goods meant that prices in the city
would rise. The trade treaty with England would be in jeopardy. Shared tax
revenues would take away funds needed to run the city government and repay
the debt owed to British bankers. All of Ferré's efforts failed. More and more
communication between Corrientes and Europe bypassed Buenos Aires, going
down the Uruguay to Montevideo, with Rosas retaliating by retaxing any goods
that came to Buenos Aires from Montevideo. When the French blockaded the
port of Buenos Aires in 1838 hostilities escalated. Genaro Berón de Astrada,

268 | Ecology on the Ground and in the Clouds

Ferré's successor as governor of Corrientes, took action, putting together an alliance he hoped would drive Rosas's forces from the neighboring province of Entre Ríos, and then continue on to challenge Rosas's rule in Buenos Aires.

In February of 1839 Berón, supported by Ferré, organized a brigade of Corrientes militia to confront Rosas's troops. Bonpland signed on as aide and chief army doctor for the armed forces of Corrientes. Visiting Berón's camp to assess the health of the troops, he was appalled: "All announces the destruction of the country whether one wishes it or not," he wrote in his journal. His worries were well founded. In the end there was little call for his medical services. A first pitched battle was fought at Pago Largo on December 31. Backup forces promised by the French and by Rivera in Uruguay failed to appear. The Corrientes army was slaughtered. Berón was killed. Eighty officers and two hundred recruits were rounded up and had their throats cut by Rosas's troops. Bonpland's newly fenced and planted fields at Santa Ana, twenty leagues from the site of the fighting, were overrun by marauding troops. The French battle ship that was to have supported the rebellion went back downriver, and France made a separate peace with Rosas, abandoning her allies upriver. Rosas reasserted his brutal control over the river provinces. In January of 1840, Bonpland wrote a despairing note in his journal: "[Rosas] is a bloodthirsty man whom any man of reason would want to be removed from power, of which he makes such a bad use" (AMF, 1733).

Barred from Buenos Aires, writing to Delessert from Montevideo some months later, Bonpland tallied up his losses. First the pension:

> The deplorable state into which this country finds itself plunged, and especially the impossibility of travel, had again prevented me getting to Montevideo, so as to obtain a certificate of life to send it to you by the time you were kind enough to indicate in your letter. (AB, 132–133)

His losses at Santa Ana were even greater: 5000 merinos, 200 horses, 500 cattle, 400 brood mules gone, slaughtered, scattered, stolen. When he had repaired some of the damage and found an overseer, he told Delessert, perhaps it would be time for him to come back to France. A day later, in a letter to Mirbel at the Muséum accompanying a shipment of seeds, he was more candid about the deficiencies of French policy:

> If the atrocious war which ravages these beautiful countries would end, I would be bothering you for many more requests for seeds. The government of Corrientes loves the French. It protects the sciences, the

arts, and neglects nothing for progress in agriculture. Our differences with Rosas brought a French squadron to La Plata. France should because of that be crowned with glory to have brought happiness to all of South America. France must act with her own forces. She alone must fight Rosas. The approach she has taken is detestable. We will end badly the most beautiful of all the questions and the same Americans who have received so much from France, whether of one party or another, will mistreat horribly the agents and the government of France. France must act alone. She must fight Rosas, whose conduct makes him unworthy to deal with her. (AB, 139)

Bonpland apologized. He had gone from agriculture to war. Though he has been away from his country for so many years, "French blood still flows in my veins." He cannot ignore France's failure to send supporting troops up river, and the shameful negotiations with Rosas to end the blockade.

He is continuing with his botanical work for the Jardin and the Muséum, he told Mirbel. He has received the digitalis seeds he asked for. When the fighting stops he will be asking for many other useful seeds. And yes he has heard of the new microscopic study of plant tissues being championed in Germany and agrees it may lead to important discoveries:

But does not one gain as much when one is seriously and appropriately involved with knowing the properties of many plants? The Chinese have discovered the very useful properties of tea, the natives of Paraguay those of *Ilex thecezans* or the herb of Paraguay, the Peruvians those of quina, etc. etc. I would think that research into the utility of plants offers great advantage. It is truly much neglected. (AB, 141)

Bonpland closed with that old question of return to France:

I thank you for your desire that I return to France. But have patience. If Corrientes is again invaded, I will take my leave and abandon all hope of bringing back what I believe is necessary for my publications. (AB, 141)

But would he? By this point few of his friends took such promises seriously. A day after he wrote his letter to Mirbel, a French officer brought news of Candolle, a friend since their student days together in Paris. Immediately Bonpland sat down to write to Candolle, restoring contact:

> After I left Paraguay, I naturally asked everyone for news of you;
> no one, absolutely no one, was able to give me any. A long time
> after, repeating my inquiries, I was told that you had traveled the
> interior of France and had designed a course in botany. In vain
> I asked where you were and what you were doing, the works
> you had published, etc. Everyone left me in the most complete
> ignorance. . . . Often in my prison in Paraguay I recalled those
> agreeable evenings on the boulevards in front of the Passage of
> the Panorama, our vertical voyage to the Creux du Vent, and our
> walks at Coppet. (AB, 135–136)[2]

Always, he wrote, he knew Candolle's work would enrich science, and his
own botanical work was ongoing with 3,000 new plants and "interesting"
commentary. This time, if he returned to Paris, he would not let himself be
persecuted by booksellers or by anyone. He would want to know what was
needed to make a work like *Plantes équinoxiales* sellable. He questioned Candolle: Would anyone be willing to invest in such a venture, advance capital
on the understanding of getting it back along with half the profits? Or should
he simply send the manuscripts? As always came back that reluctance to hand
his work over to others as he had to Willdenow and Kunth:

> That mode of publication has without doubt a great vice, because
> I have always regarded it as impossible that manuscripts could be
> published accurately by anyone other than the one who wrote them.
> When one writes on the spot, from life, not only does one see well,
> because one is completely in the moment, but at the same time a
> crowd of circumstances mix in that are not written down but that
> remain deeply graven on the memory. (AB, 137)

Only he had seen the plants, only he could do them justice, as he had tried
to do in *Plantes équinoxiales*. How much would it cost to publish such a
work, he asked Candolle, how much would he have to pay painters, printers,
and engravers? If Candolle will advise him perhaps he will give up life on the
rivers and return.

Candolle's reply was not encouraging. There was no longer much possibility of botanical publishing in Europe without institutional or government
support, and little market for serious science. Even if he found a publisher,
he might find his plants had already been described. If he were to succeed,
he would have to establish himself in a European city, and perhaps begin by

writing a travel book. As for publishing at a distance, the most that could be done would be to send some short memoirs, or some descriptions to be included in publications like his own *Prodromus*.[3]

In Montevideo Bonpland had an opportunity to meet with a relative who had recently been in La Rochelle, had visited the family there, and brought news of Olive, his nieces and nephews, and now grandnieces and grandnephews. Immediately Bonpland wrote to Olive with regret and longing. "How happy it would make me, Olive, if I could be together with you all and enjoy your happiness":

> You must be persuaded that nothing is lacking here to me but to
> see you. I live in a country in which the climate is delicious and
> the people good. As you might imagine, I frequent all the best
> company, I am valued, and without being rich, I procure for myself
> all the necessities of life. (AB, 142–143)

Bonpland went on at length to sooth Olive's worries. No, he was not lonely, old, or broken. "It is an error that one makes in Europe, the general belief that the climate of America kills men." True perhaps in some climates, but where he lives the climate is healthy and the people are kind.

It was the last that friends and family in Europe would hear from Bonpland for some time. In the decade that followed, few letters would pass between the river provinces and Europe. After the defeat at Pago Largo, fighting continued. Lavalle tried an advance on Buenos Aires and was driven back. The Unitarian general José María Paz put together an army in alliance with Ferré, serving again as governor in Corrientes. Bonpland traveled back and forth acting as liaison between various factions, trying and often failing to keep fragile alliances together. With untrained recruits and what was left of Lavalle's defeated forces, Paz managed to drive out Rosas's governor Echagüe from Entre Ríos, but then immediately declared himself governor and took military control of the province. Ferré, wary of yet another warlord on his doorstep, withdrew his forces to Corrientes. Any semblance of unity against Rosas disintegrated.

At Santa Ana the house Bonpland built on a rise overlooking the river was vandalized and the roof caved in. His livestock was scattered, and his plantings trampled. In the midst of war he married Victoriana Cristaldo, daughter of a local landowning family, both of whose parents were killed in the fighting. Births were registered of three children: Carmen in 1843, Amado Cristaldo in 1845, and Anastasio in 1847. Bonpland settled his family in the relative safety at the farmstead at São Borja, staying as close as possible to home to be with the children while they were young and before they would have to go away to school in Corrientes. Work on the land went on, if only at São Borja, driven by those motives of "proximity, social sympathy, and relative utility" that for Humboldt obscured the higher view of *Cosmos*. Bonpland's journal from 1845 records a work crew at São Borja of 16 planters, gardeners, masons, carpenters, and helpers (ABH, 368).

But soon São Borja was also deserted and poverty-stricken due to civil war in the Brazilian province of Rio Grande do Sul. The trip down the Uruguay to Montevideo to register Bonpland's certificate of life was increasingly hazardous. A second Anglo-French blockade of La Plata was lifted, but the price was rapprochement with Rosas, who kept his stranglehold on trade up and down the Paraná. Bonpland gave provisions to fleeing Brazilian rebels, and Brazilian troops raided his orchards at São Borja. Urquiza, an ally of Rosas, ruled the neighboring province of Entre Ríos with autocratic force, and there were rumors he might turn traitor and plunge the riverlands again into full-scale conflict. French troops were on guard in Montevideo, but outside the city Rosas's ally Oribe threatened to overthrow the government and make Uruguay a satellite state of Buenos Aires. Francia died, but no one was sure what would follow his rule in Paraguay.

War or peace, now in his seventies, Bonpland cared for his young children, tended his orange groves at São Borja, and continued his medical practice. As his friend Adolphe Brunel, a physician in Montevideo, described it, guests who came to dinner often found the meal interrupted. Brunel:

> Never was personal interest his guide. He had a rare disinterest-
> edness. He was content with an expression of gratitude, which
> honored him and touched him more than pay for his services as
> doctor. Bonpland was, in effect, of a passion so charitable that he
> freely provided along with his care of the sick medicines that he
> prepared for them. How many times was he seen getting up from
> the table, leaving his dinner hardly begun, to go out on horseback
> to a sufferer who sent him word! (Brunel, 127)

As much as he was the European "savant," Bonpland was now Don Amado, famous throughout the region for his knowledge of plants, his concern for the well-being of the region, his care of the sick.

Occasionally a European visitor found a way to his door. One of them in the spring of 1845 was Alfred Demersay on an official French mission to report on the state of things in Paraguay after Francia's death. At Rio de Janeiro, he had been advised by the Emperor Dom Pedro II: He must find Aimé Bonpland and get his advice on how to get into Paraguay. After a difficult trip by mule train overland through an impoverished countryside, sleeping out at night with little to eat, Demersay approached Bonpland's ranch house at São Borja with trepidation. The mule carrying his suitcases had bolted along with the servant he hired, taking both his horse and his money. He was dirty and exhausted. In his *History of Paraguay*, he tells of arriving at Bonpland's door with no introduction and covered with mud:

> It was two hours in the afternoon when I set foot on ground before
> the modest house that my guide had been able to find on the
> outskirts of town. Assailed since morning by a violent rainstorms,
> my clothes were drenched. My feet sloshed around in oversized
> boots . . . A *poncho* . . . caked with red claylike mud covered my
> shoulders. . . . The state of my garments caused me a great degree
> of anxiety. (*Histoire*, xlii)

His worries were unfounded. "That evening I was installed in Bonpland's house and in a few hours we became like old friends of twenty years" (xliii). But Bonpland had bad news for him. Given civil unrest in Corrientes and Misiones, there was no safe way to get to the Paraguayan border or any guarantee that once he got to the border he would be allowed to cross it. Hostile militias roamed the region. He should accept Bonpland's hospitality until the situation resolved itself.

A sketch made by Demersay for his *History of Paraguay* shows the modest one-story whitewashed ranch house with tile roof and attached sheds and shelters where he spent several pleasant and productive months in company with Bonpland. In the foreground, ready for emergency medical calls, is tethered the "little horse" that Bonpland used to make his rounds. Demersay would accompany him, visiting native settlements and learning the geography of the region. Reported Demersay: "regardless of Bonpland's old age he was tireless on horseback" (*Histoire*, xlv). Demersay was given free access to Bonpland's journals and records and would use much of the material he found there in later publications on Paraguay and the missions, always giving full credit to Bonpland. Afternoons they spent writing together, with Bonpland advising Demersay on issues to address when he got to Paraguay. They went on camping trips into the forests, sleeping in the open and devoting themselves to natural history. Bonpland would talk about how their forays revived memories of his travels with Humboldt. Bonpland took Demersay to meet Ferré, now in exile in Brazil, and Demersay was able to meet and consult with Jesuits just arrived from Paraguay. Still the fighting continued. Bonpland suggested that Demersay might wait out the time by exploring the ruins of missions on the left bank of the Uruguay, and when Demersay returned there was good news. His letter to the new president of Paraguay, Carlos López, had been safely delivered. Demersay was granted permission to enter Paraguay.

Martin de Moussy, a French geographer hired by the federal government in Buenos Aires to do a survey of the Plata provinces, stopped to see Bonpland at Santa Ana and at São Borja only to find that Bonpland was away on his yearly trip to Montevideo. Moussy was given a tour of the São Borja property by Bonpland's close friend and confidant Abbé Gay, who had worries about Bonpland's collections and papers. Moussy found the collections in good order but with insect damage, which he helped Gay to mitigate. Later he met and consulted with Bonpland in Corrientes.

Bonpland continued to make the often difficult trip down the Uruguay to present his certificate of life and send shipments to the Muséum in Paris. At the request of the French colonial authorities he was now gathering collections of plants and seeds to send to French colonies in Algeria. There was maintaining the orchards at São Borja, and when possible traveling to Santa Ana to assess damage there. There was bringing up the children, keeping his botanical diary, recording names and locations and descriptions of new and interesting plants. Given the unsettled state of affairs in the provinces, there was little to no communication with Europe. After years of silence, his friend the botanist Delile wrote him from Montpellier: "As we have not received any news from you, you have been taken as dead for the past eighteen months. . . . You spoke to me at sixty-three of being tempted to return to Paris? So what do you say today?" (ABH, 133). As always, such overtures bought back yearnings to see old friends. Bonpland wrote to Delile in June 1849, "I share with you, my very old and good friend, the strong desire to see you and embrace you. Wait two years and we will arrange a very long meeting." As for his collections, he told Delile, they were in good order. And yes, he planned to publish. But then, as always, came the old hesitation, along with memories of the fate of his collections at the hands of Willdenow and Kunth:

> I would desire very much to publish my writings, because I am convinced that no one can supply what remains in our memory, I would like especially to give to the publication of my plants (3,000) the form that I established for the publication of plants from my

first voyage. Humboldt has never been of my opinion on this point, as on many others. Perhaps he is right. (AB, 149)

"Touching and admirable good humor," wrote the secretary of the Institut de France next to that last sentence on a copy of the letter he was making for the Academy of Science. The differences between Humboldt and Bonpland on the subject of publishing were well known. Also well known was the troubled fate of their South American herbarium.

Meanwhile in Berlin, Humboldt was finishing the second volume of *Cosmos*, this time relating his "higher vision of nature" more specifically to pleasure and consolation to be gained from landscape painting, poetry, and aesthetic responses to nature. In his introduction he described some of the personal experiences that awakened in him "the first beginnings of an inextinguishable longing to visit the tropics." Georg Forster's descriptions of South Sea Islanders, William Hodges's paintings of scenes along the Ganges, a dragon tree he once saw in the Berlin botanical garden: these were the revelations that put him on the path to *Cosmos* (CO II, 5). Again Humboldt made it clear: Such insights were not for everyone.

> Such incitements are, however, only influential where general intellectual cultivation prevails, and when they address themselves to dispositions suited to their reception, and in which a particular course of mental development has heightened the susceptibility to natural impressions. (CO II, 5)

At the same time, "civilization" had its own troubles. The old King Frederick William III, who had ruled Prussia for forty-three years, was now dead, and the crown prince on whom Humboldt so often attended in the past was on the throne. All the more was Humboldt as chamberlain called into service, with the new king's character flaws more and more evident. Leaving the running of the government to his ministers, the new king looked to Humboldt not only for companionship, but for a ready source of information on a narrow range of interests in Gothic cathedrals, antique curiosities, spiritualism, and reviving the old Holy Roman Empire. Always Humboldt was on call, rewriting correspondence, giving advice, keeping the queen company. More and more he vented his contempt for court life in letters to and conversations with his friend Varnhagen von Ense. On crown princes:

> One lame in the knees, and pale; the other a drunken Icelander, the third blind, and politically raving; and the last capricious and infirm in intellect. And this is the approaching generation of the monarchial world. (LHV, 132)

On the king:

> He follows the impulses of his early received and firmly rooted impressions, and the advice which he may now and then think worthy of hearing, is nothing at all to him. . . . Love of art and imagination upon the throne, fanaticism and deceit all around, and hypocritical exaggeration in matters unworthy of attention. And with all this, the man is really ingenious, is really amiable, and inspired by the best intentions. What will come out of all of this at last? (LHV, 137)

Soon, Varnhagen reported in his diary, there was no longer any question in Humboldt's mind that trouble was on its way, with growing unrest in the streets and the king more and more removed from reality:

> Humboldt regards affairs here as desperate, as I do myself. He consoles himself with the belief that the constitution presented, though good for nothing at first, may result beneficially. He expects violence of every description—atrocities committed by the police, popular rage, and military strokes. The King, however, Humboldt thinks, has no misgivings. (LHV, 245)

For solace there was *Cosmos*, as well as the prospect of one of Humboldt's few permitted visits to Paris:

> [Humboldt] says that the King lives in a whirlpool of pleasure, that he is often extravagantly gay; thinks no longer of the Chamber, except when reminded of it, when he becomes immediately grave and sullen. . . . Humboldt is engaged on the final sheets of his second volume. He is going to Paris next September. (LHV, 247)

A steady stream of visitors now arrived at Humboldt's door, eager to meet the author of *Cosmos*. Most, if not all, were gratifying. One of those less so in the summer of 1847 was the American explorer and archaeologist John Stephens.

In a series of heroic explorations and excavations in Central America, Stephens and his partner, the artist Frederick Catherwood, discovered the previously unknown civilization of the Maya. Stunned at first, struggling to make sense of what they were seeing, Stephens dug out ruined temples and artifacts while Catherwood used his skill as an artist to draw palaces, idols, hieroglyphs, and pyramids utterly unlike anything Europe had seen before. As Stephens put it:

> It was the spectacle of a people skilled in architecture, sculpture, and drawing, and, beyond doubt, more perishable arts, and possessing the cultivation and refinement attendant upon these, not derived from the Old World, but originating and growing up here, without models or masters, having a distinct, separate, independent existence: like the plants and fruits of the soil, indigenous. (quoted in Carlsen, 286)

As a young man, like so many of his time, Stephens had been inspired by Humboldt's example. Invited to be a passenger on one of the first steam ships to cross the Atlantic, he made it a point to visit Berlin and compare notes with Humboldt on South America. He arrived to find little interest in Mayans or any other indigenous American culture.

Again had been "pangs." The February before Stephens's visit Humboldt had received a belated letter of thanks from Prince Albert in England for a complimentary copy Humboldt sent him of volume 1 of *Cosmos*. He was "gradually" reading through it, wrote the prince, and was enjoying it, but could not give an "authoritative judgment." Instead the prince sent back to Humboldt a return gift of Catherwood's collection of drawings and paintings of Mayan temples and art objects. Humboldt recoiled. He ridiculed the prince's diction and waved the gift aside. He already had the Mayan book. A gift of Lord Byron's works would have been a more "delicate compliment." "Could not make a judgment!" And to send back a picture book of Indian art? His own work read "gradually," perhaps not at all. The work of others sent to him in return? It was hardly gratifying. To Stephens's surprise, in Berlin there would be no comparing of notes on ancient American civilizations. Instead, Humboldt turned the conversation to Zachary Taylor's military tactics defending slavery in Texas, the invention of steam, and prospects for trade between Prussia and the United States.[4]

A bright spot that fall was one of Humboldt's few permitted visits to Paris, but it would be his last. Soon after his return to Berlin, barricades went up again in Paris streets, and Louis Philippe was driven into exile. A Second Republic was declared along with universal male suffrage and national workshops to ease mass unemployment. For a moment revolution seemed contagious. In Vienna Metternich resigned as minister. In Berlin angry crowds attacked the palace. The king called out the guard, wavered, procrastinated, issued a proclamation promising a move toward free elections, constitutional rule, and freedom of the press. A few days later the Prussian army shot into a group of protesters as they left a political meeting, and fury erupted. Barricades were built, arms procured. Troops attacked demonstrators; hundreds were killed and many more injured.

Stories made the rounds of Humboldt's action or inaction in the uprising. He went out to join the rebels at the barricades, but was shot at and had to retreat. Rioters broke into his house looking for weapons, but when they recognized him, they respectfully withdrew. Two public appearances are reliably documented. When angry protesters demanded that the king step out and appear before his people on the balcony of the palace, they also called for Humboldt and Humboldt was forced to step out behind the king. On the balcony, the king called for calm. The soldiers, he said, had fired in self-defense. He promised free elections, a parliament, a new constitution. The protesters demanded more. The king had to honor the dead. To show his good faith he had to wear the black, red, and gold sash of revolution. Bloody bodies were lined up in the courtyard of the Berlin palace, and the king was made to walk down the rows in his revolutionary sash. More still was required: The king had to lead a funeral procession of the dead through the streets. More proved beyond the king's power. Chamberlain Humboldt put on the sash instead and led the procession as the king's representative. The next day he accompanied a shaken monarch back to seclusion in the palace at Sans Souci.

As always *Cosmos* provided consolation, as Humboldt wrote to Berghaus the following summer:

> I am glad to take refuge as often as I can, from the everlasting complaints to which I am condemned to listen upon the ingratitude of this degenerate race, and from the perpetual state of indecision ever before me, in the inexhaustible study of Nature, finding in the contemplation of her phenomena and the discovery of her

laws that peace which at the close of a restless life I feel to be so necessary. (CB II, 344)

Writing to Arago in Paris, who was deeply involved in the republican cause, even the safe joys of literary creation seemed to pale:

> I grieve to see your generous devotion to public affairs. . . . How grateful I feel that your health has not suffered from such long continued strain. I am still working with true German constancy at the last volume of this interminable "Cosmos." (CB II, 344)

Humboldt had little patience with activist protest, as he made clear in a letter to a friend in Paris less committed to republicanism than Arago:

> While on one hand the attempt is made to consolidate liberty by despotism and an absolute government, all attempt to reinstate order in the streets is viewed as a reaction in favour of aristocracy, and one cannot even go to spend the evening with one of the ministers without running the risk of being hit on the head with stones or brickbats. I hope some principles will nevertheless be left to us, and that at least the long-established prejudices in favor of morality, family ties, and the sacredness of marriage will remain. . . . In the midst of these tumultuous agitations I am more than ever filled with a zest for work and literary distinction. (CB II, 344–345)

As his biographer and friend Alfred Dove put it,

> Arago's friend was by no means himself an Arago; of the passionate fire that gleamed in the eyes of that child of the South, there was scarcely a trace in the good-humoured countenance of the man of science of the North; it might be almost unhesitantly asserted that Humboldt would never have accepted even an honorary position in the provisional government, had such a proposal been made to him. (CB II, 340)

In Berlin, Humboldt counseled concessions. He urged the king to resist the influence of clerics and ministers intent on restoring religious conformity and absolutist government and to promote gradual reform. If Arago remained friendly with radicals like Karl Marx, Humboldt had little sympathy with such excesses. In 1845, asked by the Prussian government to take a letter to his friend Guizot in Paris requesting that Marx and other German émigrés living in Paris be expelled for criticizing the Prussian government, Humboldt had no difficulty complying. Nor did he seem aware of the role his friend Guizot had played in provoking the 1848 revolution when, as prime minister, Guizot tolerated rampant corruption, insisted that the vote be restricted to those with property, and banned public meetings of groups demanding wider suffrage.

In Prussia there was little lasting result from the king's promises of liberalization. A parliament was elected and a constitution written that left significant prerogatives to the king. By the end of 1848 even that much concession had disappeared. The parliament was dissolved and the constitution rewritten. Through it all, Humboldt's loyalty and affection for the royal family remained. For him, liberalism meant reform, enlightened monarchy, constitutional guarantees, a degree of freedom of speech, a larger view of global politics. For the rest one could trust to history. The emancipation of workers, the mingling of the classes, the redistribution of wealth and privilege were not in question. As he put it at the end of that first volume of *Cosmos*, "All are in like degree designed for freedom; a freedom which, in the ruder conditions of society, belongs only to the individual, but which, in social states enjoying political institutions, appertains as a right to the whole body of the community" (CO I, 358). For that body and community to hold together, order was necessary, and a head of government that was the symbol of that order. If there was hope for safety from violence and anarchy, Humboldt did not look for it in the streets or in the fields, but to the advice of intelligent educated men like himself. It was the message of *Cosmos*. Taking the high road, even the incompetence of a particular king could be transcended. As one enthusiastic London critic put it in a review of volume 2 of *Cosmos*:

> Never since the world began has there been an epoch so marked as the present day by the wonderful application of the powers of nature to the wants of man. We hold the key by which we may lock in one common, brotherhood all the nations of Europe—and finally the world, making peace the universal desire and the interchange of thought the universal instinct of every people. (*Athenaeum*, January 12, 1848, 162)

It was a vision that was carrying Humboldt to the peaks of fame. In Germany the first edition of volume 1 of *Cosmos* sold out in two months. Translations appeared in English and in eleven different languages. Part of the success was due to Humboldt himself, to his charm, his mastery of many languages, his prominence in fashionable circles, his encyclopedic knowledge. In France there was muted praise for the scope of his treatment and his grasp of many areas of science, although it was noted that no new discoveries had been made or new scientific insights revealed. In Britain reviews were mostly favorable, especially of volumes 1 and 2, although there were complaints from clerics that there was no mention of God, and from scientists that not enough British science had been cited.

Fame was far from Bonpland's mind given the sorry state of affairs in Corrientes and São Borja, so sorry that he was ready to look elsewhere for partners and a place he could put his knowledge to some use. When news of the 1848 revolution in France reached Montevideo there had been some hope that France might reengage on the side of progressive reform in the provinces upriver. That hope quickly disappeared when the new French republic renewed the treaty with Rosas. But in the neighboring Brazilian province of Rio Grande do Sul, there were now new possibilities. There also, bloody conflict had broken out between federalists wanting regional independence and an imperial government in Rio de Janeiro. But now peace had been restored and concessions made under a new Provincial governor. In the summer of 1849 Bonpland wrote to Demersay from the provincial capital of Rio Grande do Sul, Porto Alegre, about a new and ambitious project he was contemplating in forests and highlands between the Atlantic coast and the Uruguay River.

Cultivating yerba and at the same time tending and preserving natural stands of forest yerba had been on Bonpland's mind since his first forays on Martín García. Now, he wrote, he had found the perfect site for such a venture. The government of Rio Grande do Sul was building a *picada* or cart road through a large tract of virgin forest and was offering to sell lots to settlers who would help build the road and develop the land on either side. With the river provinces of La Plata torn apart by factional fighting, with his plantings and pastures at Santa Ana overrun and his houses and barns ruined, in his seventies Bonpland was redirecting his energies to the forests of Brazil. There, in partnership with a provincial government interested in science, entrepreneurship, and enlightened development, it might be possible to create a new kind of beneficial agroforestry and develop that important resource, yerba mate. Here was a plant growing wild in the heart of native forests, a plant acutely sensitive to its environment and requiring specific conditions to flourish, a precious plant that brought not only profit, but pleasure and relaxation, a plant deeply embedded in human social relations in many parts of South America. Yerba was ceremony, stimulant, comfort, sociability, and respite at the end of a hard day. On the pampas, rough hard-riding gauchos lived on beef and yerba. In cities, Creole elite sipped maté from silver cups served with petits fours. In the countryside farmers drank mate from a reed straw at the end of a workday. For its sake thousands of Indian cutters had dropped dead from hunger on forest treks. For its sake the Jesuits had been expelled from their Guarani missions. For its sake Bonpland's workers were mowed down by Francia's troops at Santa Ana. Here was green gold as valuable as any precious metal.

Why should there be only the wild-gathered unsustainable inferior product that came out of the forests of Brazil? After his early explorations on Martín García, Bonpland had approached the government in Buenos Aires. Why not attempt a managed plantation on the island? Intent on armaments and defense, fighting off rebellion in the provinces, there had been little interest in such a project. At Santa Ana and Candelaria before his abduction to Paraguay, yerba he might have cultivated and maté he might have fabricated would have benefited both Corrientes and Paraguay. A fruitful exchange might have resulted with profit to both regions. Instead, his overtures to Francia were resented and his efforts seen as sedition. Now with an enlightened provincial government interested in the welfare of its people, and with partners willing to make an investment in time and money, something might be done. Now he hoped he had found such a government in Rio Grande do Sul and such a partner in Pedro Chavez, a wealthy Portuguese landowner and rancher who expressed interest in a joint endeavor. Bonpland's contribution would be botanical science, his ability to organize and inspire workers, and, as always, a zeal for productive enlightened labor.

Delivering a herd of merinos to Chavez's ranch on a trek from São Borja through Brazilian territory, Bonpland surveyed for yerba. He found groves at the site of an old Jesuit mission, and was told of many more in the forests. Two weeks later he was deep into yerba country testing the soil and scouting for possible sites for planting. At night sitting beside the wagons, he wrote in his journal by lantern light. The growing of maté should be combined with intelligent fabrication of the finished product, rather than fabrication as it was currently done with little expertise or care. Nor should such an enterprise depend on monoculture. Growing and harvesting could be combined with animal husbandry and food production. A dispensary could provide medical care for workers, and a garden could provide food, with excess sold in local markets for ready cash. Of great importance would be the choice of administrator: someone who understood diverse kinds of agricultural work and who would give all of his time to the kind of labor that offers both profit and honor to anyone who undertakes it. Another requirement was capital. Enough for an original investment in land, and also for tools, livestock, sheep, draft animals, seeds, and a beginning stock of food. Third, and vitally important, would be the right kind of workers—not the usual cowboys and poor whites who, with a misguided sense of racial superiority, demanded high pay for poor work, but inhabitants from the old mission territories who knew the land, and who had introduced yerba to the Spanish. As important as their skill and habits would be to treat them well and lead them effectively:

> The native people are adapted to the work that is proposed here. Moreover they are so willing and adroit that one can use them for everything; Indians love the solitary agricultural life, all like working with animals, and especially like preparing maté. One would be able to teach the young boys and girls growing up on the farm to one's own taste, in a way that conforms both to the good of the establishment, and to their own good. It would be easy for me with the relations I have always had with these people and the manner in which I have always dealt with them. I would bring together several families that I would choose and with whom I would clearly establish my conditions. The Guayana Indians newly arrived in the province of Corrientes who lived by making maté in the woods above Corpus and Trinidad on the banks of the Paraná would come gladly to a place where they would find themselves occupied with their previous work, have activity that suits their education and would pass here no doubt a happier life. (*Journal: Voyage*, 21)

The poor handling of stands of yerba and the inefficient ways in which leaves were dried always angered Bonpland. At Santa Cruz in the heart of maté country he was taken into forests and shown trees ruined by mistreatment: cuts made at the height of the growing season, older trees deprived of half their branches, young seedlings trampled. Some stands were clear of undergrowth; others languished under a canopy of larger trees or were choked by brush. Here a negotiation could be established between clearing and planting, a bargain struck to the advantage of both humans and forests. Cultivating and regulating existing stands of yerba could protect the forest at the same time as it guaranteed a superior product. In an existing stand of yerba, taller trees could be cut down so that sunlight reached younger trees, brush cleared for ease of access and so that trees did not have to compete for nutrients. The ground beneath existing trees could be worked and improved, with new cultivated plantings made of thinned wild seedlings.

Exploring the yerbas around Santa Cruz, he recorded in his journal questions that needed to be researched and addressed. Would trees do better in sun or partial shade? How many transplants could be taken from any given grove? A census should be taken of the numbers of producing mature trees. Techniques of germinating seed had to be tried, attention paid to different species of yerba and their botanical properties, careful tasting done to determine the effect of flavor additives. Always he was on the lookout for new varieties and species, searching for specimens in fruit and flower so as to record precise descriptions of each kind. Always he made note of Guarani names. "Teyu-caá," "yerba de la concession": because the Indians thought it made you immune to snakebite. "Cauna": used by the locals for a variety with superior flavor.

Not only planting and cutting but also the preparing of yerba leaves was stupidly and wastefully done. Visiting a defunct mill built on a river bank for crushing yerba leaves, he noted that the builder would have profited from some botanical knowledge. He had used for construction the wood of *Araucaria brasiliensis*, trees that sit half the year on flooded banks, becoming so soft the wood rots in a few years. In addition to rotting timbers, the mill was poorly designed. The grinders would put so much pressure on the leaves that they would be reduced to dust. Gears have to be carefully adjusted to get the highest quality product. In his journal, Bonpland calibrated the mechanics of an efficient mill at some length. It would not be run by waterpower—the builder of the mill had not accounted for the changing force of the river, which would make the running of the waterwheels impossibly difficult. As he put it in his letter to Demersay,

> If I go to work on the picada, I will render a great service to the Brazilians. Not only will I help them understand how to conserve their forests of maté, which they are in the habit of destroying . . . I hope to put into practice a new manner of cutting and fabricating the herb, from which in time they would draw an immense advantage. (AB, 149)

But, he warned, it all took time. The government was planning to sell off small lots; he would need a large tract and was preparing a proposal to that end.

In October a detailed proposal with facts and figures went from São Borja to the president of the province of Rio Grande do Sul. In it Bonpland reviewed the history of maté gathering and fabrication as it had been taught to the Spanish by the Guarani, the deterioration in methods and product, the sorry state of wild stands of yerba, the danger that a valuable resource might soon be lost, calculations of acreage and profits, and a request for large holdings on either side of the cart road. Success in such a venture was impossible, he argued, for one settler. It required the support of enlightened administrators and an organization run according to scientific principles for the good of both workers and owners. He described in detail methods of cultivating wild stands of yerba and planting new ones. He explained the botanically correct method of cutting that should replace existing practices "completely contrary to agricultural method." Above all it was necessary, he warned, to protect valuable trees in all parts of the forest with some sort of official conservation authority (AB, 152–156).

Polite acknowledgment came back from the president along with a request for permission to publish his proposal. Bonpland immediately responded yes to publication, although his proposal had not been written for publication. More important, he wrote, if the project was to go on, the details would have to be settled soon. The amount of land he would have needed to be specified before he could enlist investors. Again he said that the size of lots proposed was too small for the kind of sustainable agro-forestry he recommended. Again he laid out the amount of acreage needed. Again in even stronger terms came the warning: A great many inhabitants of the surrounding area would go into the forests as soon as the road was finished and begin indiscriminately cutting, destroying the value of the land and the trees. It was urgent to take steps now to prevent this from happening.

A year later, small lots were divided up and sold off to German settlers, who cleared the land and planted crops. Receiving a letter from his old friend and supporter Delessert chiding him for not sending memoirs to the Institut and comparing him to the prolific Humboldt taxed even Bonpland's patience. He wrote to Delessert:

> I see that M. de Humboldt continues on with admirable perse-
> verance publishing his learned, interesting, and useful works. I
> have the pleasure of seeing his name sometimes in the papers. I
> understand perfectly that I ought to send some memoirs to the
> Institut. It is not material I am lacking; it is first the resolution,
> and then a more important reason: I find myself behind in the
> current state of science, and fear to offer as new what has already
> been done. (AB, 162)

Shipments had been sent to Paris. Letters, reports, catalogs were sent. No response came back, sometimes due to naval blockades and armed conflict and other times due to the fact that the person to whom Bonpland addressed materials was either dead or gravely ill.[5] His collections were at the Muséum, he told Delessert, anyone who wished could use them, and refer questions to him. He has new collections but no time to arrange them—"the sad affairs of La Plata keep me as if paralyzed" (AB, 163).

15

A Last Exchange of Gifts

Back in Berlin, Humboldt was brooding over death. He wrote to Gauss. If he died before he finished the last volumes of *Cosmos* would Gauss and others finish them for him? On the occasion of the death of his friend Leopold von Buch, he wrote to Varnhagen:

> His funeral appeared like a prelude to my own, C'est comme cela que je serai dimanche [It is like this you will find me on Sunday]. And in what a condition do I leave the world—I who lived in 1789? But centuries are as seconds in the mighty development of advancing humanity. The swelling curve, however, has its little indentations, and it is irksome to be found in such an interval of decadence. (LHV, 275–276)

Not even the success of the first three volumes of *Cosmos* could ease his frustration with affairs at court. With Varnhagen he freely expressed scorn for the "disconnected ebullitions" that were the king's idea of a speech, for "the brutality and insolence," "hatred of all science," and "pernicious activity" of one of the ministers, for a king who "delights in playing the part of a constitutional monarch, [but] absolves himself from all responsibility when the matter is a delicate one" (LHV, 282–283). He gave full vent to bitterness and disdain for those around him: clerics wanting to restore apostolic authority; ministers demanding the removal of liberal-minded professors and Jews from the university. Visitors to his study were shown a live chameleon he kept in a box. "Did they know," he would ask them, "the chameleon is the only animal that can cast one eye upward and the other down at the same time?" Then came the joke. "Just like our Prussian clerics, one eye on God and another down on the things of this earth" (see LHV 340–341). Always he felt malicious gossip behind his back. He was a Jacobin, anti-religious, a danger to the state—the first untrue, the second hardly true given his diligence in sidestepping questions about the origins of life, the third ridiculous given that he gave over all his daylight hours to the court. A chance remark at a dinner party as far away as Belgium could have repercussions.[1] He was a godless republican like his friend Arago. He did not believe, as every good Christian must, that science has no authority to contradict the Christian creed. All when he was so careful to talk only of science and avoid such questions.

His old comrade Bonpland had to seem very far away. Then, in the summer of 1853, after years of silence, Humboldt received a gift from a professor of botany in New York. In the mail arrived a daguerreotype of Bonpland recently taken by some young photographers traveling down the Uruguay to Montevideo.[2] Bonpland, in his late seventies, a bit disheveled perhaps from having had to dress up for the occasion, looked out at him from the frame. Laugh lines etched deeply around the mouth. The eyes, bright and piercing, expressed sadness and intelligence along with a glimmer of questioning expectation. Immediately Humboldt sent a letter addressed to Bonpland to the Prussian consul at Montevideo, hoping that the letter would eventually reach Bonpland: "I recognized your noble features, worked no doubt by age, but just as I saw them at Esmeralda and at Malmaison." He showed the daguerreotype around, he said, to everyone who met Bonpland when he was in Berlin. All had happy memories of him, all were glad to know he was alive and well. And along with the letter, Humboldt sent a gift of his own:

Though I have little hope that these lines and the book that accompanies them (a good French translation of the new edition of my *Tableaux de la Nature*) will reach your hands, I try nevertheless, very near to my eighty-fourth birthday, finding myself healthy, to give you a small sign of life, that is to say rather of friendship, affectionate devotion, and lively appreciation. (AB, 234–235)

He was happy, he said, to see that Bonpland remained happily and intelligently active. As for himself, he maintains his health by regular work. A fourth volume of *Cosmos* was soon to be published. Even more important, he told Bonpland, the journals used by Kunth in compiling *New Genera and Species* were now at the Muséum in Paris, "complete and with care," deposited as "Bonpland's property and by his wish." Humboldt added a plea: "I beg you on bended knee, Bonpland, to leave them in Paris at the Jardin des plantes, where your name is venerated."

As for himself, Humboldt told Bonpland, he had not been to Paris since the revolution of 1848, and in any case was now persona non grata there given his friendship with the Duchess of Orléans and his close relations with the exiled monarchy. Certainly, wrote Humboldt, he understands why Bonpland might not want to come back to France:

> The intimate relations that I have had with Madame the Duchess of Orleans prevent me from appearing at the Tuileries, as does the warmth you know I have for liberal institutions. I have never been one of those who could have believed that you would let yourself be tempted, my dear and excellent friend, by the current state of Europe, to leave a magnificent climate, the vegetation of the Tropics, and happy solitude in the midst of domestic affections that I very much approve. . . . Perhaps these lines that I am giving to a young doctor . . . going to Buenos Aires will get to you. I would wish to see your writing before my soon-to-come death. (AB, 235–236)[3]

Humboldt was in no way mortally ill—he would live on for years yet—but more and more death was on his mind, along with decline and senility. He added a postscript:

> Poor Arago, almost blind, is in a very sad state of health. I know that you, with the same laudable ardor, continue to add to your immense collections. (AB, 236)

A sad little note to Bonpland a month later told of yet another death:

> It is not very probable that this little sign of life, of friendship, and of recognition will reach you. . . . I cry at the death of Arago. We cry together for Adrien Jussieu and Auguste Saint-Hilaire. We survive them all. But alas! The immensity of seas separates us. (AB, 234)

Meanwhile, in La Plata there was reason for optimism. Rosas was gone. Threatened by Urquiza, the powerful of governor of Entre Ríos, and by Portuguese in Brazil advancing in Uruguay, Rosas rashly declared all-out war on his enemies. In February 1852, defeated by Urquiza's militia, he had been forced to retreat to Buenos Aires, and soon after to leave by ship for exile in England. In Buenos Aires a new liberal order was declared, an Argentine Federation with free trade on the rivers, a national museum, and a federal constitution. Communication between the river provinces and the rest of the world was restored. Juan Pujol, a liberal jurist trained in the law, was elected governor of Corrientes and was rounding up the last of rebels and looters. Corrientes was to have a provincial constitution and a civil administration devoted to the public good. Bonpland wrote with renewed optimism to a rancher friend in Mercedes. The friend's choice to settle in Buenos Aires province rather than in Corrientes might have been a mistake, wrote Bonpland; Corrientes had suffered badly, but things were looking up.

> By God's grace, the governor D. J. Pujol (whom I know well and have met with frequently at Curazaquatia) is a man rich, honorable, and of an enlightened patriotism, a true liberal who wants the best for the people. . . . It is to be supposed that Corrientes will have before it a long period of peace and I will be able to put into effect the yerba projects about which I have talked so often. (AB, 166–167)

Better still, at Santa Ana Bonpland was back at work re-fencing and planting. Again there would be oxen, mules, milk cows, cross-bred sheep foraging, and a large assortment of fruits and vegetables. Christmas of 1853, in Montevideo presenting his certificate of life for his pension, Bonpland reestablished relations with friends in Europe, including Humboldt, whose letter he found waiting for him along with Humboldt's gift of *Tableaux de la nature*.

Bonpland immediately replied. Since 1850, he had heard nothing from his friend. Finding no mention of Humboldt even in the papers, he had been reduced to rereading Humboldt's old letters:

> Thank you, dear Humboldt, for giving me your dear news, and especially for your continuing kindness. Our advanced age makes us live in a continual meditation on our fate, which might be decided from one moment to another. It is very hard, after having lived and worked so many years together, it is hard, I say, not to be near each other. It seems to me you would take as much pleasure as I do in remembering Cumana, the Guayquery Indians, the Cocollar, Caracas, our privations and our joys on the Orinoco. Dear Humboldt, so present in my memory are all the circumstances of your celebrated voyage, that it would be easy for me to write my own "narrative" of our travels. (AB, 169–170)

Even more welcome, Bonpland went on, were the volumes of *Tableaux*, which he had begun reading. As for *Cosmos*, it had a great reputation in La Plata, but he had only seen the first volume and even that was quickly shown to him by an acquaintance—"It is inconceivable, the rarity not to say the nullity of your learned books here." But he now has Humboldt's *Tableaux,* and where better to read them than traveling up a wide river surrounded by the beauties of nature? "On my next navigation on the Uruguay, this excellent work will be continually before my eyes, and I can meditate on it at leisure in the midst of the unsurpassable charms offered by navigation of the most beautiful of all the rivers I have ever seen."

He understands, he told Humboldt, that his botanical journals from their voyage are at the Muséum, adding somewhat vaguely, "all that you say to me in this regard will be carried out." Again came back that old hesitation. Would the journals be used responsibly? Can journal notes ever have the same meaning to someone who has never seen what is being described? As he put it to Humboldt,

> It is for me, just between us, a question very important to answer whether a traveler must give to the public his notes and manuscripts. What one writes while traveling can never be complete. The notes a traveler takes can be well rendered only by the traveler himself, who keeps in his spirit a multitude of things that are recalled to him by a note, or a much-abbreviated and therefore incomplete description. Still, our botanical manuscripts and our sketches and drawings I am convinced have great interest. In our botanical manuscripts we were particularly intent on describing plants minutely because at each moment we believed that even the most common plants were poorly described. I do not doubt that M. Kunth and you were able to clarify those doubts by the careful reading of notes taken in place. (AB, 171)

But were they? Humboldt was unlikely to have remembered much about individual plants, and, in any case, he left the botanical work to Kunth. Nor is it clear from Kunth's treatment of the journals that the notes had been read very carefully. Bonpland had seen the first installments of Kunth's *New Genera and Species* with descriptions written in scientific Latin and without the commentary he provided in *Plantes équinoxiales*. He knew the confusions in naming and the disputes that were caused by indiscriminate use of the collection given to Willdenow, although he would never know the mess that Kunth had made of some of his journals. As for plant specimens and journals from his botanical work in Argentina and Brazil, he temporized. He was working on ordering his collections. He had Candolle's *Prodromus* and Endlicher's *Genera Plantarum* to use as reference. In short, there would be no giving away of doubles of his recent collections and copies of his descriptions to others until he had been able to put them in order himself and could answer questions from his own experience:

> If these fertile lands could have stayed peaceful, if the celebrated Rosas whom I know personally, along with all the men who have figured here, had not taken up murderous and destructive arms in the province of Corrientes, a long time ago I would have had great wealth, and for many years would have been in Paris. Today I am too old, and must only think of passing the rest of my days as peacefully as possible. (AB, 172)

Rather than end his letter on such a sad note, he could not resist, as he put it, "going on a bit more" as if they still were camped out on the Orinoco with an evening of quiet talk before them. He reminded Humboldt of the geology catalog he made especially for Humboldt's use, two copies sent to the Muséum indexed to his collection of rocks from the banks of the Uruguay, La Plata, and the Jesuit missions all also sent to the Muséum. He now has 249 specimens and will again tell the Muséum to set doubles apart for Humboldt and send them to Berlin. He is discovering new plants, not as many as they discovered on their travels given the relative lack of vegetation, but in his present work he has been able to study each plant closely, see it in its most perfect state in order to get a more exact understanding of its properties and make useful notes on its virtues. As for São Borja, due to the fighting in Rio Grande the town is still deserted and poverty stricken. But on his property there are 1,600 oranges trees he planted, 300 already bearing well and more about to bear, and also peaches, citrons, quince, and many other fruits and vegetables. As for the property at Santa Ana, there he has real hopes—"that is if this beautiful country will now be peaceful and ranchers will not be ruined like they have been for the past 13 years." In three months he has been able to gather up much of his scattered livestock, rebuild fences, plant fields of grain, fruit trees, timber trees, vines, and vegetables. Once he returns upriver, he hopes to find there 3,000 newborn cross-bred sheep. "If peace continues or rather if the troubles cease completely, as it is presumable to suppose, I will soon have repaired a small part of my losses, and I will have enough to satisfy my needs to the end of my days." He apologizes. He has been writing on for so long. "Continue your learned and useful work, but guard your health, and keep for me always the tender friendship of which you have given me repeated proof" (AB, 173–175).

The next day, as he wrote a long letter to Delessert in Paris, plants were again on Bonpland's mind. Even with Rosas gone, unrest continued to interrupt his collecting. The past June he started out from São Borja planning to go to Montevideo by way of the Paraná River though Corrientes, Santa Fe, and Rosaria to collect plants, but due to fighting along the river he immediately had to turn back. Again he reminded Delessert of the two species he had studied closely now for more than thirty years. First there was maize of the water, the giant water lily. He rehearsed for Delessert the story of his long relationship with this extraordinary plant: his discovery of it in 1820, descriptions and specimens sent to Paris, updates after his return from Paraguay, then hearing nothing in reply.[4] He had news of the discovery of a similar plant in French Guiana, but the description was incomplete. In any case he is now sure of a few things. There are at least two species of the plant, the one from Guiana slightly bigger in leaf than the one he discovered in Corrientes. And the genus is not *Nelumbium*, but a similar genus he named *Nymphaeae* although he now hears that in England it has been renamed *Victoria* after the British queen. He has found more individuals growing on the Miriñay River, which flows into the Uruguay, and is working on naturalizing the plant in his lakes at Santa Ana:

> I am occupied at the moment with making a special three-pronged fork so as to dig deep on the Miriñay for living plants to take to my lakes at Santa Ana. Cultivating this precious plant on my own land will make it easy for me to furnish it, either seeds or living plants, to the Jardin in Paris. (AB, 178–179)

Then there was the "tea plant." Here again his most reliable source of information had been the Guarani. The individual that Saint-Hilaire described and misnamed is the species they call simply "coa," a word meaning both generally "plant" and, in relation to *Ilex*, "the plant," meaning a plant of unique importance. This is the species most often used for maté. But also well known to the Guarani were other species: one called "coa-iro," meaning "bitter" plant, and another "coa-mi," "small-leafed." As a result, Bonpland told Delessert, he could now reliably identify at least three species from which maté is made and was mapping the geographical distribution of those species. Again he noted the importance of Guarani names. "The Guarani might not be 'botanists' in the European sense, but they know very well how to distinguish a species both by a plant's form and its useful properties, and it is rare to find a plant that does not have an Indian name that reflects some aspect of the plant" (AB, 181). The moral was clear. European botanists ignore local knowledge at their peril. To name plants arbitrarily after queens and patrons did little to advance useful botanical knowledge.

In January, still marooned in Montevideo, Bonpland wrote again to Humboldt:

> My dear friend, after a stay of two months in the capital of Cis-platina I am finally, to my great joy, near to my departure, but before returning to the calm waters of the Uruguay, I wanted to give myself the satisfaction of getting together again with you. The very successful translation of your *Tableaux de la nature* occupies me every day and evokes many impressions which for us were both joyous and painful, and which your descriptions recall with so much life before my mind. The expression of your profound grief at the news of Arago's death has equally very much touched me. (AB, 181–182).

Again he described his many activities. He is arranging and organizing his plant and other natural history collections and will work hard to finish by July or August. He is sending seeds and cuttings requested by the French minister of war to French colonies in Algeria. He is continuing his research on maize of the water and working to make clear the difference in species between the slightly smaller Corrientes species and the one discovered in Guiana.

A few days later, returning from a botanizing excursion, Bonpland found that the Prussian chargé d'affaires, Gulich, had arrived from Prussia with another letter from Humboldt and more gifts. This time it was pictures of Humboldt, a miniature taken from a portrait of Humboldt by Gérard and a recently made daguerreotype. Immediately Bonpland responded. As for the miniature taken from Gérard's portrait—"it's not you"—but the daguerreotype—"I see a respectable old fellow with white hair. Your features are perfectly recognizable, but especially your forehead and the disposition of your hair, which naturally appears white and adds a note of profound respect."[5]

Separated for thirty-eight years, the two of them now in their eighties, each pores over the other's portrait, struggling to reconcile what he sees with what he remembers. In a note sent to the journal *Bonplandia* along with a copy of Bonpland's daguerreotype, Humboldt commented on the difference thirty years can make in a face.[6] Yes, he saw a resemblance in the image, but also a hardness about the mouth, perhaps due to old age. Sitting in Montevideo, viewing a "respectable old fellow with white hair" brought Bonpland as close as he would ever come to seriously contemplating return to Europe: "I burn with desire to bring my collections and my new manuscripts to Paris. We would join our 165 years. We would embrace tenderly; we would cast our eyes rapidly on so many places full of happy memories" (AB, 185).

But there was too much left to do. He was happy and honored to hear about the journal *Bonplandia* founded in his honor and would help in any way he could. As for writing articles, it was not clear how it would be possible in the middle of the forest with few books, no access to current science, and the many new plants and descriptions published back in Europe. There was the mission he had undertaken for the French government to send seeds and plants to Algeria, and seeing to his collections, and restoring plantings and herds at Santa Ana; when all that was accomplished, perhaps then he would return for a visit. Bonpland must have anticipated Humboldt's skeptical smile because immediately came an apology: he regrets being so old and loving so much the banks of the Uruguay, which are truly admirable. And he has a new compatriot and collaborator, Juan Pujol, governor of Corrientes, "smart, rich, knowledgeable, who loves his own country and also foreigners" (AB, 187). And as always in August he must be in São Borja for the preparation of orange flower water because he has very little left from the year before, to say nothing of making a trip to Paraguay now that Francia is dead. And at Santa Ana he is beginning the culture of Chinese tea and thinking of working again on the Melastomataceae.

In October Bonpland, now back upriver, wrote to Humboldt to say that he finally had learned from Delessert that Humboldt was not in Paris, but living permanently in Berlin. He himself had just turned eighty-two, he told his old friend, and was still hard at work. "I work as if I were twenty-five . . . in the hope of repairing some small part of the enormous losses I suffered, so as to leave some traces of my agricultural work of use to the country I inhabit" (AB, 188). He has moved permanently to Santa Ana. He has heard that Humboldt sent volumes of *Cosmos* that are waiting for him in Montevideo. "This work as well as all those others that carry your respectable and learned name are incomprehensibly rare here. Why are the booksellers so negligent?" He was supposed to have gone to Montevideo again in September but had to postpone the trip until March to gather seed to send to Algeria, something that he can trust to no one else and that requires waiting until fruit ripens on trees. Still, he admits, he gets tired. After only five or six hours in the saddle he has to stop and rest. Recently his longest journey was only twenty-five miles. His eyesight is getting weak. "Still I read, I write, I shave my beard without glasses in the light of a bad suet lamp" (AB, 188–189).

A year later two volumes of *Cosmos* in French translation were waiting for Bonpland when he arrived in Montevideo to register his certificate of life. Immediately he wrote to Humboldt:

> My first care has been to open the packet, and already I have begun to read this immortal work. After I get to Santa Ana, which will be in few days, *Cosmos* will be my sole occupation along with the *Tableau de la nature*. I like to involve myself in the reading of your works. It seems to me often that I hear you speaking and that gives me pleasant memories. How many times, dear Humboldt, have I regretted our separation! I believe that both of us would have gained and that we would delight in it still. Man has a need for a sincere friend. He has a need to pour out the secret sentiments of his heart. A thousand circumstances have determined that I live in isolation far from any city. (AB, 199–200)

But the imagined venue for that "being-together from which they both would gain" is no longer Berlin, or Paris, or even Montevideo, "where the air is heavy with dust"; it is São Borja at the time of the winter oranges, bringing back memories of their walk across Spain.

> You were full of ecstasy at the oranges and manifested a desire to live in the shade of these precious trees, which all year are covered in leaves of a deep green and in August with flowers with an odor exquisite but also intoxicating, and all the year with oranges which have the name *invernizas*, because they ripen only in the winter. (AB, 199)

Humboldt's living situation in his apartment at Sans Souci could not have been more different. To build the palace and park, Frederick the Great had the surrounding forest cut down and a formal garden laid down in the style of Versailles with Greek statues and manicured hedges. There were orange trees, but trimmed into tight balls and rolled out on wheels from the Orangerie in summer, they had little of the intoxicating scent and lush leaves of those at

São Borja. Nor is there any indication that Humboldt took any pleasure in them or in any other plant beyond the few potted palms in his apartment he told guests reminded him of the tropics. By the 1850s Humboldt was unsteady on his feet and needed help to go upstairs. He felt the cold and needed his rooms heated to a degree often difficult for visitors to bear. Why did he stay there and in Berlin? Why not go to Tegel, the family estate where he experienced that first rush of passion for the beauty of nature? In a 1846 letter to the mathematician Gauss, Humboldt gave a sort of answer to a question that was asked by many of his friends:

> The life I am leading here is wearisome, distracting, and arduous.
> I can scarcely secure more than the hours intended for repose for
> the prosecution of my literary pursuits. You will naturally inquire
> why, at the age of seventy-six, I do not seek another position? The
> problem of human life is rather a complex one. Good nature, the
> force of habit, and foolish hopes, often prove a hindrance. (CB
> II, 259–260)

Varnhagen offered another explanation:

> Humboldt is oppressed by his multifarious occupations, but he
> would be sorry to be without them; society and the court have
> become to him like a familiar tavern, where men are accustomed
> to spend their evenings and enjoy their pipe. (CB II, 260)

Loyalty to the king, inertia, hope that he might influence policy, all kept Humboldt trapped in the hothouse of court politics. And the truth was, said Varnhagen, who knew his friend as well as anyone did, Humboldt craved the turmoil and even the often irritating sociality. When he was not invited to some court festivity he would complain. An even less flattering explanation came from Bismarck, who in those days was often at the Prussian court: Humboldt was a pathetic hanger-on, always wanting to read from his own works, miffed if anyone else held the floor, and boring everyone present.[7]

There was also the question of money, with Humboldt dependent on his salary and on the small sums the king advanced to him when he was in need. There was loyalty and patriotism. If there was fault in the government, Humboldt blamed it not on the befuddled king but on the king's ministers, the clergy, and a wave of reaction that was stifling any liberal gains left over from the rebellion of 1848. A courtier at heart, Humboldt loved the king for all his foibles and believed in his "noble character." And given the king's tendency to change his mind, there was always the chance he might be prodded in a good direction. And there were some areas in which Humboldt had real influence: the promotion of science, the giving of awards, the financing of scientific endeavors, and support for the many young men who came to him for help. Here he had unqualified success.

Too often, eating away at any satisfaction he might have had was murmuring gossip. He was a republican, an atheist, worse: a bore who talked on and on, a figure of fun. Even the chorus of acclaim could sour. He received as many as 1,000 to 2,000 pieces of mail in a year, letters from acquaintances, expressions of love and admiration from strangers, answers from scientists to whom he wrote for information. He complained to Varnhagen. He had to read 400 letters in one month, some beginning gallingly: "Noble old man." Most he answered in one way or another. Visitors arrived, screened and admitted by the valet Seifert, who made up Humboldt's schedule and escorted callers in and out of the apartment. When it was quiet again and he was no longer expected at court, Humboldt worked on into the night to finish the last volumes of *Cosmos*, struggling to include new findings in every branch of science.

In the summer of 1854 as Bonpland moved the last of his personal belongings across the river to Santa Ana, Humboldt's spirits sank even lower. He wrote to Varnhagen. He was surrounded by people who were "sick with mental poverty, bear[ing] the stamp of cowardly malice" (LHV 302). Even the United States, where he was so acclaimed, had failed him:

> In the United States there has, it is true, arisen a great love for
> me, but the whole there presents to my mind the sad spectacle
> of liberty reduced to a mere mechanism in the element of utility,
> exercising little ennobling or elevating influence upon mind and
> soul, which, after all, should be the aim of political liberty. Hence
> indifference on the subject of slavery. But the United States are a
> Cartesian vortex, carrying everything with them, grading everything
> to the level of monotony. (LHV, 305)[8]

Always Humboldt had been eloquent in his condemnation of slavery. Never had he forgotten that moment in Cumaná, when he looked down from the balcony to see slaves groomed for sale as if they were domestic animals. Discipline might be necessary to force Indian workers to carry skeletons from burial caves, or keep Indian interpreters on duty, but nothing could justify treating human beings like property. Writing to Jefferson back in 1808, Humboldt apologized for saying unkind things about slavery in the United States in his *Political Essay*, but only because he thought that steps were being taken in the United States toward its elimination. To make his position clear, he added on to the final volume of his *Personal Narrative*, the *Political Essay on the Island of Cuba*, a final chapter on slavery. Slavery was wrong, perhaps the greatest of human evils, he argued, but even if humanitarian motives were lacking, given the 1791 slave rebellions in Haiti, fear alone ought to be enough to force colonial officials to take steps to end the practice. "Calm can only spring from an authority, which, in the noble sentiment of its force and its right, knows how to direct events" (PEIC, 284). In Spanish colonies like Cuba where Spanish law allowed manumission, slavery could be gradually eliminated, with freed slaves becoming paid labor. What was needed was the effective governance by colonial officials that would ward off vengeful violent rebellion among enslaved populations.

Those steady steps to gradually eliminate slavery he thought he saw in Jefferson's United States. Laws were passed banning the import of slaves. Some states had abolished slavery. In time the liberatory impulse would spread from state to state. In this, he and Jefferson seemed to be in accord. Humboldt used the metaphor of disease. Slavery was a festering wound, which needed treatment:

> To remedy the evil, to avoid public danger, to console the mis-fortunes of a race who suffers and who are feared more than is acknowledged, the wound must be probed, for in the social body there is found, when directed by intelligence, as in organic bodies, a repairing force which may be opposed to the most inveterate evils. (PEIC, 107)

The social body could not cure itself; no internal rising up of bodily resistance could mend the evil. Ruling "intelligence" was needed, wise colonial administrators devising policy to cure an infection capable of virulent outbreak at any moment.

Writing the last chapter of his essay on Cuba in 1826, Humboldt already had fears for the United States. In the Missouri Compromise of 1820 Maine had been admitted to the Union as a free state, but Missouri, part of the Louisiana Purchase and the first state admitted to the Union west of the Mississippi, had been designated a slave state. A new state, Nebraska, north of the line dividing free states from slave states, gave free states a majority in the union, but again a compromise was allowed; Kansas, north of the line, was to be a slave state, making the so-called Missouri Compromise null and void. In the United States, where Humboldt was so admired and celebrated, it seemed that it might be slavery and not abolition that was moving west. To make matters worse, a fugitive slave law had been passed laying down harsh punishment for anyone in the North harboring runaway slaves. Now what Humboldt called the "vortex" of economic utility threatened to drag down Cuba, the island where Humboldt saw a real possibility for "intelligent" reform. A so-called Ostend Manifesto was being circulated by defenders of slavery, calling for the United States to buy Cuba from Spain, or if Spain refused, to take the island by military force.

If the United States failed him, so had Prussia. Humboldt's tongue was sharp and his wit biting, commenting on books and essays passed on to him by Varnhagen. Maddening was the realization that even as visitors praised him as the "world's greatest living man, "a throned monarch in the world of science," "the modern Aristotle," at court where his presence was constantly demanded, his own King did not look to him for advice but rather to a motley crowd of quacks promoting cures and miracles.[9] In August of 1855, with the question of Italian independence and German unification again bringing Europe to the verge of war, Humboldt freely vented his disdain for the king's obsession with spiritualists and evangelists. Varnhagen's description of some of Humboldt's complaints:

> 'The great destinies of Italy' leave the King very indifferent; but a colored pane of glass, a quaint device on an old monument, a family name, enlist his greatest interest, occupy, and amuse him. . . . 'When a man has the misfortune to be compelled to live among such wretches as this. . . .' (LHV, 312–313)

Such a man can only . . . only do what? What was such a man as Humboldt to do? Certainly there was no question of emigrating to the orange-flower groves of São Borja. Adding to Humboldt's misery, even with his salary as chancellor and handouts from the king, he was deeply in debt, most notably to his valet Seifert, whom he had to satisfy by making over to him title to most of his possessions.[10] In short, there was nothing he could do, he had no other life, and no other choice than to be what he had become: "Humboldt" who conquered Chimborazo, "a throned monarch in the world of science," "a human temple, perfect as the Parthenon" as he was called by Bayard Taylor, an American journalist who visited him in November of 1856.

Humboldt, reported Taylor, talked rapidly in a mix of English and German, and sat down for only for ten minutes before he got up and walked about the room. Humboldt praised his resilient health. In five years in South

America he had passed through epidemics of black vomit and yellow fever and been unaffected. Taylor was an admiring listener—"that trust in man, that immortal youth of heart, which made the snows of 87 years lie so lightly on his head." Humboldt, he said, asked many questions, did not always wait for an answer, and was a continual stream of knowledge.[11] A watercolor painting by Hildebrandt, "Humboldt in his interior household," shows us Humboldt in later life as he appeared to Taylor and his many visitors, sitting snowy-haired in his study surrounded by books and relics from his travels.

To help to pay off some of his debt to Seifert, Humboldt arranged for a lithograph to be made of the painting so copies could be made and sold. He sent a note to Varnhagen. Could Varnhagen come, help him decide on an appropriate inscription for the lithograph? Varnhagen, suffering from a cold, begged off, but Humboldt persisted, and a few days later in a rain storm Varnhagen arrived for consultation. For inspiration Humboldt gave him a tour of the study, pointing here and there to mementos from his travels. Humboldt complained. He was aging. He had a skin itch. The sensible Varnhagen diagnosed a common skin ailment. Humboldt grimaced. "No, senilus," he retorted. Hoping to lighten his friend's mood, Varnhagen returned a fortnight later with a poem, combining as best he could the heroic climber of Chimborazo with the aging savant in his study:

> This was the latest, the peaceful home, where the mighty explorer,
> Early ascender of summits, reposed on the heights of his glory.
> Hall of the Castle of Knowledge, the limner has deftly restored thee!
> Lofty and light, rich hung with trophies of noble endeavor;
> Treasures of nature and art, and of love, nd the weapons of science.
> While in the midst sits, earnestly glad, thoughtfully commanding
> All the profusion around, himself thy sovereign, breathing
> Speech and significant life into every shape of the picture;
> Plying the wonderful shuttle of thought, until it produces,
> Painting and painted at once, fresh images, brighter and brighter.
>   (LHV, 346)

Humboldt was delighted, his spirits restored: "Indescribably beautiful is your poetry, full of grace and delicacy," he told Varnhagen. If only his brother could have been there to witness such a family honor (LHV, 347–348).

Meanwhile, affairs at court continued to deteriorate. The king, sinking into madness, suffered a stroke that left him incapacitated. Humboldt's acidic comment on the resulting confusion: "*Alea jacta,* and the sum of intelligence at stake seems to have been doled out by nature with laudable economy" (LHV, 400).[12] The king was sent into exile. A regency was declared. Humboldt continued on as chamberlain, working on volumes of *Cosmos* late into the night. Volume 4 on celestial phenomena was finished, but yet to come was that difficult volume on earth science. Writing down some introductory remarks, Humboldt acknowledged the difficulty of this last subject. On Earth the distance between the greatest objects of science—nature considered rationally, unity in diversity of phenomena, harmony blending together all created things—and the enumeration of individual results could seem all but unbridgeable. Transition from "the all" to the celestial science of stars, galaxies, meteors, and solar systems had been relatively easy. Starry skies had always inspired in "mankind" profound thoughts, and observations of celestial phenomena lend themselves to mathematical correlations with their interlocking formulae. The Earth was different, staggering in its complexity, with a complex history and endlessly diverse forms of life. Here it might be all but impossible not to lose sight of "the all" of cosmos.

In Hildebrandt's painting Humboldt sits surrounded by notes and papers. Scattered here and there on the floor around his chair are cardboard boxes. The lid of one is pushed open, showing inside a shuffled clutter of files and papers spilling out on the floor. There are many such boxes, each labeled with a subject—"isothermal lines," "geographical distribution of plants," "geodesic observations," etc.—each filled to overflowing with notes on scraps of paper, answers to inquiries, drafts of passages, copies of letters. He would have to try to make sense of it, make sense not only of magnetism, electricity, seismic upheavals, but the intricate chemistry of plants, animals, and humans. But how in that endless play of forces would it be possible to find order or harmony?[13]

To make matters worse, in 1856 news came from the United States. One of his own works had been pulled down into the "vortex." That summer a new translation of his *Political Essay* appeared in print, but that last added chapter on the evils of slavery had not been included. Humboldt was furious. Immediately he sent letters condemning the translator, John Thrasher, who was an apologist for slavery, and also the publisher. For a few months the affair caused a sensation in the United States. Excerpts from Humboldt's letters were printed in newspapers, made into cards to pass out in the street, taken as campaign slogans by supporters of the anti-slavery candidate for president, Fremont. In November Fremont was defeated. The pro-slave candidate Buchanan was elected President, a result forecasted by Humboldt in a September letter to Varnhagen—"Most unfortunately Buchanan will be the next President, and not Fremont"—before he went on at length to vent on the folly of an escalating dispute between Prussia and Switzerland over the route of a railroad line via Neufchâtel (LHV, 324–325).

Commenting in the spring of 1857 on Friedrich Raumer's praise for remnants of enlightened rural reform in Lombardy, Humboldt saw an analogy with those who thought they saw signs of reform in America: "He has again returned with something of a hankering after the Austrian regime in Lombardy, like the Republicans when they visit the United States, where arsenic, the torture, or Fremont-worshipping negroes, cause a criminal colic to Cuba-mad Buchanan." Stories coming from America seemed nothing more than farce: Buchanan falling ill in a hotel restaurant, fearing he had been poisoned by abolitionists. Rumors spreading in Tennessee and Kentucky that bands of slaves were waiting for Fremont to come and lead them to victory (LHV, 373–374). Ending slavery seemed now no more than a joke.

In Corrientes work continued at Santa Ana restoring plantings and interbreeding livestock. Unmentioned in his September 1855 letter to Humboldt, Bonpland had also taken on other civic commitments, one of them a regional natural science museum to promote scientific education, natural history, and community development in Corrientes. Governor Pujol and Bonpland had discussed the idea as far back as 1851, and in October of 1854, Pujol sent to Bonpland a formal offer of the position of director and founder of the museum. In his acceptance letter Bonpland outlined what he saw as the aim of such an institution. The museum would collect and display products useful to the province. It would put on display "the greatest vegetal wealth now known," including his own donation of an herbier of more than 3000 plants from Argentina, Uruguay, and Banda Oriental. Nor would the museum neglect other areas of natural history such as animals and minerals. Yerba also was on Bonpland's mind, and he continued to ask questions he had been raising since his first arrival in Buenos Aires. Why could not this plant be cultivated with the same care and art as tea in China or cocoa in Peru? Again he warned that unregulated cutting of forest yerba had to be controlled. If individuals were allowed to go into the forests of the province and cut at will, wild stands of trees would disappear. Here there was real urgency, as Bonpland explained to Pujol:

> Found at the moment at San Javier are ten Brazilians . . . without counting workers. . . . I have been assured once again that they are there with the assent of the Correntine authority, that they own

> farms, one of them even claims the title of Commandant . . . In
> fact as a result of their way of working on the seven immense
> yerbals that I visited in all their splendor on the outskirts of San
> Angel, all has been lost, and recently the yerbal of Santo Christo
> seems irretrievable. (Cerruti, 228)

If cultivation was not carried out scientifically it would fail with poor harvests, poor product, and the loss of an important resource. Ordinances needed to be passed regulating the cutting of both wild and cultivated trees, surveys made, not for the purpose of attracting European speculators, but focused on the good of the province and local residents. Along with his letter accepting the post of director, Bonpland sent on to Pujol the tract on yerba he prepared for the governor of Rio Grande do Sul. Perhaps now something might come of it.

In letters to Delessert and Demersay, Bonpland described a rush of activities, arranging and cataloging shipments to Algeria, transporting his remaining possessions from São Borja, arranging collections and displays for the museum, tending to the land at Santa Ana. In addition to making him director of the museum, Pujol appointed him administrator of the yerbals, and he was completing a survey of groves and species in the province and outlining plans for their protection. He was also making surveys of possible local mercury deposits. Writing to Demersay from Montevideo, where he was filing his certificate of life and shopping for surveying equipment, Bonpland confessed that although he might still have a "desire" to return Europe it would be difficult to accomplish. Demersay sent Bonpland's letter to the *Bulletin of the Geographical Society* for publication with an attached note:

> If the details this letter contains, marked with the modesty of a
> true scholar, are of a nature to reassure the few of his friends left
> in France of the health of this famous traveler, how can one hope
> for the realization of the gigantic projects in the midst of which he
> is wandering? How count on a return which would be so profitable
> for natural science, and in particular for geography? The excellent
> old man forgets he turned eighty-two years old last August. That
> figure by itself gives voice to our fears. (AB, 203)

A few years later, a note in a local Corrientes news journal, added to the publication of a letter from Bonpland to Martin Moussy about mercury surveying, gives a different, more positive Argentinian perspective on Bonpland's activities:

Who could believe that a letter so luminous, so youthful, and so animated with the sacred fire of science could have been written by an old man of 85 years? M. Bonpland travels still like a young man and for the companion of the learned Humboldt the years have gone by without weakening his physical forces or his intellectual energy. The Argentine Confederation is proud to possess this noble old man who consecrates always his vigils and his labors to the progress of science so appreciated for the agriculture and the industry of our country. (Printed in the *Official Journal of the Argentine Confederation*; AB, 210).

In September of 1856, the museum in Corrientes opened on schedule with exhibits in mineralogy and botany prepared by Bonpland. The next spring Bonpland wrote to his friend Felipe de Normann about the possibility of a similar affiliated regional museum in Porto Alegre. They could, he wrote, set up an exchange, communicating back and forth on subjects useful to both their adjoining regions. "We will work then, my friend, so as to be useful for the museums of Porto Alegre and Corrientes, preparing in this way for young people the means of kstudying with profit the products of nature and all that is useful in our countries" (AB, 212). Traveling back and forth from Santa Ana to Corrientes, working on his collections, setting up displays and storage cabinets at the museum, for Bonpland it was a busy spring. In June came a welcome surprise. A Prussian visitor to the region, Jules Fischer, sought out Bonpland and visited with him at the museum. Delighted to see a compatriot of Humboldt, Bonpland welcomed him warmly and showed him around the exhibits. Better still, Fischer was about to return to Berlin and offered to take a letter back to Humboldt. The night before Fischer was to leave, Bonpland sat down once more to write to his old friend.

> Among the many reasons that you might have to see one of your compatriots who has traveled in America, I was persuaded that it would be agreeable to talk about Paraguay and speak to someone who saw me for several weeks. How happy I would be, dear Humboldt, if I could talk with someone who had seen you recently, how many questions I would not ask about you and your life, and on the state of your health which I assume to be always good! Very recently, my famous friend, there died here in this province a man who was one hundred years old. What a prospect for us, we who have only just passed our eightieth. (AB, 213)

He was working on his plant specimen doubles, Bonpland told Humboldt, putting them in order for a collection at the museum and also now for Greifswald University in Prussia, hard going since he only has for reference Jussieu, Schreber, Endlicher, and of course Candolle's *Prodromus*. He is continuing to make repairs at Santa Ana, somewhat interrupted because of work at the museum. He still wants to travel in parts of Argentina that he has not seen. Most important, at the invitation of the new president of Paraguay, Carlos Antonio López, he has finally made that return trip to Paraguay and while there gathered many new and rare plants. "I do not fear to say that during the course of your immortal voyage, we did not find any place that offered us such beautiful vegetation, a site so varied and enchanting as the surroundings of Asunción." He is "burning" to return to Paraguay now that he is assured of the protection of the new president and knows that the trip will produce "treasures" of botany and mineralogy. In the meantime, he is about to go to Santa Ana to plant there, then to São Borja to make orange flower water, and in the fall it will be back to Corrientes for work at the museum. He closes his letter with affection, orange trees, and memories of their travels together.

> My learned friend, seeing palms and oranges, I recall the visit we
> made to Hyères and to the coast of Cullera in Spain all lined with
> orange trees. These two species of plants aroused in you a special
> admiration and you remarked often how happy you would be to
> live in the company of palms and oranges. Today at my farm of
> Santa Ana I have groves of both of these kinds of trees but I prefer
> the oranges over the palms in respect to their look but especially for
> the foliage which is permanent and of a dark green, for the fruits,
> which are exquisite, similar to the oranges of Havana, and finally
> for the beauty of the flowers, which perfume the atmosphere and
> produce orange flower water. The orange flower water imported from
> Italy is detestable. I would wish to be able to import to Europe a
> flower water made with our bitter oranges. When it is well made
> it lasts for many years; one single spoonful is enough for a large
> glass of water and gives a taste superior to the best flower waters
> of commerce. (AB, 215–216)

Bonpland apologized for going on so long. It was ten o'clock. The letter had to be given to Fischer, who was leaving the next day. "Be good enough to send a word to me from time to time and think at times of your faithful friend," wrote Bonpland and signed his name.

When Humboldt received a message from Montevideo a year later that Aimé Bonpland was dead of fever in Argentina, he doubted its truth. There had been other reports of Bonpland's death over the years; always Bonpland survived. They both were in their eighties, but it was Humboldt who felt his age, not Bonpland, who by all reports still rode out on horseback every day, attended patients, collected plants, and made geological surveys. It seemed unlikely that it would be Bonpland, several years younger, who would be the first to die. Nevertheless, Humboldt sent the notice he received to the journal *Bonplandia* along with two letters, one the letter from Bonpland brought to him by Jules Fischer and the other a letter he recently received from one of his protégées, a young physician, Robert Avé-Lallemant. The year before, Avé-Lallemant approached Humboldt in Berlin for help in getting passage to Brazil, and Humboldt used his connections to get him a job as assistant ship doctor on an Austrian frigate. Arrived in Brazil, in deference to his benefactor, Avé-Lallemant made a detour from his travel plans to seek out Humboldt's old comrade Bonpland and send back news of him to Humboldt:

> April 10, 1858 in São Borja on the River Uruguay:
>
> As I began my journey from Porto Alegre to the Río Pardo and then on to the missions of San Miguel, San Laurenço, San Luiz, and San Angelo, I was determined to send you news of your old travel companion, that being the sole reason for taking this particular route. (AB, 285)

In his letter Avé-Lallemant went on to express dismay and pity at the state of Bonpland's property at São Borja—"All has fallen into ruin." "Everywhere one sees the hand of the master gardener but all is sad and lonely as a cemetery without a tomb and only plants for mourner." Hearing from Bonpland's friend and agent Abbé Gay that Bonpland had moved down the Uruguay to his ranch at Santa Ana, and that a message had come that Bonpland was gravely ill, Avé-Lallemant soldiered on: "Then and there I decided to visit his ranch Santa Ana near Restauracion on the Uruguay so as to be able send to Europe a more precise account of the travel companion of my dear protector and patron, Alexander von Humboldt."

Nine days later Avé-Lallemant continued his letter from the town of Uruguayana on the Uruguay:

I returned yesterday from my excursion to Corrientes and from my useless visit to Aimé Bonpland. Not finding your travel companion at São Borja I went overland to Itaqui and from there down the river to here. Soon I was at the little town of Restauración and the next morning I went on horseback eight leagues out to isolated Santa Ana where Bonpland lives today. I had heard so many things about this dear old man and of his somewhat perverse simplicity so I was not too surprised to find him in as miserable situation as I had sadly presumed.

Avé-Lallemant went on to describe in detail what he saw as the wretchedness of Bonpland's living arrangements: adobe houses, thatched roof, table made out of a board laid over two barrels. His closing remarks were thick with sentiment.

As I could not and ought not serve in any way the dear old man, I left, my heart moved and full of a profound sadness. How much I would have liked to save him, to bring him back to the civilized world. But I felt that with him his time had passed. He was not of the present day. He belonged to the first half of the nineteenth century, not to the second: a melancholy monument to all those who pursue something grand and glorious in science but forget one thing: No intellectual bloom can achieve its full perfume and éclat unless woven with a skillful hand into the crown of European civilization. (AB, 289)

Humboldt sent Avé-Lallemant's letter to the journal *Bonplandia* along with the letter from Bonpland brought to him by Fischer, but added a cautionary note.

My worry was due more to the unexpected news of the sudden collapse of this eminent man's strength than to [Avé-Lallemant's] very graphic description of Bonpland's Indian way of life—that is to say the privations that my friend for ease rather than necessity imposes on himself voluntarily. It is a particular but admirable trait of Bonpland's energetic character, a trait that I was able to observe in similar circumstances of hardship and necessity in the missions and in the forest regions of the upper Orinoco and the Casiquiare, regions almost completely uninhabited, and also a trait I observed later in in his brilliant career as intendant of the royal gardens of the Empress Josephine. In intimate conversations with me and in personal letters, Bonpland recalled with particular fondness our life in the forest, often adventurous to no small degree. (AB, 239)

Humboldt went on to remark that although it was reported Bonpland died in May, since Avé-Lallemant had seen him alive in April there was a good chance Bonpland was alive.

But there was no such chance. Gravely ill with fever at the time of Avé-Lallemant's visit, Bonpland died a few months after. Less than a year later, Humboldt took to his own bed, and died a quiet death guarded over by the valet Seifert. The last volume of *Cosmos* on human geography never appeared. Volume 5 on earth science, published posthumously, included only the beginnings of an introduction, a description of the inner structure of the earth and its magnetic qualities, some added material on earthquakes, and 237 pages on volcanoes.

16

Scattered Remains

As Bonpland's death became widely known there was concern about his papers and collections. A herbarium of plants collected on his travels with Humboldt was in the Muséum national d'histoire naturelle in Paris along with volumes of his botanical journals, number-keyed to each specimen. Another herbarium of 3,000 plants was in in the regional Museum of Natural Sciences he helped found in Corrientes. But the fate of his master herbarium was unknown. Not only did it contain the results of forty years collecting in La Plata, Rio Grande do Sul, and Paraguay, but also plants collected while traveling with Humboldt. In Berlin Humboldt immediately contacted Benjamin Delessert, Bonpland's banker and business agent in Paris, seeking confirmation of Bonpland's death and inquiring about the fate of Bonpland's possessions. He held fast, he told Delessert, to the idea of saving Bonpland's manuscripts and seeing them safe in the Muséum in Paris. Could Delessert urge the professors at the Jardin to write and alert French consuls at Buenos Aires and Montevideo to try to get Bonpland's effects sent to Paris? He had his doubts, he said, about this supposed museum in Corrientes where Bonpland put doubles from his collections, and of primary concern were plants from their voyage: "These losses would be all the more deplorable since M. Bonpland, in spite of my pressing pleas, took with him the herbarium of our expedition, which was without a doubt his property, but which I see with grief is exposed to new dangers" (AB, 241).

Some of Bonpland's papers and manuscripts were known to be at the house of the Périchon family, where Bonpland lived when he was in Corrientes. An agent of the French government was sent to make an inventory, and a deal was made. Bonpland's books and instruments went to the Corrientes museum for its library and natural history collections. His manuscripts would be returned to the Muséum in Paris, including a geology catalog, travel journals, and tracts on the cultivation of maté and tobacco. To the regret of Bonpland's friends there was no finished literary product, no best-selling *Personal Narrative*, no unifying "Views of Nature."[1] He was remembered and revered by the many patients he treated in Argentina and Brazil. He was a legend among aides, laborers, landowners, and regional officials he worked with in the river provinces of the Río de la Plata. His published botanical works—two volumes of *Plantes équinoxiales*, *Rare Plants Cultivated at Malmaison and Navarre*, and the *Monographie des melastomacées*—were in libraries and on display in museums. Soon after his death, his friend Adolphe Brunel put together reminiscences of their many conversations for a *Biography of Aimé Bonpland*, adding an appendix of Bonpland's writings. Alfred Demersay cited Bonpland as the source of much of the material in his *History of Paraguay* and *Economic Study of Maté*. As Demersay put it in his introduction to *History of Paraguay*,

> I am happy to recognize that the descriptive part of this work owes all its interest to the communications of the celebrated naturalist recently lost to the sciences. I am speaking of M. Aimé Bonpland, whose name will recur many times in the course of these pages. . . . M. Bonpland put at my disposal, without reserve, the voluminous journals where he wrote down each day for thirty years the results of his observations. I have drawn from it, with discretion, and I have kept before me the assurance that I have rarely omitted an occasion for attributing what belongs to this excellent man whose modesty equals his knowledge. (*Histoire*, xix)[2]

Certainly nothing found could ever rival the publications left behind by Humboldt when he too died a year later. Over the years Humboldt had turned out volume after volume of densely written prose, with extensive notes and appendices, published in many editions and translated into many languages.

As the centenary of Humboldt's birth approached in 1869 there was a move in Germany to enhance his memory with a three-volume official co-authored biography that would, as its supervising editor, Karl Bruhn, put it, do justice "to his labours in the various branches of science" (CB I, xi). A first volume would cover Humboldt's early life and travels in America, a second would continue with his life in Paris after his return and his later life in Berlin, and in a third volume would discuss Humboldt's scientific achievements. Given that Bonpland's name was regularly associated with Humboldt's and was listed as coauthor on so many of Humboldt's publications, Bonpland would necessarily be part of the story. To that end, Julius Lowenberg, author of the first volume on Humboldt's early life, added to his account a short biography of Bonpland in which he praised Bonpland's good nature and work in botany. As he put it,

"Aimé Bonpland stands intimately associated with Alexander von Humboldt, not only as his faithful companion during his travels in America, but also as his able coadjutor in the publication of his works" (CB I, 397). However, a section of the second volume, covering Humboldt's residence in Paris after his return from South America, was given over to Robert Avé-Lallemant, that last visitor to Bonpland's ranch at Santa Ana, who so lamented the sorry state of the botanist compared to the greatness of his travel companion. Why is not completely clear. There is no evidence for Bruhn's claim that Avé-Lallemant "spent many years amid the scientific circles of the French capital," or any indication that Avé-Lallemant spent any significant amount of time in Paris at all. He was employed at a yellow fever sanitarium in Rio de Janeiro during the years Humboldt lived in Paris. He met Humboldt briefly when he returned to Berlin from Rio and went to Humboldt for help in finding passage back to Brazil. The choice may have been simply due to desperation given the lack of contact between scientific circles in Berlin and Paris and to Avé-Lallemant's eagerness to take on the task.

For an account of Humboldt's life in Paris, Avé-Lallemant spliced together materials passed on to him by Bruhn, lists of Humboldt's publications, quotes from letters, background on the French revolution, mini-biographies of people Humboldt knew in Paris, and a chronology of Humboldt's movements. He had little to say about Bonpland's botanical work, and what he did say was based almost solely on Humboldt's 1810 letter to Bonpland complaining about the slowness of botanical copy. Avé-Lallemant:

> The dilatoriness exhibited by Bonpland in these labours, which seems to have exerted no disturbing influence on the friendship felt towards him by Humboldt, may perhaps be best explained by the supposition that he scarcely felt equal to the task of describing such a collection of botanical treasures, and that his knowledge of botany was not sufficiently extensive to enable him to fulfil in a satisfactory manner the demands made upon him by such an undertaking. (CB II, 12)

Even more damning was a separate essay written by Avé-Lallemant, "The Last Days of Aimé Bonpland," which was attached to Lowenberg's biography of Bonpland at the end of volume 1.

In the essay no trace was left of the pious sentimentality in Avé-Lallemant's letter to Humboldt from Brazil. His journey to Santa Ana, wrote Avé-Lallemant, was "useless." He had to ride across a desolate landscape with a taciturn "dusky" guide, passing nothing but a few solitary riders, wild horses, a herd of deer, and an ostrich until he finally arrived at a Bonpland's ranch house: He asked himself: "Could it be in these huts, these miserable sheds, in the midst of this dreary wilderness of Pampas, Bonpland had for so many years led the life of a cynical patriarch?" (CB I, 409). There was no silverware for the table, no proper guest quarters. Avé-Lallemant had trouble faulting Bonpland's plantings, but even there he noted weeds growing between the rows.

> Orange and peaches flourished in perfection; Bonpland's rose garden was in full bloom; fig trees and castor-oil bushes grew together in luxuriant interlacement, but weeds were also thickly springing up in every direction. (CB I, 410–411)

There was no sign, he said, of the "French wife" that Bonpland was supposed to have married. Instead the presence of "dusky" children confirmed a story he was told in a neighboring town that Bonpland had taken up with a native wife who grew tired of him and left, leaving him with half-caste offspring.

Some of the distortions of Avé-Lallemant's racially tinged account of Bonpland's family may have been due to an uncertain grasp of colloquial Spanish. He reported that he had been told in the town where he was given directions that Bonpland took a "native" "china" wife, and seems to have understood "china" as referring to an Indian tribe rather than someone with pale skin. This may have colored Avé-Lallemant's perception of Bonpland's fifteen-year-old daughter, Carmen, who met him at the door, as well as of the two younger brothers staying with their father on vacation from studies in Corrientes. All were "dusky," a derogatory term used by Avé-Lallemant to indicate mixed race, although Bonpland's wife, Victoriana Cristaldo, was of Creole descent. As for Victoriana, she had indeed "left," if not in the way that Avé-Lallemant seems to have understood. Evidence indicates that she died a few years before, leaving Bonpland to bring up their children.

But "native" wives and "dusky" children were hardly the worst of Bonpland's faults in Avé-Lallemant's eyes. Much worse was what he took as Bonpland's less-than-reverent view of Humboldt:

> It was evident that Bonpland viewed with envy the immense superiority of his friend. He thought that Humboldt had published many things as his own discoveries that had properly belonged to Bonpland; he believed that Humboldt had rejoiced to see him start for America the second time, because he had entered into

some special engagements with Kunth, and that he continued to work with him on the publication of his books without waiting for Bonpland's return to Europe. (CB I, 410)

There was no need, said Lallemant, to defend Humboldt from such attacks:

> If Bonpland failed to secure an independent position, if his name will be preserved to posterity only as an appendage to the more brilliant name of Humboldt, the reason lies in his lack of industry and his unconquerable propensity to postpone every kind of labor. (CB I, 410)

What happened at Santa Ana the night of Avé-Lallemant's visit is impossible to know. Bonpland was suffering from the fever that in a few months would prove fatal, but a note he wrote the next day to his friend Kasten, who had directed Avé-Lallemant to his door, was nothing if not lucid. He was sorry, he wrote Kasten, for not sending a response back with Avé-Lallemant, but the visit had tired him too much to write.

> [M. Lallemant] is doubtless a truly extraordinary man, considering his wide knowledge and the journey he is about to undertake. In the few hours he was with me we were able to discuss Humboldt, his earlier life, his learned works, etc. But I was already suffering greatly, and twenty-four hours spent with this intellectual increased my pains to such an extent that I was unable to write to you a word. (Bell, 216)

What Bonpland said to offend his visitor one can only guess. For Bonpland, Humboldt was a lifelong intimate friend, and, as in most such friendships, he knew both Humboldt's strengths and his weaknesses. He also guessed the unhappiness of Humboldt's last years. Perhaps fever made him more open with this unforeseen visitor than he might otherwise have been. Perhaps he mentioned that he and Humboldt had differences over publication and the aim of botanical science. Certainly Bonpland had reason to complain, although never in any letter or reported conversation did he give voice to those complaints in the terms suggested by Avé-Lallemant. Instead, his letters to Humboldt were invariably full of affection and concern for the life Humboldt had chosen to live, trapped in court politics, confined in overheated apartments, at the mercy of publishers. Perhaps for Avé-Lallemant it was simply chagrin that there in the middle of nowhere, living in an adobe hut, was the beloved comrade whom Humboldt never failed to praise and whose name would forever be paired with Humboldt's.

No one who knew Bonpland would have taken Avé-Lallemant's judgment seriously. The many scientists—Candolle, Mirbel, Delile, Jussieu, Demersay—with whom he shared seeds, plants, and information throughout his life respected and admired his work. In Brazil and Argentina he was the comrade of the famous Humboldt, but more importantly he was Don Amado, who returned for important useful work in botany, land development, indigenous medicine, and community development. He was the learned resident that visiting European scientists sought out for information on the region, including Martin Moussey, Alfred Demersay, and Charles Darwin on his famous voyage in the Beagle. Streets and towns were named for him as they were for Humboldt: a Rue Bonpland in La Rochelle and a street in Buenos Aires, a mountain in New Zealand and villages in Argentina and Brazil. Argentine and Brazilian newspapers and journals published pieces from his letters and writings. Journals printed the news of his death. A copy of his *Nomenclature*, with the names and descriptions of 5,000 tropical plants in Latin, and with Spanish, Portuguese, German, Latin, and French translation, passed from researcher to researcher in the region of la Plata until it was finally lost. Nevertheless, in successive revivals of Humboldt as national hero, discoverer of America, or more recently "inventor of Nature," it was Avé-Lallemant's story that survived.

Centennial celebrations of Humboldt's birth held in cities in Germany and the United States in 1869 were lavish affairs with bands, speeches, and parades. Atheist transcendentalists as well as liberal creationist clergy, defenders of segregation like Agassiz and fervent abolitionists, conservative republicans along with radical contingents of emigrant German workers versed in Marx and Engels, all claimed Humboldt's cosmic legacy as their own. Three volumes of the *Commemorative Biography* were published six years later in 1875, with a London edition that omitted the third volume on grounds that whatever there was of scientific interest was adequately covered in the first two volumes. Even in the second volume, Alfred Dove took a nuanced view of Humboldt's achievements in that area. Much of the science in *Cosmos* was out of date, he pointed out. Humboldt himself acknowledged as much when he remarked that he stood at some variance with "the spirit of the age" (CB II, 358). If Humboldt had lived a few years longer, would he have been able to bring *Cosmos* up to date? Dove's answer was no. *Cosmos* volumes 1 and 2 had unity of theme, but Humboldt's attempt to include new discoveries in the later volumes turned *Cosmos* into an encyclopedia almost immediately out of date. Humboldt had become a curator of scientific data, splicing together bits and pieces solicited from many sources. What resulted was "isolated data on the subjects in question gathered from various authorities and put together after the fashion of a mosaic" (CB II, 361). In short, *Cosmos* was a period piece, an unrivaled production of its time, a record of the state of science in the early nineteenth century, valuable as an exemplar of popular science writing not based on spiritualism or Ouija boards. Wrote Dove:

> Nevertheless, though unfinished, not perfectly homogeneous, displaying a want of adjustment between the claims of science and the elegancies of literature, and now to some extent obsolete, 'Cosmos' yet remains an unrivalled production. . . . In the sense perhaps in which the Homeric age is spoken of, may the future historian of the development of science speak of the present [nineteenth] century as that of Alexander von Humboldt. (CB II, 368, 416)

Everything is connected. We take joy in nature because there is an affinity between us and the natural world. Deforestation decreases rainfall, negligent camp fires destroy forests, but behind these disturbances and interruptions there is balance and harmony. By the time he wrote that last difficult volume on earth science, it was a view that Humboldt himself was finding it difficult to sustain:

> Amid, the boundless wealth of chemically varying substances, with their numberless manifestations of force—amid the plastic and creative energy of the whole of the organic world, and of many inorganic substances—amid the metamorphosis of matter which exhibits an ever-active appearance of creation and annihilation, the human mind, ever striving to grasp at order, often yearns for simple laws of motion in the investigation of the terrestrial sphere. (CO V, 8–9)

Musing on the Earth and its complex chemistry a page later, he worried that such cosmic yearnings could result in error and deception.

> As in the physical world, more especially on the borders of the sea, delusive images often appear which seem for a time to promise the

expectant discoverer the possession of some new and unknown land; so, on the ideal horizon of the remotest regions of the world of thought, the earnest investigator is often cheered by many sanguine hopes, which vanish almost as quickly as they have been formed. (CO V, 10)

Humboldt used the example of electricity, so hard to capture and understand, perhaps remembering his own failed attempt to discover a vitalizing electrical current running through all of nature. Even the new mechanical theory of light, he worried, might be illusory, with atomic theory only a mode of expression or a kind of myth (CB II, 359).

There were achievements. If Humboldt did not discover America, inspire Simon Bolivar to emancipate Latin America, climb to the top of Chimborazo, or invent nature, he was tireless in support of science and scientists. If he did not lead the 1848 revolution in Berlin or manage to convince Prussian kings to make liberal reforms, he was often able to persuade them to give financial and institutional support to traveling naturalists, scientific meetings, and research projects. He worked for and made progress in establishing a chain of international research stations around the globe mapping climate and seismic phenomena. He was a ready patron and advisor to a generation of young scientists who sought him out for contacts, posts, information, money, and encouragement. Humboldt's writings and lectures created a popular audience for science and public support for scientific research. Revolutionaries like Bolivar and Sarmiento drew on his descriptions of the beauty of South American landscapes. His descriptions of nature inspired landscape painters and echoed in the poetry of generations of romantics rebelling against the ugliness and pollution of industrial Europe. His evocation of consolation and spiritual enrichment contemplating nature inspired writers like John Muir and Henry David Thoreau, and led to movements to protect wilderness areas for elite recreation and sport.

In ethnic studies, Humboldt's influence was less benign. *Views of the Cordilleras*, argued Ernest Hamy, editor of Humboldt's *Lettres américaines*, discouraged research in South American antiquities and ancient American cultures. Publications like the Louvre's influential 1851 *Monograph on Aztec Monuments* simply repeated Humboldt's claims that the organization of Aztec society "barred the quest for beauty that comes with progress," and that Aztec art had only historical interest. Luckily, wrote Hamy, researchers were beginning to do justice to pre-Columbian South American art and culture.[3]

Humboldt was not a polygenist like his protégé Louis Agassiz, but the view of human races that he inherited from Blumenbach had its own limitations. Humboldt never varied from his opposition to slavery, but never would he have contemplated working on an equal basis with American Indians or Africans, both of whom he saw in terms of Blumenbach's racial template. What was needed with such peoples, as he saw it, was "civilizing," adopting European ways like the coastal Indians in Cumaná who learned Spanish, or like dispossessed Indian tribes on the American frontier converted to Christianity and private property. For enslaved Africans, social justice meant you assumed and pitied their degradation, supported policy that led to the abolition of slavery, and employed them as free laborers.

George Perkins Marsh, author of one of the early classic texts of environmentalism, *Man and Nature*, responded to complaints that Humboldt lacked scientific and mathematical expertise in an essay "Study of Nature" for the *Christian Examiner* in 1860.[4] One has to do justice to Humboldt, said Marsh, citing the breadth of Humboldt's knowledge and the many subjects he covered. He noted Humboldt's contributions to geography, a field to which Humboldt added a "poetry and philosophy" with special application in landscape painting. As March put it, "The popularization and general diffusion of science, of which Humboldt was the great apostle, has been of infinite service to the cause of art." In addition, Marsh went on to note, Humboldt advanced science by attracting "votaries," young men like Charles Darwin and John Stephens who read Humboldt's *Personal Narrative* and conceived a "burning zeal" for travel. In the end, it was not romantic cosmic vision that had led to discoveries like Darwin's "origin of species," but careful observant work by botanists like Bonpland, and the finely observed distinctions between habitat and station that were the basis for Candolle's critique of Humboldt's "geography of plants" in 1814.[5] Humboldt may have woven his intellectual blooms into the "crown of European civilization," but by the end of the nineteenth century that crown had lost much of its luster. Neither the "metamorphoses of plants" nor "the all" was any more considered the aim of scientific research and discovery. Goethe and Schiller were no longer in fashion. Psychology was no longer philosophy of mind. Science was no longer knowledge in general, but rather different areas of methodical experimental inquiry.

A Humboldtian current of thought continued to flow. In Nebraska, Frederick Clements studied the Midwestern prairies and saw not living things competing and coexisting in particular habitats, but Humboldt's vegetal physiognomies, higher-order organisms with a natural sequence of progressive development to a beneficial climax state of natural equilibrium. As the death of prairie grasslands in the 1930s accelerated due to drought and overgrazing, that view fell out of favor.[6] More disturbing was the use of ecological holism in South Africa as theoretical support for apartheid, with each race playing its ordained role in a greater whole.[7] By the last decades of the twentieth century damage done to plants, animals, and habitats was infinitely more catastrophic than in yerba groves along the Paraná in 1820. Enclaves of well-being existed, gated wealthy communities, wildlife refuges, hunting parks, national parks, but whole regions of fertile land were becoming desert, water reservoirs contaminated, populations of animals lost, glaciers melting, farm workers sick and dying from exposure to pesticides and weed killers. Humboldt's "cosmos" could seem no more than a last vestige of monotheism, the anomaly of a secular deity in a post-romantic age.

❧

In 1905, about the same time that Hamy was making his attempt to correct the record on Bonpland, the director of the Medical School at the University of Buenos Aires, Juan Domínguez, long an admirer of Bonpland's work in the pharmaceutical use of plants and indigenous medicine, noticed that a student with the last name Bonpland had enrolled in classes at the medical school. Hoping to find some of Bonpland's lost writings, Domínguez sought out the student, who turned out to be a descendant of Bonpland. The result was the university's acquisition of a large trove of Bonpland's papers and manuscripts that became the *Archivo del Museo de Farmacobotánica Juan A. Domínguez*. Of particular interest to Domínguez, himself a researcher in the medical uses of local plants, were Bonpland's tracts on the phytochemical properties of Argentinian plants. In addition, there was his medical journal on wound treatment in war, plans and regulations for the growing, cutting, and preparing of maté, travel journals made on various trips, botanical journals, seed inventories, and correspondence with European scientists and regional political leaders. A first volume from the archives, *28 Lettres inédite d'Alexandre Humboldt*, was published in 1914, and later three additional volumes with material on Bonpland's relations with South American revolutionaries in London, his botanical journal from the last years of his life, and medical journals.[8]

Included in the archives was a copy of a letter Humboldt sent with Bonpland's botanical journals when he deposited them in the Muséum national d'histoire naturelle in Paris.

The case I have the honor of sending you and to recommend to your kindness and solicitude contains the original manuscripts relative to descriptive botany and the geography of plants, written almost

day to day, on location during the voyage which I made conjointly
with my excellent friend M. Aimé Bonpland. . . . Although a part
of the manuscripts . . . were written by my hand, I must regard
the whole as the property of M. Bonpland. Almost a quarter of the
plants were collected by me, sometimes in very difficult circumstances; nearly 400 drawings had been made by me with crayon
and pen in the same locations, but the principal, I must say the
true merit of the botanical work done during the course of the
expedition, does not belong to me, but to the courageous zeal of
M. Bonpland. (Cordier, 460–461)

Attached to the copy of the letter, Henri Cordier, co-editor of the Buenos
Aires archives, found a handwritten note:

M. le Baron had not always rendered the same justice to my old
and excellent friend and compatriot M. Aimé Bonpland. M. le
Baron Humboldt—other than the numerous merits due to his deep
and varied knowledge—had a great talent for exploiting almost
entirely to his own profit and living scientifically for fifty years
off of the Voyage to Equinoctial Regions made collectively with
our compatriot, who was so modest and such a good type that it
never for one moment occurred to him to request any redress for
an ingratitude so flagrant. (Cordier, 462)

The writer of the letter, most probably Bonpland's friend Dominique Roguin,
had his own reasons for being resentful, as the note went on to explain. Traveling to Paris in 1819 with letters and papers from Bonpland to deliver to
Humboldt, he had called repeatedly at Humboldt's residence, but was never
admitted. Although Roguin may have exaggerated the profit Humboldt made
from his publications and minimized the many tributes Humboldt paid to
Bonpland over the years, there was truth in his claim that Humboldt regularly
exaggerated his own very minimal contribution to the work of collecting, preserving, describing, and classifying plants. Cordier, in his preface to an inventory
of the Buenos Aires Bonpland archives, wrote somewhat optimistically, "The
covering genius of Humboldt put into shadow the work of Bonpland. These
unedited papers are the beginning of his reappearance."

Another turning point came in 1955 when the Argentine botanist Alicia
Lourteig took over as curator of neglected "New World Collections" at the
Muséum in Paris. In the collections Lourteig discovered Bonpland's journals

and collections, recognized their importance, and reorganized them to make them available to researchers. But regardless of Cordier's optimism and Lourteig's efforts, a 1968 collection of essays, *Humboldt, Bonpland, Kunth and Tropical American Botany*, edited by the British botanist William Stearn, continued to portray Bonpland as the incompetent assistant. George Sarton, in an essay, "Aimé Bonpland," attributed the botanical works that resulted from Humboldt's voyage to Humboldt and to Kunth, continuing to base his evaluation of Bonpland's contribution on Humboldt's 1810 letter and on Avé-Lallemant's contributions to the *Commemorative Biography*. Bonpland, according to Sarton, was "nonchalant and lazy," but Humboldt took pity on him, procured him a pension, and got him a post as "gardener" at Malmaison. Sarton went on to give Bonpland some credit for the botanical work, but claimed that even that would have been impossible if it had not been for Humboldt's "initiative and driving power." A final comparison, meant to favor Humboldt, did little justice to either man. Humboldt, said Sarton, was an encyclopedist, a synthesizer of existing science. He did not want to be burdened with the collections, but was only interested in ideas. Once the plants that Bonpland and he collected had served the purpose of documenting new species and filling in the isothermal zones on his *Tableau physique*, he had no further interest in them. Bonpland, on the other hand, just took notes, filling up journal after journal.

An essay by the editor of the collection, William Stearn, "Humboldt's Essay on the Geography of Plants," was equally dismissive of Bonpland, whom Stearn referred to as Humboldt's "companion and secretary." Again using Humboldt's 1810 letter and Avé-Lallemant's account of Bonpland's "last days" as his sources, Stearn concluded that Bonpland was supposed to work on the collections but "failed badly." Whatever success Bonpland achieved was only due to Humboldt's "generosity."

[Procuring the pension and getting him the job as "gardener" at Malmaison] illustrates Humboldt's generosity which it is well to insist upon, for it has been doubted. The doubting was apparently justified by the fact that Humboldt became a regular courtier of the king of Prussia. . . . At the court of Berlin he learned to be smooth-spoken and his critics concluded that he was insincere and selfish. . . . Humboldt never ceased to show generosity to Bonpland in spite of the fact that the latter disappointed him. . . . The explanation of this is simply that Humboldt was a great man who could not become small even when he was a courtier; he might and did become somewhat pompous and smooth-spoken but he remained essentially generous. (Stearn, 3)

A 1955 article by McVaugh reprinted in the same collection gave a detailed account of the mismanagement of Willdenow's copies, calling the Humboldt/ Bonpland collection probably "the most important botanical collections ever made in tropical America, from the standpoint of taxonomy," but again McVaugh took no note of the detailed descriptions and comments in Bonpland's botanical journals and the use Kunth made of them to produce *New Genera and Species*.

In Paris sparks of interest continued to flare. Philippe Foucault was asked to write a script for a documentary on Bonpland's life and traveled to Buenos Aires to research the Bonpland archives. The documentary never materialized, but Foucault turned his script into a biographical novel with a romantic title, *Le pêcheur d'orchidées* (1990). A few years later, given renewed interest in Bonpland's botanical journals and in his South American collections, the Muséum national d'histoire naturelle invited Nicolas Hossard to write a monograph about the voyage of Humboldt and Bonpland. After researching the Buenos Aires archives, Hossard opted to write instead about Bonpland. *Aimé Bonpland (1773–1858): Médecin, naturaliste, explorateur en Amérique du Sud* (2001) was the result, with an appendix of further documentation on Bonpland's life and writings. Nine years later, the American geographer Stephen Bell found new relevance in Bonpland's geographical work in South America, and in *A Life in Shadow* finally gave full credit to Bonpland's careful constantly revisited field work, his willingness to cross territorial and social boundaries, and his forest conservation and land use initiatives. As Bell put it in his conclusion,

> Bonpland was ahead of his time in his pioneering of agricultural practice and plans. His attitudes to forest resources were even more farsighted, coming close to the current notion of sustainable development. A strong emphasis on the local development of natural resources in a sustainable way was always present in his writing. Bonpland's concern for the protection of natural resources was an innovation in the South America of the middle nineteenth century. Although his plea fell mostly on deaf ears, they would receive a wider hearing today. In this way he was a prophet and a visionary. (Bell, 228)

At the same time as Bell was painstakingly documenting Bonpland's geographical research, in the first decades of the twenty-first century came an even greater revival of interest in Humboldt as a visionary thinker. *Cosmos* and the *Geography of Plants* were issued in new scholarly editions. Popular biographies celebrated Humboldt's adventures on rivers and climbs up mountains. His careers as writer and statesman were celebrated. Again mention was made of his travel partner, the botanist Bonpland, who assisted on the voyage, failed as a scientist, dropped out, and went native somewhere in South America. As a wave of environmental activism from the 1960s and '70s crested, and attempts to restrain global warming stalled, there was a resurgence of hope that Humboldt's Nature, that Ephesian goddess with her hanging breasts, might inspire new hope for the environment.[9]

Afterthoughts

A Bonplandian Ethos

Answering a question from his friend Brunel as to why he did not give up the struggle and return to the "civilized" comforts of Europe, Bonpland answered simply, "Here I live in the company of plants." Bonpland came to that commitment not from any theory of vegetation but from traditions of land stewardship in provincial France, progressive science institutions in the early days of the French revolution, glimmers of possibility in ruined Jesuit missions, and—perhaps most important—personal attachment to a piece of land and to a region. To a botanist and a planter, there were few if any places where traces of human presence on that land or any land were not apparent. With that realization came not only a sense of harm that can be done to living habitats, but also the pull of what might be possible to accomplish in collaboration with honorable, like-minded workers, community officials, and landowners.

In the physic gardens of his pharmacist uncles, at the Jardin des plantes with André Thouin, with Josephine at Malmaison, in Paraguay with María, and finally at São Borja and Santa Ana with Victoriana and Indian workers and guides, the aim was more ambitious than simply restoring health to a particular piece of land. Bonpland envisioned scientists and students working for the improvement of agriculture and the beauty of gardens. He envisioned alliances between enlightened property owners, ecologically minded investors, and progressive governments. He envisioned mutually beneficial exchanges between regional cultures, and productive, diverse, and enriching local economies. If this environmental consciousness did not involve a vision of the oneness of nature, neither was it a calculation of costs and benefits. It was seeing what might be accomplished when people work together with intelligence and industry for a common good. It was belief in such a possibility that made Bonpland urge that last visitor to Santa Ana, Avé-Lallemant, to come and visit him again—visit when cross-bred merinos grazed in the pastures, the rose garden had been weeded, experiments with the cultivation of tea were ongoing—so that he might see what might be created in the new world of the Americas.

Behind these projects was an attitude, a way of seeing and responding to the natural world that Bonpland shared with Thouin, Josephine, Zea, Candolle, Demersay, and others. There is no "Nature" to be unveiled or worshiped, dominated or controlled, but rather living beings relating to each other and to the physical world around them in endlessly complex ways. Humboldt envisioned ecology written large, theory that transcended local conditions, truth independent of any use to be made of that truth, truth that soared above politics and economics. For Bonpland it was the physical marks of success and failure on the ground that were the only reliable signs of truth. In his eighties, on a last trip down the Uruguay to Montevideo, once again he noted signs that relations between humans and plants were being poorly managed. As soon as sap came up in full force in palms along the banks, locals rushed to cut open unripe fruits and boil down juice for syrup or liquor, a practice that not only prevented harvest of ripe fruit but sapped the strength of the tree. Only ripe fruit should be collected, Bonpland noted in his journal, and better methods used to extract syrup and liquor. Just as with yerba, municipal governments should issue guidelines and regulations to protect valuable local resources. Especially this was true with palms. Not only did palms have an aspect "majestic and picturesque"; they provided so many of the needs of human life in the tropics. A last undated entry in the last of his botanical journals, "Notes on the Palms of Corrientes and Paraguay," points to what might have been a wider consideration of palms and their importance in the tropics, if illness and death had not intervened.[1]

A word used often by Bonpland in connection with plants was "precious." It could be the sheer wonder and beauty of a plant like maize of the water with its harmonious adaptation to swampy wetlands, the symbiosis between its extravagant flowering and the swarms of insects that feed on its nectar, the drama of its life history and intricate phytochemistry. Plants were not things to be discovered and named. They were living beings rooted in place and time, beings that one could get to know, adopt, nurture, and live with for mutual benefit. Drifting on the Miriñay in his canoe, observing the stillness of the waters, the filtered sunlight, the texture of the mud, he shared maize of the water's habitat. He watched flower stems rise quickly to produce luxuriant blooms that lasted only two days, with a strong sweet scent coming on the second day attracting hordes of pollinating beetles. He called the plant by the name given it by local inhabitants who knew it in its "full perfection" and who ground its seeds into nourishing grain. Even more precious was yerba, so deeply implicated in the rhythms of South American social life with its affinity for the companionship of orange trees and distinctive growing habit.

Describing plants he cultivated and cared for in Josephine's hothouses and parks in *Rare Plants*, Bonpland used much of the same vocabulary he might use for persons. The pink tree peony *Paeonia moutan* "exhaled" a delicious odor. *Magnolia glauca*, used to exquisitely flavor liquors in Martinique, "likes" warm and humid places. *Magnolia macrophylla*, with the grandeur of its foliage and beautiful flowers, "asks" to be grown in a place sheltered from the wind. Little-known *Tristania neriifolia*, a lovely small woody shrub with clusters of yellow flowers from Australia, "deserves" to be cultivated in French gardens. Plants grow, flower, exhale, wither, and fail to thrive as active beings with needs and strivings. There is no holistic merger with Nature; only seeing, studying, understanding, caring for other living beings.

For Bonpland, crucial for the success of these relationships between people and plants was cooperation and exchange. America gave to Europe medicines, tanning agents, dyes, fine wools, exotic blooms. In the subtropical climate of Corrientes almost anything could grow, and Bonpland's planting lists were long and infinitely varied. After decades of war, multiple different species of oranges still made their way down the rivers to the port of Buenos Aires, along with new varieties of wool, the result of cross-breeding Spanish merinos with native Corrientes stock and thick-coated Brazilian sheep. Supporting such initiatives in Corrientes, there was the promise of progressive regional government. If Bonpland failed to persuade the governor of Rio Grande do Sul of the importance of long-term planning for forest land along the cart road, in the last years of his life with Pujol as governor of Corrientes he was on surer ground. Surveys were made of forest resources, plans made for conservation, work done to identify species and map distributions of species, alliances formed between regional government, local peoples, and landowners. The new Museum of Natural Sciences was ready to educate young people with displays and programs for community development. Decisions could be made jointly, involving elected officials, native people with historical roots in the land, settlers, landowners, and community members, creating a commonality based not on race or conquest, but on sound and proven science and past experience.

More important than any ideology in these initiatives was partnership: with María in Paraguay and Victoriana in São Borja; in Corrientes with regional authorities, native people, enterprising settlers, and networks of information and policy initiatives. Partnership might result in hybrid enterprises, privately owned but government supported, drawing on local knowledge but informed by institutional science, operated for profit but also for the common good. There might be centers for diverse land- and plant-based activities cooperatively run and administered with intelligence. There might be profit for investors and homes for workers and their families, as in Bonpland's plan for a model farm in Rio Grande do Sul. For Bonpland a key factor in the success of such initiatives was something he called "honor." Honor meant not only seeing other people clearly, but even more important was seeing oneself in the eyes of others. Honor in dealing with animals meant that when a mother squirrel was killed in a fire in Josephine's menagerie, Bonpland fed her orphan babies each morning with a bottle. Honor in cultivating and fabricating maté meant that he cared for the lives of trees the same way he cared for the lives of humans that depend on those trees for a living. It meant that workers were treated fairly and honestly. It meant that phytochemical affinities were developed into new products and new refinements of old products to enhance human health. It meant that naturalists learn from local healers time-tested remedies, and that European laboratories run tests to confirm the efficacy and effects of those remedies. Lack of communication between Europe and South America hindered so many of Bonpland's efforts. Letters went missing; collections were delivered in Paris, but sat and molded away because no one opened the boxes. Bonpland could only guess what might have been accomplished if steamship travel had come a few decades earlier.

For a moment at the end of Bonpland's life it seemed that harmonious regional cultures in fruitful communication might be possible in a new Argentine federation. Secure provincial boundaries were being established. Regulations were passed to protect valuable resources. Coordination with other provinces was in process. New kinds of goods were beginning to go down the rivers, grain from planted fields, native medicines, locally crafted furniture made from fine-grained tropical woods, resins, healing barks, teas and tisanes. The old Spanish Empire, obsessed with gold and immobilized by caste, had done little to develop such products, any more than had British merchants in Buenos Aires with their taxes and export duties. But with Rosas gone, enterprising honorable persons might acquire a piece of land, explore its possibilities, and provide employment. They might roam the forests and riverways looking for new and valuable plants, develop herds of prize sheep bred selectively for fine wool, plant fields using new varieties and crop rotation.

So much had gone wrong. Driven back into the dwindling forest reserves, beleaguered Indians slashed and burned larger and larger plots, leaving barren swaths where fragile tropical soil eroded away. Valuable products like Brazil nuts or cinchona were lost as forests were cleared for monoculture. On the llanos when the rivers flooded no attempt was made to retain water for irrigation so as to allow the planting of orchards and gardens. In Mexico City, the fill used to bury ancient Aztec canals was already giving way, undermining the foundations of colonial buildings. The productive interaction between European enterprise and native expertise in the cultivation of Brazil nut trees along the Orinoco that Bonpland hoped for did not materialize, and two-hundred-year-old forests of valuable trees were disappearing. Much of what was needed was repair, restoration, replanting of what was perhaps irreparably damaged.

To what end? Where is the divine scripture or the hidden plan of nature to guide such environmental initiatives in a grim post-Newtonian world of technical quick-fixes and selfish genes? Again comes back that Kantian antinomy that Humboldt never faced head-on. If there is no unifying "all," no God-created species forms, no underlying design to nature, no primal Edenic harmony and balance to be restored, only atomic processes, struggle for existence, the mindless survival and extinction of various forms of life, where is to be the guide for action? Who or what is to say what is beautiful or worthwhile? Is one left with only Nietzsche's "will to power" or Spinoza's "conatus," individual and ultimately futile strivings and the slim chance of becoming one of those lucky enough to profit from the labor of others? If so, neither Kant's categorical imperatives nor utilitarian calculations can have much meaning. The commandment "Do not kill," regularly qualified for war and self-defense, when extended to animals and plants and even further to rivers or mountains dissolves into vacuity. Concern for the pain of animals motivates protest against abusive commercial animal farming practices, but leaves non-sentient animals, plants, and landscapes free for exploitation. Intrinsic value can be attributed to forests and mountains, but provisos—"all things being equal" or "unless some greater harm will be done"—immediately dull the force of both proof and prohibition. Rivers should not be dammed *unless* there is some benefit in doing so. Animals should not be killed or harmed *unless* there is human need. Fracking is permissible *if* it will provide jobs. What remains is often no more than a slate of consoling politically correct actions—recycle, buy organic, make condoms available, vote green, etc.—with little effect on communities threated by soil erosion, climate change, oil spills, and air pollution.

If Humboldt's "cosmos" was something unveiled, intuited, glimpsed from on high, for Bonpland it was the result of work on the ground. It was the pull of a possible future good inherent in a degraded landscape that might be coaxed into new life. It was order in one's own thinking that insures that action taken is coherent and for the good. It is responsible ownership of land and fair and efficient government. It is the just adjudication of disputes that made Bonpland the negotiator of choice among warring factions in the river provinces. Always it is striving against what Simone Weil called "gravity": the weight of physical existence, resignation, weariness, and lack of vision. It was something like this that kept Bonpland coming back to his land at Santa Ana and at São Borja when governments failed, fighting flared up again, yerba cutters crossed the border from Brazil and decimated stands of trees. It was this that kept him dreaming of new projects on a damaged stretch of land along the Uruguay even as he lay dying of fever.

The natural world around him would never stand still enough for any rational or poetic "unveiling." It was a world in motion, populated by other striving living beings, marked everywhere with signs of human enterprise. If one of the goals of science is to map such a world, for Bonpland it was mapping in a literal sense, a guide to getting somewhere one might want to go. There is no lost Eden, no city of God, no one ideal way that humans should live, but rather what might be accomplished at a particular place and time. In some last published, but seldom read words from the unfinished introduction to the never-to-be-written last volume of +, Humboldt himself voiced what might almost be taken as a sense of this material possibility:

> Our earthly sphere, within which is comprised all that portion of the organic physical world which is accessible to our observation, is apparently a laboratory of death and decay; but that great natural process of slow combustion, which we call decay, does not terminate in annihilation. The liberated bodies combine to form other structures, and through the agency of active structures and through the agency of the active forces which are incorporated in them a new life germinates from the bosom of the earth. (CO V, 11)

What the aristocratic Humboldt missed was the role of human agency in that creative "germination" of new forms of life. Bonplandian science is cooperative active endeavor. It is a forging of paths of action in the world that can be shown to have results in experimental laboratories and in practice on the ground with farmers, miners, and hydrologists. For such a science to advance, institutions are necessary, such as were conceived in the early days of the French revolution in the heated disputes Humboldt found so tiresome.

It is in this that Humboldt and Bonpland were most at odds. Neither Bonpland nor his colleagues at the Muséum in Paris had any illusion that science could be detached from politics or economics. The mining techniques Humboldt studied in School of Mining at Freiburg, the colonial archives he researched in Mexico City, the global "voyages of silver" he mapped, his geological surveys in Siberia were not detached representations of objective fact, but integral to political, economic, and social initiatives. Limiting his interest to "the desire of exactitude and the love of truth" removed Humboldt and his readers from any responsibility for the implementation of such "truths." The appreciation of Nature was allowed to float free, sequestered from any obligation to engage in struggles with bankers, profiteering mine owners, populist leaders, or foreign nations competing for extracted wealth. Love of nature became a feel-good fix, a public relations maneuver, a rich person's hobby.[2]

Struggles on the ground with vested interests are hazardous, and success is fragile. Soon after Bonpland's death, the river provinces were again torn apart in a brutal war over territory. Paraguay lost most of its population in the conflict, and Brazil's economy was devastated. But even in the face of failure and death, seeds can be sown. The herbarium from Bonpland's voyage with Humboldt, the most extensive collection ever made of South American plants, along with Bonpland's botanical journals, is in current use today by researchers in biodiversity and the geography of plants.[3] The Museum of Natural Sciences "Amado Bonpland" in Corrientes remains open to visitors, scientists, and students with exhibits in geology, mineralogy, botany, and zoology, and was recently reinaugurated in new facilities. At the University of Buenos Aires the School of Pharmacy and Biochemistry established by Juan Domínguez in Bonpland's honor carries on Bonpland's work in natural history and regional development. The Bonpland archives continue to be mined by researchers in social and natural history.[4] Bonpland's letters, treatises, and botanical works are available for readers online and in libraries.

Perhaps as important for future of the environment is his example. Environmentalists struggle to bridge the gap between environmental philosophy and public policy, between environmental advocates and working citizens. A "duty" to preserve the life of nonhuman species, or a "calculation of consequences" to future generations, can seem remote from the struggles of those who work on the ground. There is no human life that does not kill other living things. Calculation of future pain quickly gives way to present profit. None of the usual exemplars of environmental virtue, whether Thoreau trying out the simple life for a year on Walden Pond, John Muir trekking in Yosemite, or Aldo Leopold restoring wildlife on his Sand County property, have much resonance for those struggling to make a living. For Bonpland the environment was from the beginning work, not theory and policy devised and promoted to be consistent with theory, but intimate involvement with land, and with the people and plants that depend on that land for their existence.[5] At the end of his life, in one of his last letters to Humboldt, Bonpland lamented their estrangement and their failure to stay together: "I believe that both of us would have gained and that we would delight in it still" (AB, 199). Perhaps, in some emerging new world, such a reunion of courageous striving on the ground and inspiring eloquence in the clouds may still be possible.

Notes

Preface

1. Rich, "The Very Great Alexander von Humboldt." See also a series of new edited editions of Humboldt's writings: From Cambridge University Press, *Views of Nature* (2012), *Political Essay of the Kingdom of New Spain* (2013), and the unabridged volumes 1 and 2 of Helen William's translation of Humboldt's *Personal Narrative* (2011); from the University of Chicago, *Geography of Plants* (2009); and from Johns Hopkins, *Cosmos* (1997); all with extensive biographical introductions and commentary.

1. Close Encounter at a Paris Boarding House

1. The account comes from Humboldt as he told it to his friend Heinrich Wilhelm Dove, repeated to Dove's son Alfred Dove, and described in the *Commemorative Biography* written after Humboldt's death. "How did you first become acquainted with Bonpland?" Dove asked. "In the simplest manner in the world," Humboldt replied. "You know that when giving up the key of one's apartments on going out, one generally exchanges a few friendly words with the porter's wife. While doing so I often encountered a young man with a botanist's satchel over his arm; this was Bonpland; and in this manner we made acquaintance" (CB I, 397).

2. There was some justification for Humboldt's worries. Commissioned by the Austrians to pick up an abandoned natural history collection, Baudin's ship was wrecked in a storm. Baudin eventually made it to France, where he convinced Jussieu at the Muséum to fund a trip to collect the Austrian collection for France. Three weeks out of port near the Canaries his ship was again wrecked in a storm. Baudin begged and borrowed a smaller ship from the Spanish and continued on to Trinidad but, finding the British in possession of the island, was unable to land. From there he disappeared, lost, it was thought, at sea. In June of 1798 he suddenly reappeared on the French coast, without the promised cache from Trinidad but with a natural history collection beyond anyone's expectations from St. Thomas and Puerto Rico.

3. André Thouin's *Mémoire pour diriger le jardinier dans les travaux de son voyage autour du monde*, preserved in the archives of the Muséum national d'histoire naturelle in Paris, was the authoritative guide for traveling botanists and gardeners, with detailed instructions for the collecting and sowing of seeds, the drying of plants for herbaria, and the transport of living plants both overland and at sea.

4. It is not completely clear when the name Bonpland was officially attached to the family name Goujaud. One story has Bonpland's grandfather planting a grape vine on the occasion of Bonpland's father's birth, declaring both vine and son a "good plant." Official records in La Rochelle show "Bonpland" sometimes added to the family name, sometimes not. The permanent change in Bonpland's surname dates from the time of his and his brother's classes at the Muséum, when professors began to refer to Aimé as Bonpland to distinguish him from his brother, Goujaud.

5. See O'Boyle, "Learning for its Own Sake," for a detailed description of education at Göttingen and similar universities.

6. "Memoir" (in French "mémoire") was—and still is to some extent—standard nomenclature for shorter scientific presentations and publications. It is used to refer to a presentation or writing on a scientific or academic subject on which the writer has made particular observations or experiments, as in a recent quote from the biography of a mathematician: "In 1943 Douglas was awarded the Bôcher Prize by the American Mathematical Society for his memoirs on the Plateau Problem."

2. A Walk across Spain and a Climb Up a Volcano

1. In his *Personal Narrative* Humboldt followed this excerpt from his diary with a long and detailed list of the instruments he had on board as well as tables of observations.

2. See a reproduction of a page in Humboldt's journal describing the incident in Botting, 67. The Leyden jar—typically a glass jar filled with water with a metal spike down through the stopper making contact with the water—was a portable device for storing electricity and conducting electrical experiments and was one of Humboldt's favorite instruments.

3. Louis Claude Richard was botany professor at the École de medicine in Paris. Bonpland's reference is to Richard's revision of Pierre Bulliard's multi-volume *Dictionaire élémentaire de botanique*.

4. See Humboldt's tribute to Bernadin in *Cosmos*, volume 2: "*Paul et Virginie* . . . a work as scarcely any other literature can show, is the simple but living picture of an island in the midst of the tropical seas in which, sometimes smiled on by serene and favoring skies, and sometimes threatened by the violent conflict of the elements, two young and graceful forms stand picturesquely forth from the wild luxuriance of the vegetation of the forest as from a flowery tapestry" (CO II, 66).

3. Aerial Views, Nocturnal Birds, and Wild Indians

1. *Guadua* bamboo, known as "vegetal steel," remains the most important of American bamboos from a utilitarian point of view and is still widely used in construction. There are now restrictions on forest cutting due to diminishing supplies, along with a move to managed groves as were later promoted by Bonpland for yerba in Argentina and Brazil.

2. On the congruence between "nonwestern taxonomies" and contemporary Linnean species categories see Gould, "A Quahog is a Quahog," in *The Panda's Thumb*, 204–213.

3. In 1949 the Guácharo Cave National Park became the first designated National Monument of Venezuela in a move to protect the caves and surrounding forest as habitat for the guácharos, which are now an endangered species.

4. The impression of Indian passivity and indifference would remain with Humboldt. In his 1829 *Political Essay on the Island of Cuba*, he compared anger and rebellion among African slaves in the Caribbean with the behavior of the Indian population: "The copper-colored indigenous race, however, in its timid suspicion and its mysterious indifference, has remained aloof from these movements, even though it will benefit from them in spite of itself" (*Political Essay*, 146).

5. Blumenbach: "It is allowable to suppose that the people dispersed through the various parts of the world have, according to the differences in the degree and duration of the influence of climate and other causes of degeneration, either deviated still more from the form of the primary race, or approximate more closely to it. . . . Polar nations of the Mongolian Race, have deviated considerably from the Caucasian Race; whilst on the other hand, the American, placed at a hreater distance, but in a milder climate, has in an equal degree approximated; . . . in the frozen Tierra del Fuego . . . it again recedes to the Mongolian. . . . The Ethiopian Race has passed to the extreme of variation in the burning regions of African, but passes into the Malayan in the milder climate of New Holland, the New Hebrides, & c." (Blumenbach, *A Manual of the Elements of Natural History*, reprinted in Fulford, *Romanticism and Science*, vol. 5, 110). Blumenbach meant "Caucasian" literally, from the Caucasus mountains, a choice he and others based on the Caucasus's placement between Europe, the supposed origin of civilization in Greece and Jerusalem, and on the unsubstantiated claim that white inhabitants of the Caucasus mountains were the most beautiful of human beings. Humboldt was less influenced by his earlier mentor George Forster who proposed a more pluralistic and nonhierarchical approach to human difference.

6. See Gould, *The Mismeasure of Man*, 401–412, for a detailed discussion of the racial presuppositions of Blumenbach's racial template. As Gould puts it in reference to the move away from the geographical identification of races, "J. F. Blumenbach is the focus of this shift—for his five-race scheme became canonical and he changed the human order from Linnean cartography to linear ranking by putative worth" (405).

Frameworks like Blumenbach's shaped the way individuals perceived reality, with differences seen as more or less beautiful or civilized.

4. The Eel Ponds of the Llanos

1. The executed conspirator was José Maria España, and the conspiracy an offshoot of the failed San Blas Rebellion in Spain inspired by the French Revolution. España was arrested and executed on May 3, 1799.

2. Humboldt was right to note a relative "egalitarianism" among whites. In Latin America even poor whites considered themselves superior to Africans and Indians and regularly refused the manual labor reserved in the colonies for colored races.

3. Although Humboldt did many of the plant drawings, Bonpland did watercolor sketches number-keyed to entries in the journals, which were handed over to artists who did the engravings for their botanical publications. Few have survived, but one from the collection of Turpin is reprinted in Lack, 506.

4. See recent studies of Bonpland's *Botanical Journals*. For examples: Leuenberger and Arroyo-Leuenberger: Bonpland was "one of the most important botanists of his time"; his Botanical Journals were "milestones in the domains of taxonomy and floristics." Lack: "Humboldt's statements on his share in the field work—both in his letters from America and in his first letter to the Professeurs of the Muséum, turn out to be exaggerated." Stauffer, Stauffer, and Dorr: "Aimé Bonpland played the more significant role in the botanical work of the expedition and Humboldt merely contributed a limited number of collections and field notes."

5. Later, back in Paris, where deforestation and desertification had been topics of interest and concern for some time, Humboldt added to his account of Lake Valencia in volume 2 of his *Personal Narrative* the diagnosis of the lowering of the water level on which much of his later fame as a prophet of environmentalism is based: "The shores of Lake Valencia are not famed solely for their picturesque beauties: the basin presents several phenomena whose interpretation holds great interest for natural historians and for the inhabitants. . . . The destruction of the forests, the clearing of the plains, and the cultivation of indigo over half a century has affected the amount of water flowing in as well as the evaporation of the soil and the dryness of the air, which forcefully explains why the present Lake Valencia is decreasing" (PN, 150). For a detailed critical history of theories of deforestation in early nineteenth-century France see Davis, *The Arid Lands*. Davis places theories in the context of colonial attitudes and policies, arguing that indigenous peoples were often wrongly blamed for misusing the land. Although romantics and those like Humboldt looking for universal laws of nature gravitated to the idea of an interruptible universal balance of nature, the hydrologists of the time disagreed, arguing for more local and complex interactive systems. See V. Andréassian, "Waters and Forests: From historical controversy to scientific debate," *Journal of Hydrology* 291 (1), 2004, 1–27, for a historical review of debates surrounding the issue.

5. Riverworlds

1. See volume 4 of the unabridged London edition of the *Personal Narrative of Travels to the Equinoxtial Regions of the New Continent,* trans. Maria Williams, 532–533. The passage was omitted from the abridged Penguin version.

2. The fate of Brazil nuts and the Amazonion forests that play such an important role in climate regulation is even more in question today, with more and more of the forest being cleared for large-scale farming, causing damage both to trees and to forest ecosystems. See recent Bonplandian agroforestry initiatives such as the Brazilian cooperative COOPAVA promoting the sustainable gathering of nuts and preservation of trees in forest preserves.

3. For a neutral fact-based account of these practices see Whitehead, "Carib Cannibalism." See also Pagden, *The Fall of Natural Man,* 80ff, for a detailed history and analysis of the European "obsession" with supposed American Indian cannibalism and the argument that cannibalism was in fact rare and limited to cases of survival and ritual eating of parts of dead enemies or relatives.

6. The Mountain

1. The postscript reprinted by Hamy is from a letter in the library of the archives of the Muséum national d'histoire naturelle (MNHN, 213) sent by Michel in his capacity as director of a new botanical garden in La Rochelle, January 14, 1799, to Thouin regarding an exchange of plants between the two gardens.

2. *Annales du Muséum national d'histoire naturelle,* 1804, no. 4, 477, note 1, records that the shipment had arrived at the Muséum.

3. Plate 61 in Humboldt's *Vues des Cordillères* pictures Pichincha as viewed from the marqués's country house.

4. In his diary Caldas tells a somewhat different story. On a first try, Humboldt asked Caldas to join him, but Caldas declined. On the second try, Caldas was again asked and this time agreed. "I have seen the baron on the verge of extinction. . . . An Indian who was in front of him saved this precious life from death. I followed close behind the baron and the two of us were the first to reach the peak. This traveler is courageous, but I saw him tremble at the edge of the rocks. I shared the danger with him, no less frightened. I helped make the barometric measurements and then descended" (quoted in Appel, 32). Later in the unabridged version of *Views of the Cordilleras* Humboldt identified the guide with whom he made the May 26, 1802, climb up Pichincha as "the Indian Philippe Aldas." Given the similarity between Aldas and Caldas, it is possible Humboldt simply combined Caldas and an Indian guide into one.

5. José de la Cruz is not referred to by name in Humboldt's *Personal Narrative* or in his letters but rather as "a mestizo" or servant. He remained with Humboldt throughout Humboldt's travels in South America and went with him back to Paris.

He was sent back to Cumaná in 1805 when Montúfar returned to South America and Humboldt left Paris for Rome with Gay-Lussac.

6. A translation of "On Two Attempts to Ascend Chimborazo" is online at archive.org/details/b22390820, and is reprinted in Kutzinski, *Alexander von Humboldt's Transatlantic Personae*, 136. For a detailed account of texts and legends associated with Humboldt's climb in the wider context of "German imagination" and as expressive of the "triumph of the cosmic vision of European science," see Lubrich, "Fascinating Voids: Alexander von Humboldt and the Myth of Chimborazo."

7. Weitsch's painting and a portrait made a few months before Humboldt's death by Julius Schrader with Chimborazo in the background are both reproduced in the University of Chicago's 2009 edition of the *Essay on the Geography of Plants*, 51–52, figs. 6 and 7.

7. The Changing of the Gods

1. A Jesuit of Mexican Creole descent, Clavijero was the author of a multi-volume *Historia Antigua de México* (1780) in which he vehemently denied claims of Indian inferiority, pointing out their elaborate histories, the inventiveness of their arts, and the stability and order of their political institutions. Humboldt refers here to Clavijero's speculations regarding Aztec migrations into southern regions.

2. La Condamine's report is in *Mémoires de l'Académie royale des sciences*, 1738 [1740], 226–244 (quote at 235–236).

3. See in volume 4 of Bonpland's botanical journals (MNHN, ms 2535) an extensive note before number 1767 including information from Mutis. There are also notes added at the beginning of volume 1 (MNHN, ms 1332) and at the beginning of the last volume (MNHN, ms 54). After or during his 1806 trip to Berlin, an additional note was added at the end of the last volume detailing species of cinchona bark he found in German pharmacies on his visit to Berlin, speculating on their origin and efficacy.

4. The "November 25 1802" letter reprinted in *Lettres américaines* includes sections from three separate letters from Humboldt written between his departure from Quito and his arrival in Lima. All reached Wilhelm at the same time in Rome, where he was serving as Prussian envoy to the Vatican.

5. Bonpland reported in *Plantes équinoxiales* that he distributed seed to the Jardin in Paris and to other botanical gardens, but ten years later none had germinated (PE I, 81–85).

6. *Epistles* I, i, line 39.

7. The correspondence between Jefferson and Humboldt is on line at founders. archives.gov. After his return to Europe Humboldt continued to pass on to Jefferson information on Mexico, and on such subjects as the prospect of a canal linking the two oceans, the annexation of Cuba as a possible natural extension of Florida, and the mining of gold in California.

8. For a fact-based account of Humboldt's visit to Philadelphia and Washington see Schwarz, "Humboldt's Visit to Washington and Philadelphia, His Friendship with Jefferson and His Fascination with the United States."

9. See Sluyter, "Humboldt's Mexican Texts and Landscapes."

10. For a description of the image, see Pasztory, *Aztec Art*, 157–160. For a discussion of European reactions to this and other Aztec images see "The Plumed Serpent," chapter 15 of Keen, *The Aztec Image in Western Thought*.

8. Coming Home

1. *Ceroxylon quindiense*, renamed after other species in the genus were discovered, is now the national tree of Columbia and endangered due to uses made of its wax, as well as its leaves and fruit as fodder for cattle and pigs.

2. *Les Bardes*, an opera with music by the composer Jean-François Le Sueur, was taken from the "Tales of Ossian," the pretended songs of an ancient Celtic bard written by the Scottish poet James Macpherson. Napoleon was so impressed by the production he invited the composer into his box and later awarded him the French Legion of Honor.

3. Letters from Humboldt to Pictet are available on line, "Lettres d'Alexandre de Humboldt à Marc-Auguste Pictet, 1795–1824," www.hathitrust.org.

9. Tales of Three Cities

1. See also Humboldt's explanation in his memoir, "Account of the Chinchona Forests of South America" in Lambert, *An Illustration of the Genus Cinchona*, 38: "In our expedition we had an opportunity of examining botanically the Cuspare tree, which yields the *cortex Angosturae*. We discovered it to be a new genus, on which our excellent friend Willdenow . . . has conferred the name of *Bonplandia*. This name of my travelling companion has been retained for the Cuspare plant, since we have changed the Mexican *Bonplandia geminiflora*, described by Cavanilles, to *Caldasia heterophylla*."

2. Bonpland's *C. magnifolia* is now, as he ended by concluding, accepted as the same as the plant previously named by Ruiz and Pavon. The local *Cascarilla peluda* bark that Bonpland named *Cinchona ovalifolia* is not a true cinchona, but rather a species of *Macrocnemum*, validating his caveat that it is impossible to determine plant species or even genus by bark alone. *C. scrobiculata* is his discovery and remains the accepted name of a distinct and medicinally valuable species of cinchona. Partly as a result of his efforts, in 1820 French chemists were able to isolate the alkaloid substance in the bark with the most antifebrile effect and call it *quinine*, allowing it to be sold in measured doses as an extract.

3. As part of *Voyage*, the *Atlas pittoresque* was printed in an expensive limited edition with colored engravings. Citations are to *Vues des cordillères et monuments des peuples indigènes de l'Amérique*, a popular abridged mass market edition. See for a description of the image Esther Pasztory, *Aztec Art*, pp. 157–160. For a discussion of European reactions to this and other Aztec images, see "The Plumed Serpent," chapter 15 of Keen, *The Aztec Image in Western Thought*.

4. For the history and an analysis of progressive stages of human development as an alternative to Aristotle's "natural slave" as justification for Spanish and later British rule, see Pagden, *The Fall of Natural Man*. As the doctrine of the natural slave became more and more untenable, an alternate justification for dominion was that non-European cultures were in an early stage of development and, like children, needed parental supervision and guidance.

5. The quote is from Pliny's *Natural History*, book 4, here in the translation by H. Rackham for the Loeb Classical Library (Harvard University Press, 1938).

6. Klaproth was a leading German chemist, Trailles a physician who treated Humboldt for his many maladies later in life.

7. The book was translated and published simultaneously in Paris as *Tableaux de la nature*, and in various English-language editions as *Aspects of Nature*. Different versions of the title indicate the difficulty in translating the German word *Anischten*, which indicates neither the objective "aspect" or the subjective "view" but rather both at once.

10. Botany on Demand

1. Copies of letters between Humboldt and Jefferson are available at www. Founders.Archives.gov and also in de Terra, "Alexander von Humboldt's Correspondence with Jefferson Madison, and Gallatin."

2. See Miller, *The Wolf by the Ears*. The title is taken from a letter from Jefferson to John Holmes written as abolition gathered momentum: "We have the wolf by the ear, and we can neither hold him, nor safely let him go . . . justice is in one scale, and self-preservation in the other." In other words, slaves would have to be freed, but it was not clear to Jefferson how they would be able to live under the same government as whites.

3. Parts 4, 5, and 6 of the *Political Essay on New Spain* dealt almost exclusively with the location of mines, yields from mines, and profits. Published in its entirety in 1811 in French and English, the *Essay* comprised four volumes and 2,000 pages of geography, demographics, agricultural statistics, and inventories of mineral wealth. Few bought all the volumes or got through the long tables of "statistics," but abridged versions and shorter excerpts reprinted in magazines and journals were widely read.

4. *Atlas géographique et physique*, map 19—"Routes by which precious metals flow from one continent to another."

5. *Atlas*, "Intro Geographique," LXXXIII. See an analysis of Humboldt's *Political Essay* in Brading, *The First America*, 534: "Humboldt displayed all the voracious energy of an intellectual conqueror, restlessly searching for new ranges of knowledge to survey and master. Yet, at the level of theory, he adopted a remarkably passive, almost unquestioning approach to the mass of data that he collected. He made little attempt to explain or to interpret; he eschewed all inquiry into the causes of things; all his energy went into observing, measuring, describing and compiling."

6. See Stephens's account of his visit with Humboldt in the American weekly magazine *The Living Age*, vol. 15, October–December 1847, 151.

7. The title of "intendant" dates from the fifth century, when it was used by French kings to designate a public functionary or supervisor with a permanent sinecure overseeing an area of public concern such as finance, and later civic theaters or royal gardens. Use of such titles was part of Napoleon's assumption of the trappings of royal power.

8. "Monuments" refers to Humboldt's Aztec and Inca materials in *Views of the Cordilleras*.

9. "Charles" is an Anglicized version of Carl.

11. Taking Leave

1. Quoted from *Memorias del General Daniel Florencio O'Leary: Narración*, Caracas: Imprenta nacional, 1952, I: 57.

2. See Bell, 22 and notes 14–15 (239), for references to correspondence between Bonpland and Zea.

3. "But the most precious work that we possess in the geography of plants and perhaps the only one that presents it in its full extent is the *Geography of Plants* of M. Humboldt." (*Dictionnaire de sciences naturelles*, Vol. XXVIII, 360).

4. "Geographique botanique" in *Dictionnaire des sciences naturelles*, vol. 18, Paris: F. G. Levrault, 1821, 402.

5. Ibid., 403. In his 1855 update of *Géographie botanique raisonnée* Candolle's son, Alphonse, stated somewhat less diplomatically that Humboldt's "geography of plants" was not based on empirical evidence and that his vegetal physiognomy was an aesthetic impression tainted with romantic idealism.

6. Although Darwin took with him on the Beagle Maria William's seven-volume translation of Humboldt's *Personal Narrative*, more important as a scientific mentor for Darwin was the botanist John Henslow ("the one circumstance that influenced my career more than any other"). Henslow was a student of Candolle's who taught, in addition to classification, plant physiology and the use of plants in medicine and other areas of human life. Darwin's description of meeting Humboldt years later: "I once met at breakfast at Sir R. Murchinson's house, the illustrious Humboldt, who honored me by expressing a wish to see me. I was a little disappointed with the great

man, but my anticipations were probably too high. I can remember nothing about our interview, except that Humboldt was very cheerful and talked much" (*The Autobiography of Charles Darwin*, 107).

12. A Lost Friend

1. *Quarterly Review* 1816, review of the 1815 volume 1 of the *Personal Narrative*.

2. The cult statue at Ephesus is not of Greek origin. The iconography of the statue links it to older Eastern, Minoan, and Egyptian images with similarities to Cybele or Isis. What the supposed "breasts" were originally meant to represent is not clear, but evidence indicates that the egg-shaped droppings may be simply a form of ritual breast decoration.

3. See, for details, McCosh, *Boussingault*.

4. A treaty with the United Provinces in 1811 ceded to Paraguay the Department of Candelaria, including the missions of Santa Ana, Candelaria, San Ignacio Miní, and Loreto, but when the treaty was ratified in Buenos Aires that clause was omitted. When Paraguay declared independence in 1814 Argentina disavowed the treaty altogether, and in the years that followed, the mission territory was contested and fought over with devastating results. From Francia's point of view, Ramírez, under whose auspices Bonpland was acting, was an invader of Paraguayan territory.

5. Quoted in Cerruti, 681. Lebreton, some years older than Bonpland, served as head of fine arts under the Ministry of the Interior during the Directory in Paris. Like Bonpland, he left France after the Restoration, and came to Brazil on the promise of being part of a French artistic mission that was slow to materialize. He died in 1819.

6. Letter to Lebreton, November 18, 1818, quoted in Cerruti, 640.

7. *Berliner Conversations-Blatt für Poesie, Literatur und Kritik*, no. 2, January 2, 1827.

8. If Humboldt had read Hegel's "Philosophy of Nature" (part 2 of Hegel's 1830 *Encyclopedia of the Philosophical Sciences*), he might have been less critical. In it Hegel referred over and over to discoveries in science, including some that he attributed to Humboldt: magnetic reading when passing serpentine rock, observations on galvanism, separating oxygen from the air on top of mountains, and finding mammoth bones in Peru. Nor does Humboldt seem to have realized how important it was to Hegel to disassociate himself from Schelling's imaginative constructions and to reject philosophies of nature with no relation to "facts and experiments."

9. See Wulf, 242.

10. A full description of Humboldt's trip to Siberia is given by Botting, 238–254, and by Wulf, 201–216.

11. Initially the plan was to publish an ambitious three-volume work: a first volume by Humboldt in French with a map of west Asia, observations on terrestrial magnetism, and astronomical geography; a second volume by Gustav Rose on mineralogy, geology, and chemistry; a third by Ehrenberg on botany and zoology—both of

the latter two in German. This never materialized. Humboldt read a memoir touching briefly on volcanoes, climatology, and magnetism to the Berlin Academy in 1830 soon after he arrived back from Russia, and a similar memoir to the Institut de France while visiting Paris in 1831. Also in Paris in 1831, a composite publication was gotten together titled *Fragments de géologie et de climatologie asiatiques*, and including a mix of materials: 1) The memoir read in Berlin translated into French as "Considerations sur les systèmes de montagnes volcaniques de l'intérieur de l'Asie," 2) a short piece on Asian climate, 3) an excerpt from part of a larger projected work, "Essay on the Physics of the World," with material taken from Humboldt's course in 1827–1828, 4) some notes on gold and diamonds, terrestrial magnetism, and mountain systems, and 5) an introductory piece on volcanoes. Twelve years later, in 1843, Humboldt published a work in several volumes with material from many different sources he called *Asie centrale: Recherches sur les chaînes de montagnes et la climatologie comparée*. In 1837 and 1842 Rose published his own two-volume *Mineralogical-geognostic Journey to the Urals, the Altai, and the Caspian Sea*.

12. Humboldt went on to promote and further Agassiz's career even as Agassiz's researches in human difference became more virulently racist. Agassiz opposed slavery, but insisted that given the differences between colored and white races they could not have come from common stock. For that reason, he supported strict segregation of the races and a ban on "miscegenation."

13. Warlords and Kings

1. There is little known about Bonpland's romantic life, due most probably to the reticence of biographers and keepers of archives given that none of his three marriages was legally constituted. Piecing together bits and pieces of personal records in the Bonpland archive in Buenos Aires, Philippe Foucault in his fictionalized biography *Le pêcheur d'orchidées* tells a romantic story of Bonpland and María Chirivé, the daughter of a Guarani leader, who bravely offered water to Bonpland and his wounded and captured men. He credits María with helping Bonpland set up his clinic, including a maternity ward, and working with him in his medical practice. In the town of Santa María de Fe, near to Bonpland's land at El Cerrito, there is a monument to Bonpland, and according to locals his and María's descendants still live in the vicinity. (See for example a reference to Bonpland's descendants in a 2014 Bradt *Guide to Paraguay* by Margaret Hebblethwaite). Later, there were reports that a son of his and María's sought out Bonpland at São Borja.

2. See Bell, 297. Whether Bonpland was ever able to bring his plan to the attention of Rosas is not clear. A 2011 survey, "Natural Territory, Urban Growth and Climate Change in the Parana River Delta and Rio de la Plata Estuarine System: an Overview" (Verónica Zagare, www.delta-alliance.org) refers to many of the same issues raised by Bonpland, noting that lack of planning was an obstacle to addressing problems caused by climate change.

3. Saint-Hilaire, *Histoire des plantes les plus remarquables du Brésil et du Paraguay*.

4. In 1819 in Buenos Aires, Bonpland began compiling a Guarani vocabulary and expression list (AMF, 2044).

5. Augustin Saint-Hilaire traveled widely in Brazil from 1816 to 1822 but only approached at some distance the closed border with Paraguay. Rengger and Longchamp were Swiss physicians who traveled from Buenos Aires to Asunción, were detained there by Francia, and were made to serve as medical officers in army garrisons in Asunción. They contacted Bonpland several times for advice on medical matters, but were not allowed to leave Asunción and could not have had much to say about Paraguayan plants.

6. "Chile": Humboldt's reference is to the so-called 1836–1839 War of the Confederation between a Bolivian/Peruvian alliance and Chile backed by British Navy, which in the end proved decisive.

7. Humboldt's reference is to Hegel's *Lectures on the Philosophy of World History*, in which Hegel follows Buffon's lead, arguing that indigenous peoples and animals are weaker in the Americas than in the Old World: "Even animals show the same inferiority as the human beings. The fauna of America includes lions, tigers, and crocodiles, but although they are otherwise similar to their equivalents in the Old World, they are in every respect smaller, weaker, and less powerful. We are even assured that animals are not as nourishing as the food which the Old World provides. And although America has huge herds of cattle, European beef is still regarded as a delicacy" (Hegel, 163).

8. See CO I, 76, for the passage chosen: "As intelligence and forms of speech, thought and its verbal symbols, are united by secret and indissoluble links, so does the external work blend almost unconsciously to ourselves with our ideas and feelings. 'External phenomena,' says Hegel, in his *Philosophy of History*, 'are in some degree translated in our inner representations.'"

9. The Italian-born naturalist Pedro de Ángelis met Humboldt and Bonpland in Paris and was now resident in Buenos Aires doing studies of the history and geography of the Río de la Plata. He welcomed Bonpland and Adeline when they first arrived in Buenos Aires. Waiting for Bonpland to arrive from upriver after his release from Paraguay, he wrote to Cuvier asking him to pass on a message to Humboldt that Bonpland would arrive soon and Humboldt could write to Bonpland through him (Cordier, 476).

10. The grant was given under the legal device of "emphyteusis," a long-term lease in which a leaseholder pledges to improve and add value to a landholding with his own and his workers' labor. Dating from the Roman republic, it had been instituted by Rivadavia in his early days as minister but was no longer in use in Buenos Aires province, where large landholdings were now the norm. Ferré was eager to put the policy into effect in Corrientes before all unclaimed land upriver had been handed out as political favors to Rosas's generals and cronies.

14. Cosmos and Microcosm

1. Humboldt takes liberties here. In Greek παν is not a noun but a particle that is added to other words to indicate extent, as in the English words *pandemic* and

panorama. Closer might have been the Greek philosopher Parmenides's "being" and "not being," except that Parmenides's strict monism ruled out the observed facts that were to validate Humboldt's account of "what is."

2. Passage of the Panorama, opening in 1800, was one of the first of the covered passageways of Paris. The Creux du Vent (properly Creux-du-Van) is a deep pit-like rock formation in Neuchâtel, Switzerland. In his *Mémoires* Candolle recalled fondly and at length a hazardous climb he took there with Bonpland and other young friends from the Muséum.

3. Candolle's *Prodromus Systematis Naturalis Regni Vegetabilis* was a "preliminary" summary of all known seed plants with comments on ecology, evolution, and biogeography. Candolle edited the first seven volumes. After his death in 1841 his son, Alphonse, edited the remaining ten with contributions from other researchers

4. The incident and Humboldt's reaction are described by Abraham Hayward, "Correspondence of Humboldt," *Edinburgh Review*, vol. 112, 1860, 231–236, quoted in Rupke, 49. When an 1829 Spanish degree abolished slavery throughout New Spain, Southern slave-owners who had emigrated into the Texas territory rebelled and declared Texas independent. A constitution was passed reinstating slavery, making it illegal to release a slave, and restricting the rights of free blacks. When the United States annexed Texas in 1840, slave labor predominated, with cotton a major crop. At the time of Stephens's visit to Humboldt, American forces, led by the flamboyant Taylor, a slave owner himself, were in the process of driving any remaining abolitionist Mexican forces out of Texas.

5. Bonpland mentioned Guillaume Dupuytren, chief surgeon at Hôtel-Dieu, who died in 1835, and Jean-Louis Alibert, who did crusading work in skin diseases and died in 1837, both of whom Bonpland knew at medical school, and also Mirbel at the Muséum, with whom Bonpland kept up a lively exchange of seeds and information until Mirbel fell ill and retired.

15. A Last Exchange of Gifts

1. A supposed defense of Arago at a dinner party in Brussels resulted in a homily given at the Belgian Chamber of Deputies, angry rebuttal in liberal papers, protest letters to Humboldt, and Humboldt's insistence to Varnhagen that he could not remember what he said and that although he was a liberal he was no "republican" (LHV, 342, 346).

2. Few images of Bonpland survive. Something of a likeness appears in various portraits of the two of them on the Orinoco and at Chimborazo. An engraving was made in Leipzig from a drawing probably done on Bonpland's visit to Berlin showing him with a very sour expression, and a lithograph was taken from a rough drawing by Alfred Demersay. Of them all, the daguerreotype, taken late in life, is perhaps the most reliable likeness.

3. During the reign of Louis Philippe from 1830 to 1848, whenever he was in Paris, Humboldt was a frequent visitor at the Tuileries and at St. Cloud, where he

was on intimate terms with the wife of Louis Philippe's eldest son, Helene, Duchess of Orléans, who was also a niece of Frederick William of Prussia. Their friendship continued after Louis Philippe was forced into exile, with Humboldt sending the duchess copies of *Cosmos* to console her. "The current state of Europe"—When Louis Philippe abdicated in 1848 Louis Napoleon, the nephew and supposed heir of Napoleon, was elected president. Three years later he took on dictatorial powers in the coup of 1851 and declared a "Second Empire."

4. Bonpland made no attempt to press the fact that he was the first to discover the plant that caused such a sensation in fashionable horticultural circles in England, and it is impossible to imagine him participating in the competition as amateur and professional botanists vied to come up with a name to best find favor with Queen Victoria. Two species of the genus *Victoria* were eventually distinguished, with *Victoria amazonica* somewhat larger in leaf and flower, and Bonpland's "maize of the water," from the cooler waters of Paraguay and Corrientes, given the name *Victoria cruziana* after Andrés de Santa Cruz, who funded the expedition to South American of Alcide d'Orbigny, who later also described the species discovered by Bonpland. Current botanical descriptions of *V. cruziana* note that it was Bonpland who first collected and described the plant.

5. The first was probably the lithograph made by Delpech from a portrait by Gérard in 1832, the other a daguerreotype of Humboldt made in 1847.

6. The journal *Bonplandia* was established in 1853 in Bonpland's honor in Hanover, Germany, as the official organ of the Academia Caesaro-Leopoldina, edited by Wilhelm and Berthold Seemann, and is still being published.

7. The description is from a diary kept by Moritz Busch, published as *Bismarck: Some Secret Pages of His History* (London: Macmillan, 1898).

8. Humboldt was probably reacting to the 1854 Kansas–Nebraska Act, which ruled that white male settlers moving into new territories could vote on whether slavery would be allowed. It is less clear what Humboldt means by "indifference," since in the United States the issue was hotly and violently debated. As part of the "compromise" of 1854 a federal law was passed abolishing the domestic slave trade but not slavery, and a new, more punitive Fugitive Slave Act was passed requiring the capture and return of escaped slaves. The law was the subject of the Lincoln–Douglas debates, with Douglas needing Southern consent to build a transcontinental railroad and the South demanding in return that part of the Nebraska territory as well as more of the west be open to slave holding.

9. For "the modern Aristotle" see the translator's preface to *Tableaux de la nature* (vol. 1, p.i): "History has shown us only two men whose encyclopedic genius embraces all human knowledge: Aristotle and Humboldt."

10. See, on Seifert and his hold on Humboldt, von Hagen, "Was This the Fate of the Library of Alexander von Humboldt?"

11. Taylor's essay "Alexander von Humboldt" is reprinted in Taylor's *At Home and Abroad: Life Scenery, and Men*, volume 1. Quotes from Bayard are from pages

351, 353, and 359. Humboldt's joke with the chameleon got Taylor in trouble when he mentioned it in a lecture to the Young Men's Christian Union in New York. As reported in *The New York Times* (March 5, 1860), the slur on the clergy resulted in the cancellation of a lecture Taylor was to give in Richmond, Virginia.

12. "Alea jacta est" is Latin for "The die is cast," said by Julius Caesar as he crossed the Rubicon.

13. See Dove's extended description of the contents of the boxes (CB II, 366–367).

16. Scattered Remains

1. See Demersay, "Note sur les manuscrits et collections de M. Aimé Bonpland," for a detailed inventory.

2. See Demersay, *Histoire physique, economique, et politique du Paraguay*, lix–lx, for a long footnote on Bonpland's death and measures to recover his manuscripts.

3. See Hamy's introduction to Aubin's *Mémoires sur la peinture didactique et l'écriture figurative des anciens Mexicains*.

4. "Study of Nature" is reprinted in Marsh, *So Great a Vision*, 83. Compare Andrea Wulf's claim that Marsh thought Humboldt was "the greatest of the priesthood of nature," citing as her source a passage in which Marsh calls Humboldt "the apostle of the *popularization of* science" (Wulf, 284). Wulf's further evidence for saying that Marsh "idolized" Humboldt is that there were books by Humboldt in Marsh's library at his death, although her claim that Marsh had a "whole section" on Humboldt seems somewhat strong. On Marsh's bookshelves along with a hundred other books were an edition of *Views of Nature*, several volumes of *Cosmos*, and some books about Humboldt.

5. In the introductory historical sketch Darwin wrote for *On the Origin of Species* references are to Lamarck, Geoffroy Saint-Hilaire, Buffon, Candolle, Humboldt's friend the geologist von Buch, and of course Wallace as laying the groundwork for the theory of evolution. Humboldt is not mentioned.

6. See Ronald Tobey's classic account in *Saving the Prairies*. Clements and others wrongly extended Kant's natural functional teleology of individual living organisms to supposed higher-level organisms like prairies. As Tobey put it, " 'Nature' could not guide vegetation toward the climatic climax, or repair damage, because nature, as an action of a natural world independent of man, simply did not exist—certainly not in the midcontinental grasslands. The scientist had to discover by experiment or historical inference what the path of succession would be isolated from man and then actively guide the path of succession. This was called *conservation*" (198).

7. See Jan Smuts in *Holism and Evolution* arguing on the basis of holism for apartheid in South Africa, with each race occupying the niche suitable to its natural place in human society. See also J. Baird Callicott's defense of holistic environmental ethics in "Holistic Environmental Ethics and the Problem of EcoFascism" in *Beyond the Land Ethic*.

8. Cordier's inventory of the archives with selected texts is available online: "Papiers inédits du naturaliste Aimé Bonpland conservés à Buenos Aires."

9. See Rupke, *Alexander von Humboldt: A Metabiography*, for a detailed historical account of the different forms Humboldt's patriotic legacy took in Germany, among them German *Kultur*, the ideals of National Socialism, and—for a moment in the old Soviet East Germany—Marxist revolution.

Afterthoughts: A Bonplandian Ethos

1. See Stauffer and Stauffer, "The Palm (Arecaceae) Collections Gathered by Bonpland and Humboldt in Their American Journey."

2. For a current example, see the chapter "Fruits, not Roots: The Disastrous Merger of Big Business and Big Green" in Naomi Klein's 2014 *This Changes Everything*.

3. For a recent study using Bonpland's herbarium and botanical journals, see Leuenberger and Arrayo-Leuenberger, "Humboldt, Bonpland, Kunth and the type specimen of *Rauhia multiflora (Amaryllidaceae)* from Peru," 608: "The excellent and well-documented material of the Humboldt and Bonpland collections is of permanent importance in the context of current tropical biodiversity studies." See also Leuenberger, B. E., "Humboldt and Bonpland's *Cactaceae* in the Herbaria at Paris and Berlin," and Stauffer, Stuaffer, and Dorr, "Bonpland and Humboldt's Specimens, Field Notes and Herbaria."

4. See Pennini, "Le pharmacien Juan A. Dominguez initiateur de la pharmacologie argentine," for the importance of the Bonpland archive in the Institut's collections.

5. See Joshua Howe's examples in *Behind the Curve*, 205–208, of current "bottom-up" "multi-level" approaches to environment policy in towns, counties, and regions as a reason for hope in the light of constantly stalled international and national attempts to slow global warming.

Primary Sources

Many of the primary sources are available in free online archives. Quotations from editions in French are the author's own translations.

AB   Hamy, *Aimé Bonpland, médecin et naturaliste, explorateur de l'Amérique du Sud.*

ABH   Hossard, *Aimé Bonpland (1773–1858): Médecin, naturaliste, explorateur en Amérique du Sud.*

AMF   Archivo Aimé Bonpland del Museo Farmacobotanica Juan A. Domínguez, Facultad de Farmacia Bioquímica, Universidad de Buenos Aires.

AN   Humboldt, *Aspects of Nature in Different Lands and Different Climates.*

CB   Lowenberg, Avé-Lallemant, and Dove, *Life of Alexander von Humboldt*, vols. 1 (I) and 2 (II).

CI   Humboldt, *Corréspondance inédite scientifique et litteraire*, vols. 1 (I) and 2 (II).

CO   Humboldt, *Cosmos*, vols. 1 (I), 2 (II), 3 (III), and 5 (V).

HCH   Humboldt and Bonpland, *Corréspondance, 1805–1858.*

LA   Humboldt, *Lettres américaines de Alexandre de Humboldt.*

LHV   Humboldt, *Letters of Alexander von Humboldt to Varnhagen von Ense.*

MNHN Muséum national d'histoire naturelle, Paris, Archive Aimé Bonpland.

PE   Bonpland, *Plantes équinoxiales*, vols. 1 (I) and 2 (II).

PEIC   Humboldt, Alexander von. "Political Essay on the Island of Cuba," in *Personal Narrative of Travels to the Equinoctial Regions*, translated by Helen Maria Williams.

PN   Humboldt, *Personal Narrative of a Journey to the Equinoctial Regions of the New Continent*, abridged and translated by Jason Wilson.

PR   Bonpland, *Description des plantes rare cultivées à Malmaison et à Navarre*.

VC   Humboldt, *Vues des cordillères, et monumens des peuples indigènes de l'Amérique*.

Bibliography

Andréassian, V. "Waters and Forests: From Historical Controversy to Scientific Debate." *Journal of Hydrology*, vol. 291, no. 1, 2004, pp. 1–27.

Appel, John Wilton. "Francisco Jose de Caldas: A Scientist at Work in Nueva Granada." *Transactions of the American Philosophical Society*, vol. 84, no. 5, 1994, pp. 1–154.

Aubin, J. M. A. *Mémoires sur la peinture didactique et l'écriture figurative des anciens Mexicains.* Paris: Imprimerie nationale, 1885.

Avé-Lallemant, Robert. "The Last Days of Aimé Bonpland." In Lowenberg, Avé-Lallemant, and Dove, *Life of Alexander von Humboldt*, vol. 1, pp. 407ff.

Bell, Stephen. *A Life in Shadow: Aimé Bonpland in Southern South America 1817–1858.* Palo Alto: Stanford University Press, 2010.

Bernadin de Saint-Pierre, Jacques-Henri. *Paul and Virginie.* Paris: Garnier-Flammarion, 1966. (First published in Paris (1788) as the fourth volume of a new edition of Bernardin de Saint-Pierre's *Studies of Nature*.)

Blumenbach, Johann Frederich. "Manual of the Elements of Natural History." In Fulford, *Romanticism and Science*, vol. 5.

Bonpland, Aimé. *Description des plantes rare cultivées à Malmaison et à Navarre.* Paris: P. Didot l'aîné, 1813.

———. *Journal: Voyage de San Borja à la Cierra y a Porto Alegre.* Porto Alegro, Brazil: Department of Botany, Institute de Biociencas, 1978.

———. *Monographie des melastomacées, comprenant toutes les plantes de cet ordre récueillies jusqu'à ce jour.* 2 vols. Londres: Gide 1833.

———. *Papiers inédits du naturaliste Aimé Bonpland conservés à Buenos Aires.* Edited by H. Cordier, Paris: Picard et fils, 1910.

———. *Plantes équinoxiales.* 2 vols. Paris: Schoell, 1806–1816.

Botting, Douglas. *Humboldt and the Cosmos.* London: Michael Joseph, 1973.

Boussingault, Jean-Baptiste. *Mémoires.* Paris: Chamerot and Renovard, 1892–1903.

Bowen, Margarita. *Empiricism and Geographical Thought: From Francis Bacin to Alexander von Humboldt.* Cambridge: Cambridge University Press, 1981.

Brading, D. A. *The First America: The Spanish Monarchy, Creole Patriots and the Liberal State 1492–1867.* Cambridge: Cambridge University Press, 1993.

Brunel, Adolphe. *Biographie d'Aimé Bonpland, compagnon de voyage et collaborateur d'Alexandre de Humboldt*. Paris: Guérin, 1871.

Busch, Moritz. *Bismarck: Some Secret Pages of His History*. London: Macmillan, 1898.

Callicott, J. Baird. *Beyond the Land Ethic: More Essays in Environmental Philosophy*. Albany, NY: State University of New York Press, 1999.

Candolle, Augustus Pyramus, and Jean-Baptist Lamarck. *Flore française, ou Descriptions succinctes de toutes les plantes qui croissent naturallement en France*. 3rd edition, vol. 1, Paris: Agasse, 1805.

———. *Mémoires et souvenirs (1778–1841)*. Geneva: Bibiothéque d'Histoire des Sciences, 2004 (reprint of the 1862 edition).

Carlsen, William. *Jungle of Stone: The Extraordinary Journey of John L. Stephens and Frederick Catherwood, and the Discovery of the Lost Civilization of the Maya*. New York: HarperCollins, 2017.

Cerruti, Cedric. *L'Américanisme en construction: Une pré-histoire de la discipline d'après l'expérience du naturaliste Aymé Bonpland (1773–1858)*. La Rochelle: Université de la Rochelle, 2012.

Clark, Rex, and Oliver Lubrich, eds. *Cosmos and Colonialism: Alexander von Humboldt in Cultural Criticism*. New York: Berghahn Books, 2012.

Cordier, Henri. "Papiers inédits du naturaliste Aimé Bonpland conservés à Buenos Aires." *Comptes rendues des séances de l'Academie des inscriptions et belles-lettres*, vol. 54–56, 1910, pp. 455–479.

Corsi, Pietro. *The Age of Lamarck: Evolutionary Theories in France, 1790–1830*. Translated by Jonathan Mandelbaum, Berkeley: University of California Press, 1988.

Darwin, Charles. *The Autobiography of Charles Darwin*. New York: W. W. Norton, 1969.

Davis, Diana. *The Arid Lands: History, Power, Knowledge*. MIT Press, 2016.

Deleuze, Joseph-Philippe-François. *Histoire et description du Muséum royal d'histoire naturelle*. Paris: M. A. Royer, 1823.

Demersay, Alfred. *Étude économique sur le maté ou thé du Paraguay*. Paris: Bouchard-Huzsard, 1867.

———. *Histoire physique, économiqu, et politique du Paraguay et des établissements des Jésuites*. Paris: Hachette. 1860.

———. "Note sur les manuscrits et Collections de M. Aimé Bonpland." *Bulletin de la Société de géographie (Paris)*, vol. 4, no. 19, 1860, pp. 426–429.

———. "Paraguay." *New Monthly Magazine*, vol. 119, 1860, pp. 453–457.

———. "Sur la vie et les travaux de Aimé Bonpland." *Bulletin de la Société de géographie (Paris)*, vol. 4, no. 5, 1853, pp. 240–254.

de Terra, Helmut. "Alexander von Humboldt's Correspondence with Jefferson, Madison, and Gallatin." *Proceedings of the American Philosophical Society*, vol. 103, no. 6, 1959, pp. 783–806.

———. *Humboldt: The Life and Times of Alexander von Humboldt*. New York: Alfred A. Knopf, 1955.

Dettelbach, Michel. "Global Physics and Aesthetic Empire: Humboldt's Physical Portrait of the Tropics." In Miller and Reill, pp. 258–292.

————. "Humboldtian Science." In N. Jardine, J. A. Secord, and E. C. Spary, eds., *Cultures of Natural History*. Cambridge: Cambridge University Press, 1996.

Ebach, Malte Christian. *Origins of Biogeography: The Role of Biological Classification in Early Plant and Animal Geography*. New York: Springer, 2015.

Fayet, Joseph. *La Révolution française et la science: 1789–1795*. Paris: Marcel Rivière, 1960.

Foner, Philip. "Alexander von Humboldt on Slavery in America." *Science and Society*, vol. 47, no. 3, 1983, pp. 330–342.

Foucault, Philippe. *Le pêcheur d'orchidées: Aimé Bonpland 1773–1858*. Paris: Seghers, 1990.

Fulford, Tim, ed. *Romanticism and Science, 1773–1833*. London: Routledge, 2002.

Galeano, Eduardo. *Open Veins of Latin America*. Translated by Cedric Belfrage, New York: Monthly Review Press, 1973.

Ganson, Barbara Anne. *The Guaraní Under Spanish Rule in the Rio de la Plata*. Stanford: Stanford University Press, 2003.

Godlewska, Anne. *Geography Unbound: French Geographic Science from Cassini to Humboldt*. Chicago: University of Chicago Press, 1999.

Gould, Stephen Jay. *The Mismeasure of Man*. New York: W. W. Norton, 1981.

————. *The Panda's Thumb*. New York: W. W. Norton, 1980.

Halperín-Donghi, Tulio. *Politics, Economics and Society in Argentina in the Revolutionary Period*. Translated by Richard Southern, Cambridge: Cambridge University Press, 1975.

Hamy, E. T. *Aimé Bonpland, médecin et naturaliste, explorateur de l'Amérique du Sud: Sa vie, son oeuvre, sa corréspondance*. Paris: Guilmoto, 1906.

Hegel, G. W. F. *Lectures on the Philosophy of World History*. Translated by H. B. Nisbet, Cambridge: Cambridge University Press, 1975.

Helferich, Gerard. *Humboldt's Cosmos: Alexander von Humboldt and the Latin American Journey that Changed the Way We See the World*. New York: Gotham Books, 2004.

Hossard, Nicolas. *Aimé Bonpland (1773–1858): Médecin, naturaliste, explorateur en Amérique du Sud*. Paris: L'Harmattan, 2001.

Howe, Joshua. *Behind the Curve: Science and the Politics of Global Warming*. Seattle: nUniversity of Washington Press, 2014.

Humboldt, Alexander von. *Ansichten der Natur*. Tubingen: J. G. Cotta, 1849.

————. *Asie centrale: Recherches sur les chaînes de montagnes et la climatologie comparée*. Paris: Gide, 1843.

————. *Aspects of Nature in Different Lands and Different Climates*. Translated by Mrs. Sabine, Philadelphia: Lea and Blanchard, 1849.

————. *Atlas géographique et physique des régions équinoxiales du nouveau continent*. Paris: Schoell, 1814–1834.

————. *Corréspondance inédite scientifique et littéraire*. 2 vols. Paris: Guérin, 1869.

————. *Cosmos*. Vol. 1, translated by E. C. Otté, Baltimore: Johns Hopkins University Press, 1997; vol. 2, translated by E. Sabine, London: Longman, 1849; vol. 3, translated by E. C. Otté, and vol. 5, translated by E. C. Otté and W. S. Dallas, New York: Harper & Brothers, 1866.

————. *Essai politique sur le royaume de la Nouvelle-Espagne*. Paris: Schoell, 1811.

————. *Essay on the Geography of Plants*. Edited by Stephen Jackson, translated by Sylvie Romanowski, Chicago: University of Chicago Press, 2009.

————. *Florae fribergensis*. Berlin: Berolini, 1793.

————. *Fragments de géologie et de climatologie asiatiques*. 2 vols. Paris: Gide, 1831.

————. *Letters of Alexander von Humboldt to Varnhagen von Ense. From 1827 to 1858*. Translated by Friedrich Kapp, New York: Rudd and Carleton, 1860.

————. *Lettres américaines de Alexandre de Humboldt*. Edited by E. T. Hamy, Paris: Librarie Orientale et Américaine, 1905.

————. *Lettres d'Alexandre de Humboldt à Marc Auguste Pictet (1795–1824)*. Genéve/ Carey Frères, 1869.

————. *Personal Narrative of a Journey to the Equinoctial Regions of the New Continent*. Abridged and translated by Jason Wilson, London: Penguin Books, 1995.

————. *Political Essay on the Island of Cuba, Personal Narrative of Travels to the Equinoctial Regions of the New Continent During the Years 1799–1804. Vol. 7*. Translated by Helen Maria Williams. London: Longman, 1829.

————. *Recueil d'observations astronomiques, d'opérations trigonométriques et de mesures barométriques*. Reviewed and calculated by Jabbo Oltmanns, Paris: Schoell, 1808–1810.

————. *Tableaux de la nature*. Trans. Ferd. Hoefer. Paris: Firmin Didot, 1850.

————. *Views of the Cordilleras and Monuments of the Americas*. Edited and translated by Vera Kutzinski and Ottmar Ette, Chicago: University of Chicago Press, 2012.

————. *Vues des cordillères, et monumens des peuples indigènes de l'Amérique*. Paris: Maze, 1816–1824.

Humboldt, Alexander von, and Aimé Bonpland. *Corréspondance, 1805–1858*. Edited by Nicolas Hossard, Paris: L'Harmattan, 2004.

————. *Essai sur la géographie des plantes*. Reviewed and corrected by Alexander Humboldt, Paris: Levrault, Schoell et Compagnie, 1805.

————. *Recueil d'observations de zoologie et d'anatomie comparée*. Paris: Schoell and Dufour, 1811.

Humboldt, Wilhelm. *On Language: On the Diversity of Human Language Construction and Its Influence on the Mental Development of the Human Species*. Edited by Michael Losonsky, Cambridge: Cambridge University Press, 1999.

Ireton, Sean, and Caroline Schaumann, eds. *Heights of Reflection: Mountains in the German Imagination from the Middle Ages to the Twenty-First Century*. Rochester, NY: Camden House, 2012.

Jardine, N., J. A. Secord, and E. C. Spary, eds. *Cultures of Natural History*. Cambridge: Cambridge University Press, 1996.

Keen, Benjamin. *The Aztec Image in Western Thought*. New Brunswick, NJ: Rutgers University Press, 1971.

Kellner, L. *Alexander von Humboldt*. Oxford: Oxford University Press, 1963.

Klein, Naomi. *This Changes Everything: Capitalism Is the Climate*. New York: Simon & Schuster, 2014.

Klonk, Charlotte. *Science and the Perception of Nature.* New Haven: Yale University Press, 1996.

Kutzinski, Vera, ed. *Alexander von Humboldt's Transatlantic Personae.* London: Routledge, 2012.

Lack, Walter. "The Botanical Field Notes Prepared by Humboldt and Bonpland in Tropical America." *Taxon,* vol. 53, no. 2, 2004, pp. 501–510.

Lambert, A. B. *An Illustration of the Genus Cinchona.* London: Longman, 1821.

Larson, James. *Interpreting Nature: The Science of Living Form from Linnaeus to Kant.* Baltimore: Johns Hopkins University Press, 1994.

Leopold, Aldo. *Sand County Almanac.* New York: Random House, 1966.

Leuenberger, B. E. "Humboldt and Bonpland's *Cactaceae* in the Herbaria at Paris and Berlin." *Willdenowia,* vol. 32, no. 1, 2002, pp. 137–153.

Leuenberger, B. E., and S. Arroyo-Leuenberger. "Humboldt, Bonpland, Kunth and the type Specimen of *Rauhia multiflora (Amaryllidaceae)* from Peru." *Wildenowia,* vol. 36, 2006, pp. 601–609.

Lowenberg, Julius, Robert Avé-Lallemant, and Alfred Wilhelm Dove. *Life of Alexander von Humboldt Compiled in Commemoration of the Centenary of His Birth.* 2 vols. London: Longmans, Green and Co., 1873.

Lubrich, Oliver. "Fascinating Voids: Alexander von Humboldt and the Myth of Chimborazo." In Ireton and Schaumann, pp. 153–175.

Lynch, John. *Argentine Dictator: Juan Manuel de Rosas, 1829–1852.* Oxford: Clarendon Press, 1981.

———. *Caudillos in Spanish America: 1800–1850.* Oxford: Clarendon Press, 1992.

———. *Simón Bolívar: A Life.* New Haven: Yale University Press, 2007.

Marsh, George Perkins. *Man and Nature: Or, Physical Geography as Modified by Human Action.* Cambridge: Harvard University Press, 1965. (Reprint of original 1864 edition.)

———. *So Great a Vision: The Conservation Writings of George Perkins Marsh.* Edited by Stephen Trombulak. Middlebury, VT: Middlebury College Press, 2001.

Maspero, François. *Alexandre de Humboldt.* Paris: Minguet, 1969.

McCosh, F. W. J. *Boussingault: Chemist and Agriculturalist.* Dordrecht: D. Reidel, 1984.

McVaugh, Rogers. "The American Collections of Humboldt and Bonpland, as Described in the Systema Vegetabilium of Roemer and Schultes." *Taxon,* vol. 4, no. 4, 1955, pp. 78–86. Reprinted in Stearn, *Humboldt, Bonpland, Kunth and Tropical American Botany.*

Miller, D. P., and P. H. Reill, eds. *Visions of Empire: Voyages, Botany, and Representations of Nature.* Cambridge: Cambridge University Press, 1996.

Miller, John Chester. *The Wolf by the Ears.* New York: Free Press, 1977.

Minguet, Charles. *Alexandre de Humboldt: Historien et géographe de l'Amérique espagnole.* Paris: Harmattan, 1998.

Morton, Timothy. *Ecology without Nature: Rethinking Environmental Aesthetics.* Cambridge: Harvard University Press, 2007.

Moussy, Martin de. "Notice sur la vie de Aimé Bonpland en Amerique." *Bulletin de la Societé de geographie (Paris)*, vol. 4, no. 19, 1860, pp. 414–425.

Nye, Andrea. "Aimé Bonpland: A Land Ethic in the La Plata." *Environmental Ethics*, vol. 41, no. 4, 2019, pp. 361–379.

O'Boyle, Lenore. "Learning for Its Own Sake: The German University as Nineteenth-Century Model," in *Comparative Studies in Society and History*, vol. 25, no. 1, 1983, pp. 3–25.

Pagden, Anthony. *European Encounters with the New World*. New Haven: Yale University Press, 1993.

———. *The Fall of Natural Man: The America Indian and the Origins of Comparative Ethnography*. New Haven: Yale University Press, 1982.

Page, Thomas J. *La Plata*. New York: Harper & Row, 1859.

Pasztory, Esther. *Aztec Art*. Norman, Oklahoma: University of Oklahoma Press, 1983.

Pennini de De Vega, Elena. "Le pharmacien Juan A. Dominguez initiateur de la pharmacologie argentine." *Revue d'histoire de la pharmacie*, vol. 22, no. 266, 1975, pp. 501–506.

Pratt, Mary Louise. *Imperial Eyes: Travel Writing and Transculturation*. New York: Routledge, 1992.

Robertson, William Parish, and John Parish Robertson. *Francia's Reign of Terror*. London: J. Murray, 1839.

Rich, Nathaniel. "The Very Great Alexander von Humboldt." Review of Wulf, *The Invention of Nature*. *New York Review of Books*, October 22, 2015.

Rupke, Nicolaas. *Alexander von Humboldt: A Metabiography*. Chicago: University of Chicago Press, 2008.

Sachs, Aaron. *The Humboldt Current: Nineteenth-Century Exploration and the Roots of American Environmentalism*. New York: Viking, 2006.

Sachs, Julius von. *History of Botany, 1530–1860*. Translated by Henry Gaarnsey, New York: Russell & Russell, 1890.

Saint-Hilaire, Auguste de. *Histoire des plantes les plus remarquables du Brésil et du Paraguay*. Paris: Belin, 1824–1827.

Sarton, George. "Aimé Bonpland." In Stearn.

Schwarz, Ingo. "Alexander von Humboldt's Visit to Washington and Philadelphia." *Northeastern Naturalist*, vol. 8, Special Issue 1, 2001, pp. 43–56.

Sluyter, Andrew. "Humboldt's Mexican Texts and Landscapes." *Geographical Review*, vol. 96, no. 3, 2000, pp. 361–381.

Smethurst, Paul. *Travel Writing and the Natural World, 1768–1840*. New York: Palgrave, 2012.

Smuts, Jan. *Holism and Evolution*. New York: Macmillan, 1926.

Stafleu, Frans A. *Linnaeus and the Linnaeans: The Spreading of Their Ideas in Systematic Botany, 1735–1789*. Utrecht: A. Oostock, 1971.

Stauffer, Fred W., and John Stauffer. "The Palm (Arecaceae) Collections Gathered by Bonpland and Humboldt in Their American Journey: Origin and Fate of the Specimens and Typifications." *Candollea*, vol. 72, no. 1, 2017, pp. 5–22.

Stauffer, F. W., Stauffer, J., Dorr, Laurence. "Bonpland and Humboldt's Specimens, Field Notes and Herbaria: New Insights from a Study of the Monocotyledons Collected in Venezuela." *Candollea*, vol. 67 no. 1, 2012, pp. 75–130.

Stearn, William, ed. *Humboldt, Bonpland, Kunth and Tropical American Botany*. Lehre: J. Cramer, 1968.

Stephens, John. "An Hour with Alexander von Humboldt." *Littell's Living Age*, vol. 15, 1847, pp. 151–153.

———. *Incidents of Travel in Central America, Chiapas, and Yucatan*. New York: Harper & Collins, 1841.

Stoddard, Richard Henry. *The Life and Books of Alexander von Humboldt*. New York: Rudd & Carleton, 1859.

Taylor, Bayard. *At Home and Abroad: Life Scenery, and Men*. New York: Putnam's, 1889.

Tobey, Ronald. *Saving the Prairies: The Life Cycle of the Founding School of American Plant Ecology, 1895–1955*. Berkeley: University of California Press, 1981.

von Hagen, Victor Wolfgang. *South America Called Them: Explorations of the Great Naturalists*. New York: Alfred A. Knopf, 1945.

———. "Was This the Fate of the Library of Alexander von Humboldt?" *Isis*, vol. 41, no. 2, 1950, pp. 164–167.

Walls, Laura Dassow. *The Passage to Cosmos: Alexander von Humboldt and the Shaping of America*. Chicago: University of Chicago Press, 2009.

Weil, Simone. *Gravity and Grace*. London: Routledge, 1963.

White, Richard. "Are You an Environmentalist or Do You Work for a Living? Work and Nature." In *Uncommon Ground*, edited by William Cronon, New York: W. W. Norton, 1996.

Whitehead, Neil. "Carib Cannibalism. The Historical Evidence." *Journal de la Société des Americainistes* 1984, vol. 70, no. 1, pp. 69–87.

Worster, Donald. *Wealth of Nations: Environmental History and the Ecological Imagination*. Oxford: Oxford University Press, 1993.

Wulf, Andrea. *The Invention of Nature: Alexander von Humboldt's New World*. New York: Alfred Knopf, 2015.

Zagare, Verónica. "Natural Territory, Urban Growth and Climate Change in the Parana River Delta and Rio de la Plata Estuarine System: an Overview." Delta Alliance, delta-alliance.org, 2011.

Index

Agassiz, Louis, 232, 316, 343n12 (chap. 12)

agriculture, 5, 15, 44, 128, 160, 201, 217, 241, 259–60

Artemis at Ephesus, 217, 324, 342n2 (chap. 12)

Andes, 105–6, 115

Arago, Francois, 215, 279, 289

Avé-Lallemant, Robert, 307–8, 313–16, 322

Aztec art, 127–28, 144

Bambusa guadua, 47

Baudin, Nicolas, 9, 11, 12–13, 100–1, 109, 333 n2 (chap. 1)

Bell, Stephen, 323

Bernadin de Saint-Pierre, 33–34, 75, 260, 334n3 (chap. 2)

Bertholletia excelsa (brazil nut tree) 83–85, 337n2 (chap. 5)

Bichat, Xavier, 15

Blumenbach, Johann Friedrich, 17, 40; on racial hierarchy, 57, 59, 318, 335–36n5–6 (chap. 3)

Bolivar, Simon, 200–1, 208, 224–25, 318

Bonaparte, Josephine, 181–84, 186, 189–90, 197–98

Bonaparte, Napoleon, 1, 9, 10, 131, 136–37, 162, 170, 172, 176, 182–83, 185, 189–90, 196, 209

Bonpland, Aimé:

Berlin visit, 172–73; botanical work, 2, 10, 27–28, 32, 38–39, 46–47, 48–49, 49–50, 64–66, 79–80, 81–85, 99, 101, 103–7, 139–40, 179–81, 187–88, 240–41, 253–54, 312; botanical journals, 60, 65–66, 95, 139, 257–58, 336n4 (chap. 4), 348n3; Canary Islands, first impressions, 29–31; collecting birds and animals, 75, 241–42, 258; daguerreotype of, 288; *Description des Plantes Rares Cultivées à Malmaison et à Navarre*, 198, 312; Director at Malmaison and Navarre 183–84, 185, 197–98, 199; education, 13–15; family relations, 13–14, 190, 195, 198–99, 208, 209, 271; in Buenos Aires, 226–37, 233–45; in Paraguay, 224–27, 232, 234–35; landholding at Santa Ana (Corrientes), 259–60, 268, 271, 290, 292–93, 303; letters to Humboldt, 236–37, 241–43, 244–45, 249–50, 251, 257–58, 290–93, 294, 296, 305–6; marriages, 137–38, 189–90, 235, 271–72, 343n1 (chap. 13); *Monographie des melastomacées*, 140, 312; "Notes

Bonpland, Aimé *(continued)*
for Agricultural Establishment"
(land use plan for Buenos Aires),
232; pension from the French
government, 147–48, 236, 238,
246–47, 259; *Plantes Equinoxiales*,
2, 32, 46, 79–80, 138, 156–57,
179, 180, 181, 185, 192, 312;
work with native Americans, 84–85,
59–60
Views on: Europe, 198–200, 209;
French colonial policy, 268–69;
Native Americans, 84–85, 59–60;
Guarani, 242–43, 253–54, 293–94;
Napoleonic Paris, 136–37, 149;
publishing, 155–56, 191–92, 202–
4, 244–45, 270, 274–75, 291–92,
315–16; Spanish botanists, 151
Bonplandia (Journal), 294, 295, 346n6
(chap. 15)
Bonplandia (plant) 122, 152=55, 167,
339n1 (chap. 4)
Botany, 10, 16–17, 18–19, 27–28,
38–39, 43, 46–47, 50–51, 59–60
Bougainville, Louis-Antoine de, 10, 11,
12
Boussingault, Jean-Baptiste, 112, 220–22
Bruhn, Karl, 312
Brunel, Adolphe, 5, 312
Buenos Aires, 233–34, 240–41, 243–44

Caldes, José de, 106, 107–9, 111
Calibozo, 70, 107
Canary Islands, 29–32
Candelaria, 239
Candolle, Augustin de, 188, 204–7,
216–17, 269–71
Capuchin Hospice, visit to, 49–53
Caracas: sea journey to, 63, social life,
63; European culture in, 64
Caldas, José de, 106, 107–9, 111,
337–38n4 (chap. 6)

Carlos del Pino, 34–35, 36
Casiquare Canal, 83
Cavanilles, Antonio-José, 121–22,
152–55, 167
Cave of the Guácharos, 43, 50–53,
335n3 (chap. 3)
Ceroxylon andicola (wax palm), 106–7,
134–35, 339n1 (chap. 8)
Cervantes, Vicente, 122–23
Chalchiuhthcue (Aztec deity), 128
Chimborazo, 101, 110–13, 126, 227,
266, 338n6–7 (chap. 6)
Chirivé, Maria, 235, 343n1 (chap. 13)
Cristaldo, Victoriana, 271, 314
Cinchona (yerba maté), 103–4, 117–19,
157, 244, 254–55, 281–85,
293–94, 303–4, 339n2 (chap. 9)
Clements, Frederick, 319
Coathicue (Aztec deity), 128
Community, 5, 47, 209, 280, 303, 325,
328
Condamine, Charles Marie de La, 110,
117–18
Cordier, Henry, 321
Cotta, Friedrich Johann, 140–41
Cumaná: first stay at 35–39, second stay
at 61–62
Cuvier, Georges, 163–64

Darwin, Charles, 207, 316, 319,
341–42n6 (chap. 11)
Delahay, Adele 189–90, 197–98, 201,
233, 237–38
Delessert, Benjamin, 285–86, 293, 311
Demersay, Alfred, 272–74, 312
Desfontaine, René, 10, 15
Domínguez, Juan, 320, 331
Dove, Alfred, 316–17

Ecology: agency, 330–31; economics,
325; partnerships, 327–28; vision,
330–31

Emphyteusis, 344n10 (chap. 13)
Ethnic studies, 318–19
European civilization, 54, 92

Ferré, Pedro, 259, 267, 271
Fichte, Johann Gottlieb, 202
Foster, George, 17
Foucault, Philippe, 323
Fourcroy, Antoine-Francois, 18
Francia, José, Gaspar Rodriguez, 235, 250, 342n4 (chap. 12)
Friedrich William III, 132–33, 163, 170, 275
Freiesleben, Carl, 27, 132–33
French Revolution, 9, 14–15

Gallocheau, Olive Goujaud (sister of Aimé Bonpland), 30, 136–38, 147–49, 209–10
Gay-Lussac, Joseph Louis, 140, 145, 166–67, 175
Gérard, Francois, 126
Geology, 17, 187, 215, 257, 292
Goethe, Johann Wolfgang von, 18
Guaiqueri Indians, 58–59
Goujaud, Jacques (father of Aimé Bonpland), 14
Goujaud, Michel (brother of Aimé Bonpland), 14, 99–100, 135
Grandshire, Richard, 225–26
Guácharos (oil birds). See Cave of the Guácharos
Guizot, Francois, 246, 280
Gymnoti (electric eels), 70–73

Hamy, Ernest-Théodore, 3–4, 318
Havana, 95, 100
Hegel, George Wilhelm, Friedrich, 248, 251–53, 262, 342n8 (chap. 12), 344n7 (chap. 13)
History, uses of, 5–6
Hossard, Nicolas, 323

Humboldt, Alexander von:
achievements, 318; *Asie Centrale*, 261, 342–43n11 (chap. 12); *Aspects of Nature*, 3, 67, 86, 90, 171–72, 176; at Jena, 18–19, 262, 264; *Cosmos* 4–5, 248, 249, 261–67, 275, 280, 302, 316–18, 320; botanical work, 16–17, 18–19, 27–38, 38–39, 107; duties as Chamberlain, 163, 196–97, 227, 232, 248, 249, 275–76, 278–79, 297–98, 301; education, 15–20; electricity experiments, 17–18, 29, 37, 70, 72–73, 318; *Essay on the Geography of Plants*, 23, 113; *Flora Fribergensis*, 17; *Geographical and Physical Atlas*, 126; *Geography of Plants*, 205–7, 217; images of 294–95; letters to Bonpland, 215–16; letters to Varnhagen, 247–49, 296, 287, 298; instrument readings, 19, 32, 35–36, 37–38, 43–44, 45, 49, 61–62, 67, 81, 91, 143, 171; lectures in Berlin, 228; love life, 11, 16–17, 27, 107–8, 140, 145, 166–67, 175, 220–21; "My Confession," 166; *New Genera and Species*, 288, 291; *Personal Narrative*, 181, 199; personality, 12, 13, 27; *Political Essay on the Island of Cuba*, 299–300; *Political Essay on the Kingdom of New Spain*, 126, 165, 175–79, 219; publishing results of the voyage with Bonpland, 81, 96–97, 141–45, 150–52, 157, 164–65, 168–69, 175, 180–82, 184, 185–88; relations with Spanish officials, 25–27, 92–93, 97–98, 132; romanticism, 3, 18–19, 33–34, 152, 171–72; 'Rhodian Genius," 18–19, 143; Russian Expedition, 185–86, 229–32; Spanish officials,

Humboldt, Alexander von *(continued)*
  relations with, 25–27, 97–98;
  speech to the Petersburg Academy
  of Science, 230–32; *Views of the*
  Cordilleras, 32, 112, 116, 120,
  126–27; Visit to Philadelphia and
  Washington, 124–25
  Views on: Aztec art and culture,
  126–37, 158–62; botany, 151–52;
  Capuchin missionaries, 56;
  European politics, 245, 247–48,
  278–80; Hegel, 251–53; Incan
  roads and ruins, 116–17; Mexico
  City, 120–21; mountain climbing,
  66, 70–73, 106, 107; native
  Americans, 35–37, 43, 48, 52,
  53–59, 66, 73, 79, 81, 85–90,
  92, 319, 335n4 (chap. 3); slavery,
  33, 36, 67, 143, 177, 186–87,
  188, 191, 204, 218–19, 298–300,
  302–3, 319; South American
  revolutions, 63; Spanish botanists,
  150–51; tropical degeneration,
  57–59; tropical vegetation, 44–45,
  47, 49, 85–86; volcanoes, 32–33,
  106
Humboldt, Wilhelm (brother of
  Alexander), 11, 16, 116, 132, 196,
  218, 228, 248–49

Institute de France, 1, 2, 11, 123, 133,
  134–35, 188, 216

Jardin des Plantes, 9–10, 15, 43
Jefferson, Thomas, 125–26, 131, 176,
  178, 338n7 (chap. 7)
Jena, 18–19
Jesuits, 70, 79, 87
Jussieu, Antoine de, 10, 15, 21

Kant, Immanuel, 18, 264, 329
Kunth, Carl, 189, 193, 210, 217–18,
  219, 314, 322–23

Kunth, Gottlob, 189

Lake Valencia, 67, 336n5 (chap. 4)
Lamarck, Jean-Baptiste, 10, 20
Lavalle, Juan, 240
Leopold, Aldo, 331
Life of Alexander von Humboldt compiled
  in commemoration of the centenary of
  his death, 312–17
Lima, 119
Linnaeus, Carl, on human species, 18,
  59, 118
Llanos, travel across, 67–73
Lopez, Estanislao, 234
Lourteig, Alicia, 321–22
Lowenberg, Julius, 312–13
Loxa, 117–18

Madrid, 25–27
Maize of the water, 4, 254–55, 293,
  346n4 (chap. 15)
Magdalena river, 101–2
Malmaison, 139, 181–85, 189, 197–98,
  260
Marsh, George Perkins, 319
Marx, Karl, 279–80, 316
Medical science, 14–15
Mexico, 177–78, 221–24
"Mexican silver bubble," 178
mining, 17, 26, 123, 125, 177–78, 230,
  231, 340n3 (chap. 10)
Montúfar, Carlos, 107–8, 137
Moscow Academy of Science, 230
Moussy, Martin de, 271
Mt. Silla, climb up, 66
Muir, John, 318, 331
Muséum national d'histoire naturelle,
  1, 4, 9, 10, 12, 256, 257, 311,
  321–22
Museum of Natural Science "Amado
  Bonpland," 303, 304, 305, 311,
  331
Mutis, José Celestino, 101, 103

Natural History, 9–10, 12–13, 15
Navarre, 185–86

Oltmanns, Jabbo, 170–71
Orinoco river, 76–77: travel on, 73–85;
    ship wreck on, 77–78; link to
    Amazon river system, 80–81;
    digging turtle eggs on, 86

Pago Largo (battle at), 268
Paraguay, 224–27, 232, 234–35, 312,
    342n4 (chap. 12)
Paraguay river, 234
Paraná river, 234
Pichinda, 107, 110
Pictet, Marc-Auguste, 11, 22, 141–45,
    175–76
Popayán, 106
Pujol, Juan, 295, 327
Puracé, 106
Pueyrredón, Juan Martin de, 210, 234

Quito, 107

Ramirez, Francisco, 234
Rio Grande do Sul, 281
Riobama, 115
Rivadavia, Bernardo, 208, 210, 240
Robertson, William, 160
Roguin, Dominique, 233, 321
Royal Botanical garden of Mexico City,
    123
Rosas, Juan Manuel, 240, 243, 267–69,
    271
Rose, Gustav, 229
Ruiz, Hippólito, 104

Saint-Hilaire, Augustin, 242–43, 255,
    344n5 (chap. 13)
Sans Souci, 296
Santa Ana (on the Paraná), 239–40

Santa Ana (Corrientes), 259–60, 268,
    271, 290, 292–93, 303
Santé Fé de Bogotá, 101, 102
Sarratea, Mariano, 208
Sarton, George, 322
Sao Borja, 235, 272–74, 292
Schiller, Friedrich, 18–19, 262
Schlos Tegel (Humboldt Estate), 16
South American revolutions, 200–1,
    208, 210
Spanish officials, relations with: 25–37,
    37, 92–93, 132
Stearn, William, 322
Stephens, John, 178, 277–78

Taylor, Bayard, 300–1
Tenerife, 32–33
Tenochtitlán, 127
Thoreau, Henry David, 318, 331
Thouin, André, 10, 15, 334n3 (chap. 1)

United Provinces of the Rio de la Plata,
    210, 289–90, 328; War of the
    Triple Alliance, 331
Urquíjo, Luis de, 25–26

Varnhagen, Karl August von Ense,
    247–49, 301 (See also Humboldt,
    "Letters to Varnhagnen")

Weil, Simone, 330
Willdenow, Carl, 16, 17, 27, 28, 95–99,
    121, 141, 154, 164, 167–68,
    172–73, 185–86, 189

Yerba maté (Ilex paraguariensis), 238–39,
    244, 281–85, 293–94, 303–4

Zapla, Leandro, 115
Zea, Francisco, 201, 219–20